Enjoy your snowdrops.
With Best wishes & tha[nks for?]
all your help with my plants.
Margaret Swindin

A GARDENER'S GUIDE TO
SNOWDROPS

FREDA COX

A GARDENER'S GUIDE TO
SNOWDROPS

FREDA COX

THE CROWOOD PRESS

First published in 2013 by
The Crowood Press Ltd
Ramsbury, Marlborough
Wiltshire SN8 2HR

www.crowood.com

British Library Cataloguing-in-Publication Data
A catalogue record for this book is available from the
British Library.

ISBN 978 1 84797 475 4

Dedication

For my dear friends Ann, Barbara, Caroline, Deanna, Joan, Penny, Sally, Shaunah and Sue,
who put up with my endless talk of plants and gardens, as do all my other friends.
Thank you all for your friendship, understanding, patience and support.

Typeset by Kelly-Anne Levey
Printed and bound in India by Replika Press Pvt Ltd

CONTENTS

ACKNOWLEDGEMENTS

Many people contributed help and advice to this book. It could never have been
completed without them and I very much appreciate all of their support.

Firstly an enormous debt of gratitude to the following: the anonymous reviewer for help, advice and expertise with checking and correcting the manuscript and answering many queries; Ian Christie who gave his time and expert knowledge so kindly, generously and willingly – this was so much appreciated; Matt Bishop, Aaron Davis and John Grimshaw, *Snowdrops – A Monograph of Cultivated Galanthus* (Griffin Press, 2001 and 2006) – this comprehensive and detailed monograph was an important reference source in the compilation of my book and is essential for all Galanthophiles; Aaron Davis, *The Genus Galanthus* (Royal Botanic Gardens, Kew, in association with Timber Press, 1999), the book that originally fired my enthusiasm and provided information, and also his help in kindly supplying details of *G. panjutinii* as soon as they became available; Camilla Stewart for all her help and advice in correcting and editing the manuscript; John Grimshaw for help and advice; Michael and Joan Head's invaluable help and guidance, work with snowdrop lists and data, and always being on the end of the telephone to answer my many queries; Trevor Nottle for important advice and information on Australian snowdrops and his time spent answering questions; Marcus Harvey, Hill View Rare Plants, for information on snowdrops in the southern hemisphere; and Christopher Norton and Shaunah Murrell, my computer experts, who rush to my aid in emergencies.

Others who offered help with research include Avon Bulbs; Beth Chatto Garden; Gaby Belton, Dunskey Gardens; Alice Boyd, Viscountess Boyd of Merton, Ince Castle; RHS Lindley Library; Broadleigh Gardens; Ernest Cavallo, USA; Ray and Sylvia Cobb; Patricia Cullinan, USA; David Ellis, American Horticultural Society; Hagen Engelmann; Rosemary Fitzgerald, Beggars Roost Plants; Bill and Marilyn Hammerton; Ulla Høst; Shuji Inoue, Japan; David Jordan, Anglesey Abbey; Linda Keevy, Heavens Scent Nursery, South Africa; Natasha MacFadyen, Veseys Nursery, Canada; Ann Marrison; Jane Merryman, Pacific Bulb Society; John Morley, North Green Snowdrops; Harry Pierick, Hidden City Garden, Netherlands; Yvonne Reynolds, South Africa; Peter Salmond, Hokuni Alpines, New Zealand; Jim Shields, USA; Mark Smyth; Wol and Sue Staines, Glen Chantry; Susan Tindall, Timpany Nursery, Ireland; Mike Werkmeister, Lambrook Manor; and Jill Yakas, Greece.

Many thanks to those who kindly helped with photographs of snowdrops and gardens, and the garden owners who let me take and use photographs of their beautiful gardens including: Ampthill Town Council; Michael Baron, Brandy Mount; John Bent, Weeping Ash; Anna Briggs, Burton Agnes Hall; Beth Chatto and Tricia Brett, Beth Chatto Garden; Phil Cornish; Pamela Davey, Welford Park; Rob Davison, Maple Glen; Sir Peter and Lady Erskine and Pauline Rennie, Cambo; David L. Finnis, Finlaystone; Alan Ford, Magnolia House; Jo Goode, Pencarrow House; Susie Hunt, Waterperry; Carrie Irvin, Moggerhanger Park; Sarah Lorimer-Riley, Chelsea Physic Garden; David and Margaret MacLennan, Byndes Cottage; Elizabeth Meath-Baker, Walsingham Abbey; Paul Moir, Painswick Rococo Garden; Hugo and Rebecca Nicolle, Chippenham Park; Roger and Sue Norman, Ivy Croft; Mark and Clare Oglesby, Goldsborough Hall; Richenda Oldham, Ford Abbey; John and Shirley Palmer, The Homestead; Roger Holland, Allan Pettitt and the E.A. Bowles of Myddelton House Society; Corinne Price; Deborah Puxley, Welford Park; Christina Quijano-Caballero; Carole Smith, Robinswood; Christopher Sutherns, Kings Arms Garden; James and Margaret Swinden, Beech Cottage; Lionel Taylor and the Bank Hall Action Group; Jorun Tharaldsen; Thompson & Morgan; Ken Tudor; Mike Werkmeister, Lambrook Manor; Tim Whiteley, Evenly Wood; and June Whittaker, Willesley Hall.

As well as my own photographs, I used a number of sources on which to base drawings, including Snowdrops – A Monograph of Cultivated Galanthus, Matt Bishop, Aaron Davis and John Grimshaw; The Genus Galanthus, Aaron Davis; Galanthomania, Hanneke Van Dijk; Schneeglöckchen, Günter Waldorf; www.brandymount.co.uk; www.broadleighbulbs.co.uk; www.carolynsshadegardens.com; www.engelmannii.de; www.oirlicherblumengarten.de; www.galanthus.co.uk; www.galanthusgallery.com; www.galanthusonline.de; www.growsonyou.com; www.judyssnowdrops.co.uk; www.sneeuwklokjes.nl; www.snowdropinfo.com; and www.srgs.net.com. My sincere thanks to them all.

Finally heartfelt thanks to my family and friends, who put up with endless talk about snowdrops: John, Elaine, Matthew, Christopher and Rebekah Norton; Kathy Norton and Dominic Marsden; Mark, Clare, Aimiee and Juliette Norton; Camilla, Peter, Douglas and Tristan Stewart; Lorna, Chris, Joseph, Mia, Jacob and Freya Hawthorne; Leslie, Marita and James Rawlins; Pat Cordingly; Sue Graham; Barbara Handy; Caroline Harbouri; Sandra Hawthorne and family; Arthur and Pat Lacey; Deanna Morris; Shaunah Murrell; Clive and Veronica Rawlins; Sally Razelou; John and Jay Rendall; Carol Smith; Grace and Norman Stewart; Ann Warner-Casson; Penny Westgate; and Gordon Fenn and Raymond Treasure, whose friendship and incredible Stockton Bury Garden offer peace, tranquillity, sanctuary and sanity.

PREFACE

I have loved snowdrops all my life. They are one of my greatest joys each year and I long for their appearance. But they were always simply 'snowdrops', those delicate and beautiful ice-white flowers that pierced the earth at just the moment when winter seemed at its darkest – in no time at all spreading into vast white carpets beneath the winter trees. In my parents' garden, snowdrops spilled out from the rocky face of an old quarry to naturalize in huge drifts. They were absolutely stunning as over the years they spread further and further across the garden, scenting the air with their honey perfume.

My late mother-in-law was deeply superstitious and refused to come into the house if I had snowdrops indoors. The vase had to be banished to the garden until she left as she was genuinely terrified that snowdrops brought into the house heralded bad luck. This superstition was very prevalent in certain parts of the country, and many stories and legends surround the snowdrop.

I have planted thousands of snowdrops over my lifetime. They are always the first plants to go into any new garden. But snowdrops were still 'snowdrops' until a very few years ago, when suddenly I found something different. I lived on a farm that dated back to medieval times with a correspondingly ancient nut orchard. Snowdrops grew in great drifts beneath the hazel trees and one cold winter's day, with just a hint of sun in a snow-laden sky, I found a tiny snowdrop with reflexed segments. I imagined the wind must have blown the snowdrop almost inside out and thought little of it. The following year I was amazed when the little reflexed clump came through again, and again the year after that. I moved the snowdrop into the garden, where it could be seen and admired more easily and every year it came up the same. But I still thought of it as no more than a slightly malformed snowdrop, although very beautiful.

One winter I saw a small pot of plants for sale at a local nursery. Hyacinths, a coloured primrose, tiny ivy and right at the back, half hidden by a fern, a tall snowdrop with entirely dark green inner segments. I bought the bowl for £2.50, an absolute bargain. I proudly planted the snowdrop out in the garden, where my hens promptly pecked off the only flower. But it started me thinking.

I collected a few bulb catalogues and to my surprise found numerous different snowdrops listed. Some of them had longer outer segments, some differently shaped inner markings; there were large snowdrops and small snowdrops; and I learned a host of new names to add to the two I already knew, *G. nivalis* and *G. nivalis* 'Flore Pleno'. Soon I had stately *G. elwesii* growing in my garden,

together with *G.* 'Magnet' and *G.* 'S. Arnott'. I had started a 'collection' to add to my stalwart little reflexed snowdrop and the one with the green centre (although for some reason the hens always unfailingly nipped off the dark green flowers).

Then, sadly, I moved house and my snowdrops were left behind. Why is it always more distressing to leave a garden than it is a house? Now I am careful and mark where I plant my snowdrops, and will allow plenty of time with any future move to dig them up and take them with me.

When I proposed writing a book on snowdrops, my publisher didn't think there was enough to write about, but even I was surprised when I realised it was going to be difficult to contain all the information in the confines of a single book. In the end it proved almost impossible, which is why this book became an even larger project than first anticipated.

I have done my best to list as many named snowdrops as possible, including some which are not yet available on the open market, and others that have names but no one seems to have heard of them or seen them. But new snowdrops are appearing and receiving names all the time through the feverish enthusiasm of Galanthophiles and Galanthomania. Surely sometime, someday, all possible combinations of flower and segment shape, coloration and markings will have been exhausted and no more snowdrops will be named!

Sadly, this small, very beautiful but unassuming tiny white flower also generates great hostility among certain Galanthophiles, and for the first time in all my years associated with gardens and gardening I experienced unpleasant aggression and mean-mindedness. There is no need for such angst. Perhaps they have been standing too close to *G.* 'Grumpy'? Luckily I also met tremendous Galanthophiles who offered their friendship, encouragement and support, happily sharing their knowledge and expertise. To them I say a huge 'Thank you', for as well as their help they restored my faith in human nature and the true spirit of gardeners and people who love plants.

I have a passion for plants and gardens on any day, whatever the season, whatever the weather. However, somehow nothing ever compares to the anticipation and excitement of seeing the very first tiny snowdrop shoots forcing through the frozen earth, unfurling their beautiful, delicate, white pendant flowers.

Read this book at your peril. You could soon find you too have become a Galanthophile and have fallen under the magical spell of the snowdrop.

CHAPTER 1

INTRODUCING SNOWDROPS

The humble snowdrop, such a pure and simple flower, but what elegant beauty. Each one brightens the grey gloom of a winter's day and nothing is guaranteed to lift one's spirits more than seeing the very first snowdrops. Small, undemanding and delicate-looking, they never fail to produce stunning displays, naturalizing in their millions through woodland, fields, lanes and gardens, brightening borders and spilling through hedges onto wayside verges. Within days of the first buds opening, carpets of ice-white flowers spread in great drifts beneath gaunt winter trees.

Snowdrops are heralds of new life and rebirth, appearing as the year's cycle begins anew, and marking the gentle waking of the garden from its deep winter sleep. Spring is coming. Great excitement and eager anticipation greets the arrival of snowdrops each year as snowdrop lovers wait for the first tiny shoots to pierce the ground – two grey-green leaves enclosing a small, white bud, opening into a pendant flower.

After a surfeit of dark days, leaden grey skies and below-freezing temperatures, these delicate but extraordinarily tenacious little flowers still miraculously appear year after year, as if by magic. Their strong protective sheaths force their way to the surface through unyielding, frozen earth. A delicate hint of honey perfume is borne on the breeze in the winter sunshine, while the flowers provide much-needed nectar for early insects which, in turn, aid pollination. Snowdrops make excellent cut flowers, bringing a breath of spring indoors at the time of year when we need it most.

ABOVE: *Galanthus nivalis*.

LEFT: The first snowdrops emerging from the frozen earth.

OPPOSITE PAGE: Snowdrops naturalized along the banks of the Cound Brook, Shropshire.

Snowdrops spreading through woodland.

The snowdrop is a flower most people recognize. Millions of bulbs are sold every year, and they are one of our best loved and most popular bulbous plants. To the novice all snowdrops look similar: simple white, tear-drop flowers suspended from a slender stem. Three larger outer segments surround three smaller inner segments with a green mark at their tips. It comes as quite a surprise that (at the time of writing) there are twenty known species and over 1,500 hybrids and cultivars. This number continues to rise as snowdrop enthusiasts hunt out different variations, adding new names to an already extensive list.

The main snowdrop season is between mid-January and mid-March. Mild winters bring earlier flowers, while displays last longer during cold winters. In very severe winters, such as that of 2010/11, the appearance of snowdrops can be very much delayed. It is hardly surprising that plant lovers look for the first snowdrops of the year with such hope and enthusiasm, gently brushing back fallen flurries of autumn leaves in the hope of finding those first buds that little bit sooner. A kaleidoscope of glorious flowers in every conceivable shape, size and colour will follow as the seasons unfold, but snowdrops are the first, the most welcome, the most important and eagerly awaited of all plants to flower each year, especially for Galanthophiles.

Galanthophiles

Snowdrop aficionados, or Galanthophiles, regularly travel hundreds of miles, even visiting different continents, to fulfil their desire to see specific plants and collections. Despite freezing temperatures, torrential rain and often heavy snow, they can be seen crawling about on hands and knees, or lying flat in the mud to examine a particular snowdrop's markings more closely. They flock in vast numbers to gardens opening specifically to exhibit impressive collections and acres of naturalized snowdrops, not to mention visits to see those rare and highly coveted varieties that all Galanthophiles aspire to own.

The renowned horticulturist and snowdrop enthusiast E.A. Bowles is credited with the introduction of the term 'Galanthophile' in the 1900s. In fact, more precisely he termed the new generation of snowdrop enthusiasts 'Neogalanthophiles', and applied the word 'Galanthophile' to nineteenth-century collectors. However, the attraction in Bowles's time was very low key compared to the snowdrop frenzy and crazy prices paid for bulbs today.

Although snowdrops are thought of as spring flowers, different species flower over a period of several months, between

Galanthophiles attending a snowdrop study day at Colesbourne Park, Gloucestershire.

September and April. This is a relatively long flowering period for one type of plant. Even so, this time is still all too brief for the serious Galanthophile, who will watch for the first snowdrops to appear in September and hunt down the last to fade in April.

A true Galanthophile is one who loves snowdrops for their pure and simple beauty rather than aspiring to have a vast and valuable collection at all costs. They are able to spot and select snowdrops that are slightly different from the norm in a swathe of plants which all look very much alike to anyone else. They seek out that slight variation of green marking, segment shape or arrangement of the flower. The difference between a tiny green spot placed exactly so, or the breadth of a green line is all important. The love of snowdrops might start off as a simple pleasure, but beware – interest in this beautiful plant can escalate into a hobby, a hobby can quickly become a passion, and passion an obsession. Family and friends think you are quite mad as you brave the winter elements to examine the delicate green markings of flowers, the length of spathes, or the shapes of various leaf forms.

Escalating Values

In February 2012 a single, tiny snowdrop bulb was sold on the eBay internet auction site for the astronomical sum of £725. This doubled the previous record set in March 2011, when a single snowdrop sold for £360. This in itself had been a slight increase on the previous record of £357 paid on the same site in January 2011, causing a major sensation at the time. £725 for one tiny snowdrop bulb!

This latest record was set by a distinctive Scottish snowdrop, 'Elizabeth Harrison'. It was bought by seed merchants Thompson & Morgan, who plan to propagate the bulb and eventually sell the plants to the wider public. This snowdrop is rare in that it is the only known yellow *G. woronowii* to date. 'Elizabeth Harrison' is a beautiful snowdrop with broad green leaves, bright yellow ovary and good yellow inner segment markings. It

The record-breaking 'Elizabeth Harrison', a single bulb of which sold for £725 on the eBay auction site in February 2012. (*Photo courtesy Ian Christie*)

is named after the owner of the garden in which the seedling was found by Galanthophile Ian Christie a few years ago.

The previous record of £360 was for 'Green Tear', a strong growing, beautiful virescent snowdrop originally found in the Netherlands by Gert-Jan van der Kolk in 2000. Its folded leaf edges suggest it may be a hybrid of *G. nivalis* and *G. plicatus*, and it was found growing in a large colony of *G. nivalis*. 'Green Tear' has long, broad outer segments with delicate pale green lines and inner segment markings extending almost from apex to base.

The £357 recorded in January 2011 was for a single *G. plicatus* 'E.A. Bowles'. First discovered at the former home of E.A. Bowles, Myddelton House Gardens, Enfield, in 2004, it was taken to Cambridgeshire to be propagated at Monksilver Nursery. The flowers are poculiform, with six, pure white, equally sized segments and no green markings. This gives the flower a rounded appearance instead of the more usual teardrop shape. It was named after Edward Augustus Bowles, and proceeds from sales of this snowdrop help towards restoring Myddelton House Gardens.

Before this, the record for a single snowdrop bulb was £265, while more common varieties regularly change hands for £40 or £50 a bulb. Other prices realized on the eBay auction site in the past include *G. nivalis* 'Ecusson d'Or' at £145, *G. plicatus*

'Wandlebury Ring' at £123 and *G. elwesii* 'Jonathan' at £100. However, one does not have to pay a fortune to enjoy the beauty of snowdrops. Bulbs of the simple, common *G. nivalis* are inexpensive to purchase and rapidly produce new plants.

As people are increasingly won over by the charm of snowdrops, and Galanthophile numbers soar, prices are set to escalate further and faster. Collectors seek out the latest, more unusual hybrids, snapping up bulbs as soon as they appear and paying high prices, and sadly in the process putting more uncommon snowdrops out of the reach of many enthusiasts. Specialist bulb companies dramatically increase prices for choice varieties, restricting the purchase of special snowdrops to one per order. Very rare varieties of snowdrop never even make the open market or bulb catalogue, but are swapped, exchanged and coveted by private growers.

Galanthomania

As many forecast, the passion for tulips which sparked off 'Tulipomania' in the 1600s, has hit the snowdrop world. Then the highest price paid for a tulip, 'Semper Augustus', was 6,000 florins the equivalent today of some £750,000. Now, as then, collectors are prepared to beg, borrow and steal, going to great lengths and spending vast sums of money to obtain choice bulbs for their collections. It is a form of madness, but all collectors of specific plant species know how easy it is to get hooked on something you love. But it is important to keep some perspective, and to enjoy the plant for its simple beauty, rather than being influenced by how valuable or vast your collection may become.

The Wildlife and Countryside Act (1981) makes it illegal to take wild plants without the landowner's permission, and the UK National Wildlife Crime Unit and police impose severe penalties on those caught. But when a handful of *G. nivalis* can be worth around £15, and rarer snowdrops far more, snowdrop theft is inevitably increasing. Bulbs are either sold directly to the public via garden centres and car boot sales, exported to Europe, or stolen to order by ruthless collectors. In secluded locations thieves even bring in earthmoving JCBs to dig up the ground, removing vast quantities of bulbs, but in the process completely decimating whole areas and destroying thousands of bulbs and their habitats. Lorry-loads of bulbs can sell for £50,000–£60,000 a time.

To combat snowdrop theft, large estates and gardens with important collections carefully monitor stocks and increase security. Some tag collections for safety, a process first initiated at the National Trust's Anglesey Abbey, where numerous rare snowdrops have been discovered. Locations of snowdrops are logged on a master map, making it a simple matter to identify and track plants that go missing. Wardens watch the bulbs, looking for suspicious activity or disturbed ground where snowdrops may have been looted.

It is a sad and damning reflection that a few fanatical and unscrupulous collectors are not immune to stealing. A number of gardens have reported thefts of rare snowdrops by people who obviously know exactly what they are looking for. Unfortunately, it appears that such greed-motivated thieves have little conscience and lack concern about the long-term welfare or survival of the bulbs they steal. Many gardens now remain closed, sadly denying genuinely honest and interested people the chance to see spectacular displays.

One small consolation is that very rare snowdrops are known to all serious collectors. If they are offered bulbs, they will know exactly where they were stolen from, so passing on pilfered plants is not as easy as it might appear. We are all responsible for safeguarding such an important part of our nation's heritage. If we watch and monitor areas that we know, immediately reporting suspicious activity, it makes it far more difficult for snowdrop thieves to perpetrate their crimes.

Seeing Snowdrops

Between January and March each year, despite freezing temperatures, torrential rain, mud and often heavy snow, snowdrop lovers flock in their thousands to gardens and estates opening specifically to exhibit impressive acres and collections of white blooms. Snowdrops spread beneath bare trees in deciduous woodland, star grassy meadows, grow beneath orchard trees, multiply along garden borders, carpet churchyards, old monastic sites and village verges, and edge river and stream banks. Most people who love snowdrops have their favourite haunts for seeing them, whether it is a large country estate, a local garden, or areas where snowdrops have become widely naturalized.

Snowdrop events are well publicized in the local and national press, in garden publications and on the internet. The National Trust and English Heritage have special, early season openings with guided walks and talks. Many snowdrop gardens open for the National Gardens Scheme (NGS), which produces the famous 'Yellow Book', listing gardens across the country. Each year increasing numbers of gardeners are keen to open their gates to the public specifically to show off their snowdrops.

There are snowdrop walks, talks and trails, lectures by top experts, week-long guided tours, snowdrop spectaculars and extravaganzas. Galanthophiles host private snowdrop lunches and discussions. The annual UK Galanthus Gala attracts buyers from all over the world; bulbs are swapped or sold between enthusiasts and there is a hotly contested auction. Scotland held its first Snowdrop Festival in 2007 and now over fifty gardens and estates participate; events include exhibitions, photography, talks and tours. Ireland held an inaugural Snowdrop Gala in February 2012 and other snowdrop spectaculars take place across Europe. There are internet sites, forums and chat rooms specifically on snowdrops.

Visitors going to see snowdrops at the National Trust's Bodnant Garden in North Wales can help to expand the collection in a novel way: bulbs can be purchased at £1 each to plant in the garden in memory of their visit. The Royal Botanic

Visitors to Margaret Owen's garden, Acton Pigot, Shropshire – a favourite place to see snowdrops each year.

Gardens, Kew, and its sister garden, Wakehurst Place, also have extensive snowdrop collections and visitors can sponsor displays in memory of loved ones.

Native Habitats

Snowdrops are native to central and southern Europe, from the Pyrenees to the Ukraine and Russia, and as far east as Poland, Albania, Iran, the Caucasus, the former Yugoslavia, Greece and Turkey. It is not known exactly when *G. nivalis* first arrived in Britain, and although some consider it a British native, this is unlikely. Many plants often considered native to Britain were in fact introduced at some period in their history. As late as 1952 Clapham, Tutin and Warburg's *Flora of the British Isles* classed snowdrops as probably being British natives, but goes on to say they were commonly planted and usually naturalized. Snowdrops flourished in the climate and conditions, spreading into vast colonies across the UK and northern Europe. *G. nivalis* is found abundantly throughout England, Wales and southern Scotland. It is less common in north-western Scotland and is mainly found in the east of Ireland.

Although snowdrops are generally associated with late winter and spring, different species and varieties start flowering as early as September and October, well before winter sets in. Like many autumn-flowering bulbs, these snowdrops generally appear without leaves, which follow later. Other species don't appear until as late as March or April, although in the northern hemisphere most snowdrops have flowered before the vernal equinox on 21 March. This means different species and varieties of snowdrop can extend the flowering period over seven months of the year.

There have almost certainly always been numerous variations among snowdrops in naturalized populations, most of which went almost unnoticed until Galanthomania took hold.

Galanthus byzantinus

3. 28.XI.1906.   4. 29.XI.1906.   15.I.1907.

Watercolour of *Galanthus byzantinus* by E.A. Bowles, painted during the winter and spring 1906/1907. (*Photo courtesy RHS Lindley Library*)

Snowdrops Through History

Historically, there is a possible reference to snowdrops as *Leukoion* by Theophrastus (372–287 BC.) However, as this name also applied to a number of other plants, this is not conclusive. Records show that snowdrops were cultivated in Britain in the 1500s. John Gerard (1545–1611/12) referred to them as '*The timely flow'ring bulbous violet*', stating '*Nothing is set down hereof by the ancient writers, nor anything observed by the moderne*'. His original 1597 edition of Gerard's Herball shows an unmistakable drawing and description of the snowdrop.

Despite his comments, there is actually a reference considered to refer to the snowdrop in an old glossary of 1465 under the name '*Leucis i viola alba*', the white violet, stating the flower is an 'emmenagogue', ie. stimulates blood flow in menstruation and in the pelvic regions.

Other old manuscripts list snowdrops among *Leucoium* or *Narcissus*, including Pietro Andres Mattioli (1501–1577), in his *Medici Senensis commentarii, in sex libros Pedacii Discoridis* of 1544. An illustration shows a snowdrop with numerous leaves instead of the usual two. Snowdrops are described as being '*digestive, resolutive and consolidante*'.

Snowdrops from a Victorian sketchbook.

Carolus Clusius (1526–1609), a pioneering botanist and horticulturist, remarked on the fragrance of a single bulb of *G. plicatus* received from Constantinople; this snowdrop was also known as Clusius's Snowdrop.

The name 'Snowdrop' appears for the first time in 1633, in Thomas Johnson's revised edition of Gerard's Herball, with a footnote beneath the entry for '*timely flow'ring bulbous violet*' – '*Some call them also snowdrops*', and there is an unmistakable drawing.

Galanthus nivalis was the '*Early white, whose pretty pure white bellflowers are tipt with a fine greene, and hang down their heads*'. So John Evelyn (1620–1706), in his *Kalendar of Horticulture*, listed them in 1664. Robert Boyle (1627–1691), the scientist and natural philosopher, described '*Those purely White Flowers that appear about the end of winter and are commonly call'd Snow drops*'. In 1732 Robert Furber (1674–1756) included the Greater Early Snowdrop and Single Snowdrop in *The Flower Garden Displayed*. Likewise, in Furber's 1733 *A Short Introduction to Gardening, or a Guide to Gentleman and Ladies in Furnishing their Gardens*, both the Single Snowdrop and Greater Early Snowdrop are included, as well as the Double Snowdrop. The plant received its generic name, *Galanthus*, with the specific epithet '*nivalis*', from Linnaeus in his 1753 *Species Plantarum*.

It is most likely that naturalized colonies of snowdrops evolved from garden escapes. 'Wild' snowdrops were recorded by William Hudson (1734–1793), the English botanist, in his 1778 *Flora Anglica*, as growing in meadows, hedges and orchards in Westmorland, Cumberland, Lancaster and Gloucester. William Withering (1741–1799), the English physician and botanist, noted snowdrops growing in Gloucestershire and Worcestershire. Sir James Edward Smith (1759–1828) published his extensive *Flora Britannica* in 1804, listing a number of sites for snowdrops including Malvern, Worcestershire; the River Tees near Blackwell and Conniscliffe, and Bedfordshire. In 1841 Jane Loudon (1807–1858) published *The Ladies' Flower Garden*, which listed two species of snowdrop: *nivalis*, which she considered to be an English native, and the 'Folded' or Russian snowdrop, *plicatus*, which she stated was first brought to England in 1592.

G. nivalis 'Flore Pleno' appeared in 1703. No one knows where it originated but the popularity of this double snowdrop was quickly established. Nineteenth- and twentieth-century plant hunters brought back different snowdrop species and varieties. Travellers collected bulbs to bring home, and bulbs of *G. plicatus*, for example, found their way back to Britain with soldiers returning from the Crimea.

In 1879 the *Gardener's Chronicle* recorded four available snowdrop species: *G. nivalis*, *G. elwesii*, *G. plicatus* and *G. reginae-olgae*, together with nine types of *G. nivalis*. The first accurate classification was made by the Swiss botanist Pierre Edmund Boissier (1810–1885). In his 1882 *Flora Orientalis*, he included six *Galanthus* species, *G. nivalis*, *G. graecus*, *G. reginae-olgae*, *G. elwesii*, *G. plicatus* and *G. latifolius*. By 1894 Günther Beck (1856–1931), was listing thirty-five *Galanthus*. A

Galanthus nivalis 'Flore Pleno'.

more extensive study by Paul von Gottlieb-Tannenheim in 1904 noted three species and eight subspecies. Numerous hybrids and new cultivars were now being introduced and snowdrops became increasingly popular.

The Royal Horticultural Society held its inaugural Snowdrop Conference in 1891. One of the speakers was James Allen (1832–1906), an amateur horticulturist who grew more than one hundred varieties of snowdrop at his home, Highfield House in Shepton Mallet. He also possessed the largest collection of snowdrops in England at the time, becoming known as the 'Snowdrop King'. Snowdrops enjoyed the fertile Somerset soil, naturalizing throughout his garden. Sadly, before the value of the collection was realized, much of it was destroyed when the site was redeveloped in 1981 for the headquarters of Mendip District Council. In January 1985 some snowdrops were rescued and taken to Cannington College, Bridgwater.

Edward Augustus Bowles (1865–1954), a self-taught horticulturist and botanical artist, wrote articles about snowdrops in 1914 and 1918, also contributing to the important 1956 monograph *Snowdrops and Snowflake* by Sir Frederick Stern (1884–1967).

Otto Schwarz (1900–1983) wrote a treatise on snowdrops in 1963, grouping them by leaf colour, and in 1965 Zinaida Trofimovna Artjushenko produced an even more detailed account, classifying snowdrops by their anatomical features. Her final works listed seventeen species and two subspecies. Christopher Brickell gave an account of Turkish *Galanthus* species in *Flora of Turkey* in 1984, and in 1998 Zeybeck listed twenty-four taxa in his work on Turkish snowdrops.

Aaron Davis published a major work with his 1999 monograph *The Genus Galanthus*, which gave a more concise overview of *Galanthus*, clearing up a lot of confusion surrounding snowdrops.

Schneeglöckchen (Galánthus nivális) II.
Familie: Amaryllidaceen. Blütezeit: Ende Februar, März

Frühlingsknotenblume (Leucóium vérnum) II.
Familie: Amaryllidaceen. Blütezeit: März, Anfang April

Snowdrops and snowflakes from Walter Nöldner's *Uus Wald und Flur* (1937).

This was followed in 2001 by Matt Bishop, Aaron Davis and John Grimshaw's *Snowdrops – a Monograph of Cultivated Galanthus* (reprinted in 2006), which was hailed as the 'Snowdrop Bible'. *Galanthomania* by Hanneke van Dijk was published in 2011, and *Schneeglöckchen*, by Günter Waldorf in the same year.

Many plants become fashionable and then interest in them fades as a new trend takes hold, and snowdrops are no exception. The Victorian era saw interest in snowdrops reach feverish proportions before slowly declining again. However, stalwart and passionate enthusiasts continued to grow snowdrops, discovering and breeding new hybrids, and interest began to revive again towards the middle of the twentieth century. Today snowdrops have once again captured the attention and imagination of gardeners and horticulturists, in some cases to an obsessive extent. New snowdrops and names appear almost daily; astronomical prices are achieved for rarer plants; twin scaling and micro-propagation increase saleable stocks more rapidly; specialist snowdrop events escalate; and more gardens than ever before open at snowdrop time.

Throughout the twentieth century and on into the twenty-first the impressive list of famous Galanthophiles continues. In the UK alone these include Bertram Anderson, Ruby Baker, Michael Baron, Matt Bishop, Christopher Brickell, David Bromley, Ian Christie, Ray Cobb, Phil Cornish, Cliff Curtis, Aaron Davis, Carolyn Elwes, Catherine Erskine, Margery Fish, John Grimshaw, Ronald Mackenzie, Richard Nutt, Margaret Owen, Joe Sharman and Primrose Warburg.

These simple but very beautiful flowers have seen a renaissance over the last sixty years, to arrive at the height of popularity they enjoy today. With such intense interest, it looks as if this trend will continue for many years to come.

Naming the Snowdrop

The true derivation of the name 'Snowdrop' will probably never be known. Closest is the Swedish *Snödroppe*, but some say it comes from the German *Schneetropfen*, a popular style of sixteenth- and seventeenth-century drop earring. The German *Schneeglöckchen*, and Dutch *Sneeuwklokjes* refer to snow-bells.

Other names include Fair Maids of February, Candlemas Bells, Death's Flower, Dewdrops, Dingle-Dangles, Drooping Bells, Eve's Comforters, Eve's Tears, Flowers of Hope, Mary's Tapers, Naked Maidens, Pierce Snow, Purification Flower, Snowflowers, Snowbells, White Bells and White Ladies.

In France they are known as *Galantine d'hivre* or *Pierce-neige* (snow piercer), in Italy as *bucaneve* and in Hungary as *hovirag*.

The word *Galanthus* itself comes from the Greek *gala* = milk, and *anthos* = flower, while *nivalis* means 'of the snow'.

Ecclesiastical Traditions

Snowdrops have long been associated with Candlemas Day, 2 February, the Feast of the Purification of the Virgin Mary. Young girls dressed in white hung garlands of snowdrops around their necks and carried bunches of snowdrops as symbols of their purity. Walking in procession to the church, they scattered snowdrops on the altars chanting 'The snowdrop in purest white array, first rears her head on Candlemas Day'.

This old custom may help explain why such large colonies of snowdrops are found in churchyards and around old monastic sites. Snowdrops were also probably planted by monks and nuns in their gardens as they represented purity.

In some areas of Britain bunches of snowdrops were also carried into houses in an act of purification.

Legend, Superstition and Folklore

Many superstitions surround snowdrops. In some areas it was considered extremely lucky to take the flowers indoors, but in other areas, including Derbyshire, Hampshire, Northumberland, Shropshire, Staffordshire, Sussex, Westmorland and Worcestershire, it was considered very unlucky, heralding a death. Likewise, in some areas taking indoors the first snowdrop to flower was deemed unlucky, but subsequent flowers were

Extensive colonies of naturalized snowdrops in St Peter's Churchyard, Stanton Lacy, Shropshire.

acceptable. Victorians associated snowdrops with death, saying that they grew 'closer to the dead than the living', and that they resembled shrouds or looked like a corpse in its shroud.

Whereas historical records of snowdrops can be proved and are well documented, superstitions and legends are more tenuous. Many plants were woven into mythology and folklore, and quite often different plants were adapted to the same story, passed down and changed as time and the storyteller dictated. Greek legend tells that when Persephone was taken to the Underworld, earth turned to winter until her return. Snowdrops were just one of the plants she was said to have carried back with her, bringing a breath of spring to the barren landscape. However, because the flowers came from the Underworld, many considered them unlucky.

Naturalized *Galanthus nivalis*, Cound Brook, Shropshire.

Another story tells how King Albion's son fell in love with Oberon's daughter Kenna. Oberon objected to his daughter's liaison and drove her lover from Fairyland, killing him when he tried to return. Kenna attempted to revive him by putting the herb 'Moly' onto his wounds, and as it touched him it turned into a snowdrop. The herb 'Moly' is referred to in Homer's *Odyssey*, and in 1983 Duvoisin suggested that this mysterious and magical herb was in fact the snowdrop. Because the plant does possess medicinal properties, it could therefore have acted as an antidote to the poison. Snowdrops contain the active substance 'Galantamine', which is used in a group of anticholinesterase drugs, beneficial in treating Alzheimer's Disease. Galantamine was originally obtained from wild snowdrops in the Balkans.

One of the snowdrop's colloquial names, 'Eve's Comforters', derives from the story that Eve was weeping in Eden one day because no flowers grew there in winter. Hearing her, an angel caught a passing snowflake, breathed on it and handed it to Eve, saying: '*This is an earnest, Eve, to thee, that sun and summer soon shall be*'. As the angel's feet touched the ground, snowdrops sprang up everywhere and Eve thought them the most beautiful flowers in Eden. Snowdrops were also said to have sprung up in the footsteps of the Virgin Mary as she walked across the hills.

German legend tells that the snow asked God for a colour. He told it to ask the plants and animals for one of their names. The snowdrop flower was the only one willing to share its colour, and so snow became white.

In Celtic mythology snowdrops were flowers of Brigid, triple goddess of poetry, inspiration and healing.

Garden folklore tells that before moving snowdrops, they should always be told what is happening otherwise the plants won't thrive afterwards.

In flower lore snowdrops signify 'Hope' and 'Virginity'. In Victorian times, when flower lore was strictly adhered to, young maidens wore snowdrops as a sign of purity. If a gentleman received a few of the flowers it was a warning that his advances were too ardent.

Whether one believes in the superstitions surrounding snowdrops, simply enjoys the beautiful flowers or is an enthusiastic and committed Galanthophile, snowdrops have the ability to win hearts and fire passions. These cheerful, optimistic little flowers, with their pure white blooms nodding in the sunshine, herald the gentle awakening of our gardens from their long winter sleep, and it makes them irresistible plants to grow. Plant snowdrop bulbs and you can look forward to your own patch of magic each spring. And if you don't have a garden, there is sure to be one not too far away, opening its gates and putting on a spectacular display.

SNOWDROPS IN LITERATURE

Snowdrops have inspired many poets and writers. For example, the poet Thomas Tickell (1686–1740) called snowdrops 'Vegetable snow'.

Alfred Lord Tennyson (1809–1892)
Many, many welcomes,
February fair-maid!
Ever as old as time,
Solitary firstling,
Coming in the cold time,
Prophet of the gay time,
Prophet of the roses,
Many, many welcomes,
February fair-maid!

William Wordsworth (1770–1850)
On Seeing a Tuft of Snowdrops – 1819
… Like these frail snowdrops that together cling,
And nod their helmets, smitten by the wing
Of many a furious whirl-blast sweeping by…

To a Snowdrop
Lone Flower, hemmed in with snow and white as they
But hardier far, once more I see thee bend
Thy forehead, as if fearful to offend, …
… Nor will I then thy modest grace forget,
Chaste snow-drop, venturous harbinger of Spring,
And pensive monitor of fleeting years!

Walter de la Mare (1873–1956)
The Snowdrop
From hidden bulb the flower reared up
Its angled, slender, cold, dark stem.
Whence dangled an inverted cup
For tri-leaved diadem.

Snowdrops in a garden border.

Extensive colonies of *Galanthus nivalis* naturalized in Welsh woodland. (*Photo courtesy Corinne Price*)

James Montogmery (1771–1854)
Snow-drop
At the head of Flora's dance;
Simple Snow-drop then in thee
All they sister-train I see
The morning star of flowers

Mary Webb (1881–1927)
Snowdrop Time
Ah hush! Tread softly through the time,
For there will be a blackbird singing, or a thrush.
Like coloured beads the elmbuds flush:
All the trees dream of leaves and flowers and light.
And see! The northern bank is much more white
Than frosty grass, for now is snowdrop time.

Hans Christian Anderson (1805–1875)
His story of 'The Snowdrop' tells of its journey from bulb to flower, until finally it is picked and pressed in a poetry book.

Twelve Months
This Russian/Japanese animated film tells the story of Anya, a young orphan girl who lives with her stepmother in a cottage in the woods. One New Year's Eve the queen offers a basket of gold to anyone who takes her snowdrops on New Year's Day. Anya's cruel stepmother sends her into a blizzard to find the flowers, not normally in bloom until later in that part of the world. Anya meets the spirits of the twelve months of the year. Taking pity on her, they save her from being frozen to death, and April gives her one hour of spring so she can pick snowdrops and return safely home.

CHAPTER 2

DESCRIPTION OF THE SNOWDROP

Snowdrops are bulbous perennial geophytes in the Amaryllidacea family. They are one of the most popular of all cultivated bulbous plants. The bulbs produce a pair of basal leaves, although occasionally there are more. Leaves are usually present at flowering but sometimes they only appear after the flowers have faded, especially with autumn species.

There is generally one stem or 'scape' to each bulb, occasionally two. Although many descriptions of snowdrops say the flowers have 'petals', these are in fact 'tepals', so named when the perianth cannot be clearly differentiated into a petal or sepal. (Tulips are another example.) Botanically, therefore, the flowers are described as having tepals or perianth segments. Snowdrop flowers are commonly white, solitary, pendant and suspended from a slender pedicel. Three larger outer segments surround three smaller inner segments, which usually have a green mark at the apex, just above the notch or sinus. The under surface of the inner segments is generally delicately striped green.

Contrary to popular belief, snowdrops do not all flower in the spring. Autumn species flower in September and October, and different species and varieties will flower until the following April. This provides a snowdrop season spreading across seven months of the year.

There are at present twenty snowdrop species. In addition, there are in excess of 1,500 different hybrids, cultivars and varieties of snowdrop, but this number continues to rise. While most look very similar to the untrained eye, many show distinctive differences.

Snowdrops vary in height from around 5cm (miniatures) up to 30+cm ('giant'). Flowers can be single or double, pendant or upright, and vary in shape and size. Inner segments usually have green marks at the apex but there can be one large mark, or separate marks at apex and base, or the marks can be yellow rather than the usual green. Outer segments can also have green marks, or the whole flower can be devoid of any marking, creating an 'albino' snowdrop.

OPPOSITE PAGE: Carpets of naturalized snowdrops spreading through woodland at Winsley Hall, Shropshire.

Autumn-flowering *Galanthus reginae-olgae*.
(*Photo courtesy Harry Pierick*)

Snowdrops are hermaphrodite, having both male and female organs. They produce a delicious, light, honey perfume in warm weather, or when brought into a warm room.

Serious Galanthophiles eagerly seek out 'different' snowdrops, looking for unusually shaped flowers or markings, hoping to be the first to find new varieties to name.

Galanthus nivalis

G. nivalis, the common snowdrop, is the one we think of as the *typical* snowdrop. It has pendant white flowers and green-tipped inner segments. It is native to a large area of Europe, from the Pyrenees through France, Germany, Poland, Italy and

Galanthus nivalis.

areas showing distinct climate changes, with hot summers and cold winters. They dislike very hot, dry conditions and shallow soils, tending to prefer cooler, damper, north-facing situations.

Snowdrops appear to prefer growing above calcareous-type rocks and limestone, although they happily grow in most fertile soils. In the wild they also tend to grow on sloping sites. They enjoy humus-rich soil which has a high proportion of organic matter, and shady, damp conditions, particularly in the growing season. During dormancy bulbs can cope with drier conditions providing the soil retains some moisture and does not dry out completely for extended periods.

Their natural habitat is in woodland, meadows and rocky crevices from sea level up to around 2,700m. Some are true alpine plants as they grow above 2,000m, while many species are found growing above the 1,000m line.

Snowdrops can withstand extremely cold winters and have adapted well to the northern European climate, although they are not found naturally in Scandinavia. Snowdrops are often thought to be native British wild flowers but this is unlikely. They were possibly brought into Britain by the Romans, as so many other flowers have erroneously considered to have been, or more probably they were introduced in the early 1500s.

Hardiness Zones (USDA)

Hardiness zones are geographical areas in which plants grow, depending on the plant's ability to withstand the specific temperatures of that zone. Zones are numbered one to ten. In the UK the zones are quite high, varying between seven and ten due to the moderating effects of the Gulf Stream around the coastline. Snowdrops grow best in zones three to eight.

Identification

Identification of snowdrops is a minefield, even for the most dedicated Galanthophile, as snowdrop species and cultivars are notoriously difficult to determine.

Shape of Leaf Base

Taxonomically the shape of the leaf base is the plant's most distinctive feature. Snowdrops generally produce a pair of leaves, although sometimes there are three. Certain cultivars have even more. There are three distinctive leaf forms denoting different species of snowdrop, *G. nivalis*, *G. plicatus* or *G. elwesii*. This 'vernation' is an important feature in helping distinguish between species, and also helps determine the parentage of hybrids.

This vernation is referred to as 'applanate', 'explicative', or 'supervolute'.

northern Greece to Ukraine and European Turkey. Elsewhere snowdrops have been introduced and have naturalized into huge colonies.

Most other *Galanthus* species hail from the Eastern Mediterranean, though a number come from southern Russia, Georgia and Azerbaijan. *G. fosteri* comes from Jordan, Lebanon, Syria and Turkey. There are many different forms of snowdrop, including double, poculiform, albino, spiky, virescent, donkey-eared and yellow.

Distribution

In the wild, snowdrops grow naturally throughout a large part of central and southern Europe and western Asia, with the widest diversity of species found in northern Turkey and the Caucasus. They grow in Albania, Austria, Bulgaria, the Czech Republic, France, Georgia, Germany, Greece, Hungary, Italy, Moldova, Poland, Romania, Slovakia, Spain, Switzerland, Turkey, Ukraine and the former Yugoslavia. Snowdrops grow in

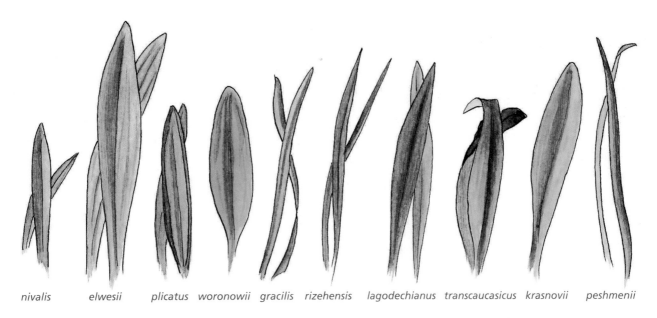

nivalis   *elwesii*   *plicatus*   *woronowii*   *gracilis*   *rizehensis*   *lagodechianus*   *transcaucasicus*   *krasnovii*   *peshmenii*

Variations in snowdrop leaf shapes.

Flower Shape and Segment Marking

Some plants are difficult to recognize as snowdrops at all. The flowers are held upright instead of pendant, with unevenly shaped segments forming an untidy ruff. Segments can all be of equal length. Some flowers form what looks like a ballet dancer's miniature tutu. Others, have a bell-shaped 'skirt' more closely resembling snowflakes, the *Leucojum* and *Acis* species. Often confused with snowdrops, snowflakes also have pendant white flowers with green markings and appear in spring. Snowflake flowers can be single or in an umbel, but the segments are all similar, forming a bell shape with green or yellow markings.

Snowdrop flowers may also be misshapen or poorly formed for no apparent reason. Again, this can be a passing aberration or it may denote a new cultivar. Many snowdrop markings appear virtually identical to the amateur, whereas experts appreciate these are individually named hybrids and cultivars.

Snowdrops typically have a single inverted U- or V-shaped green mark at the apex of the inner segments, around the notch or sinus, although the shape of these marks can vary.

There can be a tiny spot or line, or the mark can almost completely cover the whole inner segment. In some snowdrops the outer segments also carry green marks, which again can vary in size and shape.

The merest hint of a change to markings or segment shape is eagerly sought out in case it indicates a new variety. Often these changes are disappointing – simply short-term anomalies denoting that for some reason the plant is performing slightly differently for a season, often after being moved – but a few do denote a new cultivar. *G. nivalis* 'Lady Elphinstone', for instance, a beautiful snowdrop with a light apricot-yellow mark, will suddenly come up one year with green-marked flowers. In some years green tips may suddenly appear on a snowdrop but be absent the following year.

Differences that remain constant over a period of time may well denote a new variety and, as interest grows, increasing attention is paid to the markings in an attempt to determine new hybrids and cultivars. This adds more names to an already extensive list. Despite this, many 'different' snowdrops still remain unnamed as the plants can be so variable or are too poor to merit a name.

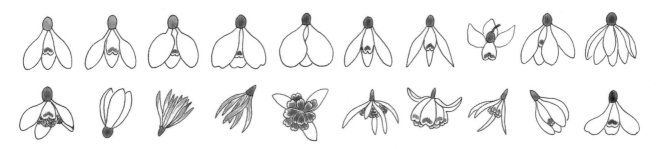

Variations in snowdrop flower shapes.

The snowdrop and its parts.

1. bulb
2. roots
3. tunic
4. sheath
5. leaf
6. scape
7. spathe
8. pedicel

9. ovary
10. flower
11. outer perianth segments
12. inner perianth segments
13. inner perianth segment
     internal view
14. immature fruit
15. flower bud

16. vertical section of flower
17. dormant bulb
18. new bulblet
19. mature fruit
20. mature fruit vertical cross section
     showing developing seeds
21. horizontal section
22. seed

23. fruiting capsule open
     showing seeds
24. ovary and style
25. filament
26. anther
27. ovary, style and anthers
28. apex of mature fruit

Bulbs

Bulbs are spherical to ovoid with a narrower neck or 'nose'. The basal plate is a flattened area at the base of the bulb from which the roots develop. Bulbs are formed from swollen leaf bases compressed together (termed bulb scales), and these store starch created by photosynthesis in the leaves above. Snowdrop bulbs are covered with a thin, brown, papery outer layer or 'tunic', although this can be missing completely, or simply have remnants of the tunic remaining. This tunic is formed from old shrivelled bulb scales which are slowly pushed outwards as new scales are formed in the middle.

Secondary shoots grow from bulb scale axils, developing into side bulbs around the basal plate. These go on to produce new plants. Snowdrops also increase from seed.

After the flowers have faded, the leaves continue to grow, supplying nutrients back into the bulb by the process of photosynthesis. A new shoot quickly develops inside the bulb for the following season, and the bulb then remains dormant throughout the summer months. With the approach of cooler autumn temperatures, new roots begin to grow, thrusting down into the moist earth. The newly forming shoot and bud are protected by a strong, cylindrical sheath, a modified leaf, which splits as the shoot reaches the surface, allowing the bud to emerge.

Each bulb usually produces a pair of leaves, a single flowering stem or scape, and one pendant flower. In some snowdrops the flowers can point upwards, or there can be two flowerheads on the stem.

Leaves

Although the shape and markings of snowdrop flowers are extremely significant, these can and do vary in the same species. This means the leaves are perhaps the most important feature in distinguishing different species and the parentage of hybrids and cultivars. Vernation of leaves is applanate, explicative or supervolute:

- Applanate: two opposite leaf blades pressed flat against each other in the bud and as they emerge.
- Explicative: leaves held flat against each other but with the leaf edges folded back, or sometimes rolled.
- Supervolute: one leaf clasped tightly around the other inside the bud, often remaining so at the point where the leaves emerge from the bud.

As the plants mature, much of this vernation becomes indistinguishable, requiring careful examination. It is usually, though not always, detectable at soil level.

Depending on the snowdrop type, leaves can either be very lax, semi-erect or upright as they develop, further aiding identification. Snowdrop bulbs generally produce a pair of leaves, although some have three or even more leaves. Each leaf has a median rib that varies from very pronounced to almost indistinguishable. Leaves are generally smooth or

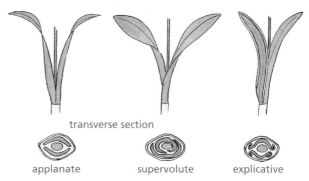

Vernation of snowdrop leaves.

transverse section

applanate   supervolute   explicative

slightly grooved or puckered, and vary in colour from light to dark green, blue-grey or glaucous – caused by a thin coating of wax. Leaves are often darker on the upper surface and paler beneath. Leaf tips vary from acute (pointed) to obtuse (rounded). They can be flat, or cucullate (slightly hooded). In most snowdrop species the leaves are present at flowering. Some species, such a *G. reginae-olgae*, have only small leaves at flowering, while in others, such as *G. peshmenii*, the leaves usually only develop after flowering. These are generally autumn-flowering species.

The leaves continue to develop after the flowers have faded, becoming longer, wider and more lax, continuing photosynthesis to supply nutrients back into the bulb. Because of this, snowdrop leaves must be left to die back naturally and should never be cut back or removed. The leaves disappear completely within a few weeks of the flowers fading.

Scape

The emerging bud is protected by a strong, almost transparent sheath, or 'spathe', which splits as the bud breaks the surface of the ground. A single, slender stem, the scape, emerges from between a pair of leaves. At the top of the scape the bud is held erect on a slender pedicel. The pedicel can be upright and short, or long and arching. In most snowdrops the bud soon drops into a pendant position. Some snowdrops produce two scapes per bulb.

Inflorescence

This refers to the flowering parts. Most snowdrop flowers are pendant and made up of six segments arranged in two whorls of three, which are not joined to each other at the base. These are referred to as the inner and outer perianth segments. Each scape generally produces one flower, but sometimes there are two flowers, and in rare instances even three. Some snowdrop flowers have long, slim, pointed segments, others are shorter and rounded, resembling a spoon, or pear-shaped. Flowers can have more than six segments, as in *G. nivalis* 'Flore Pleno', the double snowdrop, where the inner segments are multiplied to form a ruff. In some areas 'Flore Pleno' is more common than single *G. nivalis*.

The three larger, equally sized, outer perianth segments are convex, spoon or bowl-shaped (cunneate), usually white, and lightly ridged. They taper towards the base, often forming a 'claw' where they join the ovary. Very pronounced claws are referred to as 'unguiculate'. If the claw has slight furrowing, this is termed 'goffering'. Some snowdrops have green markings on the outer segments.

The outer perianth segments surround three smaller, white, inner perianth segments, generally half to two-thirds smaller than the outer segments. They are rounded or slightly pointed at the apex, with a small notch or sinus. The sinus is present in most, although not all, snowdrops. The inner segments are less curved and more tube-like than the outer, and generally have green marks at the apex, although these can be absent. These marks are usually small and take the form of an inverted U or V, or are Chinese bridge-shaped. Depending on the species or variety, the mark can be a thin line, a spot either side of the sinus, X-shaped, scissor-shaped, or heart-shaped; there may be two green marks, one at the apex and one at the base of the inner segments, or the mark can cover almost the entire inner segments, in which case it generally pales, or diffuses, towards the base of the segments. The shape and coloration of the marks are important in helping to identify different snowdrops. The underside of the inner segments is generally ribbed and finely striped with green.

Some snowdrops have yellow or apricot-coloured markings instead of green, for example 'Wendy's Gold'. In some snowdrops this yellow, apricot or orange colouring diffuses across the segments.

The temperature inside the inner segments is up to 2 degrees warmer than the outside air temperature, thus giving a further measure of protection for the delicate reproductive parts of the plant.

Snowdrop flowers remain in bloom for a long time compared to many other bulbous plants. Under normal conditions flowers will usually last for a good month or more.

Fertilization

The inner segments of the snowdrop surround six stamens, which in turn surround the slender, straight style. The filaments are straight and usually shorter than the perianth segments. Stamens are not attached to each other and are only attached to the flower at the receptacle. Orange-yellow anthers open by way of two terminal splits, which gradually extend towards the base. Anthers mature at the same time as the stigma, and the orange-yellow pollen is released when flowers are moved either in the breeze or by insects. A barely discernible nectary at the base of the style and filaments secretes nectar, attracting insects. Bees coming for the nectar touch the stigma, which is longer than the anthers, with pollen from flowers previously visited, thus effecting pollination. If the flower has not been pollinated by insects, the stalks of the anthers loosen and the anthers meet so that pollen falls onto the stigma. As the weather warms up, the flower segments open wider to allow fertilization, closing again as temperatures cool.

The small swelling at the top of the snowdrop flower is an inferior three-celled ovary made up of three fused carpels. These ripen and split into a three-celled, oval to spherical capsule, formed from the receptacle and ovary. Tiny, oval whitish seeds have fleshy tails (elaiosomes), which shrink as the seeds mature. After pollination, the flowers fade and the scape drops into a prostrate position until it touches the ground. The capsule swells, until it eventually opens to release seeds that contain substances ants find very attractive, thus helping with distribution.

Snowdrop flowers produce a delicate honey perfume as well as providing an important source of nectar for early bees, particularly bumblebees, and snowdrop flowers are specifically adapted for pollination by bees.

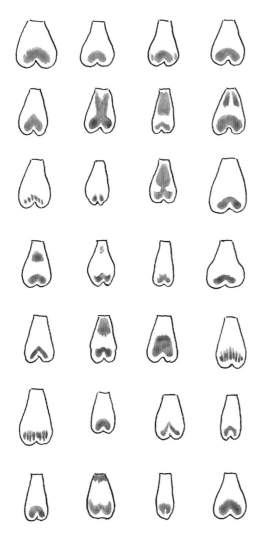

Variations in snowdrop inner segment markings.

Propagation

Most snowdrops spread quickly from small bulblets that form around the base plate of parent bulbs. These develop into new plants. Most snowdrops also reproduce from seed. Snowdrops flowering during the main period, between mid-January and mid-February, produce ripe seed between late April and June. Germinated seeds develop into a small bulb with a single leaf by the following season. The bulb increases in size, producing two leaves in the second season, followed by a flower in the third or fourth year.

Snowdrops can hybridize to form new seedlings that can continue to cross, potentially giving rise to new cultivars, which are eagerly sought by discerning collectors.

Seeing and Buying Snowdrops

Each year increasing numbers of snowdrop gardens open to the public. These special openings are widely publicized in the local and national press, on the internet and in the NGS Yellow Book. This means virtually everyone can find and visit a snowdrop garden in close proximity to where they live.

Bulbs are also frequently offered for sale at these venues. Specialist nurseries advertise and stock a wide range of rare as well as common snowdrops, cultivars and hybrids. Nurseries also exhibit at horticultural fairs and flower shows, including the world-renowned RHS spring shows in London,

Outer segments reflex back in sun and warmth.

Snowdrop sales at Colesbourne Park, Gloucestershire.

CLIMATE CHANGE

The Royal Botanic Gardens, Kew, and Wakehurst Place are conducting research into plant life cycles over periods of time, a study known as Phenology. This provides valuable insights into possible changing climate conditions. Hundreds of plants are monitored each year in the gardens and flowering times recorded. Study of *G. nivalis* shows that within the last fifty or sixty years their main flowering period is now almost a month earlier, in January.

staging spectacular and tempting displays of the best in snowdrops. There is an annual Galanthus Gala in the UK, a magnet for Galanthophiles from around the world. Special, invitation only, snowdrop lunches are hosted by serious Galanthophiles to discuss, view, sell and exchange new varieties and rare bulbs.

Internet auction sites have also become a source for bulbs, but beware of the descriptions and names given, which can be confusing and misleading. You may unwittingly pay a considerable sum of money for what turns out to be a very ordinary snowdrop.

When admiring areas of naturalized snowdrops, carefully watch for any which look a little different. Many new snowdrops have been discovered in this way by sharp-eyed Galanthophiles.

Collection of Wild Bulbs

Like many other plants, snowdrops have been massively over-collected, decimating their native habitats. The two main reasons for this are the financial rewards for supplying plants to the horticultural trade, and the encroachment of agriculture and land development.

Many bulbs such as narcissi and tulips are easily grown commercially in large fields. Snowdrops do not adapt well to this form of cultivation and many small villages obtained their main source of income from selling snowdrop bulbs collected from the wild. This trade was extremely difficult to control as millions of bulbs were collected and exported for resale. Over-collection threatened many sites, putting snowdrop species at risk.

Wild sources of *G. nivalis* have been severely depleted. For instance, it was once very common and widely distributed in the East Carpathian mountains, but within the last few years this is no longer the case. Now wild collection of *G. nivalis*

A selection of recently purchased and planted imported *Galanthus elwesii*, Colesbourne Park, Gloucestershire.

Large swathes of naturalized snowdrops colonize areas of countryside but it is illegal to dig up or remove bulbs without the permission of the landowner.

bulbs has virtually ceased after the end of exports from Hungary in 1995. In Ukraine *G. nivalis* is on the list of Rare and Disappearing Species. In some areas it is considered seriously under threat of extinction.

Galanthus elwesii bulbs have been collected and exported from Turkey since the 1800s. Between the 1960s and 1980s trade increased to such an extent that around forty million bulbs a year were exported by the mid-1980s. The fifteen or so companies involved in exporting such large numbers of bulbs are now reduced to four. Bulbs can only be collected over a two-week period in mid-May by local villagers. Legislation enabled specific quotas to be set up for the export of *G. elwesii*, and careful monitoring ensures trade is sustainable. This eased the pressure on the wild collection of *G. elwesii*, helping preserve bulbs and their natural environment.

Collection sites must be allowed to regenerate for three years before re-collection can occur at the same site. Small offsets must be replanted and *G. elwesii* cannot be collected from locations containing rarer snowdrop species. Regular inspections ensure regulations are maintained, collection is sustainable, native bulb stocks remain healthy, and harvesting has no detrimental effect on wild stocks. Collection of bulbs is carried out within the terms of the CITES agreement and at present is limited to eight million bulbs each year. *G. elwesii* bulbs from Turkey are exported mainly to the Netherlands for the commercial horticultural trade.

Over recent years schemes have been put in place encouraging the commercial cultivation of snowdrops in Turkey and Georgia. Habitats are also being destroyed by the creation of new towns, which decimates plant habitats, particularly in low foothills.

G. nivalis bulbs are sold in their millions each year. In the UK small-scale collection occurs on various large estates with extensive collections. This operates on a four- or five-year rota so stocks remain sustainable. Bulbs are sold to the horticultural trade or to private individuals visiting the estates.

Galanthus nivalis.

CITES

In the early 1990s collecting snowdrops from the wild came under the control of CITES – the Convention on International Trade in Endangered Species of Wild Fauna and Flora. This is an agreement between governments worldwide. The aim of CITES is to help ensure the survival of endangered species in the wild. In most countries it is now illegal to collect snowdrops without a CITES permit. At this stage snowdrops are not as severely threatened with extinction in the wild as many other plants, but limiting trade stops them becoming increasingly endangered.

All snowdrops are listed under CITES Appendix No. 2, categorized as plants which are not under imminent threat of extinction but which are monitored and regulated to protect wild populations and safeguard them against becoming endangered. In the UK CITES controls *G. nivalis* and all wild orchids.

CITES stipulates that international trade in *Galanthus* – whether bulbs, living or dead plants – is illegal without a permit. This applies to all species, named cultivars and hybrids. There are only three species in which CITES allows limited trade in wild collected bulbs, *G. nivalis*, *G. elwesii* and *G. woronowii* from Turkey and Georgia. People who once derived their incomes from wild bulb collection are encouraged to cultivate bulbs on a commercial basis, easing the pressure on over-harvesting of wild bulbs.

So many plants are now seriously threatened or have become extinct in their wild habitats due to over-collection and thoughtless management, and it is imperative that we do all in our power to protect and preserve plants for their benefit and the benefit of generations to come. This is why it is so important to buy only from reputable sources. Most nurseries now sell bulbs raised from offsets, chipping or seed, and not wild collected bulbs.

Code of Conduct for Conservation of Wild Plants

Digging up wild plants in the countryside is not only harmful to the plants, many of which never survive, but in many cases it is also highly illegal. Picking a small handful of primroses, bluebells or snowdrops is a joy, but if everyone followed suit there would soon be few flowers left. In some instances it is even illegal to pick certain flowering plants.

Wild plants are protected by the law in the UK. The 1981 Wildlife and Countryside Act made it illegal to dig up or remove any wild plant without the permission of the landowner. This also applied in Northern Ireland after the 1985 Wildlife (Northern Ireland) Order. Under the 1968 Theft Act it is a serious offence to remove plants from the countryside for commercial purposes without formal authorization.

Strict rules and guidelines apply to National Nature Reserves, Sites of Special Scientific Interest (SSSIs) in the UK and Areas of Special Scientific Interest (ASSIs) in Northern Ireland. Plants on these sites cannot be removed or destroyed by landowners without prior consultation and agreement with the relevant authorities – English Nature, the Countryside Council for Wales, Scottish Natural Heritage, and the Northern Ireland Environment and Heritage Service. Additional bylaws make it illegal to pick, uproot or remove plants on certain sites such as Nature Reserves, National Trust properties or Ministry of Defence land.

There are lists of endangered plants that are protected against intentional destruction, uprooting or picking without prior possession of a special licence from the relevant authority. Plants are also protected from being sold. Lists of rare species can be obtained from the Joint Nature Conservation Committee or viewed on its website. In some instances all stages of the biological cycle of certain plants, including seeds and spores, are protected, as well as mature specimens.

Schedule 8 of the Wildlife and Countryside Act covering the above is revised every five years. The aim of these laws is to encourage enjoyment of the countryside while promoting the conservation of wild plants.

National Red Data Books and Country Rare Plant Registers contain details of endangered plants. Plants which are not included on the Red lists may be collected for purely botanical purposes. In these instances only the smallest amount of material possible should be removed to enable the study to go ahead.

In some instances picking is acceptable, but if you are unsure it is better not to risk falling foul of the law. If in doubt, or if there are only one or two plants, it is safer to follow the rule not to pick. Organizers leading groups should also be aware that it is their responsibility to obtain necessary permissions and ensure groups comply with the law and follow all guidelines.

Plant photography should be undertaken with care so plants and surrounding areas remain undamaged. Sites of rare plants should not be publicized to their detriment, passed on to collectors, or the plants or areas around them damaged in any way. New finds should be reported to the local Wildlife Trust, which will take the relevant action.

Conversely plants or seeds must not be introduced into the wild. Many invasive species, introduced by well meaning bystanders who think they can improve on nature, cause severe problems, and put native plants at risk.

It is important that these codes are practised worldwide. Follow the rules, never pick endangered species or those on Red lists; when a plant can be picked, take only the smallest portion; don't pick plants unnecessarily; do not pick flowers that will wilt and die immediately, such as poppies; and be careful not to damage other vegetation when picking flowers.

Children will always want to pick flowers and gathering one or two plants of a common species is relatively innocuous. However, it is important that young people are taught to respect plants and their environment. A handful of hastily picked and then swiftly forgotten flowers does nobody any good.

CHAPTER 3

SNOWDROP SPECIES

All plants belong to the plant kingdom, *Plantae*, with a specific order of taxonomy descending through class, subclass, superorder, order, family, subfamily, genus, species and subspecies.

TAXONOMY

Kingdom: *Plantae*
Class: *Angiospermae*
Subclass: *Mesangiospermae*
Superorder: *Monocots*
Order: *Asparagales*
Family: *Amaryllidaceae*
Subfamily: *Amaryllidoideae*
Genus: *Galanthus*

In the main it is the lower ranks that are of interest to most horticulturists. Carl Linnaeus (1707–1778) was the first botanist to standardize a complicated and unregulated system for naming plants by introducing a binomial (two-part) classification in 1753.

The genus name comes first, grouping plants with a common ancestry. It begins with a capital letter, in this case *Galanthus*. Within the genus there can be a number of different species. Each has its own specific type characteristics applying to that particular species. This forms the second part of the name, written in lower case, and is usually more descriptive: examples include *Galanthus nivalis* = 'of the snow'; *Galanthus elwesii* = 'found by Elwes'; *G. ikariae* = after the Greek island of Ikaria where it was first found; *G. gracilis* = 'graceful'. Both genus and species names are usually written in italics.

The next rank below species is subspecies. These have similar characteristics to a species but morphological variations which set them apart, such as distinctively shaped marks or flower segments,

or a different flowering time. Subspecies are denoted by subsp. or ssp. after the species name: *Galanthus elwesii* subsp. *elwesii*.

In the wild most snowdrop species grow in their own distinct geographical locations, which rarely overlap. This means subspecies are fairly limited in the wild as two different species rarely get the chance to interbreed.

When a new hybrid becomes available, it is attributed a name. This is not written in italics, begins with a capital letter, and is enclosed within single quotation marks: *Galanthus nivalis* 'Bitton'. If the parentage of the plant is unknown, only the genus and cultivar names are used: *Galanthus* 'Atkinsii'.

The naming of plants is regulated by the International Code of Botanical Nomenclature for wild plants and the International Code of Nomenclature for Cultivated Plants (see Chapter 4).

Plant names regularly change. New research and information leads to plants being regrouped, placed in a new species or subspecies, or even transferred to a different genus. New names follow and the original obsolete name then becomes a synonym of the new plant. Botanists and gardeners find it extremely frustrating when a name they have known for many years suddenly disappears and a new name is coined. However, confusing as this may be, it is generally for the better, ironing out past inconsistencies to further clarify the whole system.

Snowdrop Species

In April 2012 the nineteen known species of snowdrop officially became twenty. The latest exciting addition, *G. panjutinii*, was confirmed, researched and named by Aaron Davis and Dmitriy Zubov. One other snowdrop is at present undergoing research and classification, and it is expected that a new species name will be released in the not-too-distant future.

OPPOSITE PAGE: *Galanthus plicatus*.

Snowdrop species cover a range of flowering times from September to April. *G. reginae-olgae* subsp. *reginae-olgae* is one of the first to flower, while *G. platyphyllus* is among the last, blooming from April to July, sometimes into August in the wild. Different species have their own recognizable characteristics, including different flower shapes and markings. Most common species are easy to cultivate and grow well in gardens, creating good displays and bulking up quickly. Others are less reliable, requiring specialist attention or conditions, making them less popular with all but seriously committed Galanthophiles. By concentrating on the more reliable species, which are simple and inexpensive to acquire, a good collection can be established quickly and easily. Rarer species can be found in specialist snowdrop gardens and collections, many of which open to the public, so there is usually an opportunity to see them.

Classification

There have been numerous attempts at classification, and even in recent publications varying classifications have been promulgated, muddying the already clouded waters. Despite the long history of snowdrops, and the flower's increasing popularity in the twentieth and twenty-first centuries, surprisingly few books have been written about them. *Snowdrops – A Monograph of Cultivated Galanthus*, by Matt Bishop, Aaron Davis and John Grimshaw (Griffin Press, 2001, repr. 2006 and currently being updated), is the most relevant and comprehensive, creating order from chaos. It firmly establishes a reliable classification and reference structure for the genus *Galanthus*, which should become the recognized system for the future.

The Species

Galanthus nivalis ↑15–20cm

Syns. There have been over fifty names for variants now recognized as belonging to this species.

The 'Common' or 'English' snowdrop is the best known, most easily recognized and widely grown *Galanthus* species. It is native to western, central and southern Europe from the Ukraine in the east to the Pyrenees in the west, but not the Caucasus or Asian Turkey. Now widely naturalized across Europe, including the UK, it is well suited to the colder, northern climate.

G. nivalis grows well beneath deciduous trees, its preferred habitat in the wild, receiving dappled shade from the leaf canopy in summer, followed by light and sunshine during winter when the trees are bare of leaves. It appreciates some humidity and large, naturalized populations are often found near water. It grows well on sloping sites, especially those with northern aspects, from 100 to 1,600m. It flowers from early January to mid-March in cultivation, from early January to as late as May in the wild.

Galanthus nivalis.

The type form has simple, lightly perfumed, white, pendant flowers with three larger outer segments surrounding three smaller inner segments. Bulbs produce a single, slender scape between a pair of blue-green, glaucescent leaves, often with a noticeable median stripe on the upper leaf surface. Leaves are held flat at the base of the stem, applanate. Inner segments have a single green inverted U or V mark at the apex, often slightly broader at the base on either side of the sinus. Green lines on internal faces of inner segments run from apex to base.

Size of flowers and leaf colour varies depending on plants and habitat. There are slight variations and mutations. Early cultivars were chosen because they looked different from the norm. It is probable that hybridization has occurred in certain areas.

Tough and easy to grow in wide-ranging conditions, *G. nivalis* prefers humus-rich, moist soil, but also grows well on clay, sand, limestone and chalk. It can contend with drier conditions but also withstands damp areas and even occasional flooding. Bulbs spread quickly by offsets and also seed, forming extensive colonies in very few years.

G. nivalis bulks up well and quickly, and is the cheapest snowdrop to purchase. Dividing clumps every three or four years prevents the bulbs becoming congested, which can affect reliability, the health of the bulbs and flowering. However, colonies can be left undisturbed for many years with no detrimental effect.

One of the best snowdrops for naturalizing, large and impressive *G. nivalis* colonies spread beneath trees in deciduous woodland on country estates such as Attingham Park, Shropshire (National Trust), Hodsock Priory, Nottinghamshire, Colesbourne Park, Gloucestershire, and the Cambo Estate, Scotland, as well as in thousands of gardens. Extensive colonies have also naturalized in country areas including Snowdrop Valley, Exmoor, and along the banks of the Cound Brook, Shropshire.

G. nivalis was the first snowdrop to be documented (Gerard 1597), and was most likely introduced into Britain in the early sixteenth century. Plants were uncommon even then, with scant reports by botanical writers of the era. By the eighteenth century descriptions of *G. nivalis* were slowly becoming more common, together with details of naturalized colonies.

G. nivalis was named scientifically by Linnaeus in 1753 in his *'Species plantarum'*, *galanthus* from the Greek *'gala'* = milk and *'anthos'* = flower, *'nivalis'* = of the snow.

Galanthus reginae-olgae ↑10cm

Syn. *G. nivalis* subsp. *reginae-olgae*
Native to Greece, the Peloponnese, southwestern areas of the former Yugoslavia, Corfu, Sicily, Italy, possibly Albania, these lightly perfumed snowdrops flourish in specific micro-climates, in or near deciduous and pine woodland, on shady north-facing slopes, in damp gorges, among rocks or edging streams, from 1,000 to 1,300m. They flower from September to March in cultivation, from October to March in the wild.

The leaves are applanate, with narrow, linear, flat-subrevolute margins; the upper leaf surface is darker grey-green, with an obvious grey-glaucous median stripe. The undersides are paler. The leaves are absent or small at flowering, a characteristic shared with *G. peshmenii*. After flowering the leaves grow normally. Inner segments have an inverted U or V mark broadening on each side of the sinus, and a lighter green marking often covers the whole underside of the inner segments.

Closely related to *G. nivalis* and almost as hardy, *G. reginae-olgae* prefers slightly drier, sunnier situations, and requires a little cosseting until established. It is the earliest snowdrop to flower, from around mid-September. Different forms flower between September and March, but not all are hardy. The bulbs bulk up well, quickly producing large, attractive clumps.

This snowdrop, discovered in the Taigetos Mountains in Greece in 1876 by botanist and poet T.G. Orphanides, was named in honour of Queen Olga of Greece (1851–1926), the grandmother of HRH Prince Phillip, the Duke of Edinburgh. The snowdrop's autumn flowering habit originally caused tremendous excitement. Orphanides asked a high price for the bulbs and few were therefore purchased. Later, *G. reginae-olgae* was discovered in other locations, and received a variety of different names until found to be the same as Orphanides's snowdrop.

Galanthus reginae-olgae.

Galanthus reginae-olgae subsp. reginae-olgae ↑8–12cm

Syn. *G. corcyrensis*; *G. reginae-olgae* subsp. *corcyrensis*.
Native to the Peloponnese, Greece, Corfu and Sicily, this snowdrop's leaves are small or absent at flowering. It prefers damp, shady, often north-facing situations, from 600 to 1,200m. It flowers from September to December in cultivation, and from October to December in the wild.

Galanthus reginae-olgae subsp. vernalis ↑7–15cm

Native to the Peloponnese, Greece, the former Yugoslavia, Italy, Sicily and possibly Albania. It flourishes in deciduous woodland and shady gorges. Generally spring flowering, it flowers from late December to March in cultivation and in the wild, although it is autumn flowering in some areas. It has large flowers and the leaves, which are present at flowering, have a glaucous median stripe.

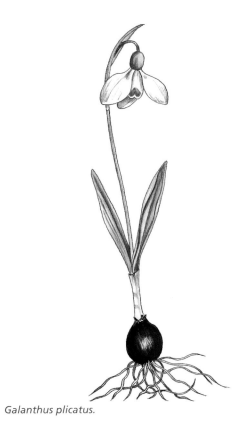

Galanthus plicatus.

Galanthus plicatus ↑25cm

Native to central and western regions of the Black Sea, Crimea, southern Russia, northern Turkey and Romania, this snowdrop thrives in deciduous and coniferous woodland, in scrub, and near rivers and streams, from 100 to 1,350m. It flowers from November to March in cultivation, and from February to April in the wild. Its leaves are explicative, green or grey-green, and glaucous, usually with a silver median stripe; the undersides are paler green-grey, with the edges conspicuously folded flat against the lower surface. Inner flower segments generally have a single apical green mark.

Cultivated since the sixteenth century, *G. plicatus* is popular. Vigorous and easy to grow. Free-flowering over long period, it naturalizes and seeds freely. It is very variable in the wild, in cultivation and in its hybrids . It hybridizes freely with *G. nivalis* and *G. elwesii*. There are some excellent named cultivars, including yellows.

Galanthus plicatus subsp. plicatus ↑10–20cm

Syns. *G. byzantinus* subsp. *brauneri*, *G. byzantinus* subsp. *saueri*, *G. byzantinus* subsp. *tughrulii*, *G. plicatus* subsp. *kara-manoghluensis*, *G. plicatus* subsp. *vardarii*.
Native to northern Turkey, Romania and southern Russia, in deciduous and coniferous woodland margins, from 80 to 1,350m. It flowers from February to April. The inner segments have a single variable apical mark, which can cover the whole segment.

Galanthus plicatus subsp. byzantinus ↑10–20cm

Syns. *G. byzantinus*; *G. plicatus* var. *byzantinus*
Native to northwestern Turkey, this snowdrop flowers from December to March in cultivation, and from late January to April in the wild. The leaves are explicative. The inner segments have a green mark at apex and base.

Galanthus gracilis ↑10–15cm

Syns. *G. graecus* subsp. *minor*; *G. elwesii* subsp. *yayintaschii*
This snowdrop is native to the Ukraine, Romania, Bulgaria, western Turkey and Greece, including the eastern Aegean islands, and favours deep fertile soil in mountainous regions, mixed woodland margins, valleys, scrub, grass, rocky areas and near rivers, from 100 to 2,000m, but usually around 800m. The northernmost wild distributions are generally found at lower altitudes. It flowers from January to March in cultivation, and from February to May in the wild.

The flower is elegant, with a long, pale green ovary, and has a light honey perfume. The leaves are applanate, grey-green, upright, narrow and often distinctively twisted. The inner segments are prominently ridged, and uniquely flared at the apex, revealing green undersides; there is a green X-shaped mark across each segment or separate marks at apex and base.

Galanthus gracilis.

A small but robust snowdrop; it bulks up well and seeds freely, and seeds freely, and deserves to be more widely grown. There are numerous variously sized and marked clones, some of them very small.

It is closely related to *G. elwesii*, with similar markings and similar distribution zones, which overlap in places.

Galanthus cilicicus ↑10–18cm

Syn. *G. nivalis* subsp. *cilicicus*

This rare snowdrop is found in the area originally known as Cilicia, between southern Turkey's Taurus mountains and the Mediterranean Sea, growing in grass, scrub and pockets in limestone cliffs and rocks, from 500 to 600m. It flowers from November to January.

The leaves are applanate, glaucous and well developed at flowering. The inner segments have a variable inverted U or heart-shaped mark at the apex.

Rare both in the wild and in cultivation, *G. cilicicus* is notoriously unreliable and difficult to propagate. It is best suited to cultivation under glass, although it may grow outside in well drained, alkaline soil in a sheltered position.

It was described by John Baker in 1897. It is closely related to the autumn-flowering *G. peshmenii*.

Galanthus peshmenii.

Galanthus peshmenii ↑9–12.5cm

This snowdrop's natural distribution covers a very small area. It was first discovered on the Aegean island of Kastellorizo in 1973 by the Greek botanist E. Stamatiadou, and was later found in small pockets on the Turkish mainland around Antalya province by H. Peşmen, B. Yildiz and O. Günes in 1978. Aaron Davis and Christopher Brickell gave it a definitive description in 1994, suggesting it was closely related to *G. cilicicus*.

It grows in north-facing shady woodland, scrub, or limestone rocks in deep fertile crevices, which provide protection from high temperatures and desiccating sunlight. It is found from almost sea level up to 1,000m. It is autumn flowering, from October to November in cultivation, and from October to December in the wild.

The leaves are applanate, narrow, grey-green glaucescent, with a grey median stripe. They are generally absent during flowering, or small. Mature leaves are long and lax. The inner segments have a variable heart or V-shaped green mark at the apex covering up to half of the segment, or a tiny spot on each side of the sinus.

G. peshmenii is challenging to grow; it dislikes wet and cold, and is not always successful under glass. It might grow outside in warm, sheltered areas with well drained soil.

It is similar to *G. cilicicus* apart from the leaves being small or absent at flowering. It is also similar (but not closely related) to *G. reginae-olgae*. *G. peshmenii* leaves are not as green as those of *G. reginae-olgae*, and they also contain an almost unique palisade layer of longer cells, denoting a significant difference between the two.

Galanthus cilicicus.

Galanthus angustifolius.

Galanthus angustifolius ↑7–14cm

Syn. *G. nivalis* subsp. *angustifolius*
This snowdrop is from the northern Caucasus, where it is found in small clumps in the rich loam edging deciduous forests and scrub, from 700 to 1,000m. It flowers from March to May.

The leaves are applanate, narrow and glaucous, with a distinct midrib and outward curve. The inner segments have a variable inverted V at the apex.

It is extremely rare both in the wild and in cultivation, but it should be hardy in northern Europe. It was introduced by J.I. Koss, the Russian botanist, in 1951. Aaron Davis differentiates this as a distinct species, although it is very similar to *G. alpinus*.

Galanthus elwesii ↑9–18cm

The second most common snowdrop in cultivation, with the widest natural distribution after *G. nivalis* and earlier flowering. It is native to Greece, Ukraine, the former Yugoslavia, Bulgaria and Turkey, with the largest wild populations in the Taurus mountains of southern Turkey, which are snow-covered in winter and cool in summer. It flourishes on north-facing sites, in deep pockets of rich soil between rocks, in deciduous and coniferous woodland, scrub, grass and subalpine pasture, from 800 to 1,600m. It flowers from October to March in cultivation, and from February to May in the wild.

The leaves are supervolute, broad, sometimes twisted, grey-green and glaucous, with vernation continuing into maturity. The flowers are large, and slender to pear-shaped, with a honey perfume. The inner segments have variable markings: a single inverted V to heart-shape; an X-shaped mark; or separate marks at apex and base, sometimes merging across the segment.

G. elwesii is free flowering and easy to grow, naturalizing and spreading well. It has striking, highly variable, flowers. Numerous strong, interesting hybrids cover a wide flowering period. The bulbs benefit from regular lifting and division, and some prefer free-draining, drier conditions.

It was probably originally collected in the Yamanlar Dagh mountains in 1854 by M. Balansa. Later plant collector Henry John Elwes (1846–1922), collected bulbs in 1874, cultivating them at Colesbourne, Gloucestershire. The snowdrop was named after him in 1875 by Sir Joseph Dalton Hooker (1817–1911), Director of the Royal Botanic Gardens, Kew. Although this snowdrop was later determined to be *G. gracilis*, the name *G. elwesii* was kept for the plant familiar in gardens today.

It was extensively harvested and imported from the wild, but not always successfully, as many failed to establish. At one stage it was seriously threatened from over-collection until trade was controlled. There is still a limited trade in wild collected *G. elwesii*, but most now originate from cultivated stocks, giving better results, as well as protecting wild plants.

G. elwesii's provenance has been subject to much discussion and confusion with other species. In the wild it is often found with (and probably hybridized with) *G. gracilis*. *G. elwesii* is differentiated by its supervolute foliage, while *G. gracilis* has

Galanthus elwesii.

applanate foliage. Plants originally known as *G. caucasicus* are likely to be single-marked *G. elwesii*, while many large *G. elwesii* var. *monostictus* have been labelled *G. caucasicus* in gardens. Aaron Davis treats *G. caucasicus* as a Syn. of *G. alpinus*, although this has been disputed.

Galanthus elwesii var. *elwesii* ↑15–18cm

Syns. *G. elwesii* subsp. *akmanii*; *G. elwesii* subsp. *baytopii*; *G. elwesii* subsp. *melihae*; *G. elwesii* subsp. *tuebitaki*; *G. elwesii* subsp. *wagenitzii*; *G. elwesii* var. *maximus*; *G. elwesii* var. *whittallii*; *G. gracilis* subsp. *baytopii*; *G.graecus*; *G. maximus*; *G. melihae*
Native to Bulgaria, Greece, Turkey, Ukraine and the former Yugoslavia, this snowdrop flowers from January to March in cultivation, and from February to May in the wild. It is vigorous, with large supervolute leaves and large flowers, and is earlier and larger than *G. nivalis*. Markings are very variable but generally the inner segments have separate apical and basal marks, or sometimes an X-shaped mark.

G. elwesii var. *elwesii* can be confused with *G. gracilis*, but there are numerous differences; *G. elwesii* generally is more robust, with larger flowers and broader leaves.

Galanthus elwesii var. *monostictus* ↑15–18cm

Syns. *G. caucasicus*; *G. caucasicus* var. *hiemalis*; *G. caucasicus* of gardens
Native to southern Turkey, flowering from October to March in cultivation, and from February to May in the wild. It is commonly found in cultivation but is rare in the wild. The inner segments carry a single apical green mark, the name *monosticus* being derived from the Greek meaning 'single spot'.

It was named by P.D. Sell in 1996, from material at the University of Cambridge Botanic Gardens. This subspecies is very confusing and requires further clarification. Originally it was mistakenly named *G. caucasicus* in cultivation, and has also been confused with *G. alpinus*, having similar characteristics, although *G. alpinus* is generally smaller.

Galanthus alpinus ↑16cm

Syn. *G. caucasicus*
Uncommon, usually isolated, wild populations are found in the mountains of the Caucasus, Transcaucasus and Pontus, Georgia, Armenia, north-eastern Turkey and possibly northern Iran, from 400 to 2,200m. It flowers from January to March in cultivation, and from February to May in the wild.

The leaves are supervolute and glaucous, with a conspicuous median stripe; narrower at the base, they widen towards the middle. The inner segments have a green inverted U- or V-shaped mark at the apex. It is relatively hardy but rare in cultivation, and usually limited to specialist collections. It is slow to bulk up but does produce seeds.

First named by the Russian botanist D.J. Sosnowsky in 1911, *G. caucasicus* is synonymous with *G. alpinus* var. *alpinus*, but *G. alpinus* is a smaller plant with smaller flowers and single apical mark. It is often confused with *G. elwesii* var. *monostictus*.

Galanthus alpinus var. *alpinus* ↑9cm

Syn. *G. caucasicus*
These small snowdrops are native to Armenia, Azerbaijan, Georgia, southern Russia and north-eastern Turkey, growing in pockets of deep soil bordering deciduous or coniferous forests, scrub and river banks, from 400 to 2,200m.

The leaves are narrow and glaucous, and generally short during flowering. The inner segments are angular, with an inverted U- or V-shaped mark at the apex.

Galanthus alpinus var. *bortkewitschianus* ↑9–16cm

Syn. *G. bortkewitschianus*
This snowdrop is found in only one region near the river Kamenka in the central Caucasus, at around 1,200 to 1,500m. It is more readily available than *G. alpinus*, and has attractive, more rounded flowers. The leaves are supervolute, narrow and glaucous, with a noticeable median stripe; they are generally short at flowering. The inner segments have a variable single green mark at the apex.

This snowdrop was named by the Russian botanist J.I. Koss in 1951, and cultivated from the 1960s.

Galanthus alpinus var. *bortkewitschianus*.

Galanthus koenenianus ↑5–14cm

Found only in limited small areas in or near deciduous and co-niferous woodland, particularly beneath hazel (*Corylus avellana*), on north-facing slopes at around 1,500m in the Pontus Mountains, Sognali Dag, eastern Turkey, receiving high rainfall and heavy snow. It flowers from February to March.

It is a small plant, usually around 7cm. The leaves are super-volute, glaucous and narrow, generally short at flowering, similar to *G. alpinus*, but in *G. koenenianus* the convolute foli-age has distinctive ribbing to the underside not found in other snowdrops. The inner segments have a variable inverted U- or V-shaped mark at the apex, often with light yellow-green stain-ing at the base. The second mark and the glaucous foliage indicate *G. koenenianus* could be closely related to *G. elwesii*. Its scent has been likened to urine or bitter almonds. It is rare and reputedly difficult to grow, and is found only in a few spe-cialist collections. It was introduced by Manfred Koenen, the German botanist, in 1988.

Galanthus fosteri.

Galanthus koenenianus.

Galanthus fosteri ↑8–16cm

Syn. *G. fosteri* var. *antepensis*

Native to central and southern Turkey, Syria, Lebanon, Jordan and possibly Israel, this snowdrop prefers cool, shady, north-facing situations in light woodland, scrub, and rocky limestone ledges from 1,000 to 1,600m. It flowers from January to April.

The leaves are supervolute, broad, mid-dark green, occasion-ally glaucescent, and can range from matt to shiny. The inner segments have an inverted U- or V-shaped mark at the apex, or a small mark on either side of the sinus, with an often paler, roughly rectangular–elliptic mark at the base. Described as bor-derline hardy, it is reputedly difficult to grow, although easier than many tender snowdrops; it does well under glass. Slow to bulk up, and often shy flowering, it should grow in southern counties of the UK given drier conditions and protection. Bulbs should be planted around 10cm deep.

Despite being cultivated for over a hundred years and large importations in the 1950s, *G. fosteri* is now rarely grown. Current plants are clones or seedlings from the original import-ed stock. It was first named in 1889 by John Baker in honour of Professor Sir Michael Foster (1836–1907), an iris expert and physiologist, who imported the original bulbs.

It has similar markings to *G. elwesii* and *G. gracilis*, although no examples have yet been found where both the inner seg-ment markings join.

Galanthus ikariae ↑10–15cm

Syn. *G. ikariae* subsp. *snogerupii*

Native to the Aegean islands of Andros, Naxos, Skyros and Ikariae, where the bulbs were first collected, hence the name. This snowdrop prefers shady, cool, sheltered habitats on slopes bordering woodland, in scrub or deep shady gorges, generally near water, between 600–900m. It flowers from February to March in cultivation, and from January to April in the wild. Plants growing in shade and rich humus are generally larger than those on drier, open ground. It dislikes long periods of freezing temperatures. It is often found growing through thick blankets of ivy (*Hedera helix*).

The appearance is very variable, with large, well marked, slender flowers. The leaves are supervolute, broad, matt, mid-dark green, occasionally glaucescent, and greener than many snowdrops; they are sometimes lightly furrowed. The inner segments have a heavy inverted U-shaped mark covering up to two-thirds of the segment, shadowed on the underside.

G. ikariae is less common in cultivation than other species, nor is it as popular as when first introduced in the early twentieth century. It grows well in milder areas, given rich, moist soil and protection, and seeds well. The plant's size depends on conditions.

G. ikariae can be confused with *G. woronowii*, but there are distinct differences, including smaller inner segment markings and greener leaves in *G. woronowii*. Many *G. ikariae* are mistakenly named *G. woronowii*.

Galanthus woronowii.

Galanthus woronowii ↑20cm

Syns. *G. ikariae* subsp. *latifolius*; *G. latifolius*

Native to north-east Turkey, the western Caucasus, southern Russia and Georgia, this snowdrop is particularly prevalent in the mountainous areas of the Black Sea's eastern coastline. It enjoys a wide range of habitats, including deciduous and coniferous woodland, shady gorges, scrub, grass, ditches, scree, rocks and river banks, from 20 to 1,400m. It flowers from January to March in cultivation, and from January to April in the wild. It grows in deep, moist, fertile soils as well as shallow soils and rocks, giving rise to two forms. Plants growing in woodland have slightly darker, reclining leaves, while those growing among rocks have long, erect, light green leaves. Other variations include semi-doubles and forms with a small pale-green mark at the apex of the outer segments.

The leaves are supervolute, bright green and usually folded, with long shallow furrows giving a pleated appearance. The inner segments have small inverted U-shaped to square marks, often little more than a tiny spot on each side of the sinus.

G. woronowii is increasingly popular; it grows well, and its beautiful green leaves remain attractive for a considerable time. It is often confused with *G. ikariae*; they do look similar, but can be differentiated by reference to leaf colour and inner segment marks. *G. woronowii*'s leaves are usually glossy, and paler green than those of *G. ikariae*, and the inner segment markings are smaller. It was incorrectly known as *G. latifolius* when it was originally cultivated in the late 1800s.

This snowdrop is named after Georg Jurii Nikolaewitch Woronow (1874–1931), the Russian botanist and plant collector.

Galanthus ikariae.

Galanthus transcaucasicus.

Galanthus transcaucasicus ↑4–12cm

Syn. *G. caspius*

Native to Armenia, Azerbaijan and northern Iran, this snow-drop is found abundantly in southern regions of the Caspian Sea area. The first to be described, in 1909, was an example from the Talysh mountains of Azerbaijan. Preferring wood-land, moist or well drained ground up to 2,000m, *G. transcaucasicus* flowers from January to March in cultivation, and from December to April in the wild. It is relatively un-known and sparsely researched.

The leaves are supervolute, broad, matt, dark-green and occasionally glaucescent, with up to four long ridges. The inner segments have a variable inverted U- to V-shaped mark at the apex.

G. transcaucasicus is one of the last snowdrops to flower. Despite being reintroduced to the UK in the early 1990s, it re-mains uncommon, and is confined to specialist collectors. It is reputedly difficult to grow, but relatively hardy.

It has been included with different taxa, including *G. rizehensis* and *G. lagodechianus*, both of which have applanate vernation.

Galanthus lagodechianus ↑20cm

Syns. *G. artjuschenkoae*; *G. cabardensis*; *G. kemulariae*; *G. ketzkhovelii*

G. lagodechianus is found at high altitudes between 1,800 to 2,400m in the eastern and central Caucasus, Armenia and Azerbaijan, in deciduous woodland and scrub. It flowers from late February to March in cultivation, amd from January to April in the wild.

The mid–dark green leaves are applanate, narrow and shiny; the underside is lighter. Segments are slim and rounded-with a variable inverted U- or V-shaped mark at the apex of the inner segments.

Another late-flowering snowdrop, *G. lagodechianus* was probably introduced into the UK in the 1960s. It is hardy and attractive, and has become well established in many gardens over a long period.

This snowdrop was originally described by the Georgian botanist L.M. Kemularia-Nathadze in 1947, while three other snowdrops from the region were classed as different species, *G. ketzkhovelii*, *G. cabardensis* and *G. kemulariae*. In 1965, how-ever, Artjushenko decided they were all *G. lagodechianus*, because all four shared the common and distinctive chromo-some number – 2n = 72, differing from all other snowdrops.

G. lagodechianus is closely related to *G. rizehensis*, and in some cases it is virtually impossible to differentiate them. Careful examination shows enough differences (including leaf colour, inner segment marking, flowering time, distribution and all important chromosome number) to ascertain that they are distinct species, but they may have shared a common ancestor.

Galanthus lagodechianus.

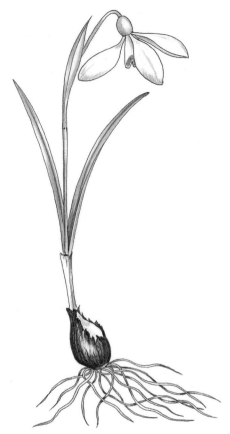

Galanthus rizehensis.

Galanthus rizehensis ↑8–12cm

Native to the western Transcaucasus, Georgia, the Krasnodor region of Russia and north-eastern Turkey, this species is very prevalent around the eastern Black Sea coast in mixed deciduous woodland, scrub, rocks, shady gorges, cliffs, river and stream banks from 25 to 1,200m. It flowers from January to February in cultivation, and from January to April in the wild.

The leaves are applanate, linear and mid-dark green, shiny-matt above and shiny below. The inner segments have a variable inverted U- or V-shaped mark at the apex.

G. rizehensis is a well established species, and easy to obtain. It flowers well and bulks up quickly, and often produces good viable seed. Most UK stocks derive from Sir Frederick Stern's garden at Highdown, Sussex, from bulbs originally imported from north-eastern Turkey. Later introductions from southern Russia make better, larger plants but these are still uncommon in cultivation.

G. rizehensis is very similar to *G. lagodechianus* but there are notable differences: *G. rizehensis* usually has matt rather than shiny leaves, with a pale glaucescent median stripe; *G. lagodechianus* usually has a V-shaped mark, *G. rizehensis* usually a U-shaped one, although this is not definitive and the marks are very similar; *G. rizehensis* flowers earlier than *G. lagodechianus*; and the all-important chromosome number varies.

Galanthus krasnovii ↑7–27cm

Found only in limited locations in western Georgia and north-eastern Turkey, mainly in eastern Black Sea coastal regions, this species grows in mixed woodland, scrub, grass, marsh, river and stream banks from 1,100 to 1,700m, and can withstand periods of flooding. It flowers from January to March in cultivation, and from March to May in the wild.

Its bulbs are longer than those of other snowdrops, especially towards the neck, and its pear-shaped buds open to distinctive, easily recognisable flowers. The leaves are supervolute, broad, shiny, light to mid-green, narrow at the base but broadening from the middle upwards, sometimes slightly ridged and puckered; vernation is maintained into maturity. It has slender, distinctive outer segments with a long claw. The inner segments are pointed at the apex, either lacking or with an indistinct sinus, and with either angular inverted U-shaped marks or two small marks.

G. krasnovii is extremely rare both in the wild and in cultivation. It was introduced into the UK in the 1990s and should be hardy, but it is supposedly difficult and disappointing to cultivate, rarely attaining the stature or beauty of its wild counterparts. It needs a light position in very moist, rich soil, and may require watering during winter and spring.

First discovered in north-eastern Turkey in 1908, it was described by the Russian botanist A.P. Khokhrjakov in 1963 and named after the Russian scientist Andrej Nikovaevich Krasnov (1862–1914).

Galanthus krasnovii.

Galanthus platyphyllus.

Galanthus platyphyllus ↑10–20cm

Syns. *G. Ikariae* subsp. *latifolius*; *G. latifolius*
This is a distinctive snowdrop from the central Caucasus, Georgia and Russia. It prefers open situations in wet ground, alpine or subalpine meadows, in snow melt regions from 1,200 to 2,700m; it is most commonly found at between 2,400 and 2,600m. A true alpine plant, it is a late flowering species, as the snow doesn't clear until July or August. It flowers from March to April in cultivation, but from April to July (occasionally August) in the wild.

The bulbs resemble *Narcissus*, with an elongated neck. The leaves are supervolute, broad, shiny, mid to dark green and larger than those of other snowdrops, narrowing towards base; vernation continues into maturity. The outer segments are slender; the inner segments have a variable, broad, inverted U-shaped mark, or two small marks at the apex, with a small light green patch at the base.

This species is still rare but its late flowering habit extends the snowdrop season. Cultivation should mimic wild habitats, with open, cool, moist growing conditions. It may require watering during growth, and is slow to bulk up and seed.

It was named by the American botanists H.P. Traub and H.N. Moldenke in 1948. It was previously known as *G. latifolius*, but that name was associated with *G. plicatus*, so could not be used. It is often confused with other green-leaved snowdrops, such as *G. woronowii* and *G. ikariae*. It is similar in appearance to *G. krasnovii*, including the absence of an apical sinus; they are obviously closely related but differences include blunt *G. platyphyllus* inner segments rather than pointed; blunt not pointed anthers; and the green staining at the base of the inner segments.

Galanthus panjutinii ↑18–25cm

Native to western Transcaucasia, *G. panjutinii* flourishes in fir and deciduous oriental beech forests, subalpine meadows, clearings, stream edges, and limestone rocks from 400 to 1,800m, flowering from March to June. The leaves are supervolute and narrow, with a conspicuous midrib and two to four longitudinal folds; they are bright mid-green, with an oily sheen. Outer segments are clawed at the base. The inner segments are rounded at the apex, and the sinus is very small or absent. Marks are variable: there may be an inverted U-shaped mark at the apex, a small mark on either side of the sinus, or no mark at all; sometimes there is a paler mark towards the base.

This exciting new addition to the genus *Galanthus* was discovered and studied on the Aibga Ridge in western Transcaucasia from 2008 to 2011.

Galanthus panjutinii.

In 1913 a snowdrop collected by G. Sakharov near Gagra, on the edge of fir forest and subalpine meadow at 1,600m, was invalidly named by P.S. Panjutin as *G. valentinae*. Despite this name being associated with *G. krasnovii*, and similarities between the two snowdrops leading some botanists to determine they were one and the same, *G. valentinae* was still considered by a number of botanists to be a distinct species in its own right. Continued research by A.P. Davis and D. Zubov revealed that the invalidly recorded *G. valentinae* and their new discovery were in fact the same. As the *G. valentinae* name was confusingly close to the hybrid *G. ×valentinei*, the new species was subsequently named *G. panjutinii* by A.P. Davis and D. Zubov in 2012 in honour of Platon Sergeyevich Panjutin (1894–1946), the chemist and botanist.

G. panjutinii is an endangered species due to its small numbers and limited locations. One habitat near Sochi has already been decimated by construction preparations for the 2014 Winter Olympic Games.

In appearance it is very similar to *G. krasnovii* and *G. platyphyllus*, and it is closely related to *G. platyphyllus*. (Information on this new species was kindly supplied by A.P. Davis and D. Zubov.)

Galanthus trojanus ↑10–20cm

This species grows in a small area of north-western Turkey, in humus-rich soil in undisturbed, open woodland and rocks, from 300 to 500m. It flowers from January to February in cultivation, and in March in the wild.

Seeds were collected in 1994, and fieldwork and further study determined it to be a new species. It was first cultivated with good results in pots at the Royal Botanic Gardens, Kew, and it should be a good, garden-worthy snowdrop.

It is similar in appearance to *G. nivalis* and *G. rizehensis*, but there are distinct differences. *G. trojanus* is larger with larger flowers; its leaves are wider and greener; the inner segment apical mark is different; and it has different areas of natural distribution.

Galanthus trojanus.

Author's note: There is on-going discussion about a number of snowdrop species and it is quite possible that more detailed research and analysis will lead some to be reclassified in the future. There is also one new species awaiting a name, and it is also possible there are still new species yet to be discovered in their native habitats.

CHAPTER 4

HYBRIDS, CULTIVARS, VARIETIES AND FORMS

Hybrids

Hybrids occur when two or more different species of the same genera are crossed sexually to produce a new plant, which shows a blend of parental characteristics, or has one more pronounced than the other. Hybridization is often carefully engineered to select and enhance specific features of the parent plants. Natural hybrids arise in the wild. Those occurring naturally in cultivation are termed spontaneous hybrids, while those created through man's intervention are known as artificial hybrids. Hybrids can also occur between subspecies of a species (known as intra-specific hybrids).

In their natural habitats most snowdrop species grow in precise locations, which are generally too far apart for hybridization to take place. However, this does not apply in gardens, where different species are often grown in close proximity. Plants can hybridize without being noticed until a difference in the flowers is spotted by a sharp-eyed Galanthophile and then the hybrid acquires a name.

Hybridization in the wild appears rare with snowdrops. To date the only fully recorded wild hybrid is between *G. nivalis* and *G. plicatus* subsp. *byzantinus*, giving rise to *G. ×valentinei* nothosubsp. *subplicatus*. Others may include *G. nivalis* × *G. reginae-olgae* subsp. *vernalis*; *G. nivalis* × *G. plicatus*; *G. plicatus* × *G. gracilis*; and *G. gracilis* × *G. elwesii*, although none of these has been fully researched and they remain as yet unproven among wild species.

OPPOSITE PAGE: An early snowdrop blooming in the garden just after Christmas.

RIGHT: In the wild species are not usually close enough together to hybridize, but this does not apply in gardens. Winter border with aconites and mixed snowdrops at Galanthophile Olive Mason's garden, Dial Park, Chaddesley Corbet, Worcestershire.

Galanthus ×valentinei

Syns. *G. nivalis* 'Valentine' – *G. nivalo-plicatus* 'Valentine'
Denotes all hybrids between *G. nivalis* and *G. plicatus*.

The leaves are generally slender, as in *G. nivalis*, with flat or explicative margins. Sometimes there is a second scape. The outer segments occasionally have a green mark at the apex. The inner segments have variable marks at the apex. This hybrid was known to both Allen and Burbidge under its synonyms. Beck gave it hybrid status under the name × *Galanthus valentinei*, now *G. ×valentinei*.

G. ×valentinei nothosubsp. *valentinei*

Hybrids between *G. nivalis* and *G. plicatus* subsp. *plicatus*
This hybrid has not yet been found in the wild, but is common in cultivation, giving rise to such well known snowdrops as 'S. Arnott', and 'Magnet'.

The leaves are applanate, matt and grey-green. The inner segments typically have a single apical mark, occasionally with a small green mark at the base, sometimes spreading across the segment. It flowers from January to March.

'Spindlestone Surprise' – *Galanthus nivalis* × *Galanthus plicatus*.

G. ×valentinei nothosubsp. *subplicatus*

Syns. *G. nivalis* subsp. *sublicatus*; *G. plicatus* subsp. *subplicatus*
Hybrids between *G. nivalis* and *G. plicatus* subsp. *byzantinus*.

This hybrid is almost identical to G. ×*valentinei* nothosubsp. *valentinei*. It is a very variable and naturally occurring hybrid, found in north-western Turkey, particularly around Istanbul, in deciduous woodland, scrub, grass, rocks and near rivers and streams, from 30 to 150m. It spreads by division of bulbs and seed.

This snowdrop shares the characteristics of both parents, although these can be very variable in different hybrid groups.

The leaves are applanate to applanate-explicative, matt, grey-green and glaucescent. The inner segments have a green inverted U- or V-shaped mark at the apex, often with one or two small green marks at the base; these marks are sometimes absent, and occasionally diffuse across the segment towards the base. It spreads by offsets and seeds, and is easy to grow, flowering from January to March.

This hybrid occurs in gardens and has been cultivated since about 1970. Different clones show distinct differences, but all are worth looking for as they form strong growing, attractive plants, well suited to the UK climate.

Note: Many garden hybrids are crosses between *G. nivalis* and *G. plicatus*.

G. nivalis × G. elwesii

The leaves are supervolute, and generally narrower than the typical *G. elwesii*. Inner segment marks tend to be stronger at the apex, paler and smaller at the base.

G. plicatus × G. gracilis

The leaves are often lax, glaucous, revolute or explicative. The outer segments are rounded; the inner segments are clasping and tube-like, with a large green mark across the segment, often to the base, above a large, narrow sinus. Often there are two scapes.

G. elwesii × G. gracilis

Crosses between these species may possibly occur in natural populations in Greece but are not common in cultivation. Examples include 'Ruby Baker' and 'Colesborne'. The plants are usually smaller, and the leaves are supervolute, with some *G. gracilis* twisting. The inner segments are tube-like, with a large sinus.

G. elwesii × G. rizehensis

Probably the only garden hybrid between these species to date is 'Early to Rize'. The leaves are supervolute, with subrevolute margins and a paler median stripe.

Galanthus ×*allenii* ↑8–12cm

This hybrid, probably a cross between *G. alpinus* and *G. woronowii*, although its precise parentage remians unknown, was discovered by James Allen. It was named in 1891 by John G. Baker in honour of James Allen (1830–1906). At the time it was considered to be either a species or a hybrid, but was later classed as a hybrid. James Allen grew this snowdrop, noting that it came via an Austrian nursery in 1883 from wild collected bulbs, possibly but not necessarily from the Caucasus. However, it is not definitively known where this hybrid originated and it is quite likely that it could be a garden hybrid. *G.* ×*allenii* is unknown or extremely rare, and so far unrecorded, in the wild.

It is widely cultivated and attractive, flowering from February to March, with a strong, bitter almond perfume. The leaves are supervolute, broad, smooth, matt, grey-green and glaucescent, with a central midrib. The inner segments have a variable green inverted V-shaped mark at the apex. Slow to bulk up, this hybrid can suddenly disappear or fail to grow for no apparent reason.

Galanthus ×*hybridus*

Syns. *G.* ×*grandiflorus*, *G.* ×*maximus*; *G. elwesii* × *G. plicatus*
This snowdrop was originally known as *G.* ×*grandiflorus*, and was supposedly a hybrid between *G. nivalis* and *G. plicatus*. It shows intermediate characteristics between *G. elwesii* and *G. plicatus*.

They are robust plants, with large, attractively shaped flowers. The leaves are applanate or supervolute, erect, broad and often glaucous, with variable explicative margins. The inner segments generally have a large mark. Often there is a second scape.

Cultivars include 'Merlin' and 'Robin Hood'.

Additional Hybrids

The following possible hybrids have also occurred: *G. ikariae* × *G. elwesii*; *G. elwesii* × *G. allenii*; *G. reginae-olgae* subsp. *vernalis* × *G. gracilis*; *G. nivalis* × *G. woronowii*.

Hybridizing

Not all snowdrops produce seed but for those that do, hybridizing can give exciting and interesting (although unpredictable) results for the enthusiast.

Many snowdrop species are inter-fertile, possibly because they originated from a common ancestor in the not too distant past. This means snowdrops will hybridize between themselves. *G. nivalis*, *G. plicatus*, *G. elwesii* and *G. gracilis* are certainly inter-fertile, and many of the other species may also cross. These have produced the numerous beautiful snowdrops we know today.

The list of snowdrop hybrids and cultivars is long and perplexing, with much misidentification. One hybrid, for example,

Galanthus × *allenii.*

The hybrid snowdrop 'Galatea'.

can be known by two or three different names. Many hybrids are very inferior and not worth growing, but some make outstanding new plants, which are eagerly sought by collectors.

Plants can hybridize naturally or can be selected for various attributes and hybridized through the intervention of man, leading to new and interesting forms. These will have the same characteristics as the parent plants but may also produce other attributes, such as larger, stronger plants, or slightly different flower shapes, colours or markings.

It is perfectly possible to breed a commercially successful new snowdrop, as is shown by the ever-expanding list of newly named plants, and the extortionate prices some achieve.

Maturing seedhead.

However, hybridizing is not always successful and the resulting plants can be weak or will not perform well, nor be different enough to be garden-worthy varieties. Careful selection of parent plants and crossing and recrossing over a number of years can develop chosen characteristics, but great patience is required due to the length of time snowdrop seedlings take to produce their first flowers.

Snowdrop seed is produced in the ovary after pollination. If fertilization has been successful, the seeds ripen in the usual way and the ovary swells. As it ripens it descends to the ground and splits, and the seed is dispersed. This usually occurs around the end of May or beginning of June. Once the capsule is ripening, it can either be left to seed naturally, covered with a small muslin bag to collect the seeds as they fall, or the whole capsule can be removed and placed in a pot of dry sand until fully ripe. Seed is best planted fresh and can be sown in labelled drills outside or potted up in a good compost mix. Under suitable conditions, the seeds will germinate a few months later, producing seedlings that usually flower between three and five years later.

In the spring, choose and carefully mark the two plants to hybridize. In the autumn, pot the plants and keep them under glass until the spring. Decide which will be the seed bearer (mother) and which the pollen bearer (male). Immediately the flower opens on the mother plant, before any pollen has been produced, carefully remove the anthers and cover the plant with a bell jar or small muslin bag to stop accidental pollination. Shortly after the stigma ripens, use a small paintbrush to collect pollen from the male plant and brush it lightly onto the stigma of the mother. Repeat this process for three to four days, keeping the mother plant covered to eliminate any possibility of cross-pollination by outside intervention such as insects or wind.

Seedhead reclined to ground.

Mother flower covered with fine muslin bag to protect against accidental cross-pollination.

Regular flowers of cultivar 'James Backhouse', which often exhibits aberrant segments.

Hybridizing can also be carried out on plants still growing in the garden, but again care must be exercised to ensure the plants are protected from unintentional cross-pollination by covering the mother.

It is important to use a methodical approach and keep accurate and detailed records of the work. Each plant should also be numbered correspondingly. Nothing is more frustrating than developing an exciting new plant, only to find there is no record of its parentage or how it came about. The name of the maternal parent takes precedence over the male and is placed first.

Hybridizing snowdrops is a long, slow process, and much research work remains to be undertaken in this area.

Cultivars

Cultivars are plants which are specifically bred or selected for certain characteristics, and retain those characteristics when propagated on.

Cultivars can be selected from wild populations or arise spontaneously; increasingly they are the product of man's intervention with careful breeding and propagation programmes on cultivated snowdrops. The resulting plant must be distinct, having its own distinguishing characteristics that are different from other named cultivars. Plants must be uniform and stable, maintaining these characteristics when repeatedly propagated from generation to generation.

Varieties

A variety comes below the species order and is denoted by the abbreviation var. (Latin *varietas*). Varieties show noticeable differences to one another in some of their characteristics, will hybridize with one another, have usually occurred naturally without man's intervention, will breed true from seed, and can only be named from wild populations. Varieties are further reduced to subvarieties (Latin *subvarietas*), denoted by the epithet subvar. Subvarieties are beneath varieties but above forms.

Forms (Latin *forma*) are denoted by the epithet f. Forms show only minor differences in one characteristic, but are still noticeably different from another form.

Clones

Clones represent a plant or group of plants derived from asexual reproduction or vegetative propagation, which are the genetically identical offspring of a single parent.

Groups and Forms

Double Flowers

Most double snowdrops are usually sterile. The inner segments form a tight or lax cluster beneath the larger outer segments. These can be regular, giving a neat shape, or irregular, giving the flowers an untidy form. *G. nivalis* 'Flore Pleno' is the most common double, and for a long time was the only double

'Gloria'.

'Welshway'.

known. A strong, attractive snowdrop, it has spread and naturalized widely. Recorded in Britain in 1703, its origins are unclear, but all double snowdrops can be traced back to a *G. nivalis* 'Flore Pleno' ancestor. It received an RHS AGM in 1993.

Worth growing:
'Ailwyn'; 'Blewbury Tart'; 'Faringdon Double'; *G. nivalis* 'Flore Pleno'; 'Gloria'; 'Hill Poë'; 'Lady Beatrix Stanley'; 'Richard Ayres'; 'Rodmarton'; *G. nivalis* 'Scharlokii'; 'Walrus'; 'Welshway'.

Greatorex Doubles

A group of snowdrops bred by Heyrick Greatorex (1884–1954). A commissioned cavalry officer in the First World War and a captain in the Home Guard in the Second, he became a recluse, living in an old railway carriage in his garden in Brundall, Norfolk. In the 1940s he began experimenting with snowdrop breeding. Pollen from *G. nivalis* 'Flore Pleno' was crossed with *G. plicatus*, producing a fine range of double hybrids. At this time the only double available was *G. nivalis* 'Flore Pleno', so these new snowdrops caused a sensation. They had large, well shaped flowers on tall vigorous plants. Most were named after Shakespearean female characters. Sadly, the lack of accurate records has led to much confusion with the names, and identification is difficult as the plants look very similar and are also very variable and unstable.

Worth growing:
'Cordelia'; 'Desdemona'; 'Dionysus'; 'Hippolyta'; 'Jaquenetta'; 'Lavinia'; 'Ophelia'; 'Titania'; 'White Swan'.

Greatorex double 'Titania'.

Greatorex double 'Dionysus'.

'Boyd's Double'.

Spiky Doubles

The first of this group was 'Boyd's Double', but numerous others followed, most with upward-facing flowers and irregular ruffs of stiff segments. They are strange not only in appearance but also because they often change characteristics when transplanted. Green coloration can be highly variable and flowers can be almost white. They require regular division as mature bulbs often do not flower. This group also appears to be limited to *G. nivalis*. Various theories have been promulgated to explain this unusual snowdrop; it may be the result of a genetic defect, but so far there is no definitive conclusion.

Worth growing:
'Alburgh Claw'; 'Boyd's Double'; 'Cockatoo'; 'Ermine Oddity'; 'Ermine Spiky'; 'Fuzz'; 'Irish Green'; 'Ragamuffin'; 'Windmill'.

Two Scapes and Twin Flowers

Numerous snowdrops produce two scapes from each bulb and a very few have two flowers on each scape, most being *G. elwesii* varieties.

Worth growing:
(Regularly produce two scapes from same bulb) 'Baytop'; 'Christine'; 'Cotswold Beauty'; 'Daglingworth'; 'Denton'; 'Dorothy Lucking'; 'Galadreil'; 'George Elwes'; 'Richard Blakeway Phillips'; 'Robyn Janey'.
(Two flowers on same scape) 'Gemini'; 'Kite'; 'Mrs Thompson'.

'Gemini'.

'Kite'.

'S. Arnott'.

Taller Snowdrops

Snowdrops are very variable and their size often depends on growing conditions as well as numerous other factors. Many snowdrops have been named specifically because of their larger size, but in some locations these can be disappointing. A number of snowdrops termed 'Large' or 'Giant' are distinctly larger than the norm, making *G. nivalis* look very diminutive; they form imposing groups.

Worth growing:
'Alison Hilary'; 'Anne's Millenium Giant'; 'Benhall Beauty'; 'Bertram Anderson'; 'Chelsworth Magnet'; 'Comet'; 'Ermine Joyce'; 'Fenstead End'; 'Fred's Giant'; 'Galatea'; 'Jaquenetta'; 'Long Tall Sally'; 'L.P. Long'; 'Mark's Tall'; 'Melanie Broughton'; 'Percy Picton'; 'Rev. Hailstone'; 'S. Arnott'; 'Sutton Court'; 'Washfield Colesbourne'; 'White Admiral'; 'Yvonne Hay'.

Autumn and Early Flowering

The typical flowering period for snowdrops is mid-late January to mid-March. However, some snowdrops bloom far earlier, considerably extending the season. Autumn-flowering snowdrops bloom from September, but are not generally as vigorous as their spring counterparts. They can also be slow to clump up and establish, or sometimes grow well for a few years and then disappear for no reason.

'Washfield Colesbourne'.

Early *Galanthus elwesii* out just after Christmas.

Galanthus reginae-olgae, an autumn-flowering snowdrop. *(Photo reproduced courtesy Harry Pierick)*

'Hill Poë'.

These early snowdrops have no leaves or only very small leaves at flowering. As there are more insects around at this time of year autumn snowdrops often set good seed. They appreciate drier conditions and more sunlight, and planting a few bulbs each year helps maintain succession. They always create a talking point, heralding the outstanding displays to follow after the New Year.

The flowers listed below bloom considerably earlier than the standard *G. nivalis*.

Worth growing:
G. cilicicus; *G. elwesii*; *G. fosteri*; *G. gracilis*; *G. peshmenii*; *G. plicatus*; *G. reginae-olgae*; 'Eleni'; 'Faringdon Double'; 'J. Haydn'; 'Jack Mead'; 'Mette'; 'Mrs McNamara'; 'Peter Gatehouse'; 'Remember Remember'; 'Three Ships'; 'Tilebarn Jamie'.

Late Flowering

These flower after the main flush in February, extending the season long after most snowdrops have faded. A few flower as late as April.

Worth growing:
'Baxendale Late'; 'Cicely Hall'; 'David Shackleton'; 'Green Ibis'; 'Greenish'; 'Hill Poë'; 'Straffan'.

Poculiforms

Known since the nineteenth century, poculiform snowdrops derive their name from the Latin *poculus* ('little cup'), and were named by the Revd. Henry Harpur-Crew (1828–1883). The inner segments are elongated so that all six flower segments are generally equal in length, forming a rounded, bowl-shaped flower. Many poculiform snowdrops are all-white. Occasionally the segment length varies and sometimes the flowers bear

Galanthus nivalis poculiform snowdrop.

'Lady Scharlock'. An albino snowdrop which also exhibits the split spathe, from the Scharlockii group.
(*Photo courtesy Harry Pierick*)

green marks. A more recent addition to this group is the 'Inverse poculiform', in which the outer and inner segments have the same markings, as in 'Trym' and its various seedlings.

Worth growing:
'Alan's Treat'; 'Angelique'; 'Bridesmaid'; 'Charlotte Green'; 'Crinolinum'; 'Danube Star'; 'E.A. Bowles'; 'Lady Mary Grey'; 'Sandhill Gate'; 'Seraph'; 'Snow White'; 'The Bride'; 'The Virgin'.

Albinos

Albinos have all-white segments, although occasionally, even in albino snowdrops, a small green mark can be detected on the inner segments. They were known to Allen as *G. nivalis albus*, but there are now many new clones.

Worth growing:
'Bohemia White'; 'Lady Scharlock; 'Sibbertoft White'; 'Snowball'; 'Snow White's Gnome'.

Scharlockii Snowdrops

In this variable group, also known as 'Donkey-eared snowdrops', the spathe splits to resemble a pair of ears. They were originally found in 1868 by Herr Julius Scharlock in the Nahe Valley, Germany. They were propagated from seed by James Allen and Samuel Arnott, giving rise to numerous variable plants. However, the split spathe and green-tipped outer segments are constant.

Worth growing:
'Doncaster's Double Scharlock'; 'Lady Scharlock'; 'Octopussy'.

Virescent and Green-Tipped

These are distinguished by various degrees of green marking on both the inner and outer segments. Some, particularly *G. elwesii*, can be very variable from season to season, also depending on where they are planted. The outer segment markings are generally found around the middle of the segment, sometimes spreading towards the base. The inner segment markings are generally larger than normal, diffusing towards the base.

Worth growing:
(Virescent) 'Fotini'; 'Greenish'; 'Green Tear'; 'Shrek'; 'Virescens'.
(Green-tipped) 'Green Brush'; 'Greenfinch'; 'Green Tips'; 'Krabat'; 'Viridapice'; 'Wodney Muž'.

'Viridapice'.

Yellow Snowdrops

Yellow snowdrops always creat interest, being suffused with varying strengths of yellow, apricot or gold shading. This can be extremely pronounced or have mid-way colouring between green and yellow. The yellow colouring can be affected when plants are moved, causing them to become more lime green than yellow. The colouring is caused by a genetic disparity affecting chlorophyll, the green colouring normally enabling photosynthesis, resulting in yellow colouring instead. It appears that these plants have no Chlorophyll B, and only one-third of the usual amount of Chlorophyll A. This normally affects the flowers, ovaries and sometimes leaves. As the plants mature, the chlorophyll levels rise to the same levels as in green snowdrops.

At one time snowdrops with yellow markings were thought to be far inferior and weaker to green-marked snowdrops, but now they are highly sought after, commanding high prices, and certain collectors specialize in them.

Yellow snowdrops come predominantly from Northumberland, although there is no apparent reason why this should be. They also grow well on the east coast of Scotland, although they are not found there naturally. They were first discovered in Northumberland in 1879 by Mr Sanders from Cambridge, and named *G. nivalis* 'Sandersii' in his honour. After the initial discovery, other yellows were found, including a larger, more vigorous form in another Northumberland garden, by W.B. Boyd. These were named 'Flavescens'.

By 1880 *The Garden* magazine was referring to them as *G. nivalis* 'Lutescens', and they became known by that name. As 'Sandersii' was the first published epithet, this, however, takes precedence. Now most yellow forms of *G. nivalis* are included under the general name Sandersii Group. Many yellow–apricot snowdrops belong in this group and there are numerous named cultivars.

Yellow coloration is primarily associated with *G. nivalis* species. In 1983 some yellow *G. plicatus* were found at Wandlebury Ring in Cambridgeshire, leading to a number of new names. A group of rare yellow *G. elwesii* gave rise to the famous snowdrop theft at Colesbourne Park in Gloucestershire in 1997. In February 2012 a yellow snowdrop smashed all previous records for snowdrops on the internet auction site eBay when a single bulb of 'Elizabeth Harrison', the first ever yellow *G. woronwii*, sold for a staggering £725. Found by Galanthophile Ian Christie, it was bought by seed merchants Thompson & Morgan.

Yellow *G. nivalis* snowdrops are noted as being difficult and slow to grow, and not vigorous, preferring a more acid soil. Many revert to green at some stage and then back to yellow later. Hybrids and *G. plicatus* yellows are vigorous.

Worth growing:
'Blonde Inge'; 'Chadwick's Cream'; 'Fiona's Gold'; 'Joe's Yellow'; 'June Boardman'; 'Lady Elphinstone'; 'Primrose Warburg'; 'Ray Cobb'; 'Ronald Mackenzie'; 'Sandersii'; 'Savill Yellow'; 'Spetchley Yellow'; 'Spindlestone Yellow'; 'Spindlestone Surprise'; 'Wandlebury Ring'; 'Wendy's Gold'.

Galanthus nivalis Sandersii Group.

'Wendy's Gold'.

'Straffan'.

'Cicely Hall'.

Irish Snowdrops

Although there are actually very few Irish snowdrops, the following originated there. Snowdrops are not native to Ireland but once introduced quickly naturalized from garden escapes. Irish folklore tells that snowdrops mark the end of winter and the beginning of spring.

Worth growing:
'Castlegar'; 'Cicely Hall'; 'David Shackleton'; 'Emerald Isle'; 'Greenfields'; 'Hill Poe'; 'Irish Green'; 'Kenneth Hall'; 'Kildare'; 'Mark's Tall'; 'Mary Heley-Hutchinson'; 'Robin Hall'; 'Ruby Baker'; 'Straffan'.

Scottish Snowdrops

Scotland has produced some outstanding snowdrops, including probably one of the best ever, 'S. Arnott', a number found by Ian Christie in the grounds of Brechin Castle, and the record-breaking 'Elizabeth Harrison'.

Worth growing:
'Boyd's Double'; 'Durris'; 'Fred's Giant'; 'S. Arnott'; 'Silverwells; 'Sir Herbert Maxwell'; 'Sophie North'; 'The Groom'; 'Wee Betty'.

Variable Inner Segment Marking

Snowdrops exhibit a tremendous range of inner segment markings from completely white to a tiny spot or heavy green colouring across the whole segment. As the outer segments flare open in sunshine, these marks are exposed in all their variety.

Worth growing:
'Bloomer'; 'Daphne's Scissors'; 'Heffalump'; 'Imbolc'; 'Lapwing'; 'Perrot's Brook'; 'Robyn Janey'.

Unusually Shaped Outer Segments

Outer segment shape varies enormously from long and slender, short and rounded, balloon-like, to spoon-, paddle- and boat-shaped. Segments can also be textured with longitudinal grooving or have a dimpled, seersucker effect.

Worth growing:
'Atkinsii' Moccas Form; 'Augustus'; 'Bertram Anderson'; 'Bushmills'; 'Comet'; 'Diggory'; 'Long Drop'; 'Mandarin'; 'Modern Art'; 'St. Anne's'; 'Shropshire Queen'; 'Trym'; 'Wasp'.

Hardy Snowdrops

Snowdrops are sturdy little plants and many will withstand whatever nature, or the gardener, throws at them, reliably appearing year after year. The following are among the hardiest and best.

Worth growing:
G. nivalis; G. nivalis 'Flore Pleno'; 'Augustus'; 'Brenda Troyle'; 'Cordelia'; 'James Backhouse'; 'Ketton'; 'Lady Beatrix Stanley'; 'Magnet'; 'S. Arnott'; 'Silverwells'.

'Heffalump'.

'Lapwing'.

'Robyn Janey'.

'Diggory'.

'Wasp'.

'Trym'.

'Augustus'.

'Lady Beatrix Stanley'.

'Silverwells'.

NAMING SNOWDROPS

New snowdrops appear every year, heralding a plethora of new names. But despite the fact there are at present in excess of 1,500 named snowdrops, many remain unnamed. It is of paramount importance that a new snowdrop proves its worth before becoming a named variety and joining the ranks of the snowdrop elite. Many snowdrops appear amidst great excitement at the prospect of discovering something new. However, a new plant might be weak or die out within a couple of seasons, the unusual characteristics might not carry through to the next season, or the plant may behave differently in diverse situations. Although it might be very tempting to leap in with a name as soon as something different appears, it cannot be stressed strongly enough that a new snowdrop MUST prove itself and be worthy of being named.

Naming a 'new' snowdrop is a metaphorical minefield. First, it must be a completely new plant, not one which has already been named as something else, and this is often not easy to prove with so many named snowdrops available. It must continue to come true each year and not be deemed to have been a 'one off' phenomenon for a particular season; most importantly, it must be different and good enough to warrant a name.

The naming of plants is strictly regulated by the International Code of Botanical Nomenclature for Wild Plants and the International Code of Nomenclature for Cultivated Plants, also known as the Cultivated Plant Code. These lay down rules, recommendations and guidelines for naming and registering new plants, which must be strictly adhered to. The ICNCP has also established a system of recording permanent reference specimens of the plant type. These can either be pressed herbarium specimens or meticulously accurate illustrations.

New, named snowdrop cultivars should be registered with the Royal General Bulb Growers Association, Hillegom, Netherlands. Established in 1860, it now has around 1,600 members. The KAVB (Koninklijke Algemeene Vereeniging voor Bloembollencultuur) maintains a database register of bulb cultivars that can be accessed via their website. The International Cultivar Registration Authority (ICRA) was set up over fifty years ago in an attempt to regulate and simplify the naming of plant cultivars and prevent the duplicate use of cultivar and group epithets. Data is updated every four years. It is a voluntary, international system and registering a cultivar name does not protect that name or infer any legal right. These are dealt with under the National Plant Breeders Rights or Plant Patents. The ICRA will check the name is not already in use in that specific genera of plants, and that it has not been used previously. It is important that a full description of the plant is submitted with the new name, including the plant's parentage, etc.

An unamed hybrid at Colesbourne Park, Gloucestershire.

The recently introduced and named 'Shropshire Queen', a superb snowdrop well worthy of a name.

The International Union for the Protection of New Varieties of Plants offers legal protection to plant breeders when introducing and registering new cultivars.

The Royal Horticultural Society's Joint Rock Garden Plant Committee makes awards for outstanding plants and will offer advice on new snowdrops.

Any new name must consist of the plant's scientific botanical Latin name (*Galanthus*), followed by a unique epithet that is generally a vernacular term enclosed in single quotation marks. Before 1959 Latin names were often also used for cultivar epithets, which led to great confusion when they were misinterpreted as botanical names. After 1 January 1959 the particular epithet had to be in a modern language.

If the new name complies with all the correct criteria, it then has to be printed in a legitimate and widely available publication before it becomes an accepted name.

Sometimes it appears that the proliferation of newly named cultivars is swamping the appeal of the humble snowdrop. However, naming new cultivars is not a problem, providing each one is good, reliable and distinct and has proven itself over a number of years. However, it is always best to err on the side of caution. Carefully check what has gone before and see if your new snowdrop will stand the test of time. It should be grown on for at least two or three years, and also perform exactly the same when grown in other locations. If the new plant satisfactorily passes all the tests, then is the time to introduce it to the world and give it a name.

There is still much confusion and disagreement, even among top experts, who all claim a particular snowdrop they grow is such and such, when someone else grows a distinctly different snowdrop with exactly the same name. Certainly there is much room for improvement in snowdrop naming and listing. This is where establishing and recording details of a basic 'Type' for each snowdrop, including an illustration, has great advantages for reference. Many old snowdrops have received new names in an effort to increase clarity and conformity among cultivar lists and names.

The present list of around 1,500 different snowdrops increases year on year. The snowdrops vary in size, flower shape, markings and period of flowering, along with other important distinguishing characteristics. Many old snowdrop cultivars are extinct although we still have their names. These are mainly snowdrops that didn't grow well, had insignificant flowers, few attributes to maintain garden worthiness, suffered disease, or were simply lost.

Once more it is imperative to stress the importance of not rushing out and naming new snowdrops without being 100 per cent certain they really are worthy of a name.

CHAPTER 5

CULTIVATING SNOWDROPS

Galanthus reginae-olgae in November in the Taygetos mountains, Peloponnese, Greece. (*Photo courtesy Wol Staines*)

Typical habitat for *Galanthus reginae-olgae* in the Taygetos mountains, Peloponnese, Greece. This snowdrop prefers woodland shade on north-facing slopes around 1000m, and running water. (*Photo courtesy Wol Staines*)

Natural Habitats

Snowdrops are among the hardiest and most tenacious of plants. In their native habitats they grow from almost sea level up to 2,800m. Some are true alpines, such as *G. platyphyllus*. Preferring light shade, they naturalize in deciduous woodland, and left undisturbed for many years they form vast colonies. The plants benefit from good light during winter, when the trees are denuded of leaves, and dappled shade in summer under the leaf canopy, providing the cooler conditions snow-

OPPOSITE PAGE: The Beeches, Tuxford, Nottinghamshire.

drops require when dormant. Snowdrops also grow in evergreen and coniferous woodland, generally towards woodland edges, and in grassland and meadows usually at higher altitudes.

In the wild they prefer the cool, moist conditions of north-facing slopes, humus-rich soils and areas of high rainfall. Many benefit from snow melt, or grow near rivers and streams. *G. platyphyllus*, for example, prefers very moist ground. Although snowdrops like damp ground and most will withstand short periods of flooding, they will not grow in ground that is constantly waterlogged. Snowdrops can withstand quite severe weather conditions and temperatures as low as −20°C but no colder than −30°C. As soon as temperatures begin to warm and the frozen ground thaws, they begin to appear, often forcing their way through snow. Some species, such as *G. peshmenii* and *G. cilicicus*, favour drier conditions and grow in hotter, more arid areas. In general, snowdrops do not like to dry out completely for extended periods during their dormant period. In Mediterranean areas they grow in cooler mountainous regions rather than lowland areas.

In their native habitats snowdrops experience marked climate changes between summer and winter, and the bulbs adapt well to northern European climates.

Cultivating Snowdrops

Although snowdrops will grow in many soil types, they prefer moist but not wet soil, deep and rich in humus, with good drainage. They like to be moist in the growing season and drier when the bulbs are dormant in summer. Neutral to alkaline soils are best, but they also grow well on chalk and on clay providing it is not too heavy. Snowdrops dislike ground that is too acidic, although yellow snowdrops tend to grow better on acid soils. The better the soil and conditions, the better the snowdrops will grow, but most tolerate a wide range of habitats and happily come up year after year to produce dazzling displays.

Good drainage is important. If the soil is sandy and light, dig in humus to give more body. On heavy clay the addition of sand, sharp sand, leaf mould or peat helps lighten the soil.

Occasionally snowdrops will not grow in an area. It may be that the soil is too acid but sometimes, for no apparent reason, snowdrops just will not grow. However hard you try and whatever measures you take to encourage them, they simply disappear over time.

Neighbouring gardens and the local countryside, particularly churchyards, will give a good indication of how well snowdrops grow in a particular area.

An outstanding winter display of snowdrops, aconites and hellebores at Dial Park, Chaddesley Corbet, Worcestershire.

Purchasing Snowdrops

For many years snowdrop growers have recommended buying or moving snowdrops 'In the green', when the flowers have faded but the leaves are still growing. Many growers still follow this practice and insist it is the best way. Bulbs do suffer a certain amount of root damage, which inevitably means the plants are weakened as damaged roots do not regrow. If the roots do not perform, the plants wilt, affecting the photosynthesis process in the leaves above. If the leaves are not able to provide adequate stores of starch for the bulb to sustain the production of new growth inside the bulb during the dormant period, the plants do not perform so well the following season. Snowdrops generally survive, and survive well, but it might take them time to settle and re-establish, meaning they will not usually perform at their best until their second year after transplanting.

Many growers now recommend moving snowdrops during the summer months when the leaves have completely died back and the bulbs are fully dormant. The advantages are that any roots left on the bulbs are easier to separate from surrounding bulbs; small bulblets around the parent bulb are easier to remove, causing less damage; and the bulbs are firm and rich with good stores of starch created by photosynthesis. This should aid the production of good, strong, healthy shoots inside the bulb during the dormant period, meaning the snowdrops should grow and settle well during their first season. However, this is not always the case and a number of growers insist that moving bulbs when they are completely dormant has a more seriously detrimental effect than moving them in the green. A number of growers have stated that when moving dormant bulbs, most have failed to re-establish and bulbs have been lost.

So, the decision to buy snowdrops in the green or when bulbs are dormant comes down to personal choice, and only experience will decide which method works best.

Some growers supply bulbs in flower, carefully packed in a little compost and damp moss; this has the added advantage of confirming that the snowdrops you have received are exactly what you ordered. Pot-grown bulbs are also available; although these are generally more expensive, the plants suffer the least amount of disturbance to their roots when transplanted into the garden.

Purchasing dry snowdrop bulbs packed in polythene at supermarkets or garden centres is not widely advocated now as the bulbs dislike being completely dried out for extended periods and will often fail to grow or establish well for some considerable time, if at all. If buying dry bulbs, make sure they are firm and healthy, not soft, shrivelled or mildewed.

By far the best way to start or increase a collection of snowdrops, whether purchasing in the green or when dormant, is to buy from specialist growers. Although there is no absolute guarantee, specialist growers are more likely to sell healthy, disease-free bulbs in the varieties you want. This is particularly important with rarer snowdrops. Of course, it is not unknown for nurseries to make mistakes, and sometimes an expensive bulb turns out to be something quite ordinary the following season; in general a good nursery will replace bulbs they have mis-sold.

Snowdrops and aconites naturalized in St James's Churchyard, Shipton, Shropshire.

Pot-grown bulbs are slightly more expensive but it causes less disturbance to the roots when transplanted.

Snowdrops take time to establish after planting before they give of their best. The Rococo Garden, Painswick, Gloucestershire.

Planting

Plant snowdrops into their permanent positions as soon as possible after receipt. If this is not possible, make sure the bulbs are stored in a cool place until they can be planted. If this is likely to be for an extended period, perhaps due to unfavourable weather conditions, for instance, plant the bulbs into pots of good compost. Bulbs should be firm to the touch, not soft.

As a general rule plant snowdrops in irregular groups about 8–10cm deep and 8cm apart, and do not allow the bulbs to dry out during planting. A light application of bone-meal and sharp sand encourages the bulbs to establish. Leaf mould is also beneficial.

Plants take time to settle after being moved or divided, so newly planted snowdrops may not flower well in their first year. Small bulblets need time to grow and establish, often taking a couple of years before producing flowers. Once established they will more than make up for it.

Autumn-flowering species are not generally as vigorous as spring-flowering species. They tend not to clump up as well, can be slow to establish, and require slightly drier conditions and a little more sunlight. They sometimes grow for a few years and then inexplicably disappear, so it is worth planting a few bulbs each year to maintain a good succession.

Naturalizing

Snowdrops are one of the best plants for naturalizing, spreading over time into huge colonies. The most spectacular and breathtaking displays are undeniably those that have become established over many years, spreading vast white carpets beneath woodland trees, or carpeting grassy areas. Most displays of this calibre are created with little if any intervention by man.

As snowdrops are naturally plants of woodland and woodland edges, they grow best in similar conditions. This means light, dappled shade rather than full sun. They do not tolerate dense shade. Even the smallest group of trees can have snowdrops naturalized beneath and around them to stunning effect.

Snowdrops such as *G. nivalis* and *G. elwesii* can be left undisturbed for many years before they become so compacted they fail to flower very well. To give nature a helping hand, dig up clumps of snowdrops every three to four years, divide them and replant. Many books and growers recommend this as standard, although snowdrops can be left far longer without any detrimental effect. Stronger, more vigorous snowdrops become congested more quickly. Single bulbs quickly form new offsets, which develop into new plants, and so the cycle continues.

Vast areas of naturalized snowdrops at Hodsock Priory, Nottinghamshire.

Whereas the common snowdrop G. *nivalis* and her sister G. *nivalis* 'Flore pleno' are most commonly found naturalized over wide areas, it is often better to plant unusual varieties in smaller clumps where their individuality can shine out rather than be lost in the crowd. This especially applies to rarer varieties where a £40 bulb would soon lose itself beneath a confusion of more common species.

Little preparation is required for planting. Where plants have been purchased in the green the planting hole should be deep enough so when filled in the surface of the soil is level with the original planting depth of the bulb. This is generally easy to see as plants remain a lighter colour below ground. A little compost in the base of the hole can encourage plants to establish more quickly.

When naturalizing bulbs, plant them in small irregular groups, placing individual bulbs roughly 5–8cm apart. Water well after planting.

If you are planting only a few snowdrops, make a small hole with a trowel and pop in individual bulbs. If the bulbs have no leaves, the usual rule of thumb is to plant at a depth roughly equalling two and a half times the height of the bulb. The tops and bottoms of snowdrops bulbs are easy to distinguish. The top has a narrow neck and the base a basal plate showing where roots have been. There is much dispute as to whether bulbs grow if planted upside down, although it probably doesn't create too many problems as the bulbs will correct themselves, even though it may take them longer to establish. If in doubt plant bulbs on their sides.

For more extensive plantings involving large numbers of bulbs, insert a spade to the required depth and fold back a spade's width of turf. It is often easier to do this first across all or part of the area, spacing the holes randomly rather than in regimented lines, before planting the bulbs and filling in. This also helps eliminate the possibility of accidentally digging up just planted bulbs.

Lightly disturb the base of the hole with a trowel and add a little compost or a mixture of compost and sharp sand to help give the bulbs a good start. Place different numbers of bulbs in uneven groups, add a little compost and replace the turf. When planting bulbs in the green make sure the leaves are angled around the edges of the hole so when the turf is replaced the original planting level of the leaves is maintained. Lightly tread the turf back into position so it is firm but not compacted.

More expensive and unusual varieties of snowdrop will benefit from extra care on planting. Remove the soil or turf to the required depth, add humus or sharp sand across the base to aid drainage, plant the bulbs and refill the hole with compost or a mixture of soil and compost. Grass will soon grow back across the bare areas, but as the turf is not as dense, the bulbs have time to establish first.

Snowdrops planted for naturalizing, now in their third year.

If necessary, mark the positions of bulbs as you go. This may look unsightly but it is necessary if you plan to add more bulbs in the near future. When the area is fully planted, the markers can be removed. With special snowdrops, markers showing names can be left in place for ease of identification.

To mark or not to mark plants is always a difficult decision. Plant labels are an intrusive addition to the garden but necessary for remembering the names of special plants, particularly bulbs that disappear below the ground when dormant. Personal preference is the deciding factor as to whether to label or not, and if so what type of labels to use.

Naturalized snowdrops require little attention. Leaves must be left to die back naturally, never cut off or removed, as this seriously threatens flowering and the strength of the bulbs, which will eventually die. Snowdrops benefit from a light mulch of leaf mould or mushroom compost in November, although this isn't strictly necessary. They do not require strong fertilizers or manure.

Snowdrops naturalized in grassland.

In the Garden

Snowdrops can be planted in borders beneath shrubs and other plants that will grow up after the snowdrops have finished, leaving no sign that the snowdrops were ever there. As snowdrops are best divided every four to five years, this ties in well with the division of herbaceous plants and the whole bed can be overhauled at the same time. Mark the snowdrops, so that the snowdrops will not get dug up mistakenly when the beds are weeded. Plant snowdrops towards the front of beds and borders so they can be seen clearly, and the delicate flowers and markings more easily examined. They can edge paths, brighten alpine beds and rockeries, or grow beneath specimen trees, and they are perfect for grassy banks, slopes and wild parts of the garden, creating good displays in difficult to manage areas.

Snowdrops in a garden border with cyclamen and aconites. The Beeches, Tuxford, Nottinghamshire.

Snowdrops and *Cyclamen coum* beneath trees, Colesbourne Park, Gloucestershire.

Although snowdrops naturalize beautifully in grassland, lawns are not generally suitable. The grass must be left until the snowdrop leaves have disappeared, around mid-June, meaning lawns become untidy while waiting to be cut. Bulbs also dislike being compacted beneath turf as lawns are regularly mown and walked on.

Unless you are a purist, and require nothing more than named varieties of snowdrop in specific areas of the garden, snowdrops mix brilliantly with numerous other plants. The contrast between the pure white flowers and the colour and foliage of their companions reveals another dimension to this simple flower altogether. Snowdrops are typical 'Cottage Garden' plants and look beautiful growing alongside other early spring bulbs such as aconites and cyclamen. Snowdrops are also good bee plants, providing an early source of nectar and pollen. This is an extremely valuable consideration now that bees seem to be on the wing earlier in the year than ever before.

Always place a few snowdrops where they can be seen from the house. As such welcome signs of spring, and such uplifting little flowers on cold, dark winter days, you need to be able to see them as soon and as often as possible.

Containers

Many experts suggest that snowdrops are better planted directly into the ground and do not make good container plants as the roots get little protection from frost in winter and penetrating heat in summer. However, snowdrops can make ideal subjects for containers, particularly in the short term, creating good seasonal displays. When displays are finished, the bulbs can be planted out into open ground.

Fill containers with compost. John Innes No. 2 mixed with extra sharp sand to improve drainage is excellent, or a fifty/fifty mix of potting compost and vermiculite. Each gardener has their own preference. Water well immediately after planting and keep moist but not wet, as overwatering can rot bulbs. Containers should not dry out during the growing season, as this has a seriously detrimental effect on snowdrops. Protect containers from severe frosts, as although snowdrop flowers and leaves are impervious to extreme cold, this does not apply to roots and bulbs.

Snowdrops can be planted on their own in containers or mixed with other plants such as hardy cyclamen, coloured primroses, polyanthus, small winter pansies and ivies.

Containers generally flower a little earlier than plants in the ground so place them where these early displays of flowers and

Snowdrops and cyclamen in an old stone trough, Colesbourne Park, Gloucestershire.

colour can easily be seen on winter days – on the patio, in view of a window, or near the front door. As pots and containers are raised, this allows the delicate flowers to be admired and examined more easily.

Unless containers are large, it is best to repot each year as the compost loses its nutrients. Use fresh compost around July–August when the bulbs are dormant. Alternatively, plants can be fed with a liquid fertilizer during the growing period.

Growing in Pots

Collections of bulbs in pots can be kept outside in a frost-free area, or in a cold frame or greenhouse. For indoor cultivation under glass, snowdrops do not require heat. They do, however, require good ventilation, so frames can be left open and greenhouse vents ajar unless temperatures fall below freezing.

Growing under glass produces earlier blooms but most snowdrops happily grow outdoors. Certain less hardy and more difficult snowdrops grow well in pots in a frost-free greenhouse; for example, *G. fosteri*, *G. reginae-olgae*, *G. peshmenii* and *G. cilicicus* all benefit from being grown under glass.

Many collectors prefer to grow snowdrops in pots. It is especially useful with rarer snowdrops that may be difficult to grow

outdoors in the ground. Specialist collectors also require different species and varieties of snowdrop to be kept well separated to avoid the risk of cross-pollination. Pots enable a careful check to be kept on the health of bulbs, and have the added advantage that you can view and examine flowers close to. Opinions vary as to whether clay or plastic pots are superior. Although plastic pots are now widely used, many collectors feel clay

Glass frames in Ray Cobb's Nottinghamshire garden.

Square pots fit together better on greenhouse staging.

encourages better root systems, although clay pots are porous so they dry out faster, leach water from the compost and require more watering. They are also more aesthetically pleasing to look at, especially for exhibition purposes. Some growers prefer square pots as these fit together better, especially on greenhouse staging, taking up less space.

Whatever your preference, the pots should be clean and sterile before planting begins. The minimum height for a pot should be around 14–15cm but taller pots are preferable to shallower ones as this allows the roots a good depth of soil, helping keep them cool. As a rough guide, 10cm diameter pots will accommodate between three and five bulbs, while 15cm diameter pots hold between six and ten bulbs.

Snowdrops in pots require sterile, free-draining compost. A standard, good quality potting compost can be used, with the addition of some fine gravel (in a mix of about 75 per cent compost and 25 per cent gravel). Alternatively a suitable mix consists of two parts good quality loam, two parts fine horticultural grit and one part humus.

Place a thin layer of clean, broken crock or gravel in the base of the pot. Put a layer of compost into the pot and place the dormant snowdrop bulbs about half way up, equally spaced and not touching. A light dusting of fungicide applied at this stage is beneficial but not necessary. Cover with compost to three times the height of the bulb, finishing 2cm below pot rim. If the snowdrops still have leaves, plant the bulbs at the same level as previously planted. The change in colour of the shoot

above and below ground level indicates a clear guideline. Top with a layer of fine grit for a clean and attractive display, as well as warding off predators such as slugs and snails. Keep pots clean, and weeds and moss at bay.

Indoor cultivation usually requires the annual repotting of bulbs to maintain healthy plants and a suitable supply of nutrients in the compost. However, this can be left to every second year.

Once the leaves have died back, pots require little water during the dormant period, beginning again in late summer.

Pots in a greenhouse receive additional protection in winter by standing them on a deep tray and infilling the tray to the pot rims with sand. Pots must also be shaded during the summer and can be placed beneath the staging or covered with newspaper.

Excessive drying out can kill snowdrop bulbs, so do not expose them to direct sunshine and water only when necessary. If temperatures fall below freezing avoid watering altogether, so pots do not freeze through, recommencing when temperatures begin to rise again.

Lattice Pots

Many specialist snowdrop growers prefer to use aquatic lattice pots of the type sold for submerging in pools for water plants. This is especially useful for growers who wish to keep special bulbs in pots but sunk into the ground outdoors. The bulbs benefit from the best of both worlds, although care should be taken to ensure that the holes in the pots are not so large that smaller bulbs fall through.

Lattice pots can be sunk into the ground and snowdrops allowed to grow naturally so the roots develop and grow out through the mesh. Grown in this way pots can be lifted as and when necessary, causing as little disturbance to plants and roots as possible. Plants grown in lattice pots generally require repotting every third or fourth year, using compost such as John Innes No. 3.

Lattice pots for aquatic plants give the best of both worlds for snowdrops. They can be sunk into the ground but are easy to lift when necessary.

Plunge Beds

Snowdrops grown in pots can be sunk into sand-filled plunge beds, which offer the advantage of protecting pots from changes in temperature and helping retain moisture. Plunge beds can be built outside, or inside on the greenhouse staging.

Outside beds are made by digging out the required area in a suitable position of well drained ground. Alternatively a wooden or brick frame can be made on top of the ground. Place the pots into the bed and carefully fill round with moist sand so the pot rims end up level with the surface. Make sure the sand does not have a high percentage of salt, which sometimes happens. Keep the sand and pots moist, watering when necessary, making sure they never dry out completely or become waterlogged.

Plunge beds can also be built on greenhouse staging, offering potted snowdrops a measure of protection as well as helping keep roots moist and cool. In both greenhouse and cold frame care must be taken to ensure the pots are not too hot in summer and there is adequate shading. Good ventilation is also essential for healthy plants.

Purpose-built plunge beds are available commercially, or they can be simply made from wooden frames, boxes, bricks or blocks.

Well constructed plunge bed at Olive Mason's Dial Park garden, Chaddesley Corbet, Worcestershire.

Snowdrops Indoors

Snowdrops do not grow or force well indoors. If you want to enjoy early blooms, snowdrops can be lifted from the ground at any stage from breaking bud to full flower. Carefully lift a clump of bulbs and plant them into compost in a pot or bowl. Cover with a layer of green moss for an attractive display. Keep cool, on a light but shady windowsill. Snowdrops will not last as long indoors, and as soon as they begin to fade replant them again outside in a permanent position. A small clump of snowdrops nestling in a bed of soft green moss brings a welcome breath of spring indoors and fills the room with fragrance.

Aftercare

Once the snowdrop leaves have died back, the old roots slowly wither below ground and the bulbs remain dormant through the summer months. Inside the bulb a new shoot quickly develops for the following season.

As summer draws to a close and the weather becomes cooler and wetter, new roots begin to develop on the basal plate, thrusting down into the earth.

In late winter the bud and leaves, protected by the sheath, push upwards through the earth. As they break the surface, the sheath splits, allowing the flower and leaves to grow and mature. When the flowers fade, the leaves elongate and photosynthesize to take nourishment back into the bulb, which is why snowdrop leaves must always be left to die back naturally.

In the middle of winter a small vase of snowdrops brings a welcome breath of spring and honey perfume indoors.

An emerging snowdrop bud enclosed in sheath.

If snowdrops do not appear to be thriving, it is always worth trying them in a different part of the garden to see if they do better.

Bulbs that bulk up quickly, such as *G. nivalis*, benefit from lifting and dividing every four or five years to prevent clumps becoming too compacted, which can affect flowering. Most snowdrops also benefit from being moved and divided on a regular basis, increasing stocks.

Snowdrops are gross feeders. A light application of bone-meal in autumn helps fertility but heavy applications of strong animal manures or fertilizers are unnecessary. Some growers consider that well rotted manure benefits snowdrops, others say it is detrimental.

Snowdrops will burst into bloom even after the hardest of winters, although flowering may be a little later than usual. In contrast, a mild winter will produce earlier blooms.

MEDICINAL PROPERTIES OF SNOWDROPS

There are no records to show when snowdrops were first used for their medicinal properties. Herbal remedies were widely used throughout the ancient world. The ancient Druids, for instance, were highly skilled in the practice of using herbs for healing, and looked upon snowdrops as potent heralds of their spring festival, Imbolc.

The whole of the snowdrop plant is toxic, and the bulbs particularly so. If ingested, they cause stomach cramps, diarrhoea, dizziness, nausea and vomiting. Although there have been recorded instances of these symptoms causing death, most people recover.

At one time rubbing snowdrop leaves on the forehead was said to relieve headaches and there are also reports from Russia that a decoction of the bulbs was beneficial in treating poliomyelitis. *G. nivalis* is reputed to be an emmenagogue, stimulating the menstrual flow, possibly resulting in abortion in the early stages of pregnancy. (Any natural or herbal treatments should only be used under the strict supervision of a qualified herbalist.)

Snowdrop leaves and bulbs contain the active substance 'Galanthamine', which is used in a group of anti-cholinesterase drugs. Much research into the properties of the alkaloid Galanthamine in snowdrops, in particular *G. woronowii*, was undertaken in Bulgaria under Communist rule. In the 1950s research began on extracting Galanthamine from the common snowdrop, *G. nivalis*, giving rise to the original drug 'Nivalin'. Galanthamine has important properties which aid the treatment and management of Alzheimer's disease, poliomyelitis, severe injuries to the nervous system, and other nerve-associated pain. Modern, anti-cholinesterase inhibitor drugs work by helping break down acetycholine in the brain, associated with memory and cognition problems. Synthetic processes were introduced, but due to the high cost, these drugs were withdrawn from patients in the early stages of Alzheimer's disease.

Galanthamine also occurs naturally in daffodils and narcissi, and trials are taking place in Wales to ascertain the viability of producing reliable supplies from this source as well. The high altitude and possibly other climatic conditions of the Welsh Black Mountains seems to increase the yield significantly. Research is on-going but if successful could dramatically cut the cost of such drugs so they become more economically viable to prescribe.

As well as Galanthamine, snowdrops also contain the glycoside scillaine (scillitoxin), and another alkaloid, narcissine (lycorine).

A derelict cottage in the middle of nowhere, with snowdrops still happily growing and spreading in the remains of the old garden.

The mannose-binding specific lectin in *G. nivalis* – agglutimin, or GNA – is used in research in medicine, bacteriology and agricultural biotechnology. It is toxic to certain insect pests such as *Hemiptera* (including aphids, leafhoppers), *Coleoptera* (beetles), and *Lepidoptera* (butterflies and moths), creating an effective insecticide. The gene was cloned in 1991. It has now been modified and transferred to a number of crops, including wheat and rice. Research continues into establishing the potential for further insect-resistant genes that can be introduced into plants to make them increasingly insect-pest resistant. Research is also under way to establish whether the snowdrop lectin GNA can be beneficial in treating HIV (Human Immunodeficiency Virus).

CHAPTER 6

PROPAGATING SNOWDROPS

Division

In the Green

Division of clumps of bulbs is the simplest way to propagate snow-drops, either 'in the green' after the flowers have finished or when the bulbs have become dormant around June and July. Carefully insert a fork around a clump of bulbs and lever them out of the ground, trying not to damage the bulbs and roots in the process. This is far easier after rain, when the ground is soft and damp. Gently shake away the soil and ease the bulbs apart, trying not to be too forceful, and breaking as few of the roots as possible. If the bulbs are soft, damaged or diseased, either dispose of the dam-aged bulbs or treat them accordingly. If diseased bulbs are found, do not replant snowdrops in the same area.

Usually small offsets grow around the base of the parent bulb and these mature into new plants. These offsets should be carefully removed, preferably when the plants are dormant, as they are easily damaged, as is the parent bulb. They can be re-moved by hand, but a safer approach is to cut away the offsets using a sharp, sterile knife, making sure you include a small section of the base plate and a few roots. A light dusting with sulphur powder can be beneficial at this stage, helping protect against rot and fungal diseases.

Offsets can be planted back into the ground in the usual fashion or, with choicer varieties of snowdrop, can be potted up and kept in a cold frame until they are more mature. They will usually reach flowering size in about two years, when they can be more successfully planted out.

OPPOSITE PAGE: Snowdrops growing between the marbled leaves of *Cyclamen hederifolium*.

Snowdrops 'in the green' ready to be planted out.

Offset removed from parent bulb.

Snowdrops divided ready for planting.

Replant the bulbs between 8 – 15cm deep, and 5 – 8cm apart, depending on the size of the bulbs. Larger bulbs require deeper planting and wider spacing. Space them irregularly so the plants look more natural. Make sure the new site is ready so they can be planted immediately. This not only limits the likelihood of bulbs drying out, but the sooner they are replanted the more chance there is that they will continue to photosynthesize.

If you plan to divide dormant bulbs, their positions should be clearly marked before the leaves die back completely after flowering. This avoids possible damage to the bulbs if their exact locations are not remembered.

Dried-out bulbs do not establish well, if at all, so it is always better to purchase bulbs in the green or in pots.

Many snowdrops produce seed in the swollen capsules that bend down to touch the ground as the flowers fade. Seed can be left to set naturally, or ripe seed can be collected and planted. Seed will not necessarily come true to the parent plant.

Chipping and Twin Scaling

These highly specialized processes involve the division of single bulbs to increase plant stocks at a faster rate, especially with rarer snowdrops. Twin scaling and chipping techniques date back to the 1930s, although they were not common even then. These techniques became popular in the 1980s, spurred on by the Glasshouse Crops Research Institute in a Grower's Bulletin published in 1982. This method is now used by both amateur and professional growers to quickly extend a stock of snowdrop cultivars. In theory, chipping and twin scaling should give identical clones of the original snowdrop, but occasionally plants show some characteristics of an earlier cross and natural mutations can and do occur.

Snowdrop bulbs are modified leaf bases compressed together on to a basal plate, from which leaves and roots grow. In simple terms chipping is a method of slicing a healthy bulb into sections, each of which then grows into a new plant. No expensive equipment or materials are required, and providing everything is sterile to limit fungal infections (and you have a steady hand) results are good. Sections consist of two or more scales and a small part of the basal plate. The number of chips that can be taken from a given bulb depends on the size of the bulb. Six to eight chips would be the maximum number for small bulbs around 1cm in diameter, or fifteen to twenty chips from a bulb around 2cm. The number also depends on whether more numerous but thinner chips are taken, or fewer but thicker. Experience is the best guide. Larger chips can also be divided into twin scales, thus doubling up on the number taken.

Method

Lift good-sized, healthy bulbs when dormant, usually around June. Mix 80mls of water into 1,000mls of vermiculite (enough for about three bulbs); stir well and set aside. Make up a solution of systemic fungicide as directed on the packet. Sterilize a glass chopping board, sharp scalpel and the bulb by wiping with methylated spirit.

Cleaned bulb prepared
ready for chipping.

Neck of bulb cut back
to top quarter.

Bulb placed cut side down
and divided into four parts.

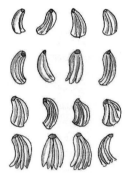

Each bulb quarter is divided again
to give eight scale sections.

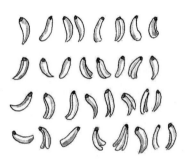

Each group of scales is further divided
again to give sixteen scales.

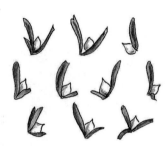

Scales after between four
and twelve weeks showing
formation of new bulblets.

Taking one bulb at a time, carefully remove the tunic. (Holding the bulb beneath gently running water facilitates this process.) Using a sharp knife or scalpel, carefully cut away the roots and the bulb's basal plate until it is level with the first scale layer. The neck can either be cut back to approximately the top quarter of the bulb, or the neck can be left on as this too often produces small bulblets. Whichever method is employed, remove any damaged or discoloured patches until the bulb is firm, clean and white, sterilizing cut surfaces with methylated spirit.

Holding the basal plate upright, slice the bulb in half vertically, and continue slicing in this fashion until it is divided into equal sections. Depending on the size of the bulb, you can finish up with between two and thirty-two sections, or chips. Each cut section must contain a small piece of the basal plate, and it is best if the chips are not too small. Larger sections can then be gently sliced down, between the scales, so each produces two scales from each section – the process known as twin scaling.

Pour a small amount of fungicidal mixture into a bowl and submerge the sections for half an hour. Then place a third of the vermiculite mix into a clean plastic freezer bag. Drain the bulb sections, wash them with sterilized water and blot off excess moisture with a small piece of kitchen roll. Place the sections into the bag of vermiculite, making sure each is separated from its neighbour. Tightly seal the bag, but leaving a good pocket of air. Label the bag with the name of the snowdrop, the date and the number of sections, and put in a warm, dark place, maintaining a temperature of around 20°C.

Clean and sterilize everything, disposing of unused fungicide, etc., before repeating the process on another bulb.

The sections should be carefully and regularly checked, immediately removing any that show signs of mould. Infected bags should have the remaining sections resoaked in fungicide for 30 minutes before being placed in a new bag with fresh vermiculite.

After approximately four weeks bulb scales begin to splay out and tiny bulblets can be seen growing between the individual scales. At around three months new bulblets are generally ready for potting. Some take a little longer, but after five or six months, if nothing has appeared, discard the material. Also discard sections which have not produced bulblets. Obviously not all chips survive to maturity; losses are inevitable, but results are generally good.

Sterilize some 7 or 9cm pots with a weak solution of household bleach and then half-fill them with a fifty/fifty mix of general purpose compost and vermiculite, or seed compost with added fine horticultural grit. Add a thin layer of sand. Insert the basal end of the sections into the sand, but make sure they are not touching. Each pot will accommodate five or six slices. Gently spray with fungicide and top up with compost.

Carefully label the pots. Water them thoroughly, then place under glass in a shady situation or plunge bed and protect from frost. Pots require little, if any, further water until growth appears, but ensure they do not dry out completely. Leaves should appear at the commencement of the normal growing season. Often bulblets do not produce any leaf in the first season and leaves only appear in the second year.

Expensive snowdrops such as 'Bloomer' can be more quickly increased by twin scaling.

Trays of new *Galanthus* seedlings.

Keep the plants moist throughout the growing season. When the new leaves have died back, repot into clean, sterilized pots, or plant out into permanent positions. New bulbs take between three

and four years to reach maturity, depending on the size of the original sections. Larger sections should produce flowering-sized plants in around three years, thinner ones need four or more.

Originally it was thought that damaged bulbs, or bulbs with fungal or viral infections, could not be propagated in this way as the disease would be perpetuated. Sometimes, however, it is necessary in an effort to prevent very rare varieties from dying out completely. Anything is worth trying, and chipping of diseased bulbs can meet with considerable success. It is important to ensure that at least part of the basal plate is intact, infected material is removed as far as is possible, and everything is sterilized to limit the infection spreading.

Most varieties of snowdrop can be propagated by chipping and twin scaling, although some take a long time to establish afterwards. Twin scaling does not appear to have any detrimental effect on the stock, and it can produce more vigorous plants. When experimenting with this method, start with common snowdrops rather than risking expensive mistakes. It is not a difficult technique to master, given a steady hand and patience, and it is always exciting to achieve success.

Should you have a special snowdrop you wish to increase but are concerned about carrying out the process, enlist the help of an expert or specialist company. At present (2012) this costs around £30 per bulb, but it can increase stock by between 10 and 40 per cent. Most companies are thoroughly reliable, returning all progeny generated. They sometimes take an agreed percentage of the resulting plants in return for their services, but reputable businesses will not risk damaging their standing by 'stealing' bulbs.

It is also worth keeping and sterilizing the top of the bulbs, and placing these in the vermiculite mixture as well. Quite often small 'pips' can be found growing around these sections, which will ultimately grow into new bulbs.

One expert snowdrop grower is disdainful about treating bulbs in such a clinical fashion. He simply slices bulbs with a sharp knife and throws them into a bag of vermiculite, and always has a good success rate.

Seeds

Snowdrops, other than the species, do not come true from seed, but can produce interesting results. Seed is produced after the plants have been fertilized. The capsule swells, bending the scape back until it rests on the ground and the ovary splits, releasing seeds into the soil.

The amount of seed produced depends on weather temperature and conditions. In some years plants produce prolific quantities of seed, in other years very little. Some clones are sterile, producing no seed at all, while other snowdrops can be extremely fertile, producing quantities of viable seed. Resulting seedlings can often be disappointing and non-descript, but sometimes the unexpected happens and a plant turns out to be something truly special. The excitement comes in never quite knowing what will happen until a flower is produced.

If using a specific plant for seed, it is best to place a small, fine, muslin bag over the seed head, gently tying it around the growing stem with cotton or wool. This should not cut into the stem but be firm enough to secure the bag and not allow seeds to escape. Seed pods can be harvested as soon as they are ripe, usually when the capsule has turned yellow, from around mid-May to mid-June. Clean the seed, store in small paper bags or envelopes and label carefully. For best results seed should be planted while still fresh. Seeds can be stored up to a maximum of one year if kept in cool and dry conditions, but seed does deteriorate with long storage. Snowdrop seed takes between four and six years to produce the first flowers.

Seed can be planted directly into prepared ground in shallow drills, but better results are obtained by sowing in pots or trays in an open frame. Light humidity through the summer months is also beneficial. Loosely fill small, clean pots with a fifty/fifty mixture of potting compost and vermiculite, or seed compost with added sharp sand, to within 2cm of the top. Scatter seed thinly across the surface and cover with a thin layer of compost, firming gently. Cover the surface with a thin layer of small, horticultural grit. Label carefully. Water well but gently, ensuring it does not disturb the surface. Keep the pots in a shady, frost-free area, out of strong sunlight, or in a cold frame or unheated greenhouse. Keep moist but not waterlogged, and ensure the pots don't dry out.

Germination takes place in late winter when a small, grass-like leaf appears, at the same time as snowdrops normally begin to show. However, germination can take up to two or even three years, so don't discard the pots if there are no signs of leaves appearing after the first year.

After germination keep the pots moist; a monthly application of a weak solution of tomato feed is beneficial. Once the leaves die back, repot the small bulbs in new sterile compost, such as John Innes No. 3, in the second year. Plant into permanent positions in the third year, when some may be producing flowers.

It is not necessary to deadhead snowdrops, and would be far too much of a nuisance as there can be many thousands of them, especially when naturalized. It would also negate the possibility of snowdrops seeding.

The only time cross-pollination might become a problem is when stray seed comes close to established groups of special snowdrops. In this instance seed heads should be removed.

Micropropagation

This is a highly skilled scientific process of tissue culture under laboratory conditions to increase plant stocks by producing numbers of identical clones. Micropropagation is a complicated and extremely expensive process, and is thus mainly used on plants that are sterile or produce little viable seed.

Due to the high demand not only for rarer snowdrops, but also for more common varieties now, the Horticulture Development Council (HDC) has been funding research into this method of increasing snowdrops with good results. Work

A selection of different snowdrops growing close together at East Lambrook Manor, Somerset. (*Photo courtesy Mike Werkmeister*)

Galanthus plicatus have been used in micropropagation research.

is carried out by skilled staff in laboratories. The main snow-drops used were species and hybrids of *G. nivalis*, *G. elwesii* and *G. plicatus*, but the same principles apply to rarer bulbs, although it will be some time before this has any major effect on the market.

The plant material must be strong, healthy and disease free. It can be a small section of plant tissue or even a single cell. The material used is thoroughly sterilized before being placed in growth medium, generally a mix of plant hormones, sucrose and agar. After the successful growth of plant tissue, multiple samples are taken and reproduced, providing thou-sands of plants from the original small sample. The resulting plantlets are encouraged to produce roots and are eventually weaned away from their specialist growing conditions and planted into compost.

Storing

If it becomes necessary for some reason to dig out snowdrop bulbs that will not be replanted for a while, the bulbs can be lifted just after becoming dormant and stored in boxes of sand or peat, in a cool dry place. Replant in the autumn.

Forcing Snowdrops

This is not usually necessary in the UK, unless you are exhibiting at shows and want snowdrops to flower out of season. In this case specialist conditions are required. Snowdrops need a period of winter cold to flower well. Where this is unavailable, plants can be forced by keeping bulbs in a refrigerator for six to twelve weeks before planting out. If planting in pots, half-fill the pots with compost mixed with sharp sand or fine horticultural grit to aid drainage. Evenly space four or five bulbs and cover with around an inch of compost. Firm down and place in a refrigerator or shaded cold frame where temperatures will not exceed 35–40°F. Leave the pots for ten to twelve weeks and then bring into a cool, light area. Keep the compost moist at all times.

Pests and Diseases

Galanthus are usually considered fairly trouble-free plants but they can suffer various problems, ranging from birds pecking off the flowers to serious virus infections. However, instances of damage by pests and disease are becoming increasingly severe, and many are resistant to the chemicals once used to treat them. With the rapid rise in popularity of the snowdrop, bulbs are increasingly moved not only around the country, but around the world, while gardens open to substantial numbers of visitors can unwittingly import disease. It is inevitable that problems will escalate.

Check all new bulbs when purchased for signs of damage, mould or virus. New bulbs can also be quarantined to make sure they do not introduce disease to established stocks. This is not generally necessary when snowdrops have been obtained from a reliable source, especially if they appear healthy, but it becomes a sensible precaution where valuable collections are concerned.

The list of available chemicals for garden use is constantly revised and changed. Most chemicals used by professional growers are unavailable to amateurs. Good garden centres can advise and recommend chemicals for specific problems. However, it is always preferable to run gardens on organic lines, without using harmful substances.

Good garden hygiene is of paramount importance in help-ing limit the spread of viral and fungal infections around the garden and from plant to plant. Many infections are spread by transferring sap from one plant to another either on the hands or on tools. Always clear up garden litter that can harbour spores, and clean and disinfect garden tools regularly, particu-larly things like secateurs when moving from plant to plant. When removing bulb offsets always clean the knife between each bulb. A quick wipe over with a good garden disinfectant helps limit the spread of disease.

The best preventatives are to practise good garden hygiene, to provide suitable growing conditions, to be vigilant, and to buy bulbs from reliable sources.

Aphids

Aphids can prove a problem, especially when snowdrops are grown under glass as the leaves and shoots are more suscepti-ble to attack. Treat with proprietary insecticide, wash plants with water containing soft soap, or remove the aphids by hand.

Mole damage in an area of snowdrops planted in grassland for naturalizing.

Birds

A number of birds peck off snowdrop flowers, especially wood pigeons and collared doves (and free-range hens). Birds do not present too much of a problem with large areas of naturalized snowdrops, but they always seem to go for the most treasured blooms. Small square mesh wire cages can be constructed inexpensively to protect rarer snowdrops.

Moles

Although moles do not appear to eat snowdrop bulbs, they can create chaos among naturalized plants, pushing up clumps when excavating tunnels, and breaking off roots, shoots and flowers. Growing bulbs in wire baskets or lattice pots can help to some extent in alleviating mole damage.

Slugs and Snails

Generally speaking, these do not present a major problem as most snowdrops flower in winter when few slugs and snails are around. Occasionally emerging shoots can be attacked in milder conditions, and autumn snowdrops are more susceptible. Slugs and snails often hibernate in groups of pots, wreaking havoc as weather improves. Practise good garden hygiene, be vigilant, remove predators on sight, or use appropriate chemical treatment.

Note that hedgehogs eat slugs and snails, and most chemical controls have a seriously detrimental effect on hedgehogs, whose numbers are declining rapidly.

Squirrels

Squirrels dig up bulbs when burying nuts, and will often dig up newly planted bulbs. Planting bulbs slightly deeper (at 10cm) generally alleviates the problem, as does firming the ground well after planting. In areas seriously prone to squirrel attack wire hanging baskets inverted over recently planted bulbs offer some protection, although they can look unsightly. Lattice pots can prove useful, especially if the tops are covered with small-mesh wire netting. An 'invisible' alternative is to remove areas of turf or soil to a depth of around 5cm. Make individual holes to a depth of a further 5cm and plant the bulbs. Refill the planting holes and cover the area with a square of fine-mesh wire netting, then replace the topsoil or turf.

Mice

Mice can attack and eat bulbs, although this problem is not usually too severe. Use bait or traps or plant bulbs in lattice pots, covered with wire mesh.

A pot of snowdrops showing slug-damaged leaves.

Large Narcissus Fly – *Merodon equestris*

A type of hoverfly that mimics a small bumble bee in appearance but can be differentiated by the very high-pitched whine when flying, Large Narcissus Flies are around 13mm long, hairy, and vary in colour from creamy-brown to orange and dark brown, often striped. Native to the British Isles and Europe, the Large Narcissus Fly lays a single egg beneath the soil at the base of dying foliage. Around two weeks later a large larva eats into and

Large Narcissus Fly - *Merodon equestris*. A type of hoverfly that mimics a small bumblebee, and lays a single egg at the base of dying foliage. (*Photo courtesy Mark Smyth*)

Large Narcissus Fly - *Merodon equestris* larvae eats into snowdrop bulbs, eventually destroying them. (*Photo courtesy Mark Smyth*)

eventually destroys the bulbs. It is more prevalent when bulbs are grown in pots. Dispose of infected bulbs and move pots to a different area, or plant bulbs directly into the ground. Always examine bulbs carefully when repotting or planting for signs of larval damage, indicated by a hole in the base plate. Bulbs can be treated with insecticide, but prevention is by far the best method of control. Make sure the areas around the bulbs are always well firmed. Investigate leaf damage and yellowing by digging up the bulb to see whether larvae are present. If so, dispose of them and remove and burn any damaged bulbs, leaves, etc.

Small Narcissus Fly – *Eumerus strigatus, E. tuberculatus*

There are two species of the small Narcissus Fly: *Eumerus strigatus* and *E. tuberculatus*. Smaller than the Large Narcissus Fly at around 7mm long, they are smooth, shiny black in colour and produce a number of small cream-white larvae, all of which eat into the bulb. Unlike the larvae of the Large Narcissus Fly, which attack healthy bulbs, small Narcissus Fly larvae generally attack bulbs already weakened by damage or disease. Treat as above, although there is often no alternative but to destroy infected bulbs as they are generally too badly damaged.

The Swift Moth (*Korscheltellus lupulina*) can lay up to 700 eggs on dying snowdrop foliage.
(*Photo courtesy © Entomart, Wikipedia Commons*)

The Swift Moth caterpillar has a distinctive red head, making it easily recognizable.
(*Photo courtesy ©Jeffdelonge, Wikipedia Commons*)

Narcissus Eelworm – *Ditylenchus dipsaci*

This microscopic nematode is causing increasingly severe problems. Symptoms include distorted, yellowing leaves, stunted stems, aborted flowers and bulb damage showing concentric brown rings with no larvae present. Eelworm remains in the soil for many years. Dig up infected areas, including a one metre radius of healthy bulbs. Dispose of damaged bulbs and replant healthy bulbs in another area. No chemical treatments are available for amateur gardeners. Bulbs can be treated with hot water but specialist equipment is usually required to achieve any success. Bulbs are immersed in a thermostatically controlled, insulated water tank for three hours at a temperature of 44.5°C. The temperature is critical: too cold and the eelworm survives, too hot and the bulbs are damaged. Replant bulbs into new areas after treatment.

Swift Moth – *Korscheltellus lupulina*

This moth lays up to 700 eggs in early summer on dying leaves. The caterpillar larva has a distinctive red head, making it easily recognizable. They burrow into the soil, feeding on roots and bulbs during the winter. Spray the ground around the bulbs with a general insecticide in the autumn to kill the larvae.

Bulb Mites – *Rhizoglyphus echinops, Steneotarsonemus laticeps*

These may not be as serious as they sound and could simply only move in when plants and bulbs have already been damaged or weakened. They are around 2mm long, and grey-white in colour, and they create scars and brown patches on bulbs. Badly infected material should be burnt; lighter infestations treated with pesticide.

Nematodes

These small organisms are found in the soil; they multiply quickly and can be harmful to bulbs. Treat with an appropriate chemical. It may be helpful to move snowdrops around, rather than keeping them in the same position over many years.

Fungal Infections

Red Fire – *Stagonospora curtisii*

Known as 'Red fire', 'Red blotch', or 'Red leaf spot', this fungal infection shows up as bright red or brownish spots or streaks on any part of the plant – roots, bulbs, shoots, leaves or flowers. The fungus is spread by air- and water-borne spores, and is particularly prevalent in cold and wet conditions. In severe cases this can wipe out whole colonies of snowdrops.

Always remove suspicious-looking leaves. Treating the plants often has little effect as they are immediately reinfected. Treatment includes digging up infected plants, together with the adjacent soil. Remove and burn the outer tunics from bulbs, and any parts of the plant showing telltale red blotches or streaks. Soak the bulbs for an hour in proprietary fungicide or disinfectant, or water containing ½ per cent of bleach or hydrogen peroxide. Replant and regularly spray newly emerging foliage until the bulbs become dormant. Alternatively, after treatment the bulbs can be replanted in pots and kept away from other snowdrops.

When growth commences, it soon becomes apparent if the treatment has worked. The fungus generally first appears with reddish-brown blotches or streaks on the leaves following a fungal attack on the bulbs. In the second season the leaf damage is more severe, with increased red marking, withered leaves and aborted or discoloured flowers. The bulbs are usually completely destroyed by the third year. Infection can be more severe and faster acting in wet summers or in very damp conditions. When lifting bulbs for division, discard soft or shrunken bulbs and any showing brown or red staining. If fungal infection is suspected, follow the treatment guidelines on healthy bulbs to kill off any dormant spores. At the first sign of the fungus, or in severe cases where treatment has failed, remove and burn the infected bulbs, and clear the area of soil where the bulbs were growing.

The best preventative is not to plant bulbs in situations where they experience very wet, cold conditions. Increasing drainage also helps. Always buy bulbs from reputable suppliers, and practise good garden hygiene.

Other fungal infections can cause the basal plates of bulbs to rot, and give rise to orange staining on bulbs when they are lifted. If left, the discoloration spreads through the bulb, eventually killing it.

Grey Mould – *Botrytis galanthina*

This occurs in mild, wet winters, or on bulbs grown under glass when conditions are too wet and humid. Fluffy, grey patches appear on young foliage and flowers, and the plants eventually collapse. In the early stages an application of mild fungicide may help, but in severe cases there is no adequate solution. Remove and destroy all infected bulbs and do not replant in the same area, as Botrytis remains in the ground and new plantings can become infected. A light dusting of sulphur when lifting and storing bulbs may be beneficial but there is no hard evidence for this. Regular repotting of bulbs under glass and good air circulation are important factors in helping to prevent Botrytis.

Botrytis cinerea

This is a less damaging grey mould.

Bulb Rot – *Penicillium spp.; Soft Rot – Rhizopus spp.*

Generally a disease of plants under propagation, this shows as patches of white fungus or decaying foliage. Good hygiene habits and sterile propagating conditions are beneficial. Treat with appropriate fungicide.

A group of snowdrops decimated by the effects of *Botrytis*.

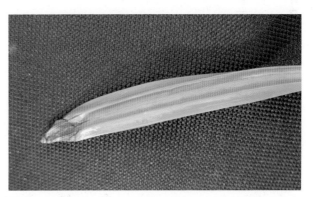

Red/brown patches on snowdrop foliage here indicate the presence of Botrytis, but can also be indicative of Red Fire - *Stagonospora curtisii*.

Viral Infections

Viral infections can distort and weaken plants. Some snowdrops seem more prone to virus attack, while others happily thrive despite being infected. Signs to look out for are discoloration and streaks on leaves, stem and ovary, scapes unable to support flowers, and flowers that fail to open properly. Once snowdrops are infected with a virus, the best solution is to destroy and burn all infected plants as there is no cure. Always keep a careful eye on snowdrops, removing infected material and plants immediately. In the case of viral attacks on rarer snowdrops, move the plants and grow them well away from other snowdrops in the hope they survive. In severe cases even these bulbs should be destroyed in an effort to stop disease spreading into other bulbs. If virus infections are discovered, do not plant snowdrops in the same area or in close proximity.

CHAPTER 7

CREATING A SNOWDROP GARDEN

Other than specialist growers, who tend to keep their collections of snowdrops strictly segregated, most gardeners are happy to use snowdrops as part of mixed planting schemes where all the plants enhance and complement one another. This also has the added advantage of utilizing space to the best advantage, as there is always something of interest, whatever the time of year.

Mixed plantings of *Galanthus* and *Cyclamen coum* in the garden at Ivy Croft, Ivington Green, Herefordshire.

Snowdrop leaves must not be removed until they have completely died back, by which time the seasonal growth from herbaceous plants covers any bare areas. The object is to establish continuous waves of plants following on one from the other, but it is important to ensure the plants that follow appreciate similar conditions to snowdrops if they are all to thrive.

Although snowdrops do not like heavy shade, they grow well and look delightful in open shrub borders. Make sure smaller snowdrops are not overshadowed by dense shrubs, although larger snowdrops stand out well growing between

OPPOSITE PAGE: The colourful winter garden at Dial Park, Chaddesley Corbet, Worcestershire.

taller shrubs and trees. Snowdrops can be used to form clumps towards the front of borders, or to edge paths; they naturalize well on steep grassy banks and in woodland, and create delightful seasonal displays in containers, placed prominently so not a moment of their beauty is missed.

Rock gardens are ideal for plants requiring extra drainage. Niches against rocks provide added protection for tender species, as well as creating a natural environment for snowdrops, which are often found growing between limestone rocks and boulders in the wild. Rock gardens are also commonly mulched with fine gravel which aids drainage, as well as giving extra protection to bulbs and providing some deterrent to slugs and snails.

In areas where snowdrops do not grow well raised beds can be filled with suitable growing medium which also has the advantage of being free-draining.

Snowdrops, spring bulbs and colourful winter shrubs at The Patch, Acton Pigot, Shropshire.

Raised beds are useful in areas where snowdrops do not grow well. Filled with a suitable growing medium, they also have the advantage of offering good drainage.

Orchards and wild flower meadows are also good areas in which to naturalize snowdrops. The grass is generally not too rampant or compacted and is not cut until well after the snowdrop leaves have disappeared.

Another method of displaying special snowdrops in pots is to make a 'theatre', of the type originally used to display *Auricula*. The same principles apply to snowdrops. Arranging the pots on shelving with a dark background will show off the snowdrops to perfection, while allowing each individual flower to be examined at close quarters.

It is always sensible to mark snowdrops, especially rarer ones, so the bulbs are not inadvertently disturbed or, even worse, destroyed when digging. Unfortunately, labels are never an attractive feature in gardens, but there are many more unobtrusive alternatives on the market today.

Many larger gardens opening to the public have created stunning winter gardens over the last few years, specifically including plants and flowers that bring colour and perfume to the garden in winter, as well as large collections of snowdrops.

Good Companions

Snowdrops grow beautifully through ivy, *Hedera helix*, a combination often seen in woodland or around old cottages where ivy sprawls across the ground. The foil of the dark green, attractively lobed leaves shows off the white snowdrops to perfection. More robust snowdrops easily grow through this mat of ground cover. Various ivy cultivars also offer interesting combinations of leaf shape and colour.

Other good combinations include snowdrops and winter flowering Iris, particularly *I. unguicularis*, *I. reticulata*, *I. histrioides* and their cultivars. *G. elwesii* grows well with miniature Iris and looks particularly good with *I.* 'Katherine Hodgkin' with its pale blue-grey flowers, darker blue veining and a tiny splash of brilliant yellow. *G. nivalis* 'Viridapice' makes an ideal partner for *Arum italicum* 'Marmoratum'. The arum's silver-mottled, heart-shaped leaves unfurl as the snowdrops reach perfection, making a simple but stunning combination.

Taller snowdrops such as 'Colossus', 'Comet' and 'S. Arnott' integrate beautifully with hellebores and are not dwarfed by them. For a subtle colour wash, plant snowdrops with white hellebores, or, for contrast, with colours such as yellow, pink, or dark purple-black. Many hellebores also have intricately shaped and patterned leaves.

Taller snowdrops also integrate well with gently moving grasses, such as *Stipa tenuissima*. The grass forms a delicately moving screen, revealing glimpses of ghost-like white flowers. Dark-coloured foliage, such as the purple-black *Ophiopogon planiscapus* 'Nigrescens', black Mondo grass, creates a dramatic contrast for white flowers.

Mixed borders with snowdrops, miniature iris and cyclamen at Ivy Croft, Ivington Green, Herefordshire.

Snowdrops and white hellebores create a bright but subtle colour scheme.

C. coum, spring cyclamen, with their attractively rounded and marbled leaves and white, pink or magenta flowers, bloom at the same time as snowdrops. A combination of cerise *C. coum*, yellow winter aconite *Eranthis hyemalis*, lavender *Crocus tomassinianus*, planted together with green-tipped white snowdrops creates stunning displays. Other good combinations are snowdrops planted with *Corydalis*, *Erythronium*, *Euphorbia* and most early flowering spring bulbs, including *Scilla*, *Eranthis hyemalis*, *Anemone blanda*, *Fritillaria* and *Crocus*. Tier the display using low-growing *G. nivalis* and *G. gracilis* together with *C. coum* and *Ajuga reptans*, backed by taller snowdrops and hellebores, against the coloured stems of *Cornus* in front of white-stemmed birch.

Creating a Woodland Garden

Light woodland creates one of the most natural and effective habitats for snowdrops, where they can be left to spread and naturalize undisturbed. Different species require slightly different conditions and some prefer more open situations and sunlight, but most common species grow well in woodland. Deciduous woodland is typically made up from a wide variety of trees, including oak, ash, maple, chestnut, beech, lime, hawthorn, holly, hazel and elder. If you are creating a woodland garden you could also include flowering cherries; Magnolia; early flowering trees and shrubs such as *Malus*, crab apple; *Mahonia*; *Chimonanthus praecox*, wintersweet; *Cornus mas*, Cornelian cherry; *Sarcococcas*, Christmas box; and *Daphne*.

Most winter- and spring-flowering bulbs appreciate a woodland setting, and when the snowdrops and other spring bulbs fade the wide variety of foliage shapes and colours of the trees and shrubs takes over, also providing the dappled shade necessary during the hotter months of the year when the snowdrop bulbs are dormant. Smaller species of daffodils, including *N. pseudonarcissus*, the wild daffodil, always look more at home in woodland than the larger varieties. Then come the plants that carpet the woodland floor: primroses, violets, wood anemone, sweet woodruff, wild arum, wild garlic and triangular-stalked garlic. An azure sea of bluebells extends the flowering season into May, as mosses spread a rich green carpet and ferns push tightly coiled fronds through fading bulb leaves, unfurling long green stems of divided, feathery foliage.

Epimedium offers attractively shaped and coloured leaves, many of which turn red and bronze in winter. Hellebores include *H. foetidus*, with apple-green flowers. *Trilliums* add an air of mystery with their strangely shaped flowers and large leaves often mottled deep red. Kidney-shaped, dark-green *Asarum* leaves also make a good foil for woodland flowers. *Pachysandra terminalis*, another good ground cover plant, has short stems and whorls of evergreen leaves. *Vinca*, periwinkle, carpets light woodland, and many different ivy species thrive in shady conditions. Certain lilies also love dappled shade, including *Lilium martagon* and the striking *Cardiocrinum giganteum*, giant wood lily.

In your woodland garden you could also include summer-flowering shrubs, simple climbing and wild roses and honeysuckle. Fruits and berries follow in the autumn, together with the vivid reds, oranges and yellows of autumn leaves, *Colchicum*, and the first autumn-flowering snowdrops, although these need to be planted on the woodland fringe where they receive more light. Finally as the leaves fall, adding rich humus to the ground, the delicate pink and white flowers of *Prunus subhirtella autumnalis*, winter cherry, brighten bare branches, holly berries shine red, and the winter shrubs begin to flower again.

Wild and cultivated plants harmonize together beautifully in the woodland garden, creating rich patterns of texture and colour so there is always something of interest.

Few gardens boast areas of natural woodland, but snowdrops grouped beneath two or three carefully chosen trees or shrubs can also be very effective on a smaller scale.

Cyclamen coum naturalize beautifully, spreading into bright carpets, as do snowdrops.

Snowdrops, *hellebores*, spring bulbs and colourful winter-interest shrubs in the woodland garden at the Beth Chatto Gardens, Colchester, Essex. (*Photo courtesy Beth Chatto Gardens*)

Galanthus.

Galanthus and species crocus.

Galanthus beneath shrubs.

Galanthus and daffodils..

Magnolia

New spring foliage.

Primula vulgaris (primrose) and *Arum maculatum* (wild arum).

Hyacinthoides non-scripta (bluebell), *Allium ursinum*

Azalea.

Lilium martagon (Turks cap lily)..

Cardiocrinum giganteum (giant wood lily).

Digitalis purpurea (foxglove).

Autumn colour with Acers.

Crataegus orientalis (hawthorn).

Callicarpa bodinieri.

Ilex aquifolium (holly).

Prunus subhirtella autumnalis (winter-flowering cherry).

Hamamelis mollis (witch hazel).

Ilex aquifolium.

Evergreens

Evergreen shrubs and trees make good backgrounds for white flowers, but plant snowdrops in front of dense evergreens rather than directly beneath them. The dark green of holly and yew, and paler green box, create seasonal foils for emerging snowdrops, while the soft blue flowers of rosemary often open well before snowdrops have finished.

Buxus sempervirens, Common box, 1–8m. Small mid-dark green leaves, forming hedges or specimen shrubs, also regularly trimmed for topiary. **'Suffruticosa'** 30cm, trimmed into low hedges creates an attractive backdrop to clumps of snowdrops but is also a feature in its own right when snowdrops disappear in summer.

Cupressus arizonica var. *glabra*, **'Blue Ice'**, 25m. Evergreen tree, blue-grey leaves. **'Compacta'**, dwarf rounded or conical tree, blue-green leaves.

Garrya elliptica 'James Roof', 4m. Shrub or small tree, dark green-grey leaves, spectacular long dangling silver-grey catkins in winter.

Ilex aquifolium 'Pyramidalis', 5m. Conical shrub or small tree, self-fertile, yellow-green leaves, bright red berries. *I.* 'J.C. van Tol', reliably produces brilliant scarlet berries. *I.* 'Ferox', Hedgehog Holly, male, old variety with spiny leaves forming neat small bush. *I. crenata* 'Golden Gem', 60 cm. Low shrub or hedge, golden leaves.

Garrya elliptica.

Viburnum tinus.

Pieris japonica 'Christmas Cheer', Lily-of-the-valley bush, 4m. Lime free soil, leathery evergreen leaves, pendulous clusters of small bell-shaped, scented white flowers late winter.

Pinus densiflora 'Alice Verkade', 1.2m. Dwarf Japanese red pine forming dense, rounded bush, dark green needles.

Podocarpus nivalis, Alpine Totara, 3m. Spreading mounded shrub, olive green leaves.

Prunus lusitanica, Portuguese laurel, 20m. Bushy evergreen shrub or tree, red bark, large, shiny, leathery leaves.

Rosmarinus officinalis 'Prostratus'. Procumbent spreading branches, aromatic, small linear leaves, whorls of blue flowers in spring.

Ruscus aculeatus, Butcher's broom, 125cm. Densely branched, small evergreen, dark green leaves, white flowers in spring followed by red, cherry-like berries.

Taxus baccata 'Fastigiata', Irish yew, 20m. Slow-growing, upright columnar tree, dense branches, small, narrow dark-green leaves. 'Standishii', Golden yew, densely packed golden leaves.

Thuja plicata 'Rogersii', Western red cedar, 70cm. Dwarf conical tree, bronze winter foliage.

Viburnum tinus, Laurustinus, 3.5m. Evergreen, rounded shiny leaves, clusters of small white-pink flowers throughout winter, followed by tiny black berries.

Camellia.

Winter-flowering and Berried Shrubs and Trees

Many winter-flowering trees and shrubs are highly perfumed to attract insects. Delicate branches wreathed with white, cream, yellow or pink flowers make an ideal canopy for groups of pure white snowdrops. Many shrubs and trees also carry bright fruits and berries well into the winter months. A long established and very popular combination of plants are snowdrops growing beneath witch-hazel and Cornelian cherry, both having attractive golden flowers in late winter. Most winter interest shrubs and trees perform equally well in summer with attractive foliage, giving interest throughout the year.

Callicarpa bodinieri, 3m. Deciduous shrub, small shiny, bead-like purple berries throughout winter.

Camellia japonica. Many cultivars, leathery evergreen leaves, vibrant, single or double flowers from mid-winter. Acid soil.

Chimonanthus praecox, Wintersweet, 4m. Deciduous shrub, winter bare branches wreathed in small, creamy yellow, highly perfumed flowers. A few flowers can scent a whole garden.

Clematis armandii, 9m. Scrambling climber, dark-green leaves, dense clusters of fragrant white flowers late winter.

Cornus mas, Cornelian cherry, 5m. Deciduous spreading shrub or small tree smothered with tiny golden-yellow flowers along bare branches in late winter.

Cotoneaster frigidus 'Cornubia', Tree contoneaster. Semi-evergreen, masses of red berries against bright green leaves. C. 'Pendulus', shrub or small tree, pendulous branches heavily laden with red berries.

Daphne bholua 'Gurkha'. 2–4m. Very hardy deciduous shrub, deliciously perfumed white, pink or purple flowers. 'Jacqueline Postill', hardy, usually evergreen, pink-purple buds opening to highly perfumed, large, pale pink flowers. *D. odora*, highly perfumed pink-purple flowers.

Edgeworthia chrysantha, Paper bush, 1.5m. Upright shoots, silky buds opening into clusters of highly perfumed yellow flowers in winter, smothered with silky white hairs.

Clematis armandii.

Jasminum nudiflorum

Mahonia aquifolium 'Atropurpurea'.

Elaeagnus x *ebbingei*, Oleaster, 3m. Usually evergreen, very small, well perfumed cream flowers hidden beneath leaves late autumn-early winter. *E. pungens*, 4m. Evergreen, often spiny shrub, young branches covered with brown scales, silver-green leaves, fragrant white flowers.

Hamamelis mollis, Witch-hazel, 5m. Large deciduous shrub or small tree, bare branches smothered in thread-like, yellow, gold, russet, or deep red-purple flowers in winter. Delicious perfume.

Jasminum nudiflorum, Winter jasmine, 3m. Sprawling shrub, slender, arching, green branches, solitary, star-like yellow flowers throughout winter. Frost-damaged flowers are soon replaced with new.

Lonicera x *purpusii* 'Winter Beauty', 3m. Shrubby, semi-evergreen winter honeysuckle, strongly perfumed small waxy creamy-white flowers on slender sprawling branches, mid-winter to early spring.

Mahonia aquifolium 'Atropurpurea', 2m. Reddish-purple leaves in winter, short racemes of yellow flowers. *M. japonica*, 3m. Evergreen, blue-green, spiny-edged leaves, sprays of pale yellow, lily-of-the-valley perfumed flowers. *M.* x *media* 'Winter Sun', shiny green leaves, horizontal racemes of perfumed, bright yellow flowers.

Malus 'Red Sentinal', Crab apple, 5m. Spring blossom, magnificent small red crab apples in autumn, holding well through winter. *M. transitoria*, crab apple, 8m. Small tree, very small golden fruits.

Prunus incisa 'February Pink', Fuji cherry, 5m. Pale pink flowers from February. *P. subhirtella* 'Autumnalis', Winter cherry, 5m. Spreading, deciduous tree, pink buds opening to masses of delicately ruffled, small white flowers through winter. Good autumn colour. 'Rosea', pink flowers.

Pseudowintera colorata, 2–6m. New Zealand shrub, pale-coloured leaves bordered orange, red or purple, paler beneath.

Sarcococca confusa, Christmas box, Sweet box, 2m. Small evergreen shrub, pointed leaves, tiny highly perfumed tassels of cream flowers. 'Purple Stem', good purple stems. *S. ruscifolia*, 1m. Suckering shrub, slightly thicker leaves, beautiful red berries.

Symphoricarpos x *doorenbosii* 'Mother of Pearl', Snowberry, 1.5m. Semi-pendulous stems clustered with white-marbled pink fruits in winter.

Viburnum x *bodnantense* 'Dawn', 3m. Clusters of sweetly perfumed, deep pink flowers on bare branches throughout winter. *V.* 'Deben', shell-pink flowers fading to white. *V.* 'Charles Lamont', deep pink flowers larger than most winter flowering Viburnums.

Coloured Barks and Stems

For contrast use trees and shrubs with coloured or textured barks and stems which look stunning especially when caught by rays of low winter sunshine. Many also have attractive foliage, flowers and berries for year-round value.

Acer × conspicuum 'Phoenix', 9m. Beautifully marbled bark glowing with reds and browns. *A. griseum*, Paperbark maple, 10m. Cinnamon coloured bark peels and twists, rustling in the breeze. *A. palmatum* 'Sango-kaku', Coral-bark maple, 8m. Deciduous tree, coral red branches, attractive bark. *A. rufinerve*, 10m. Bright green striped bark.

Arbutus × andrachnoides, 10m. Large shrub or small tree, peeling, bright orange-red bark. *A. unedo*, Strawberry tree, 10m. Shrub or small tree, flaking red bark, clusters of small, pendant white-pink flowers, red fruit.

Betula albosinensis 'Bowling Green', Chinese red birch, 18–25m. Rich honey-brown attractively peeling bark. *B. utilis* 'Silver Shadow', Himalayan birch, 20m. Thin, peeling, papery white-brown bark forming good focal point for groups of white snowdrops.

Cornus alba 'Kesselringii', 3m. Suckering shrub, striking purple-black stems. *C.* 'Sibirica', Siberian dogwood. Bright coral-red stems. *Cornus sanguinea* 'Midwinter Fire', 4m. Yellow stems shading to deep pink, vibrant red tips, good autumn colour. *C. stolonifera* 'Budd's Yellow', 2–3m. Deep golden stems. Prune *Cornus* March-April as new growth has stro ngest colouring.

Corylus avellana 'Contorta', Corkscrew hazel, 6m. Twisting, spiralling branches, yellow catkins late winter and spring.

Eucaluptus gunnii, Cider Gum, 10–25m. Erect, spreading tree, creamy green bark, sheds in late summer revealing silvery-green new bark. Mid-green to glaucous leaves, umbels small white flowers.

Prunus maackii 'Amber Beauty', Manchurian cherry, 7m. Highly polished trunk, peeling orange-yellow bark, white blossom in spring, good autumn colour *P. serrula*, Tibetan cherry, 15m. Good tree for smaller gardens, highly polished mahogany-red peeling bark gleams in winter sunshine.

Movement

Certain taller snowdrops such as *G.* 'Magnet' have exceptionally long, slender pedicels, allowing flowers to gently swing in the breeze creating delicate movement. Carry this movement through to other plants growing above and around the snowdrops.

Trees

Betula pendula 'Tristis', Silver birch, 25m. Slender tree, slim weeping branches, plenty of gentle movement.

Populus tremula 'Pendula', Weeping aspen, 15m. Small tree, slim delicately moving pendulous branches, long purple-grey catkins late winter.

Grasses

Carex buchananii, Leatherleaf sedge 10–75cm. Densely tufted, slim arching, reddish-brown-purple fronds. *C. comans*,

Acer griseum.

Prunus serrula.

6-40cm. Delicate, densely tufted sedge shading pale green-bronze to purple-brown. *C. morrowii* 'Fisher's Form', 40cm. Evergreen, arching, variegated cream and green foliage, makes excellent ground cover. *C. oshimensis* 'Evergold'. Good golden colour for open spaces. *C. testacea.* Bronze foliage.

Hakonechloa macra, Japanese mountain grass, 75cm. Red-brown stems, loose, nodding, creamy-brown panicles. Most grasses look a little battered by late winter but this holds up well.

Luzula nivea. Plant in drifts in dappled shade *L. sylvatica.* Dappled shade.

Miscanthus 'Silberfeder', architectural, free flowering, withstands harsh winter conditions.

Stipa tenuissima, Needle grass, 70cm. Tall tufted grass, fine hair-like foliage, large, soft, nodding panicles giving plenty of movement, holding well.

Flowers and Foliage

A large range of foliage and flowering plants mix well with snowdrops. Hellebores are a classic combination and many snowdrop gardens combine these two to great effect. Single or double Hellebores flower around the same time as snowdrops in a range of colours from white, cream, pink and purple to almost black. Many have freckled faces. Remove dead and weather-damaged foliage to reveal newly emerging snowdrops. Most hellebores seed well although seedlings will not come true. Many hardy geraniums have attractive foliage, and flowers appear after snowdrops have faded giving an ongoing display. All appreciate light shade but take care strong rhizomatous roots and leaves don't smother snowdrop bulbs. *Hosta* enjoy dappled shade and have a wide range of beautifully coloured and textured leaves which cover ground after spring bulbs have finished. Many ferns are suitable as foliage appears after snowdrops have finished, filling bare gaps. Winter flowering heathers act as a backdrop to groups of snowdrops but care should be taken to ensure snowdrops do not get swamped by spreading branches.

Ajuga reptans 'Atropurpureum', Bugle, 15cm. Good, carpeting ground cover, dark purple-bronze leaves, low spikes of blue flowers.

Arum italicum subsp. *italicum* 'Marmoratum', 15–35cm. Attractive, broad, crinkled, heart-shaped leaves, glossy dark-green with paler veining, late autumn to spring, spikes of bright orange seeds. *A. italicum* 'Tiny Tot' 15cm. Miniature with narrow, bright-green leaves heavily marked silver from autumn through winter *A. maculatum*, wild arum 25cm. Large, dark-green, arrow-head shaped leaves, short stems, pale green spathe enclosing purple or green spadix, bright red fruits in autumn.

Asarum europaeum, Asarabacca, 2–10cm. Broad, kidney-shaped dark glossy-green leaves with paler veining, late winter - early spring, good ground cover.

Athyrium filix-femina, Lady fern. 1m. Crown-forming fern with upright, spreading, pinnate to pinnatifid fronds.

Bergenia 'Bressingham Ruby', Elephant's ears. 30cm. Large, rounded leaves turning deep red-purple in winter followed by early pink flowers. *B.* 'Eric Smith' deep shining red leaves, pink flowers. *B. stracheyi*, smaller with upright leaves, pale pink flowers.

Cardamine quinquefolia, good ground cover, attractive leaves, purple-pink flowers.

Corydalis malkensis, Finely-cut green foliage, beautiful spurred white flowers. *C. solida*, 25cm. Perennial, attractive unevenly dissected and lobed leaves, pale pink, red or mauve flowers in spring.

Dryopteris affinis, 'Cristata', Upright semi-evergreen frilly fronds. *D. erythrosora*, Japanese shield fern, 30–60cm. Rhizomatous fern for acid soils, orange coloured fronds fading to green in winter.

Epimedium × *rubrum*, Bishop's hat, 25–35cm. Beautiful mahogany-red leaves throughout winter, small cream and red flowers in spring. *E.* × *versicolor* 'Neosulphureum', Leaves turn deep-red to burgundy in winter, coppery-red foliage in spring and pale yellow flowers.

Erica carnea, 'Ann Sparkes', Winter heath, 25cm. Dense, yellow-bronze winter foliage. *E.* 'Winter Beauty', 15cm. Dense, compact, spreading, pink flowers in winter. *E.* 'Myretoun Ruby', dark-green leaves, intense wine-coloured flowers. *E.* 'Vivellii', bronze foliage, pale pink flowers.

Euphorbia amygdaloides 'Purpurea', Wood spurge, 85cm. Purple-red leaves, lime green flower heads. *E. amygdaloides* var. *robbiae*. Rosettes of dark green leaves, yellow-green flower heads, makes good foil for taller snowdrops. *E. characias* 'Silver Swan', 1.5m. Ivory edged, narrow green leaves. *E. myrsinites*. Smaller Euphorbia, spirally arranged, blue-grey leaves, sulphur yellow flower heads in spring.

Bergenia and snowdrops.

Galium odoratum, Sweet woodruff 12cm. Stems bear whorls of small, narrow, pointed leaves, open heads of starry white flowers early summer.

Geranium clarkei 'Kashmir White', 50cm. Deeply cut and divided basal leaves, numerous cup-shaped white flowers veined purple. *G. lambertii*. Procumbent trailing perennial, divided, hairy, kidney-shaped leaves, shallowly cup-shaped, pink or white flowers, black anthers. *G. pyrenaicium*. 60cm. Hairy, lobed leaves, deeply notched, pink-purple flowers spring-autumn. *G. wallichianum* 'Buxton's Variety'. Dense, compact, spreading stems, small leaves delicately veined, blue flowers with white eye in summer. Geraniums form good spreading cover, cut foliage back in autumn making way for bulbs beneath.

Hedera helix, Ivy. Spreading evergreen, good ground cover in shady areas or for covering fence or wall. Lobed leaves. Numerous attractive cultivars including variegated forms.

Helleborus argutifolius, 1m. Tall green stems, evergreen much-divided foliage, clusters of cup-shaped green flowers in

Euphorbia griffithi 'Dixter'.

Helleborus × hybridus.

Helleborus niger (Christmas rose).

Euphorbia characias.

Iris foetidissima seeds.

Primula vulgaris (primrose).

Viola odorata (violet).

winter. *H. foetidus*, Stinking hellebore, 80cm. Erect leafy stems die back after flowering, green or grey-green leaves, large clusters of pendant pale-green flowers banded red. Seeds freely. *H. niger*, Christmas rose, 30cm. Dark-green divided leaves, ice-white flowers from mid-winter. *H. niger* 'Double Fantasy' 30cm. Semi-double, pure white, early. *H. × hybridus*, Lenten rose, 45cm. Coarsely serrated, divided green leaves, single or double flowers in a wide range of colours, many freckled red and purple.

Heuchera 'Chocolate Ruffles', Evergreen, rounded tooth-edged much ruffled purple-maroon leaves. *H.* 'Green Spice'. Red-veined green leaves in winter. *H.* 'Stormy Seas'. Silver-veined pewter and purple leaves stand well throughout winter. *H.* 'Venus', silver leaved.

Iris foetidissima, Stinking iris, 30–90cm. Basal fan of sword-shaped leaves, attractive yellow flowers marked purple in summer, followed by splitting capsules of brilliant orange seeds carrying well through winter.

Ophiopogon planiscapus 'Nigrescens', 35cm. Outstanding purple-black, grass-like leaves, spikes of small white, blue-lilac flowers. Good foil for snowdrops.

Polystichum setiferum 'Congestum', Soft shield fern, 30–50cm. Bushy green fronds, orange brown scales. *P.* 'Cristato-gracile Moly', 30–50cm. Lightly crested dark-green fronds. *P.* 'Plumosum Bevis' 30–50cm. Open elongated fronds. Ferns have attractive unfurling fronds in spring, filling gaps left by winter flowering bulbs.

Primula vulgaris, primrose 10–15cm. Rosettes of crinkled, toothed leaves, slender stems bearing flat pale-yellow flowers.

Pulmonaria angustifolia 'Johnson's Blue', 20cm. Blue flowers. *G. longifolia*, 'Bertram Anderson', Long narrow, silver-spotted leaves, blue flowers in spring. Good with Galanthus 'Bertram Anderson'. *P. montana* 'Albocorollata', 30cm. Pale-green leaves, pure-white flowers, early spring. *P. montana* 'Barfield Ruby', 30cm. Spreading, usually unmarked leaves, wine-coloured flowers.

Tellima grandiflora 'Rubra Group', Fringe cups. Dense clumps of rounded leaves, deep coral-red in winter.

Viola odorata, Sweet violet 10-15cm. Spreading, heart-shaped dark-green leaves, small fragrant spurred blue, white or purple flowers.

Bulbs, Corms and Tubers

Snowdrops combine beautifully with most other spring flowering bulbs creating colourful displays in the winter garden, naturalised beneath trees or spreading beneath shrubs. Golden winter aconites, native to France and introduced into Britain over 400 years ago are a classic combination with snowdrops. In the right situation they spread and seed freely into golden carpets, forming great naturalized colonies. Cyclamen are an outstanding combination of both leaf shape and flowers, contrasting well with snowdrops, and cyclamen and snowdrops commonly grow together in their native habitats. Hardy cyclamen start flowering in autumn and go through winter to spring with white, pink and magenta flowers and beautifully shaped and marked leaves. Long-lived plants, cyclamen seed freely and corms can reach dinner-plate size. Species crocus come in a range of colours opening to bright stars from mid-winter. *C. tommasinianus* naturalizes and mixes well with snowdrops with its early, pale lavender flowers. For a show of white combine snowdrops with white crocus and hellebores.

Anemone blanda, Windflower, 18cm. Deeply-cut, divided foliage, small, white, pink or blue daisy-like flowers. *A. nemerosa*, wood anemone 10–30cm. Finely divided leaves, slender open star-shaped white flowers.

Eranthis hyemalis, Winter aconite, 15cm. Cup-shaped golden-yellow flowers backed by green ruff. Much divided, bright-green leaves follow after flowering.

Cardiocrinum giganteaum, Giant wood lily, 2–4 m. Leafy stems, fragrant, funnel-shaped flowers.

Chionodoxa luciliae, Glory of the snow, 14cm. Narrow, often re-curved leaves, scapes of white-centred, pale-blue flowers early spring.

Crocus chrysanthus, 8cm. Early species crocus multiplying freely in white, cream, yellow and mauve. *C. sieberi*, 8cm. Pale mauve flowers from mid-winter. *C. tommasinianus*, 8cm, Pale lavender blue buds opening to star-shaped flowers from January.

Crocus 'Yellow Giant'.

Cyclamen coum.

Cyclamen coum.

Cyclamen coum. Rounded to kidney-shaped leaves silver-grey to dark-green, often with silver marking and red or green undersides. Five-petalled white to magenta reflexed flowers with darker basal blotch, **C. hederifoilum**, 7cm. Ivy-like rounded or pointed, light to dark-green leaves, marbled and veined with silver, green or purple-red beneath. Small, five-petalled, reflexed white, pink or deep carmine flowers, autumn and winter.

Fritillaria meleagris, Snake's head fritillary 12–30cm. Nodding, chequered, white, pink or purple flowers on slender stems, long narrow leaves. Damp situation.

Hyacinthoides non-scripta, Bluebell 20–40cm. Strap-shaped leaves, drooping racemes of slender, bell-shaped blue flowers.

Ipheion uniflorum 'Wisley Blue', Starflower, 25cm. Slender strap-shaped leaves, clear blue flowers. **I. 'Charlotte Bishop'**, pink flowers.

Iris histrioides 50cm. Blue flowers, paler falls spotted blue and yellow blotch. **I. reticulata**, early flowering bulbous iris, slender grey-green, four-angled leaves, attractive blue and purple flowers. **'George'**, deep purple flowers, almost black falls. **'Harmony'**, blue flowers. **'Katherine Hodgkin'**, short stems, large pale blue-grey flowers with yellow splash. **I. unguicularis**,

Iris 'Katherine Hodgkin'.

Algerian iris, 60cm, Upright evergreen leaves, mauve and yellow perfumed flowers from early winter.

Leucojum vernum, Spring snowflake, 20cm. Upright scapes, pendant white flowers, green mark at apex. Sometimes confused with snowdrops.

Lilium martagon, Martagon lily, 2m. Tall stems, numerous pendulous flowers with recurved petals. Dappled woodland.

Muscari armeniacum, Grape hyacinth 20cm. Lance-shaped, mid-green leaves, often lax, dense raceme of small, bell-shaped blue flowers.

Narcissus pseudonarcissus, wild daffodil 20–35cm. Erect mid-green leaves, pale golden flowers with darker trumpet. *N.* **'Cedric Morris'**, 25cm. Narrow green leaves, golden flowers from mid-winter. *N.* **'Tête-à-tête'**, small, bright-yellow flowers late winter. *N.* **'February Gold'**, golden flowers, late winter.

Scilla mischtschenkoana 15cm. Shiny bright-green leaves, star-shaped flowers with blue centre band. *S. sibirica*, Siberian squill 15cm. Strap-like, glossy-green leaves, three-four star-shaped blue flowers.

Beginning a Snowdrop Collection

Snowdrops are such beautiful and intriguing plants to grow that, once started, it will not be long before you want more. When beginning a collection, it is better to concentrate on a few stronger and simpler snowdrops rather than risking failure with expensive, rare bulbs that are generally more difficult to grow anyway. Given even half reasonable conditions, most common snowdrops soon spread into sizeable colonies, and prove a joy in any garden, even the smallest.

Once you have strong, well established clumps of *G. nivalis* and *G. elwesii*, and you feel a little more experienced and adventurous, and want to move on, there is a phenomenal range of hybrids and cultivars available, as well as species snowdrops that make essential additions to any collection. Look for plants in which the differences are immediately apparent, such as varying flower shapes, all-green centre segments, or perhaps gold or yellow markings, as well as a selection of snowdrops of different heights, from the petites, at around 5cm high, up to the 'giants', at around 30cm.

Most gardens are able to grow snowdrops, although there are a few areas in the UK where they do not grow well. It is always wise to check first before expending money and energy on plants that may not thrive. In these instances snowdrops can still be grown in raised beds or specially prepared rockeries. It is far more rewarding and satisfying to see large clumps of healthy snowdrops, which grow well and spread quickly, rather than struggling to grow a single, tiny, capricious bulb that may or may not flower, and may not even survive its first season.

At the present time you can expect to pay from around £5.00 for fifty *G. nivalis* bulbs, and £8.00 for fifty *G. nivalis* 'Flore Pleno'. Many hybrids and cultivars reach that sort of price for a single bulb, with many more retailing at between £35 and £40, and rarer snowdrops far, far more.

From the small *Galanthus* 'Tiny' . . .

. . to the tall 'giant' *Galanthus* hybrid.

Snowdrops that spread and bulk up quickly are highly rewarding.

First Snowdrops

G. nivalis and *G. nivalis* 'Flore Pleno', blooming mid-January to March, are good value for money and very satisfying snowdrops with which to begin a collection. They are very hardy, easy to cultivate, grow almost anywhere and bulk up quickly to create good displays within three or four years. You may already have well established clumps of these in your garden, which can be divided further and spread around.

G. elwesii is another good contender. A slightly larger snowdrop, it flowers from January to March, often a little earlier than *G. nivalis*. It is the second most common snowdrop in cultivation, is extremely free-flowering and a very variable species producing many interesting plants.

G. plicatus, the Crimean Snowdrop, flowers from late winter into early spring. It is a vigorous species, growing up to 25cm tall, and has been cultivated since the sixteenth century.

G. woronowii, sometimes known as the Green Snowdrop from its brighter than average green leaves, flowers from February to March. It was introduced in the late 1800s and grows well, even in quite severe winters.

G. reginae-olgae, an autumn-flowering species, blooms from late September to November, and is almost as hardy as *G. nivalis* (to which it is closely related). However, it will not tolerate very wet conditions and sometimes requires care and attention to establish.

Autumn-flowering snowdrops add a new dimension to a collection, always creating great interest when in bloom, as well as extending the snowdrop season. With careful planning, using different species and cultivars, snowdrops can be in flower for almost seven months each year, so snowdrop collections are not just limited to a couple of months in winter.

Collecting any plant is always an exciting and rewarding hobby for the gardener and plantaholic. Snowdrops have an added allure, being the first flowers to appear each year, and it is a simple matter to build up an interesting and worthwhile collection of beautiful and very different snowdrops at not too extortionate a cost.

Most gardeners are a munificent, helpful species, and those with large areas of naturalized snowdrops are noted for their generosity in often handing out bulbs to interested beginners. Nor is this generosity unknown even with more unusual snowdrops. Plants obtained in this way always have the added memory of how, where and when they were obtained, and the kindness of the gardener who gave them.

Very old gardens with well established drifts of snowdrops can be prime hunting grounds for seeking out new varieties of snowdrop, and are always well worth looking at more closely.

A Beginner's Collection

There are very many beautiful and fascinating snowdrops which cover a whole range of sizes, segment shapes and markings, but the snowdrops suggested below have noticeable differences and represent a good selection with which to begin a collection.

Species

G. elwesii; G. nivalis; G. nivalis 'Flore Pleno'; G. plicatus; G. reginae-olgae; G. woronowii

Hybrids and Cultivars

'Anglesey Abbey'; 'Atkinisii'; 'Augustus'; 'Barnes'; 'Bertram Anderson'; 'Bill Bishop'; 'Bitton'; 'Brenda Troyle'; 'Cedric's Prolific'; 'Comet'; 'Curly'; 'Diggory'; 'Dionysus'; 'Durris'; 'Galatea'; 'Hill Poë'; 'Hippolyta'; 'James Backhouse'; 'John Gray'; 'Lady Beatrix Stanley'; 'Lady Elphinstone'; 'Lowick'; 'Magnet'; 'Merlin'; 'Mighty Atom'; 'Mrs Macnamara'; 'Mrs Thomson'; 'Pusey Green Tips'; 'S. Arnott'; 'Three Leaves'; 'Trumps'; 'Viridapice'; 'Wendy's Gold'.

'S. Arnott'.

'Augustus'.

'Brenda Troyle'.

'Cedric's Prolific'.

'Diggory'.

'Dionysus'.

'Galatea'.

'George Elwes'.

'Hill Poë'.

'James Backhouse'.

'Lady Elphinstone'.

'Little Ben'.

'Mighty Atom'.

Galanthus nivalis.

Galanthus plicatus.

'Pusey Green Tips'.

Galanthus reginae-olgae subsp. *vernalis.*

'Wendy's Gold'.

CHAPTER 8

SNOWDROPS AROUND THE WORLD

Although native to Europe, snowdrops are now also grown in many other countries, including Australia, Canada, Japan, New Zealand, North America and Tasmania. Galanthophiles travel to Europe from around the world during the snowdrop season.

Snowdrops prefer a temperate climate and do not generally thrive in climates that have warm, mild winters, but can grow with temperatures as low as −30°C. They dislike hot arid areas in full sun, which dry out for long periods of time, preferring humus-rich soil in dappled shade. Like most plants, snowdrops grow best in a suitable environment and of necessity plants fit into the environmental conditions they require if they hope to survive. To some extent habitats can be manipulated to provide plants with suitable conditions, but even then they may not thrive and may not even survive. Obviously the further plants move away from their favoured habitats and growing conditions, the more difficult will be their cultivation.

Author's Note: It is important to emphasize that snowdrops cannot be removed from the wild or transported between countries other than EU member states without a valid CITES permit.

Hardiness Zones

Trying to formulate any standard rating for plant hardiness is a complex issue and many factors have to be taken into consideration. These issues still require much work. The US Department of Agriculture (USDA) formulated numbered hardiness zones in 1960 in an attempt to standardize information. Data are periodically revised and updated. Zones numbered one to ten denote the climatic conditions of geographical areas in which specific plants will grow, depending on the plant's ability to withstand the temperatures in that zone. Zones are calculated in degrees Celsius with reference to the average annual minimum temperature, as defined by latitude, altitude and coastal regions. A number of factors can affect conditions in certain areas within a set hardiness zone, resulting in higher or lower readings that must be taken into consideration. This method of zoning is now widely used across the world.

The American Horticultural Society developed the AHS Heat Zone map, denoting the average number of days in each year that temperatures in given areas exceed 30°C. For a more accurate picture of conditions applying to set areas, the two charts should ideally be used in conjunction.

Snowdrops grow best in USDA hardiness zones four to seven, but can grow in zones two to nine.

OPPOSITE PAGE: Trevor Nottle's Australian garden, Walnut Hill, in winter.

RIGHT: G. 'Munchkin'.

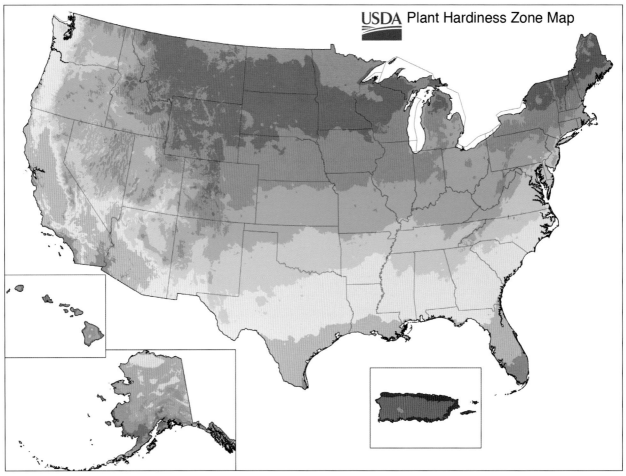

United States Department of Agriculture (USDA) Plant Hardiness Zone Map. (*Courtesy USDA*)

Average Annual Extreme Minimum Temperature
1976-2005

Temp (F)	Zone	Temp (C)
-60 to -50	1	-51.1 to -45.6
-50 to -40	2	-45.6 to -40
-40 to -30	3	-40 to -34.4
-30 to -20	4	-34.4 to -28.9
-20 to -10	5	-28.9 to -23.3
-10 to 0	6	-23.3 to -17.8
0 to 10	7	-17.8 to -12.2
10 to 20	8	12.2 to -6.7
20 to 30	9	-6.7 to -1.1
30 to 40	10	-1.1 to 4.4
40 to 50	11	4.4 to 10
50 to 60	12	10 to 15.6
60 to 70	13	15.6 to 21.1

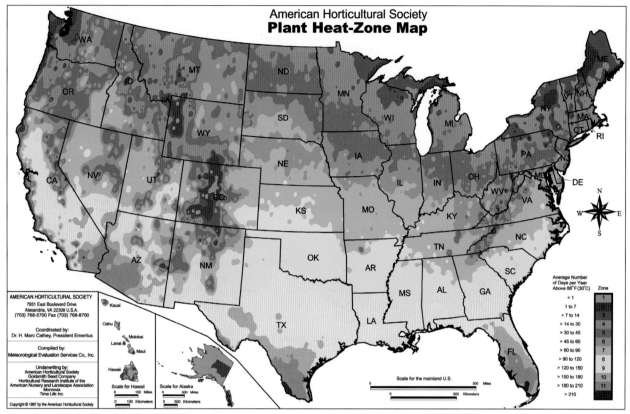

American Horticultural Society Heat Zone Chart.

European Hardiness Zones

UK zones are high on the USDA scale, varying between seven and ten, due to the moderating effects of the Gulf Stream around the coastline. However, the heat zone rating is only between one and two.

The Royal Horticultural Society zones are fairly limited in their usage. They vary between Fully hardy (**H**), hardy to −15°C; Frost hardy (**FH**), hardy to −5°C; Half-hardy (**HH**), hardy to 0°C; and Frost tender (**FT**), not hardy below 5°C.

Central Europe shows the transition from an oceanic climate to that of a continental climate, and the zones mainly decrease eastwards. Along the Dutch and Belgian coasts the hardiness rating is eight, decreasing to five on the far eastern border between Poland and Belarus. Within these zones, certain areas such as the Alps and Carpathian mountains may fall to zones three or four, due to their high elevations. Again, due to the effects of the Gulf Stream, some areas such as Arctic parts of Scandinavia are higher than expected, not falling below zone three, apart from one small area, Karajok in Norway, which is zone two.

Obviously there are inconsistencies within these zones. Certain areas may be higher or lower, or an area may experience an above or below average extreme at some period.

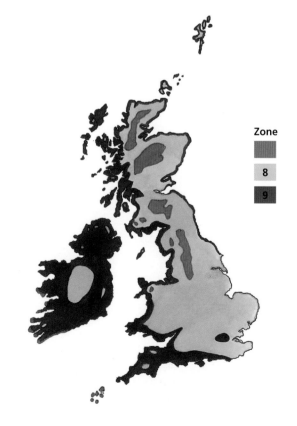

United Kingdom Hardiness Zone Map.

Northern Hemisphere

North America

Given North America's very wide diversity of climate and conditions, snowdrops grow well in many areas, but not everywhere. In some places humidity and summer temperatures prove too high, and winters are either too mild or too severe. Snowdrops are still not as popular as in Britain and Europe, and Galanthomania has not yet taken hold to any great extent, possibly because of the difficulty in obtaining bulbs. Those that are available are generally sold dry and many fail to establish. Some specialist nurseries in the USA now sell snowdrops 'in the green' and some list a selection of cultivars imported from Holland. However, American bulb companies tend to push bigger, showier bulbs, such as daffodils, tulips and lilies, rather than smaller bulb species, and gardeners also tend to want big and beautiful rather than small and simple.

Nevertheless, there are large areas of naturalized snowdrops and many private gardens grow them. There are notable collections in Delaware, Maryland, Massachusetts, New Jersey, New York State, North Carolina, Ohio, Oregon, Pennsylvania, Rhode Island, Utah, Virginia and Washington. In particular, snowdrops have naturalized over many years into vast colonies in Washington and Utah, and in eastern North America from Ontario to North Carolina, and also in Newfoundland.

In south-west Idaho, zones six to seven, snowdrops start flowering in the last week in January and have naturalized well. In Pennsylvania, zone five, snowdrops peak in April. In central Indiana, zone five, *G. nivalis* and *G. elwesii* grow well, as, to a lesser degree, does *G. woronowii*, but many snowdrops are not hardy in this climate. In the eastern USA snowdrops appear as soon as the snow melts, coming into bloom around mid-February with early *G. elwesii*. The main flowering period for snowdrops in the USA is late February to April, with *G. nivalis* being the most common. *G. elwesii* is also very popular, and *G. reginae-olgae* is widespread in cultivation.

Where temperatures and weather conditions are too extreme, some collectors grow snowdrops in cold frames to protect them from the worst of the problems. In very hot areas bulbs can be chilled in a fridge for six to twelve weeks before planting out when the weather cools, ensuring they get the requisite cold conditions to force them into flowering. Using the USDA hardiness zones chart and the AHS heat zone chart provides a simple way of calculating locations where snowdrops will grow given an 'average' winter, although common sense must be exercised because of the wide climate diversity within different regions.

Notable snowdrops associated with the USA include the tall, robust 'Theresa Stone', *G. elwesii* var. *elwesii*, from Louise Parsons' garden in Corvallis, Oregon, found in 1975 and named after the previous owner of the garden; 'Poseidon', a regular Greatorex double found in the late Molly Grothaus's garden in Oregon; 'Potter's Prelude', *G. elwesii* var. *monostictus*, developed by Jack Potter in the 1960s; and 'Christmas Cheer', a good *G. reginae-olgae* hybrid.

The Pacific Bulb Society produces regular newsletters, often containing information on snowdrops. Other societies include the International Bulb Society, the Great Lakes Bulb Society, the North American Rock Garden Society (NARGS), and one of the oldest, the American Horticultural Society.

Hitch Lyman at Temple Nurseries purportedly has the largest collection of snowdrops in the USA. A veteran Galanthophile, his 5-acre garden outside Ithaca, NY, has snowdrops edging paths, and growing beneath shrubs and woodland trees. He sells snowdrops in the green, and insists that spring is the best time for division and replanting, and autumn the worst. His passion began after attending an RHS show many years ago, and his first snowdrops came from two Cornell University professors.

Edgwood Gardens in Exton, 35 miles from Pennsylvania in the north-eastern USA, is a private garden developed since 1995 by John and Eleanor Lonsdale from the UK. At just under 2 acres, the garden is 700ft above sea level on a steeply sloping site. The temperatures can be as low as –20°C in winter and as high as 38°C in summer, but there is also high humidity. It is a woodland garden, which also has raised beds, trees, shrubs and numerous other bulbs as well as snowdrops.

Galanthophile Carolyn Walker of Bryn Mawr, Pennsylvania, has a 2.5-acre garden and nursery specializing in shade-loving plants, including numerous bulbs and snowdrops, which she also sells by mail order.

Canada

Canada is another immense country with wide-ranging terrain and climates and a vast diversity of microclimates within different zones. Snowdrops are still uncommon but grow well and have naturalized in British Columbia, Vancouver and Victoria. In Toronto their main flowering period is March. They are grown in Alberta but often struggle due to the inhospitable conditions. The most common type is *G. elwesii*, which enjoys the cold winters and dry conditions in summer.

South-west British Columbia, zone seven, has a climate similar to that of the UK but with more Mediterranean-like summers. *G. nivalis*, *G. elwesii*, *G. woronowii* and *G. ikariae* all grow well here, and *G. nivalis* in particular has increased and naturalized into large colonies.

G. reginae-olgae can be grown outdoors in Vancouver but here snowdrops can be prone to slug attacks, as the wet climate provides a perfect breeding ground. Sprinkling coffee grounds over and around the bulbs is said to act as a good deterrent, while heavily mulching the bulbs offers some protection from severe weather.

Snowdrops with Canadian associations include 'Snocus', a *G. elwesii* hybrid from Al and Shirley Smith of Victoria, British Columbia; the tall, vigorous 'Canadian Winter'; and the attractive, virescent 'Rosemary Burnham', *G. elwesii* var. *elwesii*. This was found by Rosemary Burnham in an old garden at Burneby, British Columbia, in the early 1960s and awarded the RHS PC in 2006. Bulbs from Canada were imported into the

UK in the early 1990s but failed to survive. In 1994 a similar snowdrop was found in Robert Marshall's garden in Norwich, and was named 'Marshalls Green'. This too failed to survive. In 1998 the Canadian snowdrop reappeared at an RHS show and is now very popular.

Northern Europe

Snowdrops are native to southern Europe and their exact range in more northerly countries is not known definitively before they became naturalized rather than native. They adapted to the northern European climate, growing and naturalizing well. Many botanical gardens have built up extensive collections of naturalized bulbs in woodland settings.

Nordic Countries

These comprise the five northern European countries of Denmark, Finland, Iceland, Norway and Sweden, where the climate is moderated by the action of the Gulf Stream. Although snowdrops require a period of winter cold to flower, in some areas the winters are just too severe and snowdrops fail to establish.

Stockholm, Sweden, has the warmest summers, with temperatures rising to around 23°C, while winter temperatures average between –6°C and –1°C across Sweden as a whole. Denmark's winter average is between –2°C and 4°C, while Norway's coastal regions have mild winters averaging between –6°C and 3°C. Snowdrops generally appear from late February to March, often pushing through the snow. Norwegian tradition says snowdrops were introduced by monks in the fifteenth century.

Naturalized snowdrops at the University of Vienna Botanic Garden. (*Photo courtesy Christina Quijan-Caballero*)

A Danish spring tradition is to send a tiny posy of snowdrops, or a pressed snowdrop in a special card called *Gaekkebrev* for Easter and Valentine's Day. The card is cut into an intricate pattern, with a short poem written inside. The recipient has to guess who it is from or forfeit a small gift.

The Netherlands

The Netherlands is renowned for its horticultural industry and vast bulb-fields, and has long cultivated snowdrops among many other bulbs. Harry Pierik's wonderful 'Hidden City Garden' is a haven of peace and tranquillity filled with mature trees, shrubs, plants and flowers, including an extensive snowdrop collection. *Paradijselijke Tuinen* is a book about the garden and

Snowdrops emerging through snow in Oslo, Norway, March. (*Photo courtesy Jorun Tharaldsen*)

Snowdrops in Harry Piericks' Hidden City Garden, Netherlands. (*Photo courtesy Harry Pierick*)

there is also a superb film, *Garden of Eden Snowdrops in the Hidden City Garden*. *Galanthus* introductions include 'Lady Scharlock', a beautiful albino poculiform, and 'Ragini'.

Tom Koopman has introduced numerous snowdrops, including 'Green Diamond'; 'Maximus'; 'Splendid Cornelia'; 'Tommy' and 'White Dream'. Dineke Logtenberg's garden and nursery at De Boschhoeve, Wolfheze, begins the year with a Snowdrop Festival inaugurated in 2001, while Gerard Oud organizes snowdrop days at Zaanse Schans and also sells snowdrops.

Annie Fallinger holds the Dutch National Collection, Nederlandse Planten Collectie Galanthus, with over five hundred different species, hybrids and cultivars. The collection is displayed at the annual *Sneeuwklokjesfeest*. Spectacular clumps of snowdrops have built up in her garden, which she feeds with organic fertilizer and compost.

Belgium

The climate in Belgium is similar to that of other countries in north-west Europe, with an average winter temperature of 3 °C. Snowdrops are naturalized in many areas and there are collections in estates and gardens including the National Botanic Garden of Belgium at Meisse, which has large drifts of naturalized snowdrops. Many nurseries sell snowdrops and the

Kalmthout Arboretum hosts a Snowdrop Show with lectures and plants available for sale.

In Brugge Cathy Portier and Jan Van de Sijpe's 'Alpenplantenkwekerij' at Vordenstein, a well established alpine nursery, has a collection of around three hundred different snowdrop species and hybrids in the show garden. They organize snowdrop weekends and events at the nursery. Introductions include 'White Cloud' and 'Funny Justine', a strange, rounded, upward-facing, little snowdrop with heavily green marked outer segments.

The Belgian Galanthophile Valentin Wijnen began collecting snowdrops when he was seven years old and has named numerous snowdrops under the Grakes prefix, while nurseryman Koen Van Poucke grows snowdrops and hellebores as well as having the largest collection of Epimedium in Europe.

Germany

Germany has a typical northern European climate with average winter temperatures of around −1.5°C. The North Sea coastal regions average around 1– 5°C in winter, while temperatures are inevitably lower in the mountainous regions to the south at around −2°C. Snowdrops, 'Schneeglockchen', are widely grown and naturalized in many areas.

Snowdrop days are held at Nettetal-Oirlich, attracting Galanthophiles from around the world. The Oirlicher Blumengarten boasts a collection of over two hundred different snowdrops carefully nurtured by the late Günter Waldorf. They host a widely attended annual Snowdrop Festival with numerous stands and specialist nurseries in attendance selling snowdrops and other plants.

Slovenia

Slovenia in eastern Europe has a wide range of terrain and climate conditions, including sub-Mediterranean and central European-Alpine. *G. nivalis* is the only snowdrop native to Slovenia, with many different forms widely distributed across the country. Because of the variable and wide-ranging climate, snowdrops enjoy a long flowering period in large naturalized colonies spreading through forests, along woodland edges and in meadows. The Botanical Garden of Ljubljana carefully monitors snowdrop populations, noting various anomalies that arise with plants growing in their native habitats. *G. nivalis* can vary in size, with variably sized and shaped segments; the outer segments can have variable green markings; leaves can be long and slender or shorter and more rounded, as well as exhibiting various green-blue colorations; plants can produce two scapes; and there are poculiform and malformed flowers. Some variations appear stable, while others change from year to year, often depending on where the plants are growing. Many revert to type when moved into a garden setting, while some are obvious mutations. The university has established a collection of snowdrops and also holds a Snowdrop Show with lectures and open days for snowdrop study.

Russia

This immense country mainly enjoys a continental climate, but has a subarctic climate in the northern regions, while Sochi on the Black Sea is subtropical. Several snowdrop species are found in southern Russia, including *G. plicatus*, *G. angustifolius*, *G. alpinus*, *G. woronowii*, *G. lagodechianus* and *G. rizehensis*.

Georgia

G. woronowii is the most common snowdrop here and is particularly prevalent in the wild in western Georgia, although its range extends from north-eastern Turkey to eastern Georgia. It enjoys the almost year-round damp, humid climate. Wild populations of *G. woronowii* cover vast acres of woodlands and valleys in this mountainous region. Georgia exports large quantities of *G. woronowii* but the trade requires careful monitoring so that realistic quotas can be set to make sure the harvesting of wild collected bulbs is sustainable. The trade is carefully governed by CITES. *G. woronowii* is also grown as a sustainable cash crop in Georgia where 15 million snowdrop bulbs are exported every year to Turkey and then on to the horticultural trade in the Netherlands. This goes a long way to easing the pressure on collecting snowdrops from the wild, while also providing a valuable source of income for farmers in the area. *G. alpinus*, *G. lagodechianus*, *G. rizehensis* and *G. krasnovii* also grow in Georgia.

Azerbaijan

Azerbaijan in the southern Caucasus, on the western coast of the Caspian Sea, borders Russia, Georgia, Turkey and Armenia and is home to the Caucasian snowdrop, *G. alpinus*, which now grows in ever-decreasing habitats. *G. transcaucasicus* comes from the southern Caucasus region and is also found in northern Iran and Armenia.

Southern Europe

G. nivalis is native to the Pyrenees, northern Spain and southern Italy, while a number of *G. nivalis* variants have been found in the Czech Republic. *G. reginae-olgae* and *G. gracilis* are found in the former Yugoslavia; *G. elwesii* and *G. gracilis* in Bulgaria; *G. gracilis* and *G. elwesii* in southern Ukraine; *G. fosteri* in central and southern Turkey, Jordan, Syria and Lebanon; and *G. transcaucasicus* in northern Iran and Azerbaijan, with small populations in Armenia.

Turkey

The Turkish climate ranges between Mediterranean, with hot dry summers and cool wet winters; Oceanic, with warm wet summers and cool to cold wet winters; and Continental in the central regions, which experience harsh conditions. Snow falls around the Black Sea coast and Sea of Marmara but rarely lasts long, while Anatolia province experiences very harsh winters with temperatures down to −30°or − 40°C with extensive, long-lasting snow for almost half the year.

Turkey has a very wide diversity of wild flora and is home to a number of snowdrop species, including *G. cilicicus*; *G. elwesii*; *G. gracilis*; *G. fosteri*; *G. koenenianus*; *G. krasnovii*; *G. peshmenii*; *G. plicatus*; *G. rizehensis*; *G. trojanus* and *G. woronowii*. Bulbs were originally harvested from the wild but now legislation limits this trade, helping preserve wild populations and habitats. *G. elwesii* is increasingly grown commercially. In the village of Dumlugoze in southern Anatolia the snowdrop crop provides a steady income. Originally they traded in bulbs harvested from the wild in the Taurus mountains, but overharvesting seriously depleted natural stocks. As it became increasingly difficult to make a living from wild harvested bulbs, people moved away from the area. Now, under the auspices of the Indigenous Propagation Project (IPP), supported by the World Wildlife Fund, villagers receive an income for cultivating and harvesting sustainable bulbs which are sold to exporters. Gathering *G. elwesii* bulbs from the wild has now fallen to 6 million, rather than the previous 40 million bulbs each year. CITES legislation also limits the number of bulbs collected from the wild.

Greece

With its Mediterranean climate, many parts of Greece prove too hot and arid for *Galanthus*. *G. reginae-olgae*, the autumn-flowering snowdrop, is found in the Peloponnese and Corfu, and its unusual flowering time caused a great sensation when it was first discovered by Orphanides in 1876. The earliest of the group are now classed as *G. reginae-olgae* subsp. *reginae-olgae*. *G. gracilis* and *G. elwesii* are also found in Greece, while *G. ikariae* was discovered on the Aegean island of Ikaria.

Southern Hemisphere

Australia

Southern hemisphere seasons are opposite to those of the northern hemisphere. Snowdrops are cold climate plants but grow in certain areas in the southern hemisphere and have adapted to this change of season. Australia has a vast diversity of climatic conditions; snowdrops grow better in the southern regions and elevated areas where the climate tends to be cooler.

Galanthus elwesii var. *monostictus* at Walnut Hill. (*Photo courtesy Trevor Nottle*)

wet springs, low humidity in summer and long daylight hours. 'Hughes Emerald' is a New Zealand hybrid from Denis Hughes of the Blue Mountain Nursery, Tappanui, where they hybridize their own snowdrops.

Dunedin Botanic Garden grows a number of different snowdrops. The Jury Garden at Waitara, North Island, has grown snowdrops for many years, including *G. nivalis*, *G. nivalis* 'Flore Pleno', *G. elwesii*, 'Magnet' and 'S. Arnott', which does exceptionally well, creating excellent displays. Conditions here are very mild and snowdrops thrive in an area which also grows oranges, avocados and numerous subtropical plants, and hardly ever sees snow or heavy frost.

Maple Glen at Southland, South Island, is a 25-acre garden and nursery with woodland and lakes, in USDA zone eight. Bob and Muriel Davidson began the garden in 1966, and it has seen on-going development into the spectacular displays of today. The extensive collection of snowdrops, flowering in July and August, has naturalized into vast drifts beneath woodland trees and through garden borders. Bulbs are also sold through the nursery. The collection originated from five single bulbs purchased in the garden's infancy, which have been divided and multiplied over the years.

Japan

In Japan snowdrops are called *Matsu-yuki-soo* ('Plant waiting for snow) and *Yuki-no-hana* ('Snow flowers'). Japan's climate varies from subtropical in the south to cool temperate in the north, with four distinct seasons. Northern areas down to the central highland region have cold winters and hot summers with high rainfall and humidity. The country is rugged and mountainous.

Japan has a great gardening culture with very beautiful gardens in their own distinctive style and a number of collectors grow *Galanthus*.

G. elwesii starts blooming in February. *G. nivalis*, *G. nivalis* 'Flore Pleno' and *G. elwesii* are readily available commercially. Wider varieties of snowdrop are grown in botanical gardens.

Snowdrops in this Japanese garden start flowering in early January. (*Photo courtesy Inoue Shuji*)

South Africa

The South African climate varies between subtropical and Mediterranean, and is not conducive to growing snowdrops. Some gardeners do try, not usually successfully, and snowdrops are rare in the country. One gardener at Elgin, near Cape Town, says the bulbs require a great deal of nurturing and also take time to adapt to the reversed seasonal changes. Snowflakes, *Leucojum aestivum*, are again more common here and grow well in cooler parts of the country; they are often called snowdrops.

Snowdrops at the Kyoto Prefectural Botanic Gardens, late March.
(*Photo courtesy Inoue Shuji*)

CHAPTER 9

GALANTHOPHILES

Late winter and early spring is an exceptionally busy time for Galanthophiles, with galas, lunches, shows and tours. There are snowdrop gardens to visit both in the UK and abroad, field trips to see snowdrops in their native habitats, the constant hunt for something new and of course, growing and propagating snowdrops. Each year new events are planned and increasing numbers of people become involved.

The UK Galanthus Gala, organized by Joe Sharman in a different part of the country each February, offers celebrity lectures, snowdrop exchanges and sales. Transcripts are available from when the galas began in 1997. Snowdrop lunches are by invitation only. The RHS London Spring Show in February each year attracts a wealth of magnificent snowdrops, along with collectors. Scotland likewise hosts a massive Snowdrop Festival, with many gardens opening on the snowdrop trail, while Edinburgh hosts a biannual Snowdrop Conference. The Cottage Garden Society has a snowdrop group that organizes lectures and garden visits, while the Hardy Plant Society held the inaugural meeting for their new Galanthus Group in February 2012.

In De Boschhoeve, Holland, the annual *Sneeuwklokjesfeest* has been held since 2001, together with a newer festival at Zaanse Schans. Belgium hosts spectacular snowdrop days at Arboretum Kalmthout, and in Germany the Oirlicher Blumengarten at Nettetal has a big snowdrop festival.

Galanthomania would not have existed had it not been for the great botanists, plant hunters and horticulturists who fanned the initial flames, and the passionate and committed Galanthophiles and plant breeders who followed in their footsteps.

ABOVE: Members attending the inaugural meeting of the Hardy Plant Society's *Galanthus* Group visited Dial Park, Chaddesley Corbet, Worcestershire, February 2012.

LEFT: Galanthophiles of the old school: Ray Cobb, Richard Nutt and Primrose Warburg. (*Photo courtesy Eric Webster and Ray Cobb*)

OPPOSITE PAGE: Painswick Rococo Garden, Gloucestershire.

Allen, James (1832–1906)
This Victorian plantsman was known as 'The Snowdrop King'. For most of his life he lived at Highfield House, Shepton Mallet, Somerset, and he propagated and named over one hundred snowdrops, although many of these were very similar. In 1891 he was invited to speak at the RHS conference on snowdrops. He wrote papers and grew all known snowdrops available at

G. 'Magnet', a James Allen introduction which has stood the test of time and is perennially popular.

G. 'Mighty Atom' originated in Bertram Anderson's Gloucestershire garden.

that time, creating the largest collection in England. These included 'Balloon'; *G. plicatus* 'Maximus' and *G.* 'Omega'. Other of Allen's introductions included *G.* 'Magnet' and *G.* 'Merlin', still widely collected today. Snowdrops naturalized throughout the garden but sadly much of the collection was destroyed by botrytis and narcissus fly. In 1981 the garden was further decimated by redevelopment to make way for the headquarters of Mendip District Council. The significance of the snowdrops had not been realised, but once the damage became known, a campaign began in 1985 to rescue what remained of the collection, which was taken to Cannington Horticultural College, Bridgwater.

Anderson, Edward Bertram (1886–1971)
Renowned plantsman, horticulturist and author of numerous books on plants and gardens, Anderson introduced many new plants from his extensive travels, and has many plants named after him, including *G.* 'Bertram Anderson'. He was a founder member of the RHS Alpine Garden Society, and served as its president between 1948 and 1953. He moved to Bales Mead, Somerset, in 1950, the former home of Walter Butt. He later moved to Gloucestershire, where he grew alpine plants and bulbs. *G.* 'Mighty Atom' originated here and the garden has subsequently produced numerous excellent seedlings.

Arnott, Samuel (1852–1930)
Samuel Arnott was born in Dumfries and worked there until ill-health forced his early retirement in 1884. Then he began gardening at his new home on the Solway coast, writing books and articles for various publications, notably the *Gardener's Chronicle*, including a review entitled '*The Fair Maids of February*'. He became a Fellow of the RHS in 1893 and subsequently its Honorary Treasurer, and from 1915 to 1926 served as Provost of Maxwelltown, Dumfries & Galloway. *G.* 'S. Arnott' is named after him.

Atkins, James (1804–1884)
A Northamptonshire nurseryman, Atkins retired to Rose Cottage in Painswick, Gloucestershire, on the estate of the now well known Painswick Rococo Gardens, one of the foremost snowdrop gardens in the country. Around 1870 Atkins came across a snowdrop, *G. imperati*, believed to have originated in southern Italy. It was eagerly sought after and in 1891 its name was changed to *G.* 'Atkinsii'. These snowdrops still grow in the Painswick garden.

MAULL & Cº
62 CHEAPSIDE
AND
187ª PICCADILLY

James Atkins. (*Photo courtesy RHS Lindley Library*)

Baker, Ruby
Ruby Baker has always been fascinated by snowdrops. Like many people, she thought there were only two types, single and double, but once she realised her mistake she began collecting in earnest, travelling far and wide with her husband David to see snowdrops in the UK and abroad. Their discoveries include *G.* 'Irish Green', *G.* 'Kildare' and *G.* 'Faringdon Double'. A number of snowdrops have been named for her, including *G.* 'Ruby Baker'. *G.* 'David Baker' is named after her husband.

Ballard, Philip (1909–1987) and Helen (1909–1995)

Philip was the son of well known nurseryman Ernest Ballard. At their home, Old Country in Herefordshire, Philip concentrated on snowdrops and his wife Helen on hellebores, making significant contributions to both species. Philip distributed both G. 'Greenish' and G. 'Danube Star', while Helen's important pioneering work with hellebores elevated their prominence and popularity.

Baron, Michael

Michael Baron was a former Plant Heritage Collection Holder of *Galanthus* and *Daphne* at his garden Brandy Mount, Arlesford. The one-acre town centre garden is crammed with plants, including over two hundred different snowdrops. Among those he has selected and named are G. 'Headbourne', G. 'Lulu', G. 'Rose Baron', G. 'Rose Lloyd' and G. 'Springvale'.

Michael Baron.
(*Photo courtesy Michael Baron*)

Baxendale, Martin

Martin developed his love of snowdrops from a young age, when living at Hambutt's Orchard of Herbert Ransom fame, where his father collected snowdrops. Martin's father, Leo Baxendale, discovered G. 'Baxendale's Late'. Martin collects snowdrops, researches and breeds tetraploid snowdrops, and has also written a novel, *The Snowdrop Garden* (Silent But Deadly Publications, 2009).

Bishop, Matt

Co-author of *Snowdrops* with Aaron Davis and John Grimshaw, Matt Bishop is one of the world's most prominent snowdrop experts, travelling widely to photograph and record snowdrops. He first became interested in snowdrops in 1985 when at the age of sixteen he became a student at RHS Wisley. From Wisley he attended the Somerset College of Agriculture and Horticulture, and then took a degree in Landscape Architecture at the University of Greenwich. He worked in a number of gardens before becoming head gardener of The Garden House, Devon. His interest in snowdrops has led to the development of various new seedlings, including G. *elwesii* 'Tricorn', in which the outer segments resemble a tricorn hat.

Bowles, Edward Augustus (1865–1954)

Known as 'Gussie' to his close friends, Bowles was a keen naturalist and gardener from childhood. He was born and lived throughout his life at Myddelton House, Enfield, devoting his time and horticultural expertise to his garden there and adding to it from parkland. A self-taught gardener, talented botanical artist, botanist and plant hunter, he generously gave plants, bulbs and cuttings to visitors. He wrote books about the garden in spring, summer, autumn and winter, while *Garden Varieties of Galanthus*, written in conjunction with Sir Frederick Stern, was published posthumously in 1956. Many plants are named after this great man, including G. 'Augustus', G. 'Bowles Large', and G. 'E.A. Bowles'. In 1992 the E.A. Bowles of Myddelton House Society was formed to promote knowledge and appreciation of Bowles, his work and his garden.

Boyd, William Brack (1831–1918)

An amateur botanist, Boyd became President of the Edinburgh Botanical Society, and he gave a presidential address to Berwickshire Naturalists' Club in 1905 on snowdrops. G. 'Boyds Double' is named after him.

E.A. Bowles photographed between 1900 and 1910. (*Photo courtesy E.A. Bowles of Myddelton House Society*)

Brickell, Christopher

A leading horticulturist and writer, in 1976 Chris was awarded the RHS Victoria Medal of Honour for services to Horticulture, and was made a CBE in 1991. He was director of RHS Wisley from 1969 to 1985, and Director General of the RHS from 1985 to 1993. He also held several other important posts, including Chairman of the International Commission for the Nomenclature of Plants and President of the International Society for Horticultural Science. In 1978 he was influential in initiating the formation of the National Council for the Conservation of Plants and Gardens, now called Plant Heritage, setting up national plant collections. He continues his interest and research into *Galanthus* and also into the system of stabilizing plant names.

Bromley, David

A respected Galanthophile, his Shropshire garden is a tribute to all plants but particularly snowdrops, and he was a former Plant Heritage Collection Holder of *Galanthus*. Interested in snowdrops as a young man, he contacted gardener and plantswoman Margery Fish of East Lambrook Manor in 1965. An invitation to visit her garden followed, and she gave him plenty of encouragement and his first snowdrops, *G.* 'Scharlockii', *G.* 'Hill Poe' and *G.* 'S. Arnott'. His introductions include *G.* 'Moortown', *G.* 'David Bromley' and *G.* 'Louise Ann Bromley'. He abhors the escalating prices paid for snowdrops, firmly believing it leads to greed rather than love of the plants. He is known for his generosity in exchanging and swapping rarer snowdrops.

Brown, Mark

Now living in France, Brown was given early snowdrops by Richard Nutt and now has around four hundred different snowdrops in his garden. His introductions include *G.* 'Ecusson d'Or' and *G.* 'Flocon de Neige', an expensive snowdrop looking like a delicate snowflake with six outer segments.

Burbridge, Frederick William Thomas (1847–1905)

Burbridge originally worked as a plant collector for the great Veitch Nursery, and regularly wrote about plants. As Curator of Trinity College Dublin Botanical Garden from 1879 to 1905, he recorded cultivars grown at the time and was the first to draw attention to the importance of snowdrop leaves as a means of identification.

Butt, Walter (1872–1953)

Butt created a magnificent garden at Hyde Lodge near Stroud, Gloucestershire, between the early 1920s and 1940, planting the best trees and shrubs he could find. Being particularly fond of snowdrops, he naturalized these beneath the trees, obtaining many from Colesbourne. Ill-health forced him to leave his beloved garden and he moved to Porlock, a garden later belonging to E.B. Anderson. Hyde Lodge became home to the Giant Snowdrop Company. An obituary described Butt as 'one of the greatest plant enthusiasts that ever lived'.

Chatto, Beth

A world-renowned gardener, garden designer, plantswoman and author, Beth Chatto developed her magnificent garden at Elmstead Market, Essex, in one of the driest parts of the UK. The garden includes a wide range of habitats, including dry, gravel, water and woodland areas. She has written various books about her garden and plants, has a large collection of snowdrops and also sells snowdrops in her nursery. The snowdrop *G.* 'Beth Chatto' was discovered in the garden and named for her.

Ian Christie with Margaret Owen at Acton Pigot. (*Photo courtesy Ian Christie*)

Beth Chatto. (*Photo courtesy Beth Chatto Gardens*)

Christie, Ian

A seasoned grower of alpines, Ian Christie discovered colonies of *G. nivalis* and *G. plicatus* growing together in woodland at Brechin Castle, Angus, Scotland, giving rise to variable hybrids including *G.* 'Betty Hamilton', *G.* 'Castle Green Dragon', *G.* 'Lady Alice', *G.* 'Lady Dalhousie', *G.* 'Little Emma', *G.* 'Mona', *G.* 'Wee Betty' and *G.* 'Yvonne'. Further investigation on country estates revealed other exciting finds, including *G.* 'Annielle', *G.* 'Cinderella', *G.* 'Ethiebeaton', *G.* 'Kingennie' and *G.* 'Elizabeth Harrison', of which a single bulb sold on eBay for £725 in February 2012.

Cobb, Ray

A renowned Nottinghamshire horticulturist, plantsman and gardener, Ray Cobb has a passion for plants and the many snowdrops in his Nottinghamshire garden. A 'Snowdrop Immortal' (see the end of this chapter), he has held many important plant collections, including Galanthus. He is now working on completing collections of Muscari and British ferns.

Ray Cobb.

Collins, Norman

This Australian snowdrop specialist lives near Melbourne, and has named many Australian cultivars.

Cornish, Phil

A keen gardener and plantsman, Cornish's initial inspiration for snowdrops came from Herbert Ransom and the Giant Snowdrop Company, which fired his enthusiasm. He has introduced and named numerous snowdrops, including *G.* 'Ballerina', *G.* 'Bungee', *G.* 'Edith', *G.* 'Egret', *G.* 'Elfin', *G.* 'Gloucester Old Spot', *G.* 'Ladybird', *G.* 'Lapwing', *G.* 'Little Dancer', *G.* 'Octopussy' and *G.* 'The Bride'.

Cross, Veronica

Veronica Cross moved to Lower Hopton Farm, Herefordshire, in 1992, where she created her garden from a field. She has a large snowdrop collection, many of which came from Sutton Court Garden. Snowdrops found and named by her include *G.* 'Sutton Court' and *G.* 'Wasp'.

Culp, David

An American Galanthophile from Pennsylvania, David Culp is said to hold the second largest collection of snowdrops in the USA after Hitch Lyman's Temple Nursery. Snowdrops are naturalized on the hillside, edge paths and grow in borders. He has more than ninety species and cultivars as well as spectacular hellebores.

Curtis, Cliff and Joan

These Galanthophiles from Hacconby, Lincolnshire, have over four hundred different snowdrops in their collection. They obtained permission to look in the gardens of The Cottage, Rutland, now a retirement home, and found numerous different snowdrops, including *G.* 'Peardrop', *G.* 'Squire Burroughs', *G.* 'Little Joan', named after Joan, and *G.* 'Cliff Curtis', named after Cliff.

Davis, Aaron

Co-author of *Snowdrops* with Matt Bishop and John Grimshaw, Aaron Davis is a plant taxonomist and research

The snowdrop named for him, *Galanthus nivalis* 'Ray Cobb'. (*Photo courtesy Michael Head*)

Phil Cornish.

G. 'Ballerina' one of Phil Cornish's introductions.

botanist working at the Royal Botanic Gardens, Kew. His PhD, achieved at Reading University in 1994, formed the basis for his book *The Genus Galanthus*, Botanical Magazine Monograph (Timber Press, 1999), the most comprehensive study on snowdrops at that time. He travels the world looking for and recording plants, and has taken part in many and varied plant-hunting expeditions, including numerous trips to study snowdrops growing in their native habitats. Together with D. Zubov and a team of botanists, he researched and named the latest snowdrop species, *G. panjutinii*, in 2012.

Aaron Davis. (*Photo courtesy Aaron Davis*)

Elwes, Carolyn

Carolyn became a committed Galanthophile after marrying into the Elwes family at Colesbourne, Gloucestershire, in 1962. She discovered on the estate spectacular snowdrops that had originally been collected by Henry Elwes, and attended early snowdrop lunches. Colesbourne's first Snowdrop Gala in 1995 was held in aid of the church bell fund. Visitors saw a yellow *G. elwesii*, later named *G.* 'Carolyn Elwes'. Sadly the bulbs were stolen after the open day, although luckily a few bulbs had been kept elsewhere, so the snowdrop was not completely lost. Now thousands of people flock to Colesbourne each year for special snowdrop openings and study days.

Elwes, Henry John (1846 – 1922)

A great Victorian traveller, writer and plant hunter, Henry Elwes found the snowdrop later named after him, *G. elwesii*, in Turkey in 1874. Moving to Colesbourne Park in 1891, he assembled a world-renowned collection of bulbous plants. The garden became neglected after his death until Sir Henry and Lady Elwes instigated its restoration, extending the magnificent snowdrop collection.

Engelmann, Hagen

A garden designer and German Galanthophile with over four hundred different snowdrops in his collection at 'Garten in den Wiesen' (Garden in the Grasslands). He prefers conspicuous, taller snowdrops. Some of his introductions include *G.* 'Dickerchen', *G.* 'Gruner Splitter', *G.* 'Hologram', *G.* 'Ring's Rum' and 'Schorbuser Blut'.

Erskine, Catherine

The Cambo Estate in Fife, Scotland, is famous for its snowdrops, spectacularly naturalized throughout the woodland and gardens on the estate. Much of this was generated by Catherine Erskine, who moved there with her husband and children in 1976. The estate is a Plant Heritage Collection Holder of *Galanthus*. Snowdrops are sold through the nursery, and the estate opens for an annual Snowdrop Spectacular, including a lantern-lit trail through the woodland, 'Snowdrops by Starlight'.

Fallinger, Annie

A Dutch Galanthophile from Rotterdam, Netherlands, Annie Fallinger is a holder of Nederlandse Planten Collectie Galanthus. Her spectacular snowdrop garden has over five hundred different species and cultivars of *Galanthus*. She exhibits her snowdrops at the annual *Sneeuwklokjesfeest*, and also raises snowdrops from seed with many still waiting to be named, provisionally called Annie 1, Annie 2 and so on.

Fauser, Otto

This Australian plant collector is especially interested in bulbs, with a well established woodland and hillside garden near Olinda, in the Dandenongs, Victoria. The moist woodland shade creates conditions ideally suited to many cooler climate plants, including hellebores, crocus and snowdrops, many of which he either raised from seed or imported. Numerous plants carry his name, including *Helleborus* 'Otto's Plum', and the Australian-raised *Galanthus* hybrid 'Otto Fauser'.

Sir Peter and Lady Erskine.
(*Photo courtesy Cambo Estates*)

Margery Fish. (*Photo courtesy RHS Lindley Library*)

Fish, Margery (1889–1969)

Margery Fish was influential in promoting the 'cottage garden style', introducing many new plants into cultivation from her East Lambrook Manor garden, Somerset. Snowdrops were a particular passion and she grew numerous superb and different varieties, many from the Giant Snowdrop

G. 'Margery Fish'.

Company. She especially loved virescent snowdrops, naming one found in her garden after her nephew Sir Henry Boyd-Carpenter. She grew snowdrops in troughs as well as in the garden, where most grew in the long ditch by the woodland garden. G. 'Margery Fish', a beautiful green snowdrop from the garden, was named for her by the Norton family, later owners of the house.

Garnett, Trevor

An Australian grower from Blackwood in the Wombat State Forest, Trevor Garnett was originally from Cornwall. He became principal of the prestigious Geelong Grammar School, and created a wonderful garden with many snowdrops; he was generous in passing on his wide knowledge, experience and plants.

Genat, Eric

Another Australian Galanthophile and grower, with many plants named after him.

Greatorex, Heyrick (1884–1954)

A commissioned cavalry officer in the First World War and a captain in the Home Guard in the Second World War, Greatorex later became a recluse, living in an old railway carriage in his garden in Brundall, Norfolk. In the 1940s he experimented with snowdrop breeding, and produced a fine range of double hybrids. These caused a sensation at the time with well shaped flowers on tall, vigorous plants, mostly named after female Shakespearean characters. Sadly, a lack of accurate records has led to much confusion with names and identification.

Grimshaw, John

Co-author of Snowdrops with Aaron Davis and Matt Bishop, John Grimshaw obtained a degree in Botany and his PhD at Oxford University. His interest in snowdrops was encouraged by Primrose Warburg and Richard Nutt, and he is now a leading Galanthophile and authority on snowdrops. A former garden manager at Colesbourne Park, the famous Gloucestershire snowdrop garden, he continued to plant and develop the extensive snowdrop

John Grimshaw.

collection, welcoming thousands of visitors each year as well as hosting snowdrop study days. In the summer of 2012 he took up a position as Director of the Castle Howard Arboretum Trust in Yorkshire, where no doubt he will be planting more snowdrops.

Harvey, Marcus

Tasmanian bulb importer, snowdrop grower and propagator at the re-nowned Hillview Rare Plants nursery, offering a wonderful range of plants including a good selection of named snowdrops. Harvey also has an important and spectacular collection of crocus, which is probably the largest in the southern hemisphere.

Marcus Harvey.

Greatorex double G. 'Jaquenetta'.

Irving, Craig

An Australian grower with a good collection of snowdrops in his garden, Sunnybrae, in the foothills of the Australian Alps and Snowy Mountain region, north-eastern Victoria.

Koopman, Tom

A Dutch Galanthophile growing and breeding snowdrops, including G. 'White Dream' (a beautiful pure white, later blooming snowdrop), G. 'Tommy', G. 'Green Diamond', G. 'Maximus' and G. 'Splendid Cornelia'.

Lecore, Janet

A snowdrop enthusiast in the Midlands, Janet Lecore set up a website called 'Judy's Snowdrops' in memory of her faithful Labrador dog Judy. She has an extensive collection of snowdrops, although fewer than previously because of the difficulty in maintaining such a large collection of plants. She sells snowdrops by mail order.

Leeds, Rod and Jane

Rod and Jane Leeds have over four hundred different snowdrops in their Suffolk garden. Rod, who has written books on bulbs, is a former President of the Alpine Garden Society, and Chairman of the RHS Joint Rock Garden Plant Committee. Rod and Jane began collecting in the 1970s, growing plants in

G. 'Fiona Mackenzie' named by Ronald Mackenzie.

Margaret MacLennan. (*Photo courtesy David MacLennan*)

G. 'Winifrede Mathias', the snowdrop named for Mrs Mathias.

pots as well as naturalized in the garden. Snowdrops they have named include G. 'Naughton' and G. 'White Perfection'.

Logtenberg, Dineke
A Dutch Galanthophile with a nursery and garden at De Boschhoeve, Wolfheze, Netherlands, Dineke Logtenberg organizes an annual Snowdrop Festival (begun in 2001), and sells snowdrops in pots and in the green.

Lyman, Hitch
American Galanthophile and prominent visitor to Europe during the snowdrop season, Lyman's collection of snowdrops is said to be the largest in the USA with over four hundred types in his 5-acre garden outside Ithaca, NY. He is the proprietor of Temple Nursery, supplying and selling snowdrops.

Mackenzie, Ronald
A GP for over thirty years and one of the UK's most prominent Galanthophiles, Ronald Mackenzie was interested in plants from early childhood and was particularly inspired by Sir Frederick Stern's book *Snowdrops and Snowflakes*. When building his own collection of snowdrops, he became frustrated by hearing of bulbs he was unable to find and so established the Snowdrop Company in 1991. This made many rare snowdrops available to the general public for the first time. He was an early pioneer of 'Twin-scaling', and hosts snowdrop lunches. His immaculately maintained Oxfordshire garden contains over seventy different kinds of snowdrop, with remnants of the first snowdrops he purchased as a child from Woolworths. Among the snowdrops he has named are G. 'Fiona Mackenzie' and G. 'Ronald Mackenzie'.

MacLennan, Margaret
A Plant Heritage Collection Holder of *Galanthus*, with an extensive collection of snowdrops in her 7-acre garden at Byndes Cottage, Pebmarsh, Essex. The collection has been extended by chipping and twin-scaling special snowdrops, processes at which Margaret has become

expert. The snowdrop collection spreads through the garden borders, as well as being grown in dedicated plunge beds, greenhouse and cold frames.

Mason, Colin

Colin became interested in snowdrops after meeting Richard Nutt. He lives in the Midlands and is proprietor of Fieldgate Snowdrops. He also offers an expert twin-scaling service for snowdrops. His numerous *G.* 'Fieldgate' snowdrop introductions are well known, including *G.* 'Fieldgate Fugue', *G.* 'Fieldgate Prelude' and *G.* 'Fieldgate Superb'.

Mason, Olive

A long-time plant collector and Galanthophile, with a spectacular garden at Dial Park, Worcestershire, which includes a superb winter garden full of plants, colour and interest, including an extensive collection of snowdrops.

Mathias, Brigadier Leonard (1890–1972) and Mrs Winifrede (1898–1985)

Brigadier Mathias and his wife purchased Hyde Lodge near Stroud, Gloucestershire, and its derelict garden in 1947. With their chauffer/gardener Herbert Ransom, they restored the garden, uncovering masses of giant snowdrops up to around 35cm high, which were exhibited at the RHS in 1951. Walter Butt, the original owner of Hyde Lodge, told them the snowdrop was *G.* 'Arnott's Seedling', which he had acquired from Colesbourne. The snowdrop received an RHS AM and was later renamed *G.* 'S. Arnott'. The couple established the Giant Snowdrop Company, and from 1951 to 1968 exhibited many more snowdrops, receiving numerous Gold Medals. When ill-health forced the closure of the business, they moved to Hanbutt's Orchard, Stroud. Herbert Ransom moved to Falkland House after the deaths of his employers, taking many snowdrops with him.

Melville, David (1870–1924)

Melville worked for the Dukes of Sutherland, becoming head gardener at Dunrobin Castle, Scotland. He found the first poculiform snowdrop in the grounds of the castle, *G. nivalis* 'Poculiformis'. He also discovered *G. nivalis* 'Melvillei', which was originally known as 'Dunrobin Seedling' and was exhibited in 1878.

Miyashita, Tomoko

A Japanese Galanthophile and plant collector, Miyashita is a prominent visitor to Europe during the snowdrop season and has a large personal collection of snowdrops at his home in Japan.

Morley, John

A distinguished artist, wood engraver and horticulturist, John Morley has lived for over thirty years on the east coast of England. He grows over three hundred varieties of snowdrop, which he uses with other plants as subjects for his beautiful paintings. As proprietor of the North Green Snowdrop Company, he also supplies bulbs by mail order.

Norman, Sue and Roger

The Normans began creating their beautiful Ivy Croft Garden in Leominster, Herefordshire, in 1997, and it is now home to a wide collection of snowdrops, planted out in borders as well as naturalized beneath winter-flowering shrubs and trees. They sell snowdrops through their nursery and by mail order, and the garden opens for NGS.

Nottle, Trevor

An Australian gardener, garden historian and horticulturist, Trevor Nottle grows snowdrops on the slopes of Mount Lofty

Trevor Nottle, Walnut Hill, Australia. (*Photo courtesy Trevor Nottle.*)

in southern Australia. Among his wide collection of plants, he grows numerous snowdrops, many from seed, in his 'no-dig' garden, and prefers snowdrops that flower over a long season.

Nutt, Richard (1929–2002)

A passionate plantsman, celebrated horticulturist and gardener of the old school, Richard Nutt was one of the 'greats' of the snowdrop world. He was known for his generosity and the inspiration and encouragement he gave to many generations of gardeners and Galanthophiles. A long-time member of the RHS, he regularly attended their shows and was a member of the Rock Garden and Alpine Group Committee. He travelled widely to satisfy his interest in plants, including field trips to study snowdrops in their native habitats. He was also the originator of the famous snowdrop lunches, which he began many years ago.

Oud, Gerard

A Dutch Galanthophile, whose family have been in the bulb business for five generations. He has around two hundred and thirty different snowdrops in his collection, concentrating on more unusual varieties, which he propagates by twin-scaling. He organizes snowdrop days at Zaanse Schans, in the Netherlands, where he sells snowdrops.

Owen, Margaret

A passionate gardener and Galanthophile, Margaret Owen carved her magnificent garden in Shropshire from a field. The garden opens for snowdrops on the last Sunday in February each year in aid of the Multiple Sclerosis Society, raising vast sums of money over the years. An extensive collection of snowdrops spreads beneath witch hazel, *Cornus* and hellebores. *G.* 'Godfrey Owen', a beautiful snow-drop with six outer and six inner segments, was named after her late husband, and Ray Cobb named *G.* 'Margaret Owen' for her.

'Margaret Owen', named in her honour by Ray Cobb.

Shirley Palmer.

Harry Pierick, Netherlands.
(*Photo courtesy Harry Pierick*)

Margaret Owen. (*Photo courtesy Ken Tudor*)

Palmer, Shirley

Shirley and her husband John have been avid Galanthophiles for many years, with a large collection of snowdrops in the borders and naturalized beneath trees in their Nottinghamshire garden. They run a small nursery with mail order sales for snowdrops and also Heliotropes, another of their specialities.

Peters, Louise

Louise has been interested in plants since childhood. Her nursery, Foxgrove Plants in Berkshire, initially specialized in alpines but before long her passion for snowdrops took over. The nursery sells many different snowdrops, and swathes of snowdrops carpet the garden. She is a regular exhibitor of snowdrops at RHS shows.

Pierik, Harry

A Dutch garden designer and snowdrop grower with a large collection of snowdrops, many thousands of which are naturalized in the peace and tranquillity of his highly acclaimed Hidden City Garden at Zwolle in the Netherlands. He conducts special snowdrop tours, has written a book, *Paradijselijke Tuinen*, about the garden, and has also made a film called *Garden of Eden Snowdrops in the Hidden City Garden*. His Galanthus introductions include G. 'Lady Scharlock', a beautiful albino poculiform, and G. 'Ragini'.

Portier, Cathy, and Jan Van de Sijpe

These Belgian Galanthophiles and growers have a well established alpine nursery at Vordenstein with a collection of around three hundred varieties of snowdrops. They also organize annual Snowdrop Sundays and other snowdrop events. Their introductions include G. 'White Cloud' and G. 'Funny Justine'.

Poucke, Koen Van

A Belgian Galanthophile, snowdrop grower and nurseryman who travels the world to see snowdrops and meet like-minded people. He prefers early snowdrops and although he enjoys having rarer snowdrops, he dislikes today's hype. He also has the largest European collection of Epimediums.

Raines, Keith and Libby

Australian Galanthophiles with a large collection of snowdrops and snowflakes in a cool climate garden at Mount Wilson, near Sydney. Merry Garth, which is set in an area of natural rainforest with woodland and rock gardens, regularly opens for Australia's Open Gardens Scheme.

Herbert Ransom after receiving his award for services to horticulture.
(*Photo courtesy Phil Cornish*)

Ransom, Herbert (1909–1985)

As chauffer/gardener to Brigadier Leonard and Winifrede Mathias of the Giant Snowdrop Company, Ransom too had a great knowledge of snowdrops, later moving much of the collection to Falkland House. Noted for his kindness and generosity, he then distributed his own snowdrops. Together with E.B. Anderson, they named four snowdrops found growing around a clump of G. 'S. Arnott' in the garden: G. 'Armine', after the Mathias's daughter; G. 'Sally Ann', after Ransom's daughter; G. 'Winifrede Mathias' after his former employer, and G. 'Ransom', although he himself considered it the least worthy of the snowdrops they found.

Richardson, Gill

Gill Richardson at Manor Farm, Lincolnshire, has collected snowdrops for many years, with thousands naturalized in her garden, as well as numerous 'special' snowdrops. She also specializes in *Astrantia*, including the 'Gill Richardson series'. She offers snowdrops for sale.

Sanham, Chris

A former Plant Heritage Collection Holder of *Galanthus*, Chris Sanham retired from banking and moved to Sussex in 1999, to a property where much of the garden had been an old orchard. There is an extensive collection of snowdrops in woodland areas, Chris advocates lattice pots for planting, and reputedly grows all the named snowdrops.

Sharman, Joe

A leading Galanthophile, whose Monksilver Nursery in Cambridgeshire specializes in snowdrops. He supplied around seventy different varieties for London's Chelsea Physic Garden's collection, as well as having an extensive personal collection, although probably only about half are named. He was the instigator and organizer of the annual Galanthus Gala, which he began in 1997; it is now attended by enthusiasts from around the world.

Smyth, Mark

The Irish Galanthophile Mark Smyth specializes in bulbs, with a particular interest in snowdrops and crocus, of which he has a good collection. He is also in the process of trying to establish a definitive list and collection of Irish snowdrops.

Mark Smyth.
(*Photo courtesy Mark Smyth*)

Staines, Wol and Sue

They became interested in snowdrops well over twenty years ago and now have an extensive collection at the famed Glen Chantry garden, Essex. They concentrate on very distinct varieties and plant in lattice pots. Having opened their garden for many years, they recently decided to retire and concentrate on the pleasures of gardening but they still exhibit and sell snowdrops at shows.

Stanley, Lady Beatrix (1877–1944)

A great collector of bulbs, including numerous snowdrops, at Sibbertoft Manor, Northamptonshire. The double snowdrop G. 'Lady Beatrix Stanley' is named for her, and G. 'Barbara's Double' is named for her daughter. Her daughter married Sir Charles Buchanan, and they grew snowdrops at St Anne's Manor, Nottinghamshire. The family tradition continues with Barbara's son, Sir Andrew Buchanan and his wife, who have established a magnificent snowdrop and winter garden at Hodsock Priory, Nottinghamshire.

Stern, Sir Frederick (1884–1967)

A valued member of the RHS, Stern served on numerous committees and the Council. He was knighted in 1956 for services to horticulture. In 1909 he began creating a garden in an old chalk pit at Highdown, Sussex, now owned and managed by Worthing Borough Council. He received many plants and bulbs from plant hunter E.K. Balls, and published numerous works, including the memorable *Snowdrops and Snowflakes* (1956).

Street, Alan

Alan Street is the nursery manager at Avon Bulbs, with a collection of around five hundred different snowdrops. He instigated the 'Snowdrop Immortals', a group of people with snowdrops named after them. Alan does not really qualify as the snowdrops should carry the full name, whereas G. 'Alan's Treat' is only a play on his name. His finds include G. 'Blewbury Tart'; G. 'Ding Dong'; G. 'Green Fingers'; G. 'Bankside'; and G. 'Ghost'.

Tobin, Paddy

Paddy Tobin gardens in Waterford, south-east Ireland, and is a member of the Irish Garden Plant Society (IGPS).

He has a long-standing interest in alpine plants and small bulbs, and has numerous snowdrops in his collection.

Tonkin, Shirley and Jane

The Tonkins run Sylvan Vale Nursery in the Dandenong Ranges, Melbourne, Australia. Bryan Tonkin, their late father, established the nursery, raising *Galanthus* hybrids sold under the 'Sylvan Vale' prefix.

Van der Kolk, Gert-Jan

He began collecting snowdrops in 1999, with over six hundred and fifty different varieties, not all named. He discovered G. 'Green Tear' in Holland and G. 'Envy' in the UK. He moved to England in 2001 as head gardener at the Oppenheimer Estate, Waltham Place, Berkshire, where he discovered the snowdrop he named G. 'Beany'.

Vockins, Audrey

Audrey was inspired to start collecting snowdrops in the 1960s after buying G. elwesii from Boots. She later contacted Richard Nutt, who gave her G. 'Lady Beatrix Stanley'. She was instrumental in starting Foxgrove Plants with an extensive snowdrop list,

and also has a good collection of witch hazels, which are perfect companions to her snowdrops.

Waldorf, Günter (1946–2012)

A German Galanthophile and author who published *Schneeglöckchen* (2011). Around four hundred different snowdrops are grown in lattice pots sunk into his garden. He organized the German equivalent of the Snowdrop Gala, the Oirlicher Schneeglockchentage at Oirlicher Blumengarten, along with Snowdrop Days, attracting hundreds of Galanthophiles from around the world.

Warburg, Primrose (1920–1996)

Primrose was married to the eminent botanist E.F. Warburg, who collected crocus. Her reputation among Galanthophiles is prodigious, and there are many and varied stories about her, her garden and her snowdrops. The garden and woodland at South Hayes, Oxfordshire, were carefully managed on semi-wild lines, allowing the bulbs to multiply and spread, producing many good seedlings. After her death Dr John Grimshaw was asked to catalogue the collection and arrange for its distribution. New seedlings named at this time included G. 'Primrose Warburg' and G. 'South Hayes'.

Way, David and Anke

The Ways have introduced numerous snowdrops, including G. 'Hunton Herald'; G. 'Hunton Early Bird' and G. 'Hunton Giant', the G. 'Hunton' prefix being derived from the name of their village in Kent. Another introduction was G. 'Anika', named after their granddaughter. Inveterate gardeners, they have received many Wildlife Gardening awards from the Kent Wildlife Trust.

Whinfield, Angela

A keen Galanthophile, Angela's renowned Snape Cottage garden is a plantaholic's paradise. It includes over three hundred different snowdrops, which enjoy the free-draining, moist soil, and produce outstanding displays during the snowdrop season.

G. 'Green Fingers', an Alan Street introduction.

Oliver Wyatt in his garden. (*Photo courtesy RHS Lindley Library*)

Wijnen, Valentin

A Belgian Galanthophile who began collecting snowdrops at the age of 7. He has named numerous snowdrops under the 'Grakes' prefix, including *G.* 'Grakes Gold', a good yellow with yellow leaves; *G.* 'Grakes Yellow'; *G.* 'Grakes Green Bells', with green tinted segments; and *G.* 'Grakes Monster', a variable snowdrop appearing differently each year. He also named *G.* 'Valentines Day', *G.* 'Looking Around', *G.* 'Robert Wijnen', *G.* 'Golden Boy' and *G.* 'Golden Sunrise'.

Wilson, Judy

Judy began her snowdrop collection with a hundred *G. nivalis* and *G. nivalis* 'Flore Pleno', which she planted 'in the green'. Next came *G.* 'Magnet', *G.* 'Merlin' and

G. 'S. Arnott'. There are now in excess of seventy different varieties in her collection, many naturalized in the old orchard of her Norfolk garden.

Wyatt, Oliver (1898–1973)

Oliver Wyatt was treasurer of the RHS and President of the Alpine Garden Society from 1967 to 1971. E.A. Bowles referred to him as the first Galanthophile. He was introduced to snowdrops by Lady Beatrix Stanley, and created a beautiful garden at Maidwell Hall School, Northamptonshire, during his time as headmaster. Many spring bulbs including numerous snowdrops were naturalized beneath the trees. He used the 'Maidwell' prefix for seedlings, many of which continue today. He also grew and preserved many of the older snowdrops.

Snowdrop Immortals

Galanthophile Alan Street initiated the 'Snowdrop Immortals', based on the French Immortals, a group of like-minded people who meet in Paris each year and are dedicated to keeping the French language pure. You qualify as a Snowdrop Immortal if you have a snowdrop named after you. The name must include both Christian and surname. Alan doesn't strictly qualify as his snowdrop, 'Alan's Treat', is a play on his name.

Immortals include Ruby Baker, Matt Bishop, Bill Boardman, June Boardman, David Bromley, Ray Cobb, Veronica Cross, Carolyn Elwes, Fiona Godfrey, Yvonne Hay, Bryan Hewitt, Chris Ireland Jones, Jörg Lebsa, Dorothy Lucking, Robert Mackenzie, Brian Mathew, Sally Passmore, Celia Sawyer and Audry Vockins.

CHAPTER 10

GARDENS INDEX

Below are some of the many hundreds of gardens and nurseries specializing in snowdrops. Before visiting please check current opening times and charges.

Gardens, Nurseries, Societies and Collections

Gardens and estates, large and small, open each year at snowdrop time. Collections of rare snowdrops, naturalized snowdrops, snowdrop trails, walks, talks and tours attract thousands of visitors. Many old monastic sites and churchyards also have good displays of snowdrops which have naturalized over a considerable time.

Bedfordshire

**King's Arms Garden,
Ampthill, MK45 2PP
Tel. 01525 755648**
1½-acre woodland garden in Ampthill, created by distinguished horticulturist William Nourish. Now maintained by Friends of the Garden for Ampthill Town Council. Special snowdrop openings, also hellebores, aconites and Pulmonaria.

OPPOSITE PAGE: Kings Arms Garden, Bedfordshire. (*Photo courtesy Christopher Sutherns and Friends of Kings Arms Garden*).

RIGHT: Welford Park, Berkshire. (*Photo courtesy Paul Sievers LRPS*)

**Moggerhanger Park, Park Road, Moggerhanger, MK44 3RW
Tel. 01767 641007**
Award-winning heritage site extensively restored with help from the National Lottery and English Heritage. 33 acres of parkland, originally landscaped by Humphrey Repton. Woodland walks and extensive drifts of snowdrops throughout Garden Wood. Mainly *G. nivalis* 'Flore Pleno' and *G. elwesii*.

Berkshire

**Ankerwycke Priory,
Nr Runnymede (National Trust)
Tel. 01784 432891**
Stunning snowdrops carpet the ancient ruins near the famous Ankerwycke Yew. *Also* 'Snowdrop Spectacular'.

**Welford Park, Newbury, RG20 8HU
Tel. 01488 608691
www.welfordpark.co.uk**
Historic garden on monastic site of

Magnolia House, Buckinghamshire. (*Photo courtesy Alan Ford*)

Abingdon Abbey. Snowdrop openings for over fifty years. Renowned snowdrop walk, with vast areas of naturalized snowdrops including rare and unusual varieties.

St Mary's Church, Church Road, Shaw, Newbury, RG14 2DS
Tel. 01635 40450

Buckinghamshire

Cliveden, Taplow, Maidenhead, SL6 0JA (National Trust)
Tel. 01494 755562
info@clivedonhouse.co.uk
Grade 1 listed garden and woodland with stunning snowdrops. Guided tours and walks.

Magnolia House, Grange Drive, Woodburn Green, HP10 0QD
Tel. 01628 525818
Thousands of snowdrops beneath mature trees in secluded ½-acre garden developed over the last twenty-five years. Numerous varieties, also hellebores.

Cambridgeshire

Anglesey Abbey, Quay Road, Lode, CB25 9EJ (The National Trust)
Tel. 01223 810080
Renowned snowdrop garden on old monastic site. 114 acres of formal and informal gardens include ¼-mile Winter Walk with shrubs, colourful barks, spring bulbs and snowdrops. 240 varieties of snowdrop planted and naturalized throughout grounds. Many new seedlings

originated here, including the uncommon *G. lagodechianus,* discovered on an old Victorian rubbish tip. Aconites, cyclamen and miniature iris.

Chippenham Park, Chippenham, Ely, CB7 5PT
Tel. 01638 720221
www.chippenhamparkgardens.info
Extensive gardens in the Anglo-Dutch style dating back to the seventeenth century. Canals, parkland and woodland walks with one of the best displays of snowdrops and aconites in East Anglia.

Peckover House and Gardens, North Brink, Wisbech, PE13 1JR (National Trust)
Tel. 01945 583463
www.nationaltrust.org
Georgian merchant's town house with outstanding 2-acre Victorian garden and beautiful displays of snowdrops.

6 Robins Wood, Nr Peterborough, PE8 6JQ
Tel. 01780 783094
Small woodland garden with over 200 varieties of snowdrop, together with spring plants and bulbs. Open for NGS.

Cheshire

Dunham Massey, Altrincham, WA14 4SJ (National Trust)
Tel. 01619 411025
www.nationaltrust.org.uk/ dunhammassey
Large estate with recently developed, extensively planted 7-acre Winter Garden. The largest in the UK with over 200,000 bulbs, 700 plant species and 1,600 shrubs planted for winter interest and colour. Thousands of single and double snowdrops covering sixty-one varieties along the snowdrop walk and naturalized beneath trees.

Rode Hall Gardens, Scholar Green, Congleton, S17 3QP
Tel. 01270 873237
www.rodehall.co.uk
Grade 2 listed park and 10-acre garden, in the Wilbraham family since 1669.

Chippenham Park, Cambridgeshire. (*Photo courtesy Hugo and Rebecca Nicolle*)

Snowdrops first introduced in the nineteenth century are now the highlight each year. Mile-long snowdrop walk and over fifty varieties of snowdrop.

Weeping Ash Garden, Warrington Road, Glazebury, Warrington, WA3 5NT
Tel. 01942 266300
www.bents.co.uk
Breathtaking garden with imaginative planting, designed and created by nurseryman John Bent, with ponds, borders and woodland. Magnificent displays of snowdrops. Guided walks.

Cornwall

Coombegate Cottage, St Ives, Nr Liskeard, PL14 3LZ
Tel. 01579 383520
mike@coombegate.wanadoo.co.uk
1-acre garden specifically planted for winter colour and perfume. Witch hazels, Daphne, early rhododendrons, unusual plants and well established drifts of snowdrops.

Pencarrow House, Washaway, Bodmin, PL30 3AG
Tel. 01208 841369
www.pencarrow.co.uk
50 acres of formal and woodland gardens with probably one of the best displays of snowdrops in Cornwall. Snowdrop Sundays.

Pentillie Castle and Estate, Paynters Cross, St Mellion, Saltash, PL12 6QD
Tel. 01579 350044
www.pentillie.co.uk
Breathtaking setting overlooking Dartmoor and River Tamar. Special February openings and Snowdrop Walks.

Pinetum Park and Pine Lodge, Holbush, St Austell, PL25 3RQ
Tel. 01726 73500
www.pinetumpark.com
30-acre estate and gardens including 3-acre winter garden. 'Snowdrop Fortnight' with fabulous displays of snowdrops.

Robins Wood, Cambridgeshire. (*Photo courtesy Carole Smith*)

Trebah Garden, Mawnan Smith, TR11 5JZ
Tel. 01326 252200
www.trebah-garden.co.uk
26-acre south-facing garden with in excess of 60,000 snowdrop bulbs planted in the last few years to create carpets of white flowers.

Pencarrow House, Cornwall. (*Photo courtesy Pencarrow House*)

Cumbria

**Summerdale House, Nook,
Nr Lupton, LA6 1PE
Tel. 015395 67210
sheals@btinternet.com**
Part-walled 1½-acre country garden and
nursery with herbaceous borders,
woodland and spring bulbs including
snowdrops.

Denbighshire

**Chirk Castle, Chirk, Wrexham,
LL14 5AF (National Trust)
Tel. 01691 777701
chirkcastle@nationaltrust.org.uk**
Award-winning garden with herbaceous
borders, shrubs, clipped yews and
mature parkland, with thousands of
snowdrops carpeting the Pleasure
Ground Woods. Special snowdrop walks
in February.

Derbyshire

**Cherry Tree Cottage, Sutton Lane,
Hilton, DE65 5FB**
¹/₃-acre cottage garden. Interesting
plants and special snowdrop openings.

**Hopton Hall, Hopton, Wirksworth,
Matlock, DE4 4DF
Tel. 01629 540458
www.hoptonhall.co.uk**
Extensive parkland with hidden
snowdrops revealed by mid-1990s
restoration. Thousands of snowdrops
and aconites, increasing every year,
create one of the best snowdrop
gardens in the country.

Devon

**Cherubeer Gardens,
Dolton, EX19 8PP**
Over 150 named varieties, including
doubles, yellows and more unusual
forms. Drifts of larger snowdrops,
including G. 'S. Arnott', G. 'Magnet' and
G. 'Dionysus'.

**Hartland Abbey, Hartland, Bideford,
North Devon, EX39 6DT
Tel. 01237 441282/234
www.hartlandabbey.co.uk**
50 acres of walled and woodland
gardens in Area of Outstanding Natural
Beauty. Swathes of snowdrops, many
planted centuries ago. February
Snowdrop Sundays.

**Little Cumbre, 145 Pennsylvania
Road, Exeter, EX4 6DZ**
1-acre garden with views across
Dartmoor and Exe Estuary. Displays of
around thirty different varieties of
snowdrop beneath highly perfumed
winter-flowering shrubs.

**Pikes Cottage, Madford, Hemyock,
EX15 3QZ
Tel. 01823 680345**
19 acres of bluebell woods, arboretum
and 6-acre garden with winter-flowering
shrubs, snowdrops and spring bulbs.

**The Garden House, Buckland
Monochorum, Yelverton, PL20 7LQ
Tel. 01822 854769
www.thegardenhouse.org.uk**
Outstanding and romantic 8-acre garden
in heart of Devon countryside. Large
specialist collection of snowdrops,
snowdrop walks and lectures.

**St Mary's Church, Newton Abbot,
TQ12 1EL**

Dorset

**Kingston Lacey, Wimborne Minster,
BH21 4EA (National Trust)
Tel. 01202 883402
www.nationaltrust.org**
Formal gardens and naturalized
woodland with displays of snowdrops.
Special openings January–February.

**New Lawsbrook, Brodham Way,
Shillingstone, DT11 0TE
Tel. 01258 860148
Cne7obl@aol.com**
6 acres of wooded grounds with over
200 tree species, extensive snowdrops,
spring bulbs and hellebores.

**Snape Cottage, Bourton, SP8 5BZ
Tel. 01747 840330
www.snapecottagegarden.co.uk**
Outstanding all-season garden. Extensive
collections of snowdrops. Also snowdrop
sales.

The Beth Chatto woodland garden, Essex, in spring.
(*Photo courtesy Beth Chatto Garden*)

Essex

Beth Chatto Gardens, Elmstead Market, Colchester, CO7 7DB
Tel. 01206 822007
www.bethchatto.co.uk
Renowned garden including woodland and winter walks with emphasis on coloured barks, spring bulbs and numerous snowdrops.

Byndes Cottage, Pebmarsh, Halstead, CO9 2LZ
Tel. 01787 269500
Outstanding 7-acre rural garden and arboretum. Extensive collection of snowdrops and Plant Heritage Collection Holder of *Galanthus*.

Easton Lodge, Little Easton, Great Dunmow, CM6 2BB
Tel. 01371 876979
www.eastonlodge.co.uk
Open for many years for snowdrop celebrations. Grant by Life Raft Trust aids open days with proceeds towards garden restoration. Open February–March for snowdrops.
Volunteer opportunities.

Marks Hall Garden and Arboretum, Coggeshall, CO6 1TG
Tel. 01376 563796
www.markshall.org.ukj
Landscaped gardens with woodland walks and vistas. Special snowdrop openings.

Gloucestershire

Cerney House Gardens, North Cerney, Cirencester, GL7 7BX
Tel. 01285 831205
www.cerneygardens.com
Peaceful, romantic organic garden in 40 acres of Cotswold countryside. White carpets of massed snowdrops. 200 varieties of unusual snowdrops, increasing each year.

Colesbourne Park, Nr Cheltenham, GL53 9NP
Tel. 01242 870567
www.colesbournegardens.org.uk
One of the country's foremost snowdrop gardens. Fabulous

Byndes Cottage, Essex. (*Photo courtesy David MacLennan*)

snowdrops collected over many years by members of the Elwes family, begun in 1874 by eminent Victorian plant hunter Henry John Elwes. Following his death in 1922, the garden lay neglected until Sir Henry and Lady Elwes began restoration in 1962. Passionate Galanthophiles, they have amassed many choice species and varieties, with thousands of snowdrops naturalized beneath mature trees. Snowdrops begin flowering from early autumn right through to late March and April. Dr John Grimshaw was garden manager between 2003 and 2012, contributing his expertise and horticultural experience. Snowdrop study days, weekend openings, February–early March, guided snowdrop walks.

Colesbourne Park, Gloucestershire.

Painswick Rococo Garden, Gloucestershire.

**Cotswold Farm Garden,
Duntisbourne Abbots, Nr Cirencester,
GL7 7JS
Tel. 01285 821857
www.cotswoldfarmgardens.org.uk**
Historic gardens in secluded valley. Special snowdrop collections and swathes of naturalized snowdrops in woodland.

Snowdrops in Brandy Mount garden.
(*Photo courtesy Michael Baron*)

**Home Farm, Huntley, GL19 3HQ
Tel. 01452 830210**
Hillside garden with views across the Vale of Gloucester. Mile-long walk through fields and woodland carpeted with snowdrops. Larch Corner, Snowdrop Wood and Spring Spinney have thousands of snowdrops flowering from Christmas.

**Painswick Rococo Gardens,
Painswick, GL6 6TH
Tel. 01452 813204
www.rococogarden.org.uk**
The only complete Rococo garden in England, originally developed mid-eighteenth century by Benjamin Hyett, restored by Painswick Rococo Garden Trust. Snowdrops naturalized through grass, beneath trees and cascading down banks, with extensive new plantings. Different species and varieties include many G.'Atkinsii' of nurseryman James Atkins' fame, who retired to the estate. Also G. 'James Backhouse', although mysteriously neither the estate's owners nor the Garden Trust ever purchased this snowdrop. Snowdrop walks and talks.

**Rodmarton Manor, Cuckerton,
Tetbury, GL7 6PF
Tel. 01285 841253
www.rodmarton-manor.co.uk**
8-acre Arts and Crafts garden with wide variety of rare and unusual snowdrops from October to late spring. Also hellebores, aconites, cyclamen and crocus. Special openings.

Hampshire

**Brandy Mount House Gardens,
Alresford, SO24 9EG
Tel. 01962 732189
www.brandymount.co.uk**
Secluded 1-acre town garden with mature trees. Former Plant Heritage Collection Holder of Galanthus and Daphne. 200 named varieties of snowdrop flowering from autumn through to spring. Bulb sales on open days.

**Bramdean House, Bramdean,
Alresford, SO24 0JU
Tel. 01962 771214**
6-acre plantsman's garden and old orchard massed with plants and bulbs including large collection of snowdrops, aconites and *Crocus tommasinianus*.

**The Down House, Itchen Abbas,
SO21 1AX
Tel. 01962 791054
markstephenporter@gmail.com**
2-acre garden adjoining Pilgrim Way. Walk to river with carpets of snowdrops and crocus. Open NGS.

**St George's Church, Church Lane,
Damerham, SP6 3JF**

Herefordshire

**Berrington Hall, Leominster,
HR6 0DW (The National Trust)
Tel. 01568 615721
www.nationaltrust.org**
Historic mansion and parkland, one of Capability Brown's last projects. Naturalized snowdrops in mature woodland. Special winter openings.

Ivy Croft, Herefordshire.

**Ivy Croft, Ivington Green,
Leominster, HR6 0JN
Tel. 01568 720344
www.ivycroftgarden.co.uk**
Attractive garden developed from fields since 1996. Extensive drifts of spring bulbs and over 150 varieties of snowdrops. Nursery and mail order sales. Open for NGS.

Hertfordshire

**Bennington Lordship Gardens,
Benington, Stevenage, SG2 7BS
Tel. 0143 886 9668
www.beningtonlordship.co.uk/
snowdrops**
Historic garden managed to encourage huge drifts of naturalized snowdrops throughout the grounds and around old moat. *G. nivalis* and *G. nivalis* 'Flore Pleno' together with rarer snowdrops including unusual yellow discovered near ruins.

Isle of Wight

**Highwood, Cranmore Avenue,
Cranmore, PO41 0XS
Tel. 01983 760550**
2½-acre garden with snowdrops, hepaticas and hellebores.

Kent

**Broadview Gardens, Hadlow College,
Hadlow, TN11 0AL
www.hadlow.ac.uk**
10 acres of landscaped gardens with mixed planting including snowdrops.

**Goodnestone Park Gardens, Wingham,
Goodnestone, Canterbury, CT3 1PL
Tel. 01304 840107
www.goodnestoneparkgardens.co.uk**
14 acres of romantic garden and new arboretum in heart of Kent countryside. Hellebores, Daphne, Witch hazel, Mahonias and impressive displays of snowdrops. February Snowdrop and Hellebore Extravaganza.

**Mere House, Mereworth,
Maidstone, ME18 5NB
Tel. 01622 814608
www.merehouse.co.uk**
Nineteenth-century parkland and 6-acre garden redeveloped since 1958. Naturalized snowdrops in woodland and walks. Open for NGS since 1971.

**Southover, Grove Lane,
Hunton, ME15 0SE
Tel. 01622 820876**
1½-acre garden massed with interesting plants including diverse and extensive collection of snowdrops. Open days. Also snowdrops in nearby St Marys churchyard.

**Spring Platt, Sutton Valance,
ME17 3BY
Tel. 01622 843383**
1-acre garden with collection of around 200 snowdrops, increasing each year. Open for NGS.

St Mary's Church, Hunton, ME15 0SE

Lancashire

**Bank Hall, Liverpool Road,
Bretherton, Chorley, PR26 9AT
www.bankhouseonline.2ye.com**
Parkland, arboretum and 18 acres of gardens. Bank Hall Action Group's restoration revealed extensive colonies of snowdrops originally planted after the Crimean War in 1856. On-going

Bank Hall, Lancashire.(*Photo courtesy Lionel Taylor*)

planting and development by Bank Hall Action Group and Friends of Bank House include additional rare and unusual snowdrops. Special openings.

Cobble Hey Farm and Garden, Hobbs Lane, Claughton on Brock, Garstang, Nr Preston, PR3 0QN
Tel. 01995 602643
www.cobblehey.co.uk
www.cobblehey.co.uk
Good displays of snowdrops, including unusual varieties.

Lytham Hall, Ballam Road, Lytham St Annes, FY8 4JX (Lytham Town Trust)
Tel. 01253 736652
www.lythamhall.co.uk
80 acres of mature parkland, site of twelfth-century Benedictine priory. Annual snowdrop walks with carpets of snowdrops beneath mature trees.

Leicestershire

Launde Abbey, East Norton, Leicester, LE7 9XB
Tel. 01572 717454
www.launde.org.uk
450 acres of parkland and 14-acre garden. Special snowdrop openings.

Leicestershire and Rutland Wildlife Trust, Dimminsdale Nature Reserve, Ticknall, DE73 7LE
www.lrwt.org.uk
Good displays of snowdrops on site of old cottage garden within nature reserve

Paddocks, Moira Road, Ashby de la Zouch, LE65 2TU
Tel. 01530 412606
Displays of over 150 varieties of snowdrop as well as swathes of common *G. nivalis*. Special charity openings.

Lincolnshire

Belton House, Grantham, NG32 2LS (National Trust)
Tel. 01476 566116
www.nationaltrust.org
Seventeenth-century country estate with displays of snowdrops in gardens and along lakeside walks.

21 Chapel Street, Hacconby, Bourne, PE10 0UL
Tel. 01778 570314
Galanthophile's cottage garden with many varieties of snowdrops. Also hellebores and alpines. Open for NGS.

Doddington Hall, Doddington, Lincoln, LN6 4RU
Tel. 01522 694308
www.snowdrops.co.uk
6-acre garden overflowing with spring bulbs. Good displays of snowdrops.

Easton Walled Garden, Easton, Grantham, NG33 5AP
Tel. 01476 530063
www.eastonwalledgardens.co.uk
Historic garden with carpets of snowdrops and aconites. 'Snowdrop Week', talks, and winter walks. Indoor display of rare snowdrops. Some sales.

Little Ponton Hall, Little Ponton, Grantham, NG33 5BS
4-acre landscaped garden with prairie, wild flower meadows and naturalized bulbs. Thousands of snowdrops and aconites along ½-mile snowdrop walk. Open for NGS.

Normanby Hall, Scunthorpe, DN15 9HU
Tel. 01724 720588
Country park and estate carpeted with snowdrops beneath woodland trees. Also aconites and cyclamen. Open days and guided walks.

London

Chelsea Physic Garden, 66 Royal Hospital Road, SW3
www.chelseaphysicgarden.co.uk
4-acre walled Botanical Garden founded in 1673. Winter-flowering shrubs and plants with over seventy-five varieties of snowdrop. Snowdrops also displayed in raised pots for easy viewing. Snowdrop trail guided tours.

Middlesex

Myddelton House Gardens, Bulls Cross, Enfield, EN2 9HG
Tel. 01992 702200
www.leevalleypark.org.uk
Home of the late E.A. Bowles (1865–1954), plantsman, botanist, artist and writer. The garden lay neglected until Lee Valley Regional Park Authority and

Snowdrops at Chelsea Physic Garden, London.

the E.A. Bowles of Myddelton House Society began restoration to Bowles' original design. Mature trees planted by Bowles, shrubs, alpine meadows and extensive collection of snowdrops.

Norfolk

**Chestnut Farm, Church Road, West Beckham, NR25 6NX
Tel. 01263 822241**
3-acre garden and arboretum with over sixty varieties of snowdrop, also crocus and hellebores. Open for NGS.

Lexham Hall, Nr Litcham, PE32 2QJ
Formal garden, parkland and river walks. 3-acre woodland garden massed with snowdrops and spring bulbs. Snowdrop walk and snowdrop open days for NGS.

**Walsingham Abbey, NR22 6BP
Tel. 01328 820259
www.walsinghamabbey.com**
18 acres of grounds and woodland around ruined abbey, carpeted with naturalized snowdrops. Special snowdrop walks but open throughout year.

Northamptonshire

**Beech House, 73 Church Street, Burton Latimer, NN15 5LU
Tel. 01536 723593
gloake@mac.com**
Semi-formal winter and spring garden with hellebores and over 150 different snowdrop species and varieties.

**Coton Manor, Coton, Northampton, NN6 8RQ
www.cotonmanor.co.uk**
10-acre hillside garden and orchard with collections of hellebores and snowdrops including the 'Coton' snowdrop. Annual snowdrop spectacular. Nursery and sales.

**Deene Park, Corby, NN17 3EW
Tel 01780 450278
www.deenepark.com**
Lakeside gardens with winter shrubs, hellebores and snowdrops, including many rare varieties. Famed 'Snowdrop Sundays'.

Walsingham Abbey, Norfolk. (*Photo courtesy Walsingham Estate Company*)

**Evenley Wood Garden, Evenley, NN13 5SH
Tel. 07776 307849
www.evenleywoodgarden.co.uk**
60-acre woodland garden growing approximately ninety different snowdrop varieties. One of the country's largest wholesale suppliers, selling in excess of 11,000 named snowdrop bulbs each year. Special February openings including group bookings. Sales.

Greywalls, Farndish, NN29 7HU
Mature 2-acre garden with hardy cyclamen, hellebores and over a hundred varieties of snowdrop.

**Kelmarsh Hall, Kelmarsh, Northampton, NN6 9LY
Tel. 01604 686543
www.kelmarsh.com**
www.kelmarsh.com
Grade 2 listed eighteenth-century gardens with continuing restoration aided by the Heritage Lottery Fund. Special openings for snowdrops.

**Rosemount, Church Hill, Hollowell, NN6 8RR
Tel. 01604 740354**
Over 200 different snowdrops with spring bulbs and hellebores. Open for NGS.

Hodsock Priory, Nottinghamshire.

The Beeches, Nottinghamshire.

The Homestead, Nottinghamshire.

Northumberland

**Belsay Hall, Castle and Gardens,
Nr Morpeth, NE20 0DX
(English Heritage)
Tel. 01661 881636
www.english-heritage.org.uk**
Renowned formal and woodland
gardens, wild flower meadows and
quarry with wonderful displays of
snowdrops each spring.

**Howick Hall, Alnwick, NE66 3LB
Tel. 01665 577285
www.howickhallgardens.org**
Formal and woodland gardens with
February 'Snowdrop Festival' and walks.

**Brinkburn Priory, Longramlington,
Morpeth, NE65 8AR
(English Heritage)
www.english-heritage.org.uk**

Nottinghamshire

**Felley Priory, Underwood,
Nottingham, NG16 5FJ
Tel. 07763 189771**
Naturalized bulbs and massed
snowdrops through gardens and
orchard. Nursery and snowdrop sales.

**Hodsock Priory Gardens,
Blyth, S81 0TY
Tel. 01909 591204
www.snowdrops.co.uk**
Masses of snowdrops and early spring
bulbs, iris, aconites and cyclamen in
5-acre garden. Swathes of naturalized
snowdrops beneath 100 acres of
woodland trees. Warming bonfire! In
top ten UK winter gardens. Month-long
Snowdrop Extravaganza from early
February. Snowdrop breaks in
sumptuous accommodation.

**Newstead Abbey,
Ravenshead, NG15 8NA
Tel. 01623 455900
www.newsteadabbey.org.uk**
Former Augustinian Priory. 300 acres of
parkland and gardens with special
snowdrop displays in the Monk's Garden.

**The Beeches, The Avenue, Milton,
Tuxford, Newark, NG22 0PW
Tel. 01777 870828**
Beautifully landscaped and well stocked
garden with hellebores, spring bulbs and
over 200 varieties of snowdrop.

**The Homestead, Normanton-by-
Bottesford, NG13 0EP
Tel. 01949 842745**
Attractive garden with National
Collection of heliotropes, also hellebores,
woodland plants and numerous varieties
of snowdrop. Also sales.

Oxfordshire

**Hanwell Community Observatory,
Hanwell Castle, Nr Banbury, W7 1PD
www.hanwellobservatory.org.uk**
20 acres of grounds extensively planted
with snowdrops. Stars and Snowdrops
event second weekend in February. Offsite
parking.

Waterperry Gardens, Oxfordshire. (*Photo courtesy Waterperry Gardens*)

The Patch, Shropshire. An annual opening for Multiple Sclerosis Society.

Ramsden House, Akeman Street, Ramsden, OX7 3AX
2-acre Victorian garden with mature shrubs, trees and carpets of snowdrops.

Waterperry Garden, Wheatly, OX33 1JZ.
Tel. 01844 339254
www.waterperrygardens.co.uk
8-acre garden with over thirty varieties of snowdrop naturalized in old orchard and riverside walk. Snowdrop weekend, guided tours.

Shropshire

Attingham Park, Atcham, Shrewsbury, SY4 4TP (National Trust)
Tel. 01743 708123
www.nationaltrust.org
Extensive areas of naturalized snowdrops through park and woodland.

Dudmaston, Quatt, Bridgnorth, WV15 6QN (National Trust)
Tel. 01746 780866
www.nationaltrust.org
Good displays of naturalized snowdrops around lake and dingle. Special openings.

Winsley Hall, Shropshire. An annual opening for the Lingen Davies Appeal, Shrewsbury Hospital.

The Patch, Acton Pigot, Acton Burnell, SY5 7PH
Tel. 01743 362139
Renowned Galanthophile's snowdrop garden and specialist collection. Open last weekend in February for Multiple Sclerosis Society. Snowdrop sales on open day.

Mawley Hall, Cleobury Mortimer, Kidderminster, DY14 8PN
Masses of snowdrops naturalized beneath mature trees. Snowdrop open day for charity February.

Winsley Hall, Westbury, Shrewsbury, SY5 9HB
Tel. 01743 492396
Masses of snowdrops along drive and through mature woodland. Snowdrop walks in aid of Lingen Davies Charity.

St James's Church, Shipton, Much Wenlock, TF13 6JZ
Snowdrops and aconites naturalized throughout churchyard.

St Peter's Churchyard, Stanton Lacy, Shropshire.

**St Peter's Church, Stanton Lacy,
Nr Ludlow, SY8 2AE
www.stantonlacychurch.org.uk**
Outstanding snowdrops originally
planted by Miss Armitage, sister of local
vicar, in the late nineteenth century now
cover entire churchyard. Several species
and varieties. Snowdrop weekend
mid-late February.

Cound Brook, Cound, SY5 6BE
Massed snowdrops naturalized along
banks of stream.

Somerset

**East Lambrook Manor Gardens, Easy
Lambrook, TA13 5HH
Tel. 01460 240328
www.eastlambrook.com**
Renowned Grade 1 listed cottage
garden created by the late Margery Fish
in the 1950s. Extensive collection of
snowdrops including G. 'Margery Fish'
and G. 'Sir Henry B-C'.

**Forde Abbey and Gardens,
Chard, TA20 4LU
Tel. 01460 220231
www.fordeabbey.co.uk**
40 acres of award-winning gardens on
site of old abbey. Snowdrop weekends.

**Fyne Court, Broomfield, Bridgwater,
TA5 2EQ. (National Trust)
Tel. 01628 605069
www.nationaltrust.org**
Romantic garden, mature woodland and
thousands of snowdrops. Guided walks
and snowdrop information.

**Snowdrop Valley, Wheddon Cross,
Exmoor (Badgworthy Land
Company) TA24 7DR.
www.wheddoncross.org.uk/
snowdropvalley**
Hidden valley smothered with
naturalized snowdrops, also known as
Draper's Way. An 'Environmentally
Sensitive Area', with restricted access
and park and ride scheme in snowdrop
time. Snowdrops probably introduced in
the thirteenth century by monks at
nearby Dunster.

Staffordshire

**Sugnall Hall, Sugnall,
Stafford, ST21 6NF
Tel. 01785 850820
www.sugnall.co.uk**
Parkland and walled kitchen garden with
spring snowdrop walks.

Suffolk

**East Bergholt Place,
East Bergholt, CO7 6UP
Tel. 01206 299224
www.placeforplants.co.uk**
February tours of garden and arboretum
for snowdrops and winter plants by
owner Rupert Eley. Plant centre.

**Gable House, Halesworth Road,
Redisham, NR34 8NE
Tel. 01502 575298**
1-acre garden with spring bulbs,
cyclamen, hellebores and over 200
varieties of snowdrop.

East Lambrook Manor, Somerset. (*Photo courtesy Mike Werkmeister*)

Ickworth House Park and Gardens, Horringer, Bury St Edmunds, IP29 5QE (National Trust)
Tel. 01284 735270
www.nationaltrust.org.uk/ickworth
1,800 acres of mature parkland and gardens. Open for snowdrops including numerous species and varieties.

Grey Friars Priory, Dunwich, Suffolk.

Surrey

Gatton Park, Rocky Lane, Merstham, RH2 0TW
Tel. 01737 649068
www.gattonpark.com
Royal Alexandra and Albert School. On-going garden restoration. Masses of snowdrops, snowdrop week with guided tours (advance booking).

RHS Garden Wisley, Woking, GU23 6QB
Tel. 0845 260 9000
www.rhs.org.uk/Gardens/Wisley
Flagship RHS garden. Large drifts of snowdrops in woodland, on Battleston Hill and also in Alpine House, increasing each year as new varieties added and exchanged. RHS is verifying and recording its snowdrops, creating a reference collection and programme of twin-scaling. Annual Snowdrop Splendour, snowdrop weekends, talks and sales.

Royal Botanic Gardens, Kew, Richmond, TW9 3AB
Tel. 020 833 25655
www.kew.org
One of the world's renowned botanic gardens. Snowdrops through gardens, around Temple of Aeolus, in Rock Garden and Conservation areas. Snowdrop research, assessment and plants.

Sussex

Nymans, Handcross, Haywards Heath, RH17 6EB (National Trust)
Tel 01444 405250
www.nationaltrust.org
Wonderful displays of snowdrops, spring trees, shrubs and flowers.

Pembury House, Ditchling Road, Clayton, BN6 9PH
Tel. 01273 842805
www.pemburyhouse.co.uk
2-acre, year-round interest country garden with winter-flowering shrubs, woodland, hellebores and increasing collection of snowdrops. Sales.

**The Manor of Dean, Pitshill,
Tillington, GU28 9AP
Tel. 07887 992349**
3-acre traditional English garden with
masses of spring bulbs and extensive
snowdrops.

**Wakehurst Place, Ardingly,
Nr Haywards Heath, RH17 6TN
Tel. 01444 894066**
465-acre country estate with gardens
and woodland. Thousands of
snowdrops. Sponsored displays.

Warwickshire

**Hill Close Gardens, Bread and Meat
Close, Warwick, CV34 6HF
Tel. 01926 493339
www.hillclosegardens.com**
Garden walk with displays of snowdrops.

**Ragley Hall Gardens,
Alcester, B49 5NJ
Tel. 07917 425664
www.ragleyhall.com**
24-acre gardens and woodland with
winter garden, spring meadow, and
bulbs. Massed plantings of snowdrops
and hellebores.

Wiltshire

**Great Chalfield Manor, Nr Melksham,
SN12 8NH. (National Trust)
Tel. 01225 782239
www.nationaltrust.org.uk**
7-acre gardens, grounds and orchard
around sixteenth-century moated manor.
Snowdrops and aconites naturalized
around moat walk. February charity
snowdrop day.

**Heale House Gardens, Middle
Woodford, Salisbury, SP4 6NP
Tel. 01722 782504
www.healegarden.co.uk**
Garden bordering River Avon extensively
planted with snowdrops and aconites.
Snowdrop Extravaganzas.

**Lacock Abbey Gardens, Chippenham,
SN15 2LG. (National Trust)
Tel. 01249 730459
www.nationaltrust.org.uk**
Renowned Victorian garden and
botanical collection around thirteenth-
century abbey. Mature woodland
carpeted with snowdrops, aconites and
crocus from December, peaking late
January–February.

**Stourhead, Stourton, Warminster,
BA12 6QD (National Trust)
Tel. 01747 841152
www.nationaltrust.org.uk**
2,650 acres of parkland and garden with
paths winding through naturalized
snowdrops.

Worcestershire

**Dial Park, Chaddesley Corbet,
DY10 4QB
Tel. 01562 777451**
Beautiful ¾-acre garden of rare and
unusual plants with winter garden and
large collection of snowdrops. Open
for NGS.

**The Cottage, Broughton Green,
Droitwich, WR9 7EF
Tel. 01905 391670**
½-acre plantsman's garden with mature
trees, formal hedges, topiary, snowdrops
and crocus lawn. Open for NGS.

**The Greyfriars, Friar Steet,
Worcester, WR1 2LZ. (National Trust)
Tel. 01905 23571
greyfriars@nationaltrust.org.uk**
Walled garden with spring bulbs and
snowdrops.

Dial Park, Worcestershire.

Yorkshire

**Austwick Hall, Austwick,
Nr Settle, LA2 8BS
Tel. 015242 51794
austwickhall@austwick.org**
Gardens with mature trees, shrubs, snowdrops and snowdrop walk. Hotel with regular garden openings.

**Burton Agnes Hall, Burton Agnes,
Driffield, East Yorkshire, YO25 4NB
Tel. 01262 490324
www.burtonagnes.com**
Award-winning gardens with herbaceous borders, walled garden, jungle and woodland walks. Month-long 'Snowdrop Spectacular'.

**Fountains Abbey, Ripon, Nr
Harrogate, HG4 3DY. (National Trust)
Tel. 01765 608888
www.nationaltrust.org**
Renowned World Heritage Site carpeted with snowdrops around twelfth-century abbey ruins.

**Goldsborough Hall, Church Street,
Goldsborough, HG5 8NR
Tel. 01423 867321
www.goldsboroughhall.com**
Spectacular displays of *G. nivalis* and *G. nivalis* 'Flore Pleno', together with other species and rare varieties. New Snowdrop Walk. Also hellebores and aconites.

**Mount Grace Priory, Staddlebridge,
Northallerton, DL6 3JG.
(National Trust)
Tel. 01609 883494
www.nationaltrust.org**
Remains of important Carthusian monastery carpeted with snowdrops.

Wales

**Boddysgallen Hall, Pentywyn Road,
Llandudno, LL30 1RS
Tel. 01492 584466
www.boddysgallen.com**
Restored seventeenth-century garden (now hotel) with good displays of snowdrops.

Burton Agnes Hall, Yorkshire. (*Photo courtesy Burton Agnes Hall*)

Goldsborough Hall, Yorkshire. (*Photo courtesy Mark Oglesby*)

**Bodnant Gardens, Tal-y-Cafn, Nr
Colwyn Bay, Conwy, LL28 5RE
(National Trust)
Tel. 01492 650460
www.bodnantgarden.co.uk**
80 acres of outstanding gardens and plants. Snowdrop day, sponsored snowdrop plantings.

**National Botanic Garden of Wales,
Llanarthne, Carmarthen, SA32 8HG
Tel. 01558 668768
www.gardenofwales.org.uk**
1 mile of snowdrops circling lakes.

Penrhyn Castle, Bangor, LL57 4HN (National Trust)
Tel. 01248 353084
www.nationaltrust.org
Carpets of snowdrops beneath mature trees and shrubs.

Plas-yn-Rhiw, Rhiw, Pwllheli, LL53 8AB (National Trust)
Tel. 01758 780219
www.nationaltrust.org
Large areas of naturalized snowdrops beneath woodland trees.

St Tysilio's Church, Llantysilio, North Wales

Ireland

Altamont Garden, Bunclody Road, Tullow, County Carlow
Tel. 059 915 9444
www.altamontgarden.com
100-acre estate and gardens include one of the finest collections of snowdrops in Ireland. Over a hundred varieties. Special openings, walks and guided tours.

The Argory, 144 Derrycaw Road, Moy, Dungannon, County Armagh, BT71 6NA (National Trust)
Tel. 0288 7784753
www,nationaltrust.org.uk
320-acre riverside estate with snowdrop walks.

Primrose Hill, Primrose Lane, Lucan, County Dublin
Shrubs, bulbs and fine collection of snowdrops. Special February openings.

Springhill, 20 Springhill Road, Moneymore, Magherafelt, County Londonderry, BT45 7NQ (National Trust)
Tel. 028 8674 8210
www.nationaltrust.org.uk
Guided walks through wonderful snowdrops. Sales.

Scotland

Abriachan Garden and Nursery, Loch Ness-Side, Inverness, IV3 8LA
Tel. 01463 861232
www.lochnessgarden.com
Woodland garden and nursery open for snowdrops. Mail order sales.

Cambo Snowdrops, Kingsbarns, St Andrews, KY16 8QD
Tel. 01333 450054
www.cambosnowdrops.com
Spectacular 70-acre woodland gardens carpeted with snowdrops February–March, also aconites and snowflakes. Scotland's largest specialist snowdrop garden and holder of Heritage Plant Collection of *Galanthus*. Over 300 varieties growing through woodland and in Victorian walled kitchen garden. Many doubles which multiply freely. February 'Snowdrop Spectacular', 'Snowdrops by Starlight' walk. Volunteer in exchange for accommodation and keep.

Cambo Estate, Scotland. (*Photo courtesy Sir Peter Erskine*)

Caprington Castle, Kilmarnock, Ayrshire, KA2 9AA
Tel. 07748 280036
Open for snowdrops and Scotland's annual Snowdrop Festival.

Castle Kennedy Gardens, Stranraer, Wigtownshire, Dumfries and Galloway, DG9
www.castlekennedygardens.co.uk
75 acres of extensively landscaped gardens. Guided snowdrop walks, lantern-lit snowdrop trail, talks, garden tours and sales.

Cluny House, Aberfeldy, Perthshire, PH15 2JT
Tel. 01887 820795
www.clunyhousegardens.com
Woodland garden with good displays of many different snowdrops.

Dalmeny House Estate, South Queensferry, EH30 9TQ
Tel. 0131 331 1888
www.dalmeny.co.uk
Snowdrops spreading across Mons Hill. Snowdrop day.

Dawyck Botanic Gardens, Stobo, Nr Peebles, Scottish Borders, EH45 9JU
Tel. 01721 760254
www.rbge.org.uk/the-gardens.dawyk
Stunning displays of flowers along Scrape Burn. Part of annual Snowdrop Festival.

Fingask Castle, Rait, Perthshire, PE2 7SA
Tel. 01821 670777
www.fingaskcastle.co.uk
Private garden open for snowdrops.

Finlaystone Country Estate, Renfrewshire, PA14 6TJ
Tel. 01475 540505
www.finlaystone.co.uk
Carpets of snowdrops through woodland. Ranger-guided walks, lantern-lit snowdrop trail.

Kailzie Gardens, Kailzie, Peebles, Scottish Borders, EH45 9HT
Tel. 01721 720007
www.kailziegardens.com

Finlaystone, Scotland. (*Photo courtesy David L. Finnis*)

Magnificent displays of snowdrops, especially in wild garden.

Pitumies Gardens, House of Pitumies, Guthrie by Forfar, Angus, DD8 2SN
Tel. 01241 828245
www.pitumies.com
Semi-formal walled gardens with masses of spring bulbs and snowdrops.

Royal Botanic Gardens, Inverleith Row, Edinburgh, EH3 5LR
Tel. 0131 248 2844
www.rbge.org.uk/snowdrops
70 acres of beautifully landscaped gardens with snowdrops, snowdrop events, lectures etc.

St Andrews Botanical Gardens, Canongate, St Andrews, Fife, KY16 8RT
Tel. 01334 476452
www.st-andrews-botanic.org
Hidden gem with wide range of plants including numerous snowdrops.

Torosay Castle and Gardens, Craignure, Isle of Mull, PA65 6AH
Tel. 01680 812421
www.torosay.com
Terraced gardens and mature woodland with snowdrops. Annual snowdrop events.

Where to Buy

UK Snowdrop Specialist Nurseries and Mail Order

Ashwood Nurseries,
Ashwood Lower Lane, Ashwood,
Kingswinford, West Midlands, DY6 0AE
www.ashwoodsnurseries.com

Avon Bulbs
Burnt House Farm, Mid-Lambrook,
South Petherton, Somerset, TA13 5HE
www.avonbulbs.com

Beggars Roost Plants
Lilstock, Bridgwater, Somerset, TA5 1SU
www.beggarsroostplants.co.uk

Beth Chatto Gardens and Nursery
Elmstead Market, Colchester,
Essex, CO7 7DB
www.bethchattoshop.co.uk

Bloms Bulbs UK
Primrose Nurseries, Melchbourne,
Bedfordshire, MK44 1ZZ
www.blomsbulbs.com

Broadleigh Gardens
Barr House, Bishops Hall, Taunton,
Somerset, TA4 1AE
www.broadleighbulbs.co.uk

Cambo Estates
Kingsbarns, St Andrews, KY16 8QD
www.cambosnowdrops.com

Cambridge Bulbs
40 Whittleford Road, Cambridge, CB2 5PH

Chiltern Seeds
Bortree Stile, Ulverston, Cumbria, LA12 7BP.
www.chilternseeds.co.uk (seeds only)

Colesbourne Gardens LLP
Estate Office, Colesbourne, Cheltenham,
Gloucestershire, GL53 9NP
www.colesbournegardens.co.uk

Crug Farm Nursery
Griffith's Crossing, Caernarfon,
Gwynedd, LL55 1TU
www.crug-farm.co.uk

Edrom Nurseries
Coldingham, Eyemouth, Berwickshire,
Scotland, TD14 5TZ
www.edrom-nurseries.co.uk

Elworthy Cottage Plants
Elworthy, Taunton, Somerset, TA4 3PX
www.elworthy-cottage.co.uk

Evenley Wood Garden
Evenley, Northamptonshire, NN13 5SH
www.evenleywoodgarden.co.uk

Fibrex Nursery Ltd
Honeybourne Road, Pebworth, Stratford
on Avon, Warwickshire, CV37 8XP
www.fibrex.co.uk

**Fieldgate Snowdrops
and Fieldgate Twin Scaling**
Kenilworth, Warwickshire

Field of Blooms
Ballymackey, Nenagh,
Co. Tipperary, Ireland
www.fieldofblooms.com

Foxgrove Plants
Foxgrove Farm, Skinners Green,
Enborne, Newbury, RG14 6RE
www.foxgroveplants.co.uk

Glen Chantry
Wickham Bishops, Witham,
Essex, CM8 3LG
www.glenchantry.demon.co.uk

Harvey's Garden Plants
Great Green, Thurston,
Bury St Edmunds, Suffolk, IP31 3SJ
www.harveysgardenplants.co.uk/
galanthus.asp

Judy's Snowdrops
19 Rugby Road, Long Lawford,
Rugby, Warwickshire, CV23 9DS
www.judyssnowdrops.co.uk
(mail order only)

Monksilver Nursery
Oakington Road, Cottenham,
Cambridge, CB24 8TW
www.monksilvernursery.co.uk

North Green Snowdrops
North Green Only, Stoven,
Beccles, NR34 8DG

Paul Christian Rare Plants
Orchard Nurseries, PO Box 468,
Wrexham, LL13 9XR
www.rareplants.co.uk

P. de Jager and Sons Ltd
Church Farm, Ulcombe,
Maidstone, Kent, ME17 1DN
www.dejager.co.uk

Pottertons Nursery
Moortown Road, Nettleton,
Caistor, Lincolnshire, LN7 6HX
www.pottertons.co.uk

Sarah Raven's Kitchen Garden Ltd.
2 Woodstock Court, Blenheim Road,
Marlborough, Wiltshire, SN8 4AN
www.sarahraven.com

Snape Cottage
Chaffeymoor, Bourton, Dorset, SP8 5BZ
www.snapecottagegarden.co.uk

The Snowdrop Company
Barn Cottage, Shilton, Oxfordshire

Thompson & Morgan
Poplar Lane, Ipswich, IP8 3BU
www.thompson-morgan.com

Timpany Nurseries
77 Magheratimpany Road, Ballynahinch,
Co. Down, Northern Ireland, BT24 8PA
www.timpanynurseries.com

Other Places to Buy and See Snowdrops

Netherlands

Bloms Bulbs Holland
Walter Blom and Zoon BV,
Hyacintheniaan 2, 2182 DE Hillegom
www.blomsbulbs.com

De Bolle Jist
Holdingawwei 6, 9053 LT Finkum

De Boschhoeve Garden and Nursery
Boschoeve 3, 6874 NB Wolfheze
www.boschhoeve.nl
Annual snowdrop festival and snowdrop
sales.

De Warande
Jan de Jager Road 2,
AN 6998, Low Keppel
www.dewarande.nl
Gardens and nursery with open days
and events.

The Hidden City Garden
Tuinontwerp, Groenadvies,
Assendorperstraat, 178, 8012 CE Zwolle
www.tuinharrypierik.nl.
Garden designer Harry Pierik's stunning
'Paradise' garden massed with trees,
shrubs and plants with large collection of
snowdrops. Open days and guided tours.

Belgium

Koen van Poucke
Heistraat 106, B 9110 Sint Niklaas
www.koenvanpoucke.be

Alpine Plantenkwekerij Cathy Porter
Margaret of Flanders Road 27, 8310
Cross Street, Bruges
www.alpenplanten.be
Snowdrop days and events.

**Kalmthout Arboretum
and Botanical Garden**
Heuval 2, Kalmthout, B-2920
www.arboretumkalmthout.be
Spectacular botanical garden begun in
1857, owned by Province of Antwerp.
World-renowned collection of
Hamamelis and Hamamelis festival.
Naturalized snowdrops.
Annual 'Snowdrop Show'.

Park van Beervelde
Beervelde-dorp 73, 9080 Beervelde
www.parkvanbeervelde.be
Special garden days and events,
including snowdrops.

**National Botanical Garden
of Belgium**
Nieuwelaan 38, 1860 Meisse
www.br.fgov.be
Large drifts of naturalized snowdrops.

France

B & T World Seeds (France)
Route des Marchandes, Paguignan,
34210 Olonzac
www.b-and-t-world-seeds.com

Germany

Garten in der Wiessen
Hagen Engelmann, Torgauerstrasse 11,
03 048 Cottibus
www.engelmannii.de
Garden, garden openings and specialist
collections including snowdrops.
Also sales.

Oirlicher Blumengarten
Oirlich 9, 41334 Nettetal, Hinsbeck
www.oirlicher-blumengarten.de
Private collection of over 200 different
snowdrops. Special snowdrop event
each year with numerous stands. Mail
order sales.

Staudenspezialgartnerei Jeutsch
Rayskistr 1, 01219 Dresden
www.staudengartnerei-enssner.de

USA

Temple Nursery
PO Box 591, Trumansburg, NY 14886
Probably the largest collection of
snowdrops in USA. Snowdrop events
and sales.

New Holland Bulb Co.
PO Box 134, Hooven, OH 45033
www.newhollandbulb.com
Small selection of snowdrops for sale.

Van Engelen
23 Tulip Drive, PO Box 638,
Bantam, CT 06750
www.vanengelen.com
Dutch bulb suppliers with USA nursery
and supplies.

Veseys
411 York Road, Highway 25,
York, E COA 1PO
www.veseys.com
Seed and plant supplier.

Bonnefont Garden
The Cloisters Museum and Garden, 99
Margaret Corbin Drive, Fort Tryon Park,
New York 10040
www.metmuseum.org
Branch of the Metropolitan Museum
with garden.

Edgwood Gardens
Exton, Pennsylvania
www.edgwoodgardens.net

Canada

Campbell River Garden Centre
673 Old Peterson Road, Campbell,
BC, V9W 3NA1
www.crgardencentre.com
Good range of plants and bulbs.

Van Noort Bulb Company
22264 Highway 10, Langley,
BC V2Y 2KG
www.vanoortbulb.com
Growers and wholesalers of high-quality
bulbs and plants.

Paridon Horticulture
5985 104 St. Rr 3, Delta, BC V4K 3N3
www.paridon.com
Wholesale and nursery suppliers.

Australia and Tasmania

Glenbrook Bulbs
28 Russell Road, Claremont, TAS 7011

Hillview Rare Plants
400 Huon Road, South Hobart,
TAS 7044
www.hillviewrareplants.com
Nursery specializing in rare and unusual
cool climate plants and bulbs.

Woodbank Nursery
2040 Huon Road, Longley, TAS 7150
Rare, exotic, unusual and native plants
and bulbs.

Bryan H. Tonkin
'Sylvan Vale', Olinda Creek Road,
Kalorama, VIC 3766
www.svnltd.com
Large range of unusual bulbs, corms
and perennials. High-quality plant
propagation.

Clover Hill Plants
PO Box 603, Kaloomba. NSW 2780
Specializing in woodland and hard-to-
find bulbs and plants.

Alpine Plant Society,
The Secretary, Ferny Creek Horticultural
Society, PO Box 172, Ferny Creek,
VIC 3786

Merry Garth
Davies Lane, Mount Wilson, NSW 2786
Garden open to the public with
collections of snowdrops and
snowflakes.

New Zealand

Blue Mountain Nurseries
99 Bushyhill Street, Tapanui 9775
www.bmn.co.nz

Hokonui Alpines
RD6, Gore 9776, Southland
http://users.actrix.co.nz/hokpines
Long-established, small, family nursery
specializing in alpines, small bulbs and
dwarf perennials.

Jury Gardens
589 Otaraoa Road, Waitara 4383
www.jury.co.nz
Open daily August–March. Good
displays of snowdrops July–August.

Maple Glen Gardens and Nursery
Wyndham Letterbox Road, Wyndham
www.mapleglen.co.nz
Spectacular gardens with huge drifts of
well established snowdrops in July and
August. Snowdrop sales. Open all year.

Plant Heritage Collection Holders of Galanthus

Mrs M. MacLennan, Byndes Cottage,
Pebmarsh, Halstead, CO9 2LZ
Lady C. Erskine, Cambo, Kingsbarns, St
Andrews, KY16 8QD
Mr S. Owen, 127 Stoke Road, Linslade,
Leighton Buzzard, LU7 25R

NPC Galanthus The Netherlands

Annie Fallinger, Rijksstraatweg 100,
3316 EH Dordrecht, Holland
www.nederlandse-plantencollecties.nl

CHAPTER 11

SNOWDROP DIRECTORY

Welcome to the world of snowdrops. Compiling a complete list is virtually impossible as new snowdrops are constantly being introduced and named, names can be changed, and certain snowdrops become extinct and no longer available.

Many snowdrops have been named but have rarely been seen by even highly experienced Galanthophiles, and they quite often disagree on what a particular snowdrop is or what it should look like. As this is an alphabetical list, names have been included in sequence, even when descriptions have been difficult or impossible to find. Slight variations in flowers and segment markings within the same named snowdrop also contribute to the difficulties of identification, and illustrations can only indicate the general appearance of the particular flower. Heights given are approximate as these can be affected by weather and growing conditions. I have tried to include the name of the originator of each snowdrop. This has not always been possible and to those whose names I have missed, I apologise.

A small number of names have yet to be registered or validly published according to the provisions of the Cultivated Plant Code. I have noted these where possible, and inclusion here should not be taken as establishing the name. However, it does indicate that the name is in use within the genus *Galanthus*, and such names should not therefore be used for any other clone.

'Abington Green'
(*elwesii* var. *elwesii*)
Rounded ovary, wide spreading segments. Leaves supervolute, attractive, spreading. Outer segments broad, well splayed, revealing inner marking. Inner segments mid-green slightly waisted, mark apex almost to base. Rev R.J. Blakeway-Phillips, Little Abington, Cambridgeshire, late 1970s. ↑21cm.

'Acton Pigot No 1'
(Hybrid cultivar)
Well shaped flowers, olive-green ovary. Leaves spreading, lax, flat or lightly explicative, pale-grey-glaucous. Outer segments rounded, clawed. Inner segments olive-green mark across segment, white margin. Regularly two scapes. Clumps up well. February–March. Margaret Owen, Acton Pigot, Shropshire, 1993. Similar to 'Acton Pigot No 2'. ↑22cm.

'Acton Pigot No 2'
(Hybrid cultivar)
Large, well shaped flowers, slightly shorter than 'Acton Pigot No 1'. Leaves lax, spreading, pale-grey-glaucous. Outer segments clawed. Inner segments olive-green mark, white margin. Regularly two scapes. Clumps up well. February–March. Margaret Owen, Acton Pigot, Shropshire, 1993. Similar to 'Acton Pigot No 1'. ↑19cm.

'Acton Pigot No 3'
(Hybrid cultivar)
Excellent. Full flowers well above foliage. Leaves low, lax, spreading. Outer segments large, broad, pointed. Inner segments strong mark across segment, fading towards base. Vigorous. Bulks up well. Early. Margaret Owen, Acton Pigot, Shropshire, 1993. Best of 'Acton Pigot' trio. ↑21cm.

'Ailwyn'
(Hybrid double)
Well shaped regular double. Leaves semi-erect. Outer segments slender, incurved margins. Inner segment ruff slender, spreading 'V' at apex, underside green lines to base Occasionally three unmarked segments in centre. January. Richard Nutt at Anglesey Abbey,

1994, named after Lord Fairhaven. *Elwesii* ancestry. ↑14cm.

'Aioli'

A snowdrop that is heard of but rarely seen. Said to have an unusually strong garlic odour.

'AJM 75'
(*reginae-olgae* subsp. *vernalis*)

Leaves striped, arching. Outer segments subrevolute, ridged, textured. Inner segments uniform small green 'U', rounded ends. Late. Alistair Marr, in Montenegro, former Yugoslavia, 1970. ↑16cm.

'Aladdin'

Elegant snowdrop, slender ovary. Leaves erect, blue-green. Outer segments long, pointed. Inner segments green mark across segment almost to base.

'Alan's Treat'
(*nivalis* Poculiformis Group)

Attractive, beautifully proportioned slender poculiform. Leaves applanate, blue-green. Outer segments fractionally longer than inner, green mark at apex. Inner segments good heart-shaped mark at apex. January–February. Normandy, France, 2003. Play on words for nurseryman Alan Street.

'Alanya Yayla'
(*elwesii*)

Outer segments long, pointed, lightly ridged, puckered. Inner segments 'X' mark filled in at base. Oirlicher Blumengarten, Germany.

'Albringhausen'
(*nivalis*)

'Alburgh Claw'
(*nivalis*)

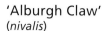

Unusual, highly variable, large spiky flowers with either regular or irregular segments. Leaves applanate, semi-erect, flat. Outer segments roughly three, narrow, pointed, variable merging green lines mainly at apex, sometimes to base. Inner segments narrow, pointed, smaller towards centre, green variable 'V' can extend to base. January–February. Robert Marshall, Alburgh, Suffolk, 1993. ↑12cm.

'Aldgate 16'

See 'Squire Burroughs'.

'Alex Duguid'
(*reginae-olgae* subsp. *vernalis*)

Distinctive, upright scape, attractive elongated flowers. Leaves semi-erect, slender, blue-green, glaucous, short at flowering. Outer segments long, slender. Inner segments 'U' or 'V' at apex. November–December, earlier than usual *G. reginae-olgae* subsp. *vernalis*. Originally 'Mr Duguid's Christmas-flowering snowdrop'. Named for former owner of Edrom Nurseries, 1998.

'Alexander the Great'
(*elwesii* var. *monostictus*)

Leaves erect, broad, grey-green. Outer segments rounded, pointed. Inner segments broad filled inverted 'U' at apex. RHS PC 2009.

'Alexandra' (*reginae-olgae*)

Sturdy shorter snowdrop. Leaves semi-erect, short at flowering. Outer segments textured. Inner segments clear inverted 'V' at apex, distinctive marking on underside with two blocks of green stripes apex–base. ↑15cm.

'Alice's Late' (*nivalis*)

Beautiful, late flowering *G. nivalis* with slender flowers. Leaves applanate, erect, dark blue-green. Inner segments inverted green 'V' at apex. Reliably flowers around a month later than other *G. nivalis*, well into March. Good Cornish variant thought to have originated on the Ince Estate, Cornwall, and named by Beggars Roost Nursery, Cornwall, although the name has not yet been officially validly published. March. ↑14cm.

'Alison Hilary'
(Hybrid cultivar)

Distinctive, upright single. Leaves arching, glaucescent. Outer segments slender, strongly clawed. Inner segments tubular, good 'H' or 'X' mark across three-quarters of segment, diffusing towards base. Vigorous. Grows well. February. Joe Sharman from Sutton Court garden, Herefordshire (former home of the Backhouse family), 1996, named after Alison Page, wife of owner. RHS PC 2006. ↑20cm.

'All Saints'

Erect scapes, curving spathes. Outer segments green mark at apex.

alpinus (species)

Syn. *G. caucasicus*
Southern Russia, north-eastern Turkey, Armenia, Azerbaijan, Georgia, possibly Iran. Leaves supervolute, erect or recurving, hooded, glaucous, conspicuous rib. Inner segments narrow 'U' or 'V' at apex. Named by D.J. Sosnowsky, Russian botanist, 1911. Rare in cultivation though should grow in UK. ↑9–16cm.

alpinus var. *alpinus* (subspecies)

Syn. *G. caucasicus*
Small snowdrop from mountains of Turkey and Russia. Leaves narrow, short at flowering. Inner segments small green inverted 'U' or 'V' at apex. January–March. Can be difficult and slow. ↑10–15cm.

alpinus var. *bortkewitschianus* (subspecies)

Syn. *G. bortkewitschianus*
North Caucasus.
Usually grows well, but increases slowly. Sterile. January–March. Named by J.I. Koss, Russian botanist, 1951, introduced late 1960s. ↑10–15cm.

'Altheia' (*nivalis*)

Leaves applanate, slender, arching, blue-green. Outer segments well shaped, bluntly pointed. Inner segments dark-green inverted 'V' at apex. February. ↑15cm.

'Amberglow'
(*elwesii* Hiemalis Group)

Unique with orange anthers glowing through inner segments. Leaves supervolute, erect, pale grey-green. Outer segments clawed. Inner segments olive-green 'U' to 'V' at apex. December–January. Phil Cornish at Longlevens, Gloucestershire, 1997. ↑15cm.

'Amigo'
(*reginae-olgae*)

Bright white flowers. Leaves applanate, slender, linear, green-grey. Outer segments long, incurved, slender. Inner segments broad dark-green inverted 'U' at apex. December–January. ↑12cm.

'Amy Doncaster'
(*plicatus*)

Popular, attractive *G. plicatus* clone (virused). Leaves arched, semi-erect. Outer segments clawed, puckered, green stripes towards apex. Inner segments broad heart-shaped green mark from apex paling towards base. Seedling from Amy Doncaster's Chandler's Ford garden, Hampshire, 1988, named for her. ↑13cm.

'Amy Jade'
(*plicatus*)

Elegant snowdrop with attractive flowers. Leaves explicative, grey-green, folded edges. Outer segments spoon-shaped. Inner segments large mid-green mark apex towards base. ↑17cm.

'Andrew Thorpe'
(*Sandersii* Group)

Yellow ovary and pedicel. Outer segments goffered at base. Inner segments inverted yellow 'U' to 'V' at apex.

'Angelfly'
(*nivalis*)

Well formed rounded flowers. Leaves applanate, blue-green. Outer segments green stripes lower third. Inner segment broad green inverted 'U' at apex, paler shading at base. January–February. Oirlicher Blumengarten, Germany, 2008.

'Angelina'
(*nivalis*)

Highly sought after. Large, weighty-looking, well shaped flowers. Leaves applanate, blue-green. Outer segments broad, pointed, large pale-green mark. Inner segments broad green mark above apex. January–February. Zlatco and Angelina Petrisevac, Croatia. ↑15cm.

'Angelique'
(*nivalis* Poculiformis Group)

Delicate, beautiful, almost full poculiform, inner segments fractionally shorter. Leaves applanate, blue-green. Outer segments long, slender, clawed. Inner segments two small green spots at apex, sometimes joined. Early. Mark Brown at M. Le Bellegard's garden, Rouen, France, 1995, named for his daughter. RHS PC 2007. ↑14cm.

'Angie'
(*nivalis* Hybrid double)

Neat double flowers. Leaves applanate, erect, slender, blue-green. Outer segments five or six, rounded, bluntly pointed. Inner segments small neat ruff, slim inverted 'V' at apex. Australian-raised selection from Otto Fauser. ↑12cm.

'Anglesey Abbey' (*nivalis*)

Variable, vigorous, free-flowering. Leaves applanate, semi-erect, glossy, bright-green. Outer segments three to five, tending to poculiform. Inner segments variable, either narrow green band, spot at apex, or no mark. February. Excellent. Formerly misidentified as *G. lagodechianus*. Graham Thomas at Anglesey Abbey, Cambridgeshire. ↑14cm.

'Anglesey Adder'

Leafy, split spathe. Outer segments long, broad, recurved margins, slender claw. Inner segments large waisted green mark across segment. Named for split spathe resembling adder's tongue. Anglesey Abbey, Cambridgeshire

'Anglesey Orange Tip' (*elwesii*)

Excellent 'orange' coloured snowdrop. Pale apricot-orange flushed segments with colour holding well. Outer segments slender, pointed. Inner segments broad inverted green 'U' at apex. Anglesey Abbey, Cambridgeshire, 2010. ↑15cm.

'Anglesey Rainbow'

Dark-green ovary. Segments varying between white or flushed orange. Anglesey Abbey, Cambridgeshire.

angustifolius (species)

Syn. *G. nivalis* subsp. *angustifolius* Southern Russia. Less well known. Rare in wild and cultivation. Leaves applanate, narrow, erect, curving, glaucous, conspicuous central line. Outer segments bluntly pointed. Inner segments green inverted 'U' or 'V' at apex. March–May. J.I. Koss, 1951. ↑14cm.

'Anika' (*nivalis*)

Good, robust, green-tipped *G. nivalis*. Leaves applanate, slender, erect, blue-green. Outer segments tipped green. Inner segments inverted 'V' at apex. January–February. David and Anke Way, Southover, Hunton, named after granddaughter.

'Anmarie Kee' (*reginae-olgae*)

Striking, outstanding snowdrop, inflated spathe. Leaves applanate, slender, flat-subrevolute. Outer segments acutely pointed, strong green mark at apex. Inner segments large broad inverted 'U' from apex to half of segment.

'Anne'

Outer segments pointed. Inner segments narrow green 'V' at apex, rounded ends. Named for Anne Johnson, snowdrop enthusiast at Bank Hall, Preston, where snowdrop originated.

'Anne of Geierstein' (Hybrid cultivar)

Beautiful, sought after. Well textured flowers. Leaves semi-erect, margins flat or lightly explicative, glaucescent. Outer segments thick, rounded, very white, with wide claw. Inner segments clasping, ridged, small spreading inverted green 'V' at apex, rounded ends. Late. William Thomson, Lanarkshire, probably named by James Allen. *G. plicatus* × *G. nivalis*. ↑17cm.

'Anne's Green Stripe' (*plicatus*)

See 'Castle Green Dragon'.

'Anne's Millenium Giant' (Hybrid cultivar)

Tall plants with well shaped, large rounded flowers on erect scapes. Leaves applanate, erect, slender, blue-green. Outer segments bluntly pointed, long claw. Inner segments narrow green inverted 'V' at apex. January. Anne Smith, 1999. ↑23cm.

'Annette'

'Atkinsii' type. No aberrant segments. Large bulbs, strong, erect scapes. Flowers well proportioned, slender. Outer segments well shaped, pointed. Inner segments shallow inverted 'V' at apex with upturned ends. Grows well. ↑10–20cm.

'Annielle' (*nivalis* Poculiformis proup)

A delicate and beautiful looking poculiform with erect scapes. Leaves applanate, erect, slender, blue-green. Six equally sized segments. ↑15cm.

'Appleby' (*nivalis*)

Small, flowers more delicate looking than standard *G. nivalis*. Leaves applanate, erect, slender, blue-green. Outer segments bluntly pointed. Inner segments green Chinese-bridge mark at apex. January–February. Hector Harrison, Appleby, Lincolnshire. ↑8cm.

'Appleby One '(*nivalis*)

Attractive snowdrop from the late Hector Harrison, Appleby, Lincolnshire, originally stocked by Potterton's Nursery in the 1990s.

'Appleby Spiky' (*nivalis*)

A spiky snowdrop raised by the late Hector Harrison, Appleby, Lincolnshire, originally stocked by Pottertons Nursery in the 1990s.

'April Fool' (*nivalis*)

Standard *G. nivalis* but later flowering than normal. Leaves applanate, erect, slender, blue-green. Outer segments slender, bluntly pointed. Inner segments green heart to inverted 'V' at apex. March. Tony Venison, Hertfordshire, early 1960s. ↑15cm.

'Armilde' (Hybrid double)

Double flower supported on erect scape with inflated spathe. Leaves applanate, erect, slender, blue-green. Outer segments long, pointed. Inner segment ruff green mark at apex. February. Netherlands. ↑12cm.

'Armine' (Hybrid cultivar)

Elegant, tall snowdrop with large, well proportioned flowers. Outer segments slender, rounded, clearly showing inner marking. Inner segments green spot either side of sinus, or horseshoe-shaped mark, wider green band or two spots at base which can be joined. Robust. Late. Easy. Good. Brig. and Mrs Matthias, Giant Snowdrop Company, Hyde Lodge, Gloucestershire, late 1950s, named by Herbert Ransom and E.B. Anderson for the Matthias's daughter. ↑22cm.

'Armistice Day' (*elwesii* Hiemalis Group)

Arching scapes, ovary tapering into pedicel. Leaves semi-erect, supervolute. Inner segments small inverted 'V' to heart-shape at apex. Variable flowering, usually mid-November. Norma Read, Pensford, Bristol, named for flowering around Armistice Day, 11 November. ↑13cm.

'Arnold' (*elwesii* var. *monostictus*)

Leaves upright, blue-green. Outer segments green-tipped. Inner segments single green mark at apex. Early. ↑15cm.

'Arnott's Seedling'
See 'S. Arnott'.

'Art Nouveau'
(*nivalis*)
Classic, beautiful flowers, pronounced curving spathe. Leaves applanate, erect, blue-green. Outer segments long, slender, pointed, pale-green marks at apex. Inner segments almost as long as outer, inverted 'V' to heart-shaped green mark at apex. January–February. Normandy, France. ↑14cm.

artjuschenkoae
Synonym for *G. transcaucasicus* but often still treated as separate plant. Leaves on *G. artjuschenkoae* applanate, and *G. transcaucasicus* supervolute. Small, elegant flowers. Outer segments slender, pointed. Inner segments tube-like, inverted green 'U' at apex. ↑8cm.

'Athenae'
(*elwesii* Hiemalis Group)
Very variable depending on weather conditions, which can badly affect flowers. Leaves supervolute, erect, small at flowering. Outer segments textured, ridged, clawed. Inner segments pale olive-green heart-shaped mark above small sinus. November–December. Broadleigh Gardens, Taunton, Somerset. ↑14cm.

'Atkinsii'
(Hybrid cultivar)

Outstanding, robust, tall classic snowdrop with elegant, pear-shaped flowers. Leaves upright, narrow, grey-green glaucous, lighter median stripe. Outer segments long, slender, pointed. Inner segments rounded 'V' at apex.

Occasional aberrant segments. Well perfumed. Bulks up well forming good drifts. January–February. James Atkins, Painswick, Gloucestershire, 1860s-70s, named by him c. 1891. RHS AM 1920. *G. nivalis* × *G. plicatus*. Similar clone has additional and aberrant segments, originally known as *G. imperati* var. Atkinsii of Backhouse, now 'James Backhouse'. *Also see* 'Moccas'. ↑20cm.

'Atkinsii of Finnis' (Hybrid)
Attractive, vigorous snowdrop with beautiful peardrop shaped flowers. January-February. Easy. Enjoys full sun or the protection of a south facing wall. Valerie Finnis.

Atkinsii 'Moccas Form'
See 'Moccas'.

'Audrey Vockins'
(*plicatus*)
Unusual albino with yellow ovary, yellow-green spathe and pedicel. Outer segments pointed, goffered at base. Inner segments rounded, white, no sinus. Named for Galanthophile Audrey Vockins.

'Augenschmaus'
Elegantly shaped flowers. Outer segments long, lightly longitudinally ridged, tapering to point at apex. Inner segments spreading mid-green inverted 'V' at apex. Garten in den Wiesen, Germany. English translation: 'Feast for the Eyes'.

'August'
(*elwesii* var. *monostictus*)
Well shaped Australian cultivar with good marks, named for its month of flowering in the southern hemisphere.

'Augustus' (*plicatus*)
Distinctive and handsome. Flowers large, globular, 'seersucker' looking (possibly from virus). Leaves lax,

plicate, short, broad, blue-green-yellow, paler midrib.Outer segments concave, rounded. Inner segments green 'H' to 'X' across segment. Vigorous. Grows, increases well. February–March. Named by Amy Doncaster for E.A. Bowles. RHS PC 1999. ↑15cm.

'Aunt Agnes'

Robust 'Trym' seedling. Leaves applanate, erect to arching, blue-green. Outer segments elegant, broad, rounded, good green mark above apex. Inner segments inverted heart to 'V' mark at apex above large sinus. Seedling from Olive Mason, Chaddesley Corbett, Warwickshire.

'Aurelia'
(Hybrid cultivar)
Large, heavy flowers which can weigh down slender scapes. Outer segments long, pointed. Inner segments green inverted 'V' at apex with rounded ends. January–February. Ray Cobb.

'Autumn Beauty'
(*elwesii* var. *monostictus*)
Very variable. Leaves supervolute, erect, matt, grey-green. Outer segments rounded, bluntly pointed. Inner segments variable mark at apex. September–October. Probably *G. elwesii* var. *monostictus* × *G. reginae-olgae*, but could be pure *G. elwesii* var. *monostictus*. Raised by Cambridge Alpines, 2009. It appears other snowdrops are also in circulation under this name, causing confusion. ↑15cm.

'Ayes and Noes' (*gracilis*)
Well shaped flowers. Leaves applanate, upright, grey-green. Inner segments marks at apex and base, can join. ↑12cm.

'Babraham'

Elegantly shaped, well rounded flowers. Outer segments rounded, pointed at apex. Inner segments green inverted 'V' at apex. *G. nivalis* × *G. plicatus*. ↑14cm.

'Babraham Dwarf' (*plicatus*)
Compact, neat plants. Rounded flowers, olive-green ovary. Leaves semi-erect, explicative, short at flowering. Inner segments tube-like, olive-green 'U' or 'V' at apex, rounded ends. Mid-February. Robin and Joan Grout, Babraham, Cambridgeshire, 1985.
G. plicatus with some *G. nivalis*. ↑8cm.

'Babraham Scented'
(Semi-double)
Well shaped semi-double flowers. Outer segments broad, bluntly pointed. Inner segment ruff, outer whorl flared at apex, variable roughly heart-shaped mark. Good perfume. Robin and Joan Grout, Babraham, Cambridgeshire, 1985. ↑12cm.

'Baby Arnott'
(Hybrid)
Similar to *G.* 'S. Arnott' but half the height. Leaves glaucescent. Outer segments, heavily textured, long, broad, rounded, clawed. Inner segments uniform inverted 'V' at apex, upturned ends. Herbert Ransom to Daphne Chappell, 1984. ↑15cm.

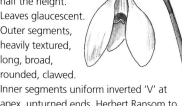

'Backhouse No 12'
See 'Mrs Backhouse No 12'.

'Backhouse Spectacles'
(Hybrid cultivar)
Syn. *G.* 'Mrs Backhouse Spectacles'
Undistinguished snowdrop. Similar to *G.* 'Atkinsii', flowering same time. Outer segments shorter, thicker, more rounded than *G.* 'Atkinsii' and no aberrant segments. Inner segment mark said to resemble spectacles. Early. Probably raised by Robert Ormston Backhouse, Sutton Court, Herefordshire, *c.* 1950s, but original hybrid possibly lost.

'Bagpuize Alexander'
(Hybrid cultivar)
Large, well shaped flowers. Leaves erect, variable flat-explicative margins, glaucescent. Outer segments bluntly pointed. Inner segments heart-shaped mark at apex diffusing towards base. Francis and Virginia Grant, Kingston Bagpuize, Oxfordshire, 2000, named after son. Probably *G. gracilis* × *G. plicatus*. ↑17cm.

'Bagpuize Virginia' (*nivalis*)
Neat, well formed double with scapes roughly same length as foliage. Leaves applanate, erect, subrevolute margins. Outer segments slender. Inner segments neatly tiered ruff, small expanded 'U' at apex. Virginia and Francis Grant, Bagpuize House, Oxfordshire, 2000. ↑17cm.

'Ballard'
Well shaped flowers. Outer segments bluntly pointed, goffered at base. Inner segments rounded mid-green inverted 'U' at apex.

'Ballard Green Hybrid'
(Hybrid cultivar)
Well shaped snowdrop with good green marked flowers. Helen Ballard.

'Ballard's No Notch'
Attractive plump, rounded flowers. Leaves broad, grey. January–February. Helen Ballard. ↑20cm.

'Ballerina'
(Hybrid double)
Attractive, sought-after shorter double. Neat, slightly upturned segments reminiscent of ballet dancer's tutu. Leaves erect, incurved margins. Outer segments pinched at apex, clawed. Inner segments inverted 'V' at apex, distinctive green lines at apex on underside.

Phil Cornish at Hatherly Manor, Twigworth, Gloucestershire, 1991. *G. elwesii* × *G. nivalis*. ↑12cm.

'Ballynahinch' (*nivalis*)
Smaller Irish *G. nivalis*. Leaves applanate, erect, blue-green. Inner segments small green inverted 'V' at apex. February–March. ↑10cm.

'Bankside' (*nivalis*)
Well shaped. Leaves applanate, erect, blue-green. Inner segments broad inverted 'V' at apex. An Alan Street introduction. ↑15cm.

'Barbara'
See *G.* 'Barbara's Double'.

'Barbara Buchanan's Late'
Smaller, late snowdrop. Slender flowers. Leaves erect. Outer segments longitudinally ridged, incurved margins. Inner segments olive-green heart-shaped mark above small sinus. ↑12cm.

'Barbara Dibley' (*nivalis*))
Leaves applanate, erect, blue-green. Well shaped flowers. Inner segments good green mark. January–February. Richard Nutt.

'Barbara Double'
See 'Barbara's Double'.

'Barbara's Double'
(Hybrid cultivar)
Syn. *G.* 'Barbara'
Attractive, neat, small double with rounded segments. Leaves spreading, narrowly explicative. Outer segments three, rounded, clawed. Inner segment ruff, well shaped symmetrical green inverted 'U' to 'V' at apex. Late. E.A. Bowles in Lady Beatrix Stanley's garden, Sibbertoft, 1944, named after her daughter. ↑10cm.

'Barbara's Hybrid' (Hybrid)
Tall, robust. Inner segments two marks. Early. Netta Stratham's garden, Erway, named by Cliff Curtis.

'Barguest' (*nivalis*)
Split spathe similar to 'Scharlockii' but

hooded. Leaves applanate, spreading, glaucous, lightly explicative base. Outer segments unmarked, occasional pale stain. Inner segments wide inverted 'U' at apex. Seedling discovered by Matt Bishop in former H.A. Greatorex's garden, Norfolk, 1996. ↑14cm.

Barnes (*elwesii* Hiemalis Group)
Flowers large, well shaped, rounded, long-lasting. Leaves supervolute, broad, erect, glaucous, developed at flowering. Outer segments large, rounded. Inner segment clear Chinese bridge-shaped mark. Light perfume. October–November, usually three weeks earlier than G. 'Earliest of All' and very similar. G. 'E.P. Barnes', from Barr Nursery, 1928, passed to Oliver Wyatt, The Old Manor, Naughton, Suffolk, c. 1960s–70s. Revd R.J. Blakeway-Phillips. ↑15cm.

'Baroness Ransonette' (*nivalis*)
Vigorous G. nivalis. Leaves applanate, erect, blue-green. Outer segments slender, elongated. January–February. Garden in the Salzkammergut, Austria. ↑17cm.

'Basalflecken' (*nivalis*)
Elegant flowers. Outer segments long, slender, pointed. Inner segments inverted green 'V' from apex to almost half of segment, two diffused marks towards base. Germany.

'Baxendale's Late' (*plicatus*)
Reliable, vigorous with attractive smaller flowers. Leaves plicate, erect, glossy, abundant. Outer segments rounded at apex. Inner segments large olive-green mark at apex diffusing slightly on basal side. Mid-late March. Leo Baxendale c. 1970s, distributed by Philip Ballard as G. 'Baxendale's Late'. ↑23cm.

'Baylham' (Hybrid)
Attractive neat double. Erect scapes, small ovary. Outer segments reflex displaying inner mark. Inner segments ruff, neat whorls, broad pale-green mark from apex towards base. Grows well. Strong perfume. Named after Suffolk village, c. 1998. G. nivalis × G. plicatus. ↑13cm.

'Baytop 34474' (*rizehensis*)
Large, robust, upright. Leaves splayed, usually three, very broad, variable margins. Outer segments clawed. Inner segments flared at apex, broad inverted 'U', fainter in centre. Usually two scapes from established bulbs. Professor Turhan Baytop, 1976. ↑14cm.

'Beany' (*elwesii* var. *elwesii*)
Outstanding green-tipped snowdrop with large, rounded flowers. Leaves supervolute, broad, erect, grey-green. Outer segments boat-shaped, pointed, merging green lines at apex. Inner segments broad green inverted 'U' at apex. ↑17cm.

'Beatrice' (*elwesii* var. *elwesii*)
Leaves supervolute, erect, broad, grey-green. Outer segments well rounded. Inner segments good 'Y' or 'X' mark across three-quarters of segment. Late. Matt Bishop in Plymouth garden, 1990, named after his great-grandmother Beatrice Popplestone. ↑21cm.

'Beechwood' (*elwesii*)
Small, short snowdrop with shapely rounded flowers. Leaves broad, erect, grey-green. Outer segments green at apex. Inner segments separate apical and basal marks. David and Ruby Baker, Surrey, 1995. ↑10cm.

'Beenak' (*elwesii* var. *monostictus*)
Australian selected cultivar.

'Bellacorolla'
See 'Sally Wickenden'.

'Belle de Waollonie' (*nivalis* Sharlockii Group)
Slim, delicate-looking flowers, split spathe. Leaves applanate, erect, blue-green. Outer segments long, slender, broad pale-green mark at apex. Inner segments broad inverted 'V' at apex, wide ends. January–February. ↑10cm

'Belle Etoile'
Highly unusual, almost poculiform double. Numerous variable, long, slender segments marked green at the apex and base. Slow. February. Belgium. ↑12cm.

'Beloglavi' (*nivalis*)
Very slender yellow. Ovary long, slender, pale yellow-green. Leaves applante, erect, grey-green. Outer segments slender, pointed. Inner segments inverted yellow-green 'V' at apex. February. ↑12cm.

'Benhall Beauty' (Hybrid cultivar)
Tall, old cultivar. Elegant long flowers, long ovary. Leaves erect-arching, flat to lightly explicative, blue-glaucous, well developed at flowering. Outer segments clawed, rounded at apex. Inner segments inverted 'V' at apex, one or two lighter green basal marks. Sometimes second scape. February. John Gray's garden, Benhall, Suffolk, named by E.A. Bowles, 1961. Possible G. elwesii ancestry. ↑23cm.

'Benthall Beauty'
See 'Benhall Beauty'.

'Benton Magnet' (*nivalis* hybrid)
Prolific, slightly shorter than G. 'Magnet' but similar markings. Leaves applanate, erect, flat or lightly explicative margins, glaucous. Outer segments bluntly pointed. Inner segments clasping, fuzzy yellowish-green inverted 'V'

with rounded ends at apex. John Morley, the late Sir Cedric Morris's garden, Benton End, Suffolk, 1982. ↑13cm.

'Berkeley'

Shapely flowers, dark green ovary, erect scape. Outer segments long, light longitudinal ridging, bluntly pointed, merging green lines. Inner segments solid inverted 'V' at apex to three-quarters of segment.↑15cm.

'Bernard Röllich'
(Hybrid double)

Good, neat, regular double. Outer segments three. Inner segment ruff with narrow inverted 'V' at apex, second mark towards base. ↑15cm.

'Bertha'

G. 'Trym' cross. Outer segments broad, paddle-shaped, bright-green mark above apex. Inner segments variable green mark at apex spreading towards base. G. 'Trym' × G. 'Hill Poe'. ↑18cm.

'Bertram Anderson'
(Hybrid cultivar)

Impressive, large, G. 'Mighty Atom' group. Flowers large, rounded, well shaped, textured. Leaves erect, broad, flat-explicative, glaucous. Outer segments small, broad claw. Inner segments inverted 'U' to 'V' at apex, paling at upper edge. Sometimes second scape. Vigorous. Seedling from E.B. Anderson's Gloucestershire garden, selected by Christopher Brickell and Eliot Hodgson, 1971, named for Anderson. RHS AM 1996. ↑25cm.

'Berwick' (plicatus)

Handsome plant with large flowers. Leaves erect, blue-green, paler median stripe. Outer segments slender, pointed, light longitudinal ridging. Inner segments slender deep filled-in 'V' at apex. ↑25cm.

'Bess' (Hybrid cultivar)

Popular, large, attractive. Leaves semi-erect, variable margins, glaucescent. Outer segments long, incurved, slightly crinkled, clawed. Inner segments longitudinally incurved, broad inverted 'V' at apex, slightly upturned. Vigorous. Daphne Chappell from Helen Milford's garden, 1990, named after the late Bess Milford.↑26cm.

'Beth Chatto'
(plicatus subsp. byzantinus)

Attractive, well shaped, rounded flowers. Leaves lax, light-green, glaucous median stripe. Outer segments rounded, clawed. Inner segments narrow green inverted 'V' at apex. Late. Beth Chatto Garden, Colchester, Essex, late 1960s, named by Graham Stuart Thomas. ↑16.5cm.

'Betty Fraser' (Hybrid)

Distinctive Irish snowdrop with large flowers. Outer segments elongated, flaring in warmth. Bulks up well, quickly. Betty Fraser's garden.

'Betty Hamilton'
(nivalis × plicatus)

Elegant flowers with distinctive marking suspended from slender pedicels. Outer segments long claw. Inner segments thin inverted 'V' at apex, oval towards base. Ian Christie, Brechin Castle, Angus, Scotland. ↑12cm.

'Betty Hansell' (Hybrid double)

Good, vigorous, regular double. Leaves supervolute, erect, hooded apex. Outer segments rounded, incurved, pinched at apex, merging green lines. Inner segments rarely aberrant, roughly 'X' shaped mark, sometimes divided longitudinally. Robert Marshall, near Hainford, Norfolk, 1994, named for aunt.↑19cm.

'Betty Page'

Small plants, large flowers. Outer segments well rounded, bluntly pointed, clawed. Inner segments green 'V' at apex, oblong mark towards base. March. ↑10cm.

'Big Bertha' (elwesii)

Tall, rounded flowers. Fast growing. September onwards. Gill Richardson.

'Big Bopper' (plicatus)

Large, attractive, well rounded flowers. Outer segments broad, bluntly pointed. Inner segments broad green inverted 'U' at apex. ↑20cm.

'Big Boy' (elwesii var. elwesii)

Beautiful and special. Very large, eye-catching flowers. Leaves supervolute, erect, broad, blue-green. Outer segments very long, large, tapering towards apex, variable inconsistent light green lines at apex. Inner segments solid, deep-green mark apex to base, narrow white margin, minute sinus. Difficult. Alan Street at Frinton-on-Sea, Essex, 1994. ↑20cm.

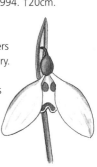

'Big Eyes'

Beautiful rounded flowers beneath dark-green ovary. Outer segments bluntly pointed. Inner segments rounded inverted 'V' at apex, two 'eye' dots towards base. ↑16cm.

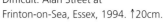

'Bill Baker's Early' (*elwesii*)

Well shaped flowers, erect scapes, inflated spathes. Leaves supervolute, broad, grey-green. Outer segments broad, rounded. Inner segments inverted broad mid-green 'U' at apex, slightly bleeding on basal side. ↑18cm.

'Bill Baker's Green Tipped' (*elwesii* Hiemalis Group)

Syn. *G.* 'Bill's Green-Tipped'
Tall, vigorous, notably early. Distinctive slender ovary. Leaves supervolute, broad, erect to arching. Outer segments variable green stripes from apex. Inner segments short, 'U' to heart-shaped green mark at apex, small sinus. Side shoot with single leaf can flower. December. Seedling from Bill Baker's garden, Tidmarsh, Berkshire. ↑18cm.

'Bill Baker's Large' (*elwesii*)

Large shapely flowers, erect scapes. Outer segments pointed at apex. Inner segments broad inverted mid-green 'U' at apex. ↑30cm.

'Bill Bishop' (Hybrid cultivar)

Syn. *G.* 'Picton's Mighty Atom'
Lovely, large, elegant, *G.* 'Mighty Atom' type similar to *G.* 'Bertram Anderson'. Leaves semi-erect, neatly folded, blue-grey. Outer segments large, long, slender, strongly clawed. Inner segments uniform dark-green 'V' at apex, paler upper edge. Flowers often weighed to ground. January–February. Bill Bishop's garden, Herefordshire, named by Christopher Brickell, 1998. RHS AM 1999. ↑22cm.

'Bill Boardman' (Hybrid cultivar)

Attractive flowers with yellow inner segment marks.

'Bill Clark' (*plicatus*)

Well shaped flowers beneath yellow ovary. Leaves splayed, pale to mid-green, channelled. Outer segments pointed. Inner

segments yellow inverted filled in 'U' at apex, small-white notch. Named after Bill Clark, warden at Wandlebury Ring, 1987. Better than other yellows from Wandlebury Ring after *G.* 'Wendy's Gold'. ↑20cm.

'Billingshurst' (Hybrid cultivar)

Syn. *G.* 'Billingshurst Lime'
Elegant with long scape, large, well shaped flowers, long, arching pedicel, slim olive-green ovary. Leaves semi-erect, flat to subrevolute, pale-green to glaucous. Outer segments bluntly pointed, puckered. Inner segments good inverted 'V', two separate paler marks at base joined by light shadow. Late. Michael Baron at Sotheby's garden, Summer's Place, Billingshurst, West Sussex, 1993. ↑15cm.

'Bill's Green-Tipped'

See 'Bill Baker's Green-Tipped'.

'Bishop's Mitre' (*nivalis* Scharlockii)

Very distinctive but elusive *G.* 'Scharlockii'. Short scape, split spathe, extremely long pedicel. Leaves applanate, erect blue-green. Outer segments long, slender, merging green lines at apex. Inner segments inverted 'U' at apex. Matt Bishop in H.A. Greatorex's former garden, Brundall, Norfolk. ↑9cm.

'Bitton' (*nivalis*)

Sturdy, small, with strong scapes, curved spathe and yellow-green ovary. Leaves applanate, lighly explicative, blue-green. Inner segments broad olive-green inverted 'U'. Early. Probably Canon Ellacombe's garden, Bitton Rectory, Bristol. ↑12cm.

'Blackthorn' (Sandersii Group)

Smaller snowdrop with peardrop-shaped flowers. Yellow ovary, yellow-green spathe. Leaves applanate, erect, yellow-green. Outer segments slender, long, rounded. Inner segments narrow yellow 'V' at apex. February. ↑8cm.

'Blaris'

Chunky, rounded flowers, well shaped segments. Outer segments broad, pointed. Inner segments inverted 'V' at apex, slightly staining outwards.

'Blasses Wesson'

Slender flowers, pale green ovary. Leaves erect, grey-green. Inner segments narrow inverted green 'U' at apex, broader ends. Germany. English translation: 'Pale Beings'. ↑12cm.

'Blewbury'

Well rounded flowers, large green ovary. Outer segments rounded, bluntly pointed, lightly ridged. Inner segments broad inverted green 'V' at apex.

'Blewbury Tart' (*nivalis*)

Curious small double with twisted, green, upward-facing flowers. Leaves applanate, grey-green. Outer segments slender, pointed, merging green lines from apex, shading towards base, shadowed on underside. Inner segments slightly reflexed, uneven, heavily marked green. Sometimes two scapes. Flowers well. January. Alan Street, Blewbury, Oxfordshire, 1975. ↑13cm.

'Blithe Spirit' (*nivalis*)

Attractive, well shaped flowers. Leaves applanate, slender, erect to arching, blue-green. Outer segments pointed, long slender claw. Inner segments light longitudinal ridging, green inverted 'V' at apex, upturned ends, narrowly joining oval towards base. January–February. ↑15cm.

'Blonde Inga' *(nivalis)*
See 'Blonde Inge'.

'Blonde Inge' *(nivalis)*
Initially similar to any small *G. nivalis*, then ovary pales and markings yellow, with yellow pedicel immediately behind ovary. Leaves applanate, semi-erect, slightly explicative. Inner segments yellow inverted 'V' at apex, sometimes dull. Difficult, or grows and bulks up well. January–February. Nicolas Top in a churchyard, Cologne, Germany, 1990s. ↑16cm.

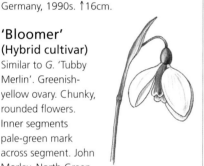

'Bloomer' *(Hybrid cultivar)*
Similar to *G.* 'Tubby Merlin'. Greenish-yellow ovary. Chunky, rounded flowers. Inner segments pale-green mark across segment. John Morley, North Green, Norfolk, 1990. ↑12cm.

'Blue John' *(reginae-olgae* subsp. *vernalis)*
Rare. Brilliant white, long flowers. Leaves lax, spreading, strong blue, contrasting silver median line. Inner segments strong green mark. Very early. John Morley, North Green Snowdrops.

'Blue Peter' *(reginae-olgae* subsp. *vernalis)*
Rounded flowers. Leaves applanate, grey-green, paler median stripe. Outer segments broad, rounded, pointed. Inner segments inverted 'V' at apex. John Morley, North Green Snowdrops.

'Bob Nelson' *(elwesii* var. *monostictus)*
Australian-raised cultivar.

'Bobette' *(elwesii* var. *elwesii)*
Large, balloon-like flowers, strong, erect scapes. Leaves supervolute, erect-arching, broad, grey-green. Outer segments well rounded, variable small green mark at apex. Inner segments scissor-shaped mark across segment, or separate marks at apex and base. Peter Nijssen, Heemsteede, Netherlands, late 1990s. ↑18cm.

'Bohemia Gold' *(nivalis)*
Rare and desirable. Unusual golden ovary and inner segment marks. North Green Snowdrops, Suffolk, from seed from a friend's woodland in Prague, 1990s.

'Bohemia Skirt' *(nivalis* Poculiformis Group)*
Attractive, elegant flowers on erect scapes. Leaves applanate, blue-green. Segments slender, white, not always of uniform length.

'Bohemia White' *(nivalis)*
Syn. *G.* 'Snow White' Small-white albino. Leaves applanate, lax, arched. Inner segments furrowed, generally pure white, occasional pale-green mark at apex, unusual among albinos with short, narrow green lines at apex on underside instead of apex to base. Wolfgang Kletzing, Czech Republic, 1990. Originally *G.* 'Snow White', renamed as already applied. ↑14cm.

'Bolu Shades' *(plicatus)*

'Boschhoeve' *(woronowii)*
Outer segments full, rounded, longitudinally ridged, flaring upwards, variable mark at apex, roughly two blotches joined by narrow line. Inner segments

broad inverted 'U' to 'V' at apex. Valentin Wijnen, Belgium. Similar to *G.* 'Cider with Rosie', slightly better. ↑10cm.

'Bowles' Large' *(plicatus)*
Well formed plicate, though not that large. Leaves plicate, grey-green, paler median stripe. Outer segments lightly ridged and dimpled. Inner segments pale-green inverted 'U' or 'V' at apex. February–March. Introduced by E.A. Bowles, Myddelton House.

'Bowles' Late' *(plicatus)*
Leaves plicate, grey-green, edges folded under. Inner segments pale-green inverted 'U' or 'V' at apex. February–March. ↑18cm.

'Boyd's Double' *(nivalis)*
Syns. *G.* 'Boyd's Green', *G.* 'Boyd's Green Double', *G.* 'Double Green', *G.* 'Green Horror'. The first spiky. Rare but constant. Spiky, upright flowers resembling shaving brush. Ovary small, wrinkled. Leaves applanate, erect, mid-green to glaucescent. Segments narrow, flattened, untidy, heavily marked green. Outer segments slightly larger, marked green, paling towards base. Inner segments similar, roughly inverted 'U' mark. Slow. William Boyd at Miss Russell's garden, Ashiestiel, Berwickshire, pre-1905. Named by Richard Nutt, 1970. ↑9cm.

'Boyd's Green'
See 'Boyds Double'.

'Boyd's Green Double'
See 'Boyd's Double'.

'Brenda Troyle' *(Hybrid cultivar)*
Popular old hybrid, *G.* 'S. Arnott' lookalike. Flowers large, rounded. Leaves narrow, grey-blue-glaucous. Outer segments

rounded, bluntly pointed. Inner segments broad green inverted 'V' at apex. Well perfumed. Easy, reliable. January–February. Origins confusing, possibly Ireland. Classed as *G. plicatus* seedling by Sir William Lawrence, first president of Alpine Garden Society, although spelt 'Brenda Troil'. RHS AM 1960. ↑20cm.

'Brian Mathew'
(elwesii)
Very large, well shaped flowers. Leaves erect, broad, grey-green. Outer segments boat-shaped, pointed. Inner segments mid-green mark apex almost to base, narrow white margin. ↑15cm.

'Brian Spence' (nivalis)
Small, delicate with well shaped flowers. Leaves applanate, erect, blue-green. Outer segments well shaped, slender. Inner segments rounded inverted 'V' at apex. January–February. ↑10cm.

'Bridesmaid'
(Poculiformis Group)
Tall, vigorous, first poculiform hybrid recorded. Large, beautifully shaped flowers. Leaves applanate, erect, flat to lightly explicative, glaucescent. Outer segments clawed. Inner segments incurved. Daphne Chappell in James and Alison Page's garden, Sutton Court, Herefordshire, 1994. Possibly *G. nivalis* × *G. plicatus*. ↑17cm.

'Brigadier Mathias'
(elwesii)
Triangular flowers. Leaves erect, slender, blue-green. Outer segments pointed, slender claw at base. Inner segments inverted 'V' at apex, rounded ends. Brigadier Mathias, wife Winifred and daughter Armine, of the Giant Snowdrop Company, all had snowdrops named after them.

'Bright Eyes'
Outer segments boat-shaped, narrow claw. Inner segments broad inverted 'V' at apex, paler mark towards base.

'Britta' (nivalis)
Rounded flowers. Leaves applanate, erect, blue-green. Outer segments pointed. Inner segments variable marks from small to none. ↑10cm.

'Britten's Kite'
(plicatus)
Beautiful large flowers. Leaves attractive, erect to arching, green-glaucous. Outer segments elongated, pointed. Inner segments olive-green mark resembling two adjacent skittles. December–January. ↑20cm.

'Broadwell' (elwesii)
Handsome. Large elegant flowers, erect scapes. Leaves supervolute, broad, pointed, grey-green. Outer segments boat-shaped, lightly ridged, clawed, small green mark at apex. Inner segments inverted 'V' thinly joining broad, upright filled in 'U' towards base. ↑20cm.

'Brocklamont Seedling'
(plicatus)
Attractive neat Irish double. Narrow ovary tapering into pedicel. Outer segments long, slender, spreading. Inner segments neat ruff, large mid-green mark from apex paling towards base.

'Bruce Lloyd'
(Hybrid cultivar)
Handsome flowers. Outer segments rounded, pointed at apex, light longitudinal ridging. Inner segments 'X' mark filled in at base.

'Bryan Hewitt'
(plicatus Poculiform)
Attractive, well shaped poculiform with slender, rounded, all-white segments. Myddelton House, Enfield, former home of E.A. Bowles.

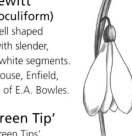

'Buck's Green Tip'
See 'Pusey Green Tips'.

'Bunch' (nivalis)
Spiky *G. nivalis* with well shaped flowers. Leaves applanate, slim, erect, blue-green. Numerous long, narrow, incurved segments, generally white, green marking on underside. January–February. Joe Sharman, Scotland. ↑10cm.

'Bungee' (nivalis)
Beautiful snowdrop. Slender ovary, unusually long slender pedicel creating delicate movement. Outer segments, long, slender, bluntly pointed. Inner segments green inverted 'V' at apex, rounded ends. January–February. Phil Cornish at Colesbourne, Gloucestershire, 1995. ↑12cm.

'Bushmills'
(Hybrid cultivar)
Triangular-shaped flowers, erect scapes. Leaves broad, grey-green. Outer segments broad, rounded, goffered claw. Inner segments slightly waisted green mark from apex to two-thirds of segment. ↑18cm.

'Butt's Form' (ikariae)
Good, robust with large, well shaped flowers. Inner segments half covered by dark green mark. Strong grower. Naturalizes, bulks up, seeds well. February–March. Probably from Walter Butt, Hyde Lodge, Gloucestershire, *c.* 1960s. ↑10cm.

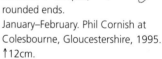

'By Gate' (elwesii)

Large flower suspended from long pedicel. Leaves broad, grey-green. Outer segments, slender, light longitudinal ridging, pointed. Inner segments green inverted 'U' at apex. ↑20cm.

'Byfield Special' (Hybrid cultivar)

Large, delicate-looking, well rounded flowers, strong scapes, long slender pedicels. Leaves semi-erect, flat to lightly explicative, glaucescent. Outer segments strongly clawed, bluntly pointed. Inner segments ridged, spreading inverted 'V' at apex. Grows well. February. Andy Byfield, 1991. ↑24cm.

'Byrkeley' (elwesii)

See 'Berkeley'.

byzantinus

See G. plicatus subsp. byzantinus.

cabardensis

Syn. G. transcaucasicus
Now synonym of G. lagodechianus but some growers still maintain difference. Leaves blue-green. Flowers good white, textured. Inner segments small green inverted 'V' at apex. February. ↑18cm.

'Calabria' (reginae-olgae)

'Cambo Estate' form (nivalis Sandersii Group)

See 'Lowick'.

'Cambridge' (reginae-olgae subsp. reginae-olgae)

Robust autumn snowdrop. Leaves short at flowering. Outer segments ridged, textured. Inner segments green inverted 'U' at apex, large for G. reginae-olgae. Wallflower perfume. Difficult or prolific.

University of Cambridge Botanical Garden, 1960s/70s, from bulbs collected in Corfu. RHS AM 1989. ↑14cm.

'Canadian Winter' (elwesii)

Vigorous, tall, Canadian hybrid. Leaves supervolute, broad, grey-green. Outer segments long, spoon-shaped, bluntly pointed, long slender claw. Inner segments broad dark-green inverted 'V' at apex narrowly joining large, deep green mark towards base. Barbara Flynn, Canada, c. 2002. ↑35cm.

'Carina' (nivalis)

Well shaped regular G. nivalis 'Flore Pleno' double, sometimes four outer segments. Leaves applanate, erect, slender, blue-green. Outer segments large, rounded, bluntly pointed, sometimes four, not consistent. Inner segments green marks at apex on inner whorls. January–February. ↑15cm.

'Caroline' (plicatus × nivalis)

Well shaped flowers, erect scapes. Leaves erect, blue-green. Outer segments long, spoon-shaped. Inner segments broad straight-sided 'V' at apex. Frequently two flowers when established. January–February. Bill Clark.

'Carolyn Elwes' (elwesii)

Good, distinctive yellow. Yellow ovary and spathe. Leaves supervolute, erect, two or three. Outer segments occasional yellow marks at apex. Inner segments flared at apex, inverted uniform yellow 'V' joining larger mark to base. Colesbourne, Gloucestershire, 1983. ↑14cm.

'Carpathian Giant' (nivalis)

Good, vigorous, large-flowered G. nivalis form. Leaves applanate, erect, blue-green.

Inner segments inverted 'V' at apex. Free flowering. Eastern Carpathian mountains, c. 1978. Originally called G. 'Maxima' but name already applied so renamed. ↑18cm.

'Carpenter's Shop'

See 'Carpentry Shop'.

'Carpentry Shop' (Hybrid cultivar)

Poorer, slimmer G. 'Atkinsii' type. Outer segments slender. Inner segments inverted green 'V' at apex. Oliver Wyatt seedling, Maidwell Hall, 1950s–60s, found near carpentry shop. ↑18cm.

'Caspar'

Tall, erect, well shaped slender flowers. Outer segments long, bluntly pointed. Inner segments small green heart-shaped mark at apex, two smaller 'eye' dots mid-way to base. Australian selected hybrid.

'Cassaba' (elwesii)

Name confusingly applied to numerous snowdrops. Among others, firstly to G. elwesii plants from Cassaba (now Turgutlu), Turkey, Edward Whittall, late 1800s; later to a G. gracilis in bulbs collected near Izmir by Colin Mason, now called G. 'Yamanlar'.

'Cassalia'

See 'Cassaba'.

'Castle Green'

Tiny plants. Large flowers, inflated spathes. Leaves broad, green, paler median stripe. Outer segments long, slender, recurved margins, pointed at apex. Inner segments green mark apex to base, narrow white border. ↑8cm.

'Castle Green Dragon' (plicatus)

Syn. G. 'Anne's Green Stripe'
Very rare, desirable virescent plicatus seedling with bell-shaped flowers. Outer segments similar to G. 'Cowhouse Green'. Inner segments green mark across segment. Ian Christie, Brechin Castle, Angus, Scotland, named after green dragon on castle flag. ↑15cm.

'Castle Plum' (plicatus hybrid)

Plum-shaped flower, particularly in bud. Outer segments long, rounded. Inner segments slender green mark. Early. Ian

Christie, Brechin Castle, Angus, Scotland.
↑15cm.

'Castlegar'
(Hybrid cultivar)
Elegant Irish snowdrop with
sturdy scapes and small
pendant flowers.
Leaves applanate,
erect, grey, central
median stripe, usually
absent at flowering.
Inner segments
tube-like, spreading
inverted 'V' at apex.
Often second scape.
November–January.
Woodland, Mahon Estate,
Castlegar, Co. Galway. ↑15cm.

caucasicus of gardens
Large flowers. Leaves broad, green. Inner
segments distinctive horseshoe mark at
apex. February–March. Name mistakenly
used for single-marked G. elwesii var.
monostictus. ↑15cm.

'Cedric's Prolific'
(elwesii)
Handsome, distinctive.
Leaves grey, acutely
pointed. Outer
segments small
green lines at apex.
Inner segments, good deep 'V' to 'X'
shaped green mark. Bulks up well,
quickly. Ideal for naturalizing. Seedling
from Cedric Morris's garden, Benton
End, named by Beth Chatto. ↑15cm.

'Celadon' (plicatus)
Elegant, scarce. Leaves
pale-green, dull, glaucescent.
Outer segments textured.
Inner segments flared,
pale-green inverted 'U'
to 'V' at apex, separate
mark fading to base,
can be joined. Amy
Doncaster selected
seedling, Chandlers' Ford garden,
named as colour reminiscent of
Celadon porcelain. ↑17cm.

'Celia Blakeway-Phillips'
(Hybrid cultivar)
Slender, rounded flowers, olive-green
ovary. Leaves semi-erect, channelled, flat to
lightly explicative, glaucescent. Outer

segments long, slender. Inner segments
olive-green heart-shaped mark at apex
diffusing towards and shadowed at base.
January–March. R. Blakeway-Phillips, Little
Abington, Cambridgeshire, late 1980s,
named for youngest daughter. ↑16cm.

'Celia Sawyer' (Hybrid cultivar)
Attractive. Large, triangular
flowers. Leaves semi-erect to
arching, spreading, glaucous.
Outer segments substantial,
pear-shaped. Inner
segments clasping,
slightly waisted mark
across segment
diffusing towards
base. Violet perfume. Early. John
Grimshaw in University of Oxford Botanic
Garden, 1992, named for Celia Sawyer in
charge of area. Good G. plicatus × G. gracilis.
↑17cm.

'Ceri Roberts' (nivalis)
Similar to, if not the same as, G. 'Lady
Elphinstone', although segments generally
regular. Leaves applanate. Netta Sharman,
Welsh hedgerow, 1996. See also G. nivalis
'Netherhall Yellow'. ↑15cm.

'Chadwick's Cream' (nivalis)
Pale-green ovary, yellow-green pedicel,
rounded flowers. Leaves applanate, lax.
Outer segments broad, cream, maturing
white. Inner segments small inverted 'V' at
apex. January–February. Nigel Chadwick,
Hainford, Norfolk, 1993. ↑9cm.

'Chandler's Green Tip'
(ikariae)
Unusually shaped flowers,
slender ovary, erect scapes.
Leaves, arching-lax, shiny,
broad, bright-green.
Outer segments
elongated, swept out
at apex with
prominent merging
green lines. Inner segments
broad inverted green 'U'
from apex to half of segment. ↑16cm.

'Chantry Green Twins' (elwesii)
Attractive snowdrop with elegant, slender
flowers. Mature scapes produce two perfect
flowers. Leaves broad, erect, green. Outer
segments pointed, dark green marks at apex.
Inner segments broad heart-shaped green
mark. Wol and Sue Staines, Glen Chantry.

'Charles Wingfield'
Elegant, well textured
flowers. Outer segments
bluntly pointed, slender
claw, lightly ridged,
textured. Inner segments
long broad inverted 'U' from apex to
half of segment. ↑20cm.

'Charlotte' (nivalis)
Attractive small G. nivalis, usually
with an extra segment. Leaves
applanate, erect, blue-green.
Inner segments mid-green inverted 'V' at
apex. February–March. Netherlands. ↑10cm.

'Charlotte Jean'
(nivalis Poculiformis Group)
Beautiful poculiform with long
split spathe. Well shaped flowers.
Leaves applanate, blue-green.
Segments slender, white, all of
equal size. Joe Sharman,
Cambridgeshire, 2004.

'Charmer Flore Pleno'
(nivalis)
See G. nivalis 'Doncaster's Double
Charmer'. Mis-named, thought to be
extinct.

'Chatterbox' (nivalis)
A G. nivalis snowdrop with flowers at an
angle to the scape, facing outwards.
Named by John Morley, North Green
Snowdrops.

'Chatton'
(nivalis Sandersii Group)
Outstanding yellow marked G. nivalis.
Named by Ian Christie, RHS PC, Scotland.
↑15cm.

'Chedworth' (nivalis)
Well shaped flowers.
Outer segments
rounded, bluntly
pointed. Inner
segments good
heart-shaped
green mark at
apex. Easy,
free-flowering,
bulks up well.
January–February. Daphne
Chappell, 1985, from Helen Milford's
garden, Gloucestershire.
↑16cm.

'Chelsworth Magnet' (*elwesii*)

Syn. *G. elwesii* 'Magnet'

Good, strong, with slender pedicel and rounded flowers. Leaves supervolute, erect. Outer segments rounded, pointed. Inner segments incurved, variable marking, large 'V' at apex and separate oval towards base, to 'X' shaped mark, small sinus. Bulks up well. Originally named G. 'Magnet' by John Morley, name already applied so renamed. Richard Britten at Chelsworth, Suffolk. ↑24cm.

'Chequers' (*plicatus*)

Large, rounded ice-white flowers resembling G. 'Gerard Parker' but smaller, can weigh down scapes. Leaves explicative, grey-green. Outer segments ridged, dimpled. Inner segments variable inverted 'U' to 'V' at apex, sometimes towards base. Christopher Grey-Wilson in the late Jenny Robinson's garden, Colchester, Essex. ↑25cm.

'Chetwode Greentip'

Elegant, elongated flowers. Leaves slender, erect to arching, blue-green. Outer segments long, slender, pointed, green mark at apex. Inner segments inverted 'V' at apex. ↑15cm.

'Chevron'
(Hybrid cultivar)

Leaves semi-erect to arching, flat to explicative. Outer segments rounded, bluntly pointed. Inner segments clasping, variable green marking, usually two inverted 'V's one above the other, paler shadow between. Phil Cornish in E.B. Anderson's former garden, c. 1992, named for double 'Chevron' marking. ↑16cm.

'Chris Sanders'

Tall and stately with attractive flowers. Leaves erect-arching, broad, grey-green.

Outer segments long, rounded, bluntly pointed, clawed. Inner segments good mid-green heart-shaped mark above apex. ↑25cm.

'Christine'
(*reginae-olgae* subsp. *vernalis*)

Robust, strong. Leaves upright, blue-green, lighter median stripe, short at flowering. Outer segments spoon-shaped, long goffered claw. Inner segments olive-green inverted 'U' at apex. Bulks up well. December–January, often before Christmas. Often smaller second scape on mature plants. Christopher Grey-Wilson, in mother's garden, named for his wife, pre-1970. ↑12cm.

'Christmas Cheer'
(*reginae-olgae* hybrid)

G. reginae-olgae cultivar from USA, bred for characteristic, distinctive glaucous central median rib on leaves. Stephen Vinisky, USA. ↑12cm.

'Christmas Wish' (*caucasicus*)

Small flowers. Leaves narrow, erect, bright green. Inner segment green mark at apex. Grows well. January. Vladikavkaz in Caucasus mountains. ↑12cm.

'Chrome Yellow'
(*nivalis* Sandersii Group)

Attractive yellow with good yellow-green ovary, spathe and scape. Leaves blue-green. Outer segments long, pointed. Inner segments broad yellow inverted 'V' at apex.

'Chubby Cheeks' (*nivalis*)

Well shaped, rounded flowers, erect scapes. Outer segments bluntly pointed, pale green lines. Inner segments inverted 'V' at apex. January–February. 2010. ↑12cm.

'Cicely Hall' (Hybrid cultivar)

Syns. G. 'Primrose Hill Special', G. 'The Stalker', G. 'The Whopper', G. 'Helen Dillon's Whopper'

Sturdy Irish snowdrop like large G. 'Merlin'. Large bulbs, thick scapes, dark green ovary. Leaves erect, slender, glaucous, flat to lightly explicative, two or three. Outer segments elegant, long, slender, thick, incurved. Inner segments dark-green mark across segment, narrow white margin at apex. March. Cicely Hall, Primrose Hill, Lucan, Ireland, 1969. G. plicatus. ↑10–20cm.

'Cicely's Tubby'
(*elwesii*)

Rounded flowers. Leaves erect, grey-green. Outer segments well shaped, light longitudinal ridging, bluntly pointed. Inner segments small triangular mark each side of sinus, broad green mark towards base. ↑12cm.

'Cider With Rosie'
(*woronowii*)

Small, low-growing flowers with slender segments. Leaves broad, green. Outer segments pale-green mark at apex. Inner segments broad inverted green 'U' at apex. Colin Mason, Warwickshire. ↑8cm.

cilicicus (species)

Syn. *G. nivalis* subsp. *cilicicus*

Southern Turkey. Autumn to winter flowering, uncommon in cultivation. Flowers over long period. Leaves applanate, grey-green-blue, glaucuous, present at flowering, lengthening in maturity. Inner segments 'U', 'V' or heart-shaped mark at apex. Related to G. peshmenii. November–December. Dry situation. First described and named by John Baker, 1897. ↑10–18cm.

'Cinderdine'
(*elwesii* Hiemalis Group)

Shorter snowdrop with well shaped flowers, olive-green scapes. Leaves

supervolute, erect. Outer segments flat, textured. Inner segments uniform inverted 'V' at apex. Bulks up well. December. Daphne Chappell selection from Helen Milford's garden, Chedworth, Gloucestershire, 1996, named after Daphne Chappell's cottage. ↑15cm.

'Cinderella'

Leaves erect, grey-green. Outer segments pointed small green mark at apex. Inner segments green inverted 'U' at apex. February. Ian Christie, Scotland. Originally *G.* 'Tinkerbell' but name already applied, so renamed. ↑10cm.

'Clare Blakeway-Phillips' (Hybrid cultivar)

Large attractive flowers, shiny, bright lime-green ovary. Leaves attractive, explicative, broad, spreading, green-blue-glaucous. Inner

segments tube-like, large pale-green variable mark across segment, diffusing towards base. Vigorous. Virus causes discrepancies with coloration, markings and streaks on foliage. Often two scapes when mature. Drier situation. Angela Marchant, Bishop's Stortford, Hertfordshire, *c.* 1960s. RHS PC 1975. RHS AM 1976. ↑23cm.

'Cliff Curtis'

Beautifully shaped, rounded flowers. Outer segments rounded, long claw. Inner segments grooved, small green mark, sometimes joined, either side of large sinus, light green flush towards middle of segments. Cliff Curtis, 2003.

'Clifton Hampden' (*nivalis*)

Leaves applanate, slender, erect, blue-green. Inner segments good green mark at apex. January–February. Clifton Hampden village, near Abingdon, Oxfordshire. ↑15cm.

'Clovis' (*plicatus* Hybrid)

Quirky, rare. Opposite to poculiform – inverse poculiform . Randomly substitutes inner segments for outer, from one to six of equal size. Leaves applanate, semi-erect, flat to explicative, green-glaucescent. Outer

segments if present, clawed, replicating inner segments with green marks. Inner segments dark-green, broad inverted 'U'. Richard Hobbs and Rosie Steele found single bulb in H.A. Greatorex's former garden, Brundall, Norfolk, 1992. Named 'Clovis' after Rosie Steele's daughter's nickname. ↑15cm.

'Clun' (*nivalis* Hybrid)

Not a spectacular snowdrop but reliable. Outer segments well shaped, slender, pointed. Inner segments broad inverted 'U' at apex. Bulks up well. January–February. Revd R.J. Blakeway-Phillips, Clun, Shropshire, c. 1980s. ↑14cm.

'Clun Green'

Name abandoned: *see* 'Clun Green Convolute' or 'Clun Green Plicate'.

'Clun Green Convolute' (*elwesii*)

Small. Well rounded flowers. Leaves supervolute, erect, very narrow, flat at apex. Outer segments broad. Inner segments solid green slightly waisted mark across three-quarters of segment. Revd R.J. Blakeway-Phillips, Clun, Shropshire, *c.* 1988. ↑10cm.

'Clun Green Plicate' (*plicatus*)

Slender. Leaves supervolute, erect, glaucous. Inner segments tube-like, flared apex, dot either side of sinus joined by narrow band, separate 'U' shaped basal mark. December–January. Revd R.J. Blakeway-Phillips, Clun, Shropshire, 5. 1988. ↑10cm.

'Clun Queen' (*nivalis* Hybrid)

Long, attractive, elegant flowers suspended beneath narrow, pale-green ovary. Leaves applanate, slender, upright,

blue-green. Outer segments long, pointed. Inner segments broad green 'V' at apex. January–February. Revd R.J. Blakeway-Phillips, Clun, Shropshire. ↑12cm.

'Cockatoo' (*nivalis*)

Well formed spiky, tending to face outwards. Leaves applanate, erect. Outer segments three or four, incurved margins. Inner segments irregular ruff, small or absent sinus, variable, misshapen green 'V' towards apex. Phil Cornish at Wallsworth Hall, Gloucestershire, 1989. ↑10cm.

'Colesborne' (Hybrid cultivar)

Syn. *G.* 'Colesbourne Seedling' Distinctive, attractive, large-flowered hybrid, taller when mature. Slender ovary. Leaves erect, stiff, glaucous. Outer segments clawed. Inner segments tube-like, large waisted mark from apex, fading towards base, narrow white margin. Often second scape. Slow. February–March. Henry J. Elwes, Colesbourne, Gloucestershire, early 1900s; modern stock Walter Butt, Hyde Lodge. Various stories as to origins, also misidentification, causing confusion. RHS AM 1951. ↑10cm.

'Colesbourne Colossus'

See 'Colossus'.

'Colesbourne Green Tips'

Showy large flowers, erect scapes. Outer segments bluntly pointed, pale-green lines at apex. Inner segments broad, well rounded, inverted 'V' at apex, two joined ovals towards base. Not recognized by John Grimshaw but listed by some growers.

'Colesbourne Seedling'

See 'Colesborne'.

'Colossus' (*plicatus*)

Syns. *G. plicatus* 'Colesbourne', *G.* 'Colesbourne Colossus' Tall, handsome 'Giant'. Large flowers.

Leaves plicate, broad, arching, flat, grey, paler median stripe. Inner segments slightly flared at apex, variable narrow green inverted 'V' paling on basal side. Often two scapes. Easy. Early, around Christmas. Caroline Elwes, Colesbourne, Gloucestershire, 1982. Name published by Phil Cornish, 1999, following change from original G. 'Colesborne', already applied. ↑23cm.

'Comet'
(elwesii var. monostictus)

Syn. G. caucasicus 'Comet'
Tall, vigorous, reliable. Large bulbs. One of the best G. elwesii. Large well shaped flowers, long arching pedicels. Leaves arching, grey-green, pointed. Outer segments inconsistent variable green stripes at apex. Inner segments large single green heart-shaped mark. February. John Morley, rock garden, RHS Wisley, 1982, name commemorates 1973 Kohoutek Comet. ↑30cm.

'Compton Court'

Tall, vigorous, similar to G. 'S. Arnott'. Well shaped flowers, erect scapes. Leaves erect, slender, blue-green. Outer segments long, rounded, clawed. Inner segments broad inverted 'V' at apex. Bulks up well. Named after garden. ↑18cm.

'Conquest' (plicatus subsp. byzantinus)

Outstanding snowdrop, maturing taller. Leaves plicate, broad, very attractive distinctive grey. Outer segments rounded, puckered. Inner segments large inverted deep-green 'U' at apex, separate basal mark which can join. Taunton, Somerset, named after garden. ↑16cm.

'Conundrum' (nivalis)

Small. Erect scape and pedicel. Similar to G. 'Blonde Inge'. Leaves applanate, arching, bright-green, pale median stripe. Outer segments strongly clawed. Inner segment green mark, pale yellow-green staining at base. January–February. French Pyrenees. Similar to G. reginae-olgae subsp. vernalis, but it is G. nivalis. Joe Sharman and Dr Alan Leslie. ↑11cm.

'Cool Ballin Taggart'
See 'Coolballintaggart'.

'Cool Ballintaggert'
See 'Coolballintaggart'.

'Coolballintaggart'

Syns. G. 'Cool Ballin Taggart', G. 'Cool Ballintaggert', G. 'The O'Mahony', G. 'The O'Mahoney'.
Good large snowdrop, similar to G. 'Straffan', possibly same although occasional differences noted. Outer segments rounded, bluntly pointed. Inner segments inverted 'V' at apex, rounded ends. Mahony, Kerry, Ireland. ↑40cm.

corcyrensis
See reginae-olgae subsp. reginae-olgae.

'Cordelia' (Hybrid double)

Tall, striking, lesser known Greatorex double. Leaves semi-erect, lightly explicative. Outer segments rounded, clawed. Inner segments dense, regular, neat ruff, inverted 'V', margins slightly staining, occasional stripes at apex. Immature markings wedge-shaped from apex halfway to base. Late. H.A. Greatorex, Brundall, Norfolk, c. 1940s. G. nivalis 'Flore Pleno' × G. plicatus. ↑20cm.

'Corkscrew'
(gracilis)

Round olive-green ovary. Leaves applanate, glaucous, much twisted, hence name. Outer segments broad, incurved margins. Inner

segments narrow green inverted 'U' at apex, broader oval towards base. John Morley, North Green Snowdrops, 1997. ↑7cm.

'Cornwood' (nivalis)

Vigorous, tall G. nivalis. Leaves applanate, semi-erect, slightly explicative. Outer segments rounded, bluntly pointed, green stripes towards apex. Inner segments inverted 'U' covering about one-third. One of the earliest green-tipped to flower. Bulks up well. January–February. Peter Glover, Delamore Estate, Cornwood, Devon. ↑16cm.

'Cornwood Gem'

Interesting quirky, untidy double with aberrant segments. Flower suspended at an angle from stiff pedicel. Outer segments variable, slender, green mark at apex. Inner segments numerous, aberrant, tipped green at apex. ↑16cm.

'Corona North' (plicatus)

Well shaped Irish snowdrop. Leaves arching, plicate, green. Outer segments spoon-shaped, merging green lines. Inner segments inverted green 'V' at apex, broad ends, paler mark towards base. Carlow, Ireland, named after former garden owner.

'Corrin' (Hybrid)

G. 'Trym' seedling. Leaves erect, slender, green. Outer segments long, broad, rounded, large mid-green mark at apex. Inner segments heart-shaped mark at apex. Early, around Christmas. ↑18cm.

'Coton Manor' (plicatus)

Sought after. Large, white flowers. Leaves broad, shiny-green, silver median stripe. January–February. Coton Manor Garden, Northamptonshire. ↑16cm.

'Cotswold Beauty'
(Hybrid cultivar)

Leaves semi-erect, explicative to mid-height, pale-green-glaucous. Outer segments slender, rounded. Inner segments tube-like, flared at apex, pale green 'X' infilled at base. Often two scapes, occasionally three. Phil Cornish from E.B. Anderson's former garden, Lower Slaughter, Gloucestershire, 1993, named by Daphne Chappell. Possible hybrid between *G. gracilis* and *G. plicatus*. ↑14cm.

'Cotswold Farm' (*plicatus*)
Outer segments broad, lightly longitudinally ridged. Inner segments broad inverted 'V' at apex, blurred in centre on basal side. 18cm.

'Cottage Corporal'
See 'Ivy Cottage Corporal'.

Cottisford'
Elegant flowers, erect scapes, long, slender ovary. Outer segments slender, pointed. Inner segments broad green inverted 'V' at apex.

'Courteenhall' (*nivalis*)
Leaves applanate. Outer segment rounded, green mark at apex, pale-green shadow at base. Inner segments inverted 'V' at apex. January–February. Oliver Wyatt, Courteenhall, Northampton, late 1960s. Many snowdrops purporting to be G. 'Courteenhall are G. 'Modern Art' as virtually identical. Also similar to G. 'Viridapice'. ↑18cm.

'Covertside' (Hybrid cultivar)
Well shaped attractive flowers, long upright pedicel. Leaves flat to lightly explicative, unusual sage-green, glaucescent. Outer segments rounded, pointed. Inner segments strong green inverted 'X' across segment, diffusing towards base. John Sales, Covertside, Cirencester, Gloucestershire, 1997. ↑23cm.

'Cowhouse Green' (Hybrid cultivar)

Tall, virescent. Leaves applanate, semi-erect, mainly explicative, glaucescent. Outer segments clawed, merging pale olive-green lines towards apex. Inner segments inverted 'V' at apex, diffusing towards base. Sometimes two or three scapes. Care. Slow. Mark Brown in Susan Cowdry's garden, Rushmere, Buckinghamshire, in mixed G. nivalis and G. plicatus colony, late 1980s. RHS AGM 2002.↑16cm.

'Crème Anglaise' (*nivalis*)
Beautiful, pristine flowers with cream-tinged buds. Mature flowers white. Leaves erect, slender, blue-green. Segments rounded, bluntly pointed, devoid of marking. January–February. ↑15cm.

'Crimea' (*plicatus*)
Run of the mill plicate. Leaves semi-erect. Outer segments rounded. Inner segments tube-like, dark-green 'V' at apex, slightly upturned. ↑12cm.

'Crimean Emerald' (*plicatus*)
Leaves semi-erect. Inner segments broad green mark apex to base. Reinhard Suckow, early 1980s, named by Antoine Hoog. ↑17cm.

'Crinkle Crankle'
Rounded balloon-like flowers, inflated spathes. Outer segments very broad, rounded, longitudinally ridged, dimpled. Inner segments inverted 'V' at apex narrowly joining heart-shaped mark towards base.

'Crinoline'

Well shaped, rounded flowers on erect scapes. Outer segments long, rounded, incurved. Inner segments rounded inverted 'V' at apex, paler lines spreading towards base.

'Crinolinum' (*nivalis* Poculiformis Group)
Elegant poculiform with six equal length white segments. Leaves applanate, erect, blue-green. Outer segments goffered at base. ↑10cm.

'Cronkhill Selection'
See 'Walloping Whopper'

'Cross Eyes' (*elwesii*)
Attractive, slender flowers. Leaves broad, grey-green. Outer segments, rounded, bluntly pointed, green marks at apex. Inner segments inverted 'V' at apex, horseshoe-shaped mark towards base, often joined by pale-green shadow. ↑18cm.

'Cryptonite'
See 'Kryptonite'.

'Curly' (Hybrid cultivar)

Large, slender, textured flowers. Leaves applanate, narrow, distinctively recurved, blue-green-glaucescent. Outer segments curved, clawed, variable merging pale-green lines. Inner segments tube-like, pale green 'X', stronger at apex, diffusing towards base, paler shading. Vigorous. Good perfume. Herbert Ransom and Richard Nutt, Hyde Lodge garden, Gloucestershire, 1960s, named by Richard Nutt for distinctively curled leaf. ↑12cm.

'Curry'
An acquired taste with unusual brown-green ovary and marking. Outer segments bluntly pointed at apex. Inner segments

brown-green inverted 'V' at apex. Germany, 2011.

'Cyclops'
Leaves slender, erect to spreading, blue-green. Outer segments boat-shaped, pointed. Inner segments broad green mark from apex to half of segment, two large 'eye' spots towards base. ↑15cm.

'Cyril Warr'
Elegant large flowers, slender pedicel. Leaves, broad, green, erect to arching, Outer segments well shaped, bluntly pointed. Inner segments broad inverted 'U' at apex. Grows well. Good perfume. ↑18cm.

'Daglingworth' (Hybrid cultivar)
Crisp elegant flowers. Leaves applanate, very erect, flat to subrevolute, glaucous, light pleating. Outer segments bluntly pointed, lightly recurved margins. Inner segments flared at apex, small dot each side of sinus which can be joined, green mark across top half of segment. Often two scapes Early. Ruth Birchall, c. 1990, in flower arrangement in Daglingworth Church, Gloucestershire, traced to nearby woodland. ↑20cm.

'Daglingworth Yellow'
Now withdrawn, as same as G. 'Ronald Mackenzie'.

'Daisy Sunshine' (Hybrid cultivar)
Attractive flowers with good yellow marks. Probably not a valid name.

'Dame Margot Fonteyn' (*nivalis*)
Quite ordinary looking. Leaves applanate, erect, blue-green. Outer segments rounded, bluntly pointed. Inner segments green mark at apex, pale green staining

towards base. January–February. Durham University student, Howick Hall, Northumberland, named after the famous ballet dancer. ↑15cm.

'Danube Star' (*nivalis* Poculiform Group)
Syn. G. 'Hololeucus' Elegant, delicate-looking poculiform. Rounded flowers with spreading segments. Leaves applanate, erect, grey-glaucous. Outer and inner segments equal, slender, all-white, textured. Late. Professor Josef Weindlmayr, Danube wetlands, Austria, 1960. Originally sold as G. 'Hololeucus', renamed as already applied. ↑13cm.

'Danube Valley' (*reginae-olgae* subsp. *reginae-olgae*)
Leaves applanate, grey-green, paler median stripe and undersides, small at flowering. Outer segments well shaped. Inner segments inverted 'V' at apex. Autumn–winter. ↑10cm.

'Daphne's Scissors' (*elwesii*)
Leaves supervolute, slender, erect to spreading. Outer segments slim, small merging olive-green lines at apex. Inner segments tube-like, distinct scissor-shaped mark. Daphne Chappell in Helen Milford's former garden, Chedworth, Gloucestershire, 1985. ↑15cm.

'David Baker' (Hybrid cultivar)
Attractive, sought after. Leaves applanate, semi-erect, variably explicative margins, glaucescent. Outer segments incurved, inverted 'U' to 'V' above apex. Inner segments uniform 'U' at apex. Early. Must establish. Michael Heard in David and Ruby Baker's garden, Farnham, c. 1987, named by David Baker, 1997. Similar to G. 'Atkinsii', first known as G. 'Green tipped

Atkinsii', but without aberrant segments and distinctively recurved. ↑20cm.

'David Bromley' (*gracilis*)
Elegant flowers, large olive-green ovary. Outer segments rounded, pointed, small green crescent at apex. Inner segments slim inverted 'U' at apex, separate large, rounded mark towards base. David Bromley, Wellington, Shropshire, 2003. ↑13cm.

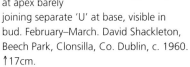

'David Bromley's Early' (*plicatus* subsp. *byzantinus*)
Handsome, very white flowers enhanced by pale-green ovary. Leaves applanate, erect. Slender, grey-green. Outer segments bluntly pointed. Inner segments roughly scissor-shaped mark of narrow, upright inverted 'V' at apex, joining paler oval to half of segment. Early. David Bromley, Wellington, Shropshire.

'David Shackleton' (*elwesii*)
Syn. G. 'Shackleton' Upright Irish clone. Large slender flowers, olive-green ovary. Leaves supervolute, erect, light green-blue. Outer segments slender, incurved, clawed. Inner segments olive-green 'V' at apex barely joining separate 'U' at base, visible in bud. February–March. David Shackleton, Beech Park, Clonsilla, Co. Dublin, c. 1960. ↑17cm.

'David Quinton' (Poculiformis group)
A recently introduced all white poculiform. Slender rounded ovary and very large attractive flowers. Early.

'David's Seersucker'
Balloon-like flowers. Leaves, broad, green. Outer segments rounded, longitudinally

ridged, puckered seersucker effect. Inner segments slightly waisted, broad green mark across segment towards base. Named for dimpled effect flowers.

'December'
(*reginae-olgae* subsp. *vernalis*)

'December Green Tip' (*elwesii*)
Leaves broad, erect to arching, grey-green. Outer segments pointed. Inner segments slightly waisted large green mark across segment towards base. November–January. ↑12cm.

'Decima McCauley'
Attractive flowers. Outer segments long, bluntly pointed, goffered claw. Inner segments broad green mark covering segment, narrow white margin.

'Decora' (*nivalis*)
Similar in appearance to G. 'Trym'. Outer segments broad, rounded, variable infilled 'U' at apex. Inner segments broad inverted 'U' at apex. January–February. Zlatko and Angelina Petrisevac, Croatia. ↑20cm.

'D'Ecouves Vert'
Erect scapes, arching pedicel. Leaves erect, green-blue. Outer segments slender, rounded, broad green mark at apex, pale-green mark at base. Inner segments inverted 'V' to heart-shaped mark at apex, diffusing and joining paler basal mark.

'Deer Slot' (*elwesii*)
Impressive snowdrop with large, elegant flowers. Leaves supervolute, erect, pressed together at

flowering. Outer segments large, flattish, clawed. Inner segments two roughly triangular or wedge-shaped dark-green marks at apex. Originally Nancy Lindsay's Persian snowdrops. ↑30cm.

'Denton' (*gracilis*)

Well rounded flowers. Leaves applanate, broad, recurved tips. Inner segments small dot either side of apex, larger triangular mark at base, sometimes narrowly joined. Two scapes from established bulbs. John Morley, former garden of Rosie Steele, Denton House, Harleston, Norfolk, 1970s. ↑13cm.

'Der Grüne Verzauberer'
Slender pedicel. Leaves green-blue. Outer segments merging green lines across centre above apex towards base. Inner segments pale-green mark covering almost entire segment. Germany. English translation: 'Green Enchanter'. ↑25cm.

'Derwish' (Hybrid cultivar)
Slender flowers, olive-green ovary. Leaves erect, flat margins, glaucous. Outer segments slim. Inner segments clasping, ridged, dark-green variable inverted 'V' at apex, occasionally 'X' shaped shadow. Nicolas Top, Cologne, Germany, 1996, in *G. nivalis* and *G. elwesii* with single marks. ↑17cm.

'Desdemona' (Hybrid cultivar)
Good, vigorous, irregular Greatorex double. Largest of the group. Leaves widely spreading, two or three, flat-explicative. Outer segments, occasionally four, nipped and hooded at apex. Inner segments good ruff with heart-shaped mark. Increases well. Early. H.A. Greatorex, Brundall, Norfolk, c. 1940s. ↑20cm.

'Devon Marble'
Elegant flowers. Outer segments slender. Inner segments variable green inverted 'V' at apex, rounded ends, paler marking channelling towards base. ↑10cm.

'Diana Broughton' (Hybrid cultivar)
Rounded flowers. Leaves supervolute, erect, two or three. Outer segments rounded, bluntly pointed, sometimes four. Inner segment ruff, outer whorl sometimes aberrant, inverted 'V' extending into oval. Ruby Baker at Anglesey Abbey, Cambridgeshire, 1994, named for Lord Fairhaven's eldest daughter. ↑14cm.

'Dicke Tante' (*nivalis*)
Large *G. nivalis*. Well rounded flowers, strong, erect scapes. Leaves applanate, erect, slender, blue-green. Outer segments broad, pointed, merging olive-green lines above apex. Inner segments broad inverted green 'U' at apex. Oirlcher Blumengarten, Germany. English translation: 'Big Aunt'.

'Dickerchen'
Very rounded, globular flowers. Outer segments, broad, well rounded, pointed. Inner segments broad inverted green 'U' at apex. Hagen Engelmann, Germany. English translation: 'Fatty'. ↑15cm.

'Diggory' (*plicatus*)
Popular, attractive, desirable. Rounded flowers. Outer segments distinctive 'seersucker' effect, incurved, giving flat-bottomed mature flower. Inner segments large light-green mark apex almost to base. Richard Hobbs, Rosie Steele, Norfolk, in colony of *G. plicatus*. Named after her late son. RHS PC 1998. AM 2009. ↑16cm.

'Diggory Like' (*elwesii*)

As the name implies, similar to *G.* 'Diggory', with globular, dimpled flowers. Leaves supervolute, broad, grey. Outer segments rounded, ridged, dimpled. Inner segments green mark across segment. January–March. ↑18cm.

'Ding Dong' (Hybrid cultivar)

Tall snowdrop with crooked pedicel. Leaves broad, flat-subrevolute, glaucous, two or three. Outer segments long, incurved, pointed. Inner segments tube-like, olive-green 'U' paling towards base. Often two scapes. Flowers over long period. Bulks up well. January–February. Avon Bulbs, Somerset. Bulbs bought as *G.* 'Robin Hood' from Herbert Ransom's son Alan, but worthwhile clone, named *G.* 'Ding Dong' by Alan Street, Avon Bulbs. Appears closely related to *G.* 'Erway'. ↑22cm.

'Dionysius'

See 'Dionysus'.

'Dionysus' (Hybrid double)

Syns. *G.* 'Dionysius', *G.* 'Sybil Roberta' Tall Greatorex double. Rounded, open flowers, occasionally single and semi-double. Leaves semi-erect, variably explicative. Outer segments rounded at apex. Inner segment ruff occasionally aberrant, green heart-shaped marks, yellowing on basal side. Vigorous. Early. Bulks up well. H.A. Greatorex's garden, Brundall, Norfolk, *c.* 1940s. Modern stock probably from R.D. Trotter. (Also mistakenly known as *G.* 'Sybil Roberta' until confirmed as *G.* 'Dionysus'.) ↑20cm.

'Doddington' (*nivalis* Sandersii Group)

Yellow *G. nivalis*. Leaves erect, slender. Inner segments yellow mark at apex. January–February. ↑14cm.

'Dodo Norton' (Hybrid cultivar)

Small plants, large, well textured flowers. Leaves semi-erect, lightly explicative margins, glaucescent. Inner segments wide inverted 'U' to 'V' at apex. Ditch garden, East Lambrook Manor, Somerset, 1990, named after previous garden owner. ↑8cm.

'Don Armstrong' (*elwesii* Poculiform)

Particularly attractive, well shaped *G. elwesii* poculiform with beautiful white segments all of equal length. Named after gardener in Victoria, British Columbia. ↑18cm.

'Don Pedro'

Smaller, almost poculiform, green-marked snowdrop with outer segments only slightly longer than inner. Outer segments slender, rounded, bluntly pointed, heavily marked green apex to base. Inner segments marked green. Johan Mens, Belgium. ↑10cm.

'Donald Sims Early' (*elwesii* Hiemalis Group)

Good, reliable. Leaves supervolute, erect, pale-green, glaucous, well developed at flowering. Outer segments long, slender. Inner segments tube-like, flared at apex, narrow inverted 'V'. Bulks up well. Early November. Donald Simms, Foxton, Cambridge, via original stock from Sir Frederick Stern's garden, Highdown, Sussex. ↑14cm.

'Donaugold' (*nivalis* Sandersii Group)

Small *G. nivalis*. Pale green-yellow ovary. Leaves applanate, erect to arching, green. Outer segments long, pointed. Inner segments narrow

yellow inverted 'V' at apex, broad rounded ends. ↑10cm.

'Doncaster's Double Charmer' (*nivalis*)

Syn. *G.* 'Double Charmer'; *G.* 'Charmer Flore Pleno' Green-tipped double, elegant, robust. Spathe inflated, sometimes split. Leaves applanate, semi-erect. Outer segments aberrant, green mark at apex. Inner segments neat ruff, small inverted 'V' at apex. January–February. Amy Doncaster's garden, Chandler's Ford, Hampshire. ↑13cm.

'Doncaster's Double Scharlock' (*nivalis*)

Syn. *G.* 'Scharlockii Flore Pleno' Curious, untidy double. Spathe erect, split. Leaves applanate, semi-erect. Outer segments slender, large green mark at apex. Inner segments usually aberrant, variable inverted 'U' to 'V' at apex. Amy Doncaster's garden, Chandler's Ford, Hampshire. ↑16cm.

'Donna Buang' (*elwesii* var. *monostictus*)

Shapely flowers. Leaves broad, grey-green. Outer segments clawed, lightly recurved margins. Inner segments 'X' shaped mark, infilled at base, to three-quarters of segment. Australian-raised selection.

'Dopey'

Arching scapes, slender pedicel. Leaves narrow, lanceolate, glaucous. Inner segments tube-like, two green marks.

'Dorothy Foreman' (*elwesii* Hiemalis Group)

Sought after, early. Leaves green, first known green in this group. Outer segments horizontal, shallow, rounded. Inner segments broad green 'U' at apex. December. Named for David Foreman's late mother.

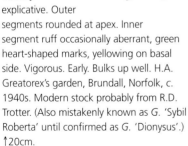

'Dorothy Lucking' (*gracilis*)

Syn. *G.* 'Cassaba' ex Dorothy Lucking
Elegant slender flowers, erect scapes.
Leaves applanate, semi-erect, slightly
twisted. Outer segments long narrow claw,
clearly showing inner segments. Inner
segments large roughly 'X' shaped mark
apex to base. Usually two scapes. Dorothy
Lucking purchased original from Jacques
Armand, 1983, passed to Ray Cobb.
Snowdrop named for her. ↑13cm.

'Double Charmer' (*nivalis*)

See 'Doncaster's Double Charmer'.

'Double Green'

See 'Boyd's Double'.

'Double Green Tips'

Green-tipped double. Outer
segments long, slender, pale
green mark at apex. Inner
segments rather untidy
ruff with variable, broad
green mark at apex,
diffusing towards base.

'Double Top' (*elwesii*)

Leaves supervolute broad, grey-green. Well
shaped flowers with good green marks.
Often two flowers to each scape.
Discovered in the garden of Helen Spencer,
Carlisle, Cumbria.

'Dragonfly'

A new snowdrop with long well-shaped
flowers. Leaves erect, slender. Outer
segments long, slender, resembling a
dragonfly's wings. Inner segments have an
infilled scissor-shaped green mark.

'Dreycott Greentip' (*nivalis*)

Slender, green-tipped flowers,
foliose spathe tending
towards Scharlockii.
Leaves applanate,
erect, blue-green.
Outer segments
green mark at
apex. Inner
segments inverted
green 'V' at apex,
rounded ends. Vigorous. Increases well. Matt
Bishop at Malcolm and Jane Tosh's garden,
Little Clandon, Surrey, 1987.

'Drummonds Giant' (*elwesii*)

Large-flowered Irish snowdrop. Leaves large,
broad, mid-green. Outer segments rounded,

tapering towards apex, pointed.
Inner segments broad green
mark apex towards base.
Corona North, former
owner of Altamont
Gardens, Ireland,
1990s.

'Drumont Giant'

See 'Drummonds Giant'.

'Duckie' (*plicatus*)

Triangular flowers. Leaves
plicate, glaucous.
Outer segments
slender,
flattened,
slight inwards curve. Inner
segments flared, heavily marked green
above narrow sinus, diffusing to base.
Late. Often two scapes. Found/named
by Alan Street in Jane Gibb's garden,
Westbury on Trym, Bristol, 1987.
↑15cm.

'Dumpy Denton'

Smaller snowdrop with well rounded
flowers on erect scapes. Leaves broad,
grey-green. Outer segments rounded,
bluntly pointed. Inner segments green
marks at apex and base. ↑10cm.

'Dumpy Green' (*nivalis*)

Pale-green rounded ovary. Leaves
applanate, slender, erect, blue-green.
Outer segments bluntly pointed, merging
green lines above apex. Inner segments
inverted broad rounded 'U' to 'V' at apex.
January–February. Named by John Morley,
North Green Snowdrops. ↑10cm.

'Dunley Hall'
(*plicatus* subsp. *byzantinus*)

Dunrobin Seedling (*nivalis*)

See 'Melvillei'.

Dunskey Talia (*nivalis*)

Quirky snowdrop which looks better in a
group. Spathe erect, foliose, often splits
like Scharlockii. Flowers angled 80–90
degrees from pedicel. Leaves applanate,
upright, blue-green. Outer segments
slender, pointed. Inner segments narrow
green 'U' to 'V'-shaped mark at apex.
Found beneath sycamore tree. Major and
Mrs Orr Ewing, Dunskey House, Scotland,
named for their grandaughter Talia.
Registered 2008. ↑15cm.

'Durris' (*plicatus*)

Large, vigorous. Leaves erect, plicate, broad,
green. Outer segments rounded, lightly
ridged, bluntly pointed. Inner segments broad
green inverted 'U' at apex. Two flowers,
separate scapes, first larger than second.
Good. Clumps up well. Noel Pritchard, Durris,
Scotland. ↑20cm.

'Dwarf Green Danube'

Delicate-looking, smaller, green-marked
snowdrop. Leaves blue-green. Inner
segments narrow inverted 'V' at apex.
↑8cm.

'Dymock'
(Hybrid cultivar)

Attractive, unusual foliage,
small flowers. Leaves,
broad, arching, flat
margins, light
puckering, distinctive
metallic sheen. Outer
segments pointed. Inner segments wide
green 'X' covering three-quarters of
segment, solid base. John Sales, at
Dymock, Gloucestershire, 1997.
Possibly *G. ikariae* parent. ↑20cm.

'E.A. Bowles'
(*plicatus* Poculiform)

Beautiful, vigorous,
expensive poculiform. Six
well shaped, pure white
segments. Leaves broad,
plicate, blue-green.
Grows well. Late.
Michael Miles in the
late E.A. Bowles's
garden, Myddelton House, Enfield,
2002, named for Bowles. ↑20cm.

'Earliest' (*elwesii* Hiemalis Group)

Thin dark-green ovary. Leaves supervolute.
Outer segments elongated. Inner segments
tube-like, flared at apex, narrow green
sharp inverted 'V' at apex. December.
Similar to *G.* 'Earliest of All'. Oliver Wyatt
from Lady Beatrix Stanley.

'Earliest of All'
(*elwesii* Hiemalis Group)

Two clones circulating:
• Leaves supervolute,
  erect. Outer segments
  flattened, ridged.
  Inner segments,
  narrow green inverted 'V' at apex.
  October–November. Richard Nutt.

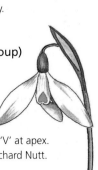

• Flowers rounded. Leaves supervolute, erect. Outer segments long, slender, rounded, clawed, reflexed. Inner segment tube-like, narrow green inverted 'V'. Similar to G. 'Barnes' but leaves wrapped around stem at flowering, around 3 weeks later, late November. ↑16cm.

'Early to Rise'
See 'Early to Rize'.

'Early to Rize' (Hybrid cultivar)
Well shaped attractive flowers. Leaves semi-erect, grey-green, glaucescent, median stripe. Outer segments long, boat-shaped, pointed. Inner segments rounded mark above apex. November–January. John Morley, North Green, Norfolk. Early 1990s. Possible *G. elwesii* Hiemalis group × *G. rizehensis*. ↑19cm.

'Early Twin' (*elwesii*)
Leaves attractive, broad, grey-green. Outer segments long, pointed, slender claw at base which lifts segments. Inner segments inverted 'V' at apex, rounded ends, paler oval towards base. Usually two scapes. December–January. Named for twin scapes. ↑18cm.

'Echoes' (*elwesii*)
Flowers large, well shaped, usually two from each pedicel. Leaves broad, erect to arching, grey. January–March. ↑12cm.

'Echoes of Christmas' (*elwesii* var. *monostictus*)
Often two flowers to each scape from separate pedicels. Outer segments well rounded, bluntly pointed, longitudinal ridging. Inner segments green marks at apex and base. November–December. ↑15cm.

'Ecusson d'Or' (*nivalis* Sandersii Group)
Tall, vigorous, yellow snowdrop. Well shaped flowers beneath yellow ovary. Outer segments

yellow marks at apex. Inner segments yellow inverted 'V' at apex. Slow to establish. February. Mark Brown, Normandy, France, 2004.

'Edinburgh Ketton' (*plicatus*)
Leaves explicative, arched, spreading, grey-green, paler median stripe. Outer segments large, rounded, clawed. Inner segments large variable green 'H' mark. Originally mistakenly supplied as G. 'Ketton' to Christopher Brickell from Royal Botanic Garden, Edinburgh, 1983; he renamed it. ↑22cm.

'Edith' (*elwesii*)
Tall with large flowers, attractive foliage. Leaves supervolute, very broad, grey-green. Outer segments long, slender, bluntly pointed. Inner segments good broad mark from apex towards base, narrow white margin. Phil Cornish, c. 2000, named for his mother. ↑20cm.

'Edward Whittall Group' (*elwesii* var. *elwesii*)
Syns. G. *elwesii* var. Whittallii, G. *elwesii* 'Whittallii' G. 'Whittallii' originally thought to be G. *elwesii* found by Edward Whittall near Smyrna, with very large bulbs, broad leaves and double basal mark. Later found to be vigorous G. *gracilis*. In 1900 a snowdrop illustrated by H.G. Moon, possibly from Taurus mountains, was also described as G. *elwesii* var. *whittallii*, with broad leaves, inner segments with apical mark, but single mark at base. Again, not Edward Whittall Group as should have two basal marks and broad leaves. To clarify matters Grimshaw, Davis and Bishop's Snowdrops created the new group.

'Egret' (*nivalis*)
Tending towards an untidy poculiform. Outer segments variable in number and shape, reflexing, some broad, some slim. Inner segments small green 'V' at apex. January–February. Phil Cornish. ↑15cm.

'Eisbär'
Textured, delicate, almost transparent, all-white flowers. Outer segments long, rounded, bluntly pointed. Inner segments pure white, no marks, large sinus. English translation:'Polar Bear'.

'Eiskristall' (*nivalis*)
Another elegant, slender, all-white snowdrop. Leaves applanate, slender, upright to arching, blue-green. Outer segments long, pointed. Inner segments pure white. Germany. English translation: 'Ice Crystal'. ↑8cm.

'Elcatus' (Hybrid)
Interesting rather than beautiful. Outer segments pointed at apex. Bulks up well. Australian-raised selection.

'Eleana Blakeway-Phillips'
See 'Eleanor Blakeway-Phillips'.

'Eleanor Blakeway-Phillips' (Hybrid cultivar)
Syn. G. 'Eleana Blakeway-Phillips' Beautiful large G. *elwesii* hybrid. Long, slim ovary. Leaves supervolute (immature bulbs applanate), broad, arching, flat to explicative, glaucous. Outer segments clawed. Inner segments clasping, tube-like, slightly waisted green mark apex to base, narrow white margin. Revd R.J. Blakeway-Phillips in Dr Nora Rink's garden, Toft Manor, Cambridge, named for his wife. RHS PC 1989. ↑20cm.

'Eleanor's Double' (Hybrid double)
Very similar to Greatorex double G. 'Ophelia' and possibly the same.

'Eleni' (*reginae-olgae* subsp. *reginae-olgae*)
Small, rounded ovary, neat, small flowers. Leaves applanate, narrow, flat-subrevolute margins, grey-green. Outer segments well

shaped, rounded, bluntly pointed. Inner segments broad inverted 'U' at apex. Good perfume. Mid-September. ↑12cm.

'Elfin' (nivalis)
Syn. G. 'Stargazer'
Small with split spathe. Leaves occasionally three, applanate, often one edge explicative. Outer segments concave, short, merging green lines at apex. Inner segments clear dark-green heart-shape mark at apex. Prolific, good, early. Phil Cornish at Wroxall, Warwickshire. Originally named G. 'Stargazer' as some flowers pointed upwards, but not consistent so renamed. ↑7cm.

'Eliot Hodgkin' (Hybrid cultivar)
Beautiful large flowers, in G. 'Mighty Atom' group. Leaves semi-erect, explicative, glaucous. Outer segments well rounded, strongly clawed. Inner segments broad inverted 'V' at apex. ↑20cm.

'Elizabeth Harrison' (woronowii)
Stunning, unusual G. woronowii. Beautifully shaped flowers, bright-yellow ovary. Outer segments slender, lightly ridged, bluntly pointed. Inner segments yellow mark each side of sinus, can be narrowly joined. Always sensational. Ian Christie, Scotland. (A single bulb fetched £725 on eBay auction site in February 2012.

'Ellen Minnet' (elwesii)
Long ovary, flowers suspended just above leaves. Leaves broad, grey-green. Inner segments broad inverted green 'U' at apex, fading slightly towards base. Phil Cornish, Gloucestershire garden, 1999. ↑11cm.

'Elles'
Yellow-green ovary and spathe. Leaves erect, slender, blue-green. Outer segments pointed. Inner segments yellow mark at apex. February. ↑12cm.

'Elmley Lovett' (elwesii)
Well shaped flowers. Outer segments slender, rounded, pointed. Inner segments broad inverted 'V' at apex, pale mark connecting to two small spots towards base, or 'X' shaped mark. ↑15cm.

'Else Bauer' (Poculiformis Group)
Heavily green-marked poculiform. Outer segments fractionally longer than inner. Outer and inner segments strong green mark at apex, upward pointing towards base. Rudi Bauer, Germany.

'Else Grollenberg' (elwesii)
Leaves erect, broad, grey-green. Outer segments long, pointed. Inner segments inverted green 'U' to 'V' at apex. W.A. Postema, 2010. ↑12cm.

elwesii (species)
Ukraine, Greece, Turkey, former Yugoslavia, Bulgaria. Vigorous, variable. Large flowers. Leaves large, supervolute, silver-grey, hooded. Inner segments generally green mark at base and apex. Sometimes green 'X' covers almost entire segment. Regular division. Imported across the world in vast quantities. Second most commonly cultivated snowdrop. Numerous named cultivars. October–March. RHS AGM 1993. ↑20–30cm.

elwesii Hiemalis Group
Narrow flowers. Leaves wrapped round scape at flowering. Inner segments single mark, narrow inverted 'V'. November. Sir Frederick Stern, Highdown, Sussex.

elwesii Hiemalis Group ex Broadleigh Gardens
One of the best Hiemalis, early flowering, single marked G. elwesii. Arching pedicel. Inner segments strong green mark at apex.

elwesii var. elwesii
Syns. G. elwesii subsp. akmanii, G. elwesii subsp. baytopii, G. elwesii subsp. melihae, G. elwesii subsp. tuebitaki, G. elwesii subsp. wagenitzii, G. elwesii var. maximus, G. elwesii var. whittallii, G. gracilis subsp. baytopii, G. graecus, G. maximus, G. melihae
Southern Ukraine, Turkey, Greece, including Aegean Islands, former Yugoslavia, Bulgaria. Elegant flowers. Leaves supervolute, generally broad. Outer segments broad, bluntly pointed. Inner segments green mark at apex and base or 'X' shaped mark. January–March. ↑15cm.

elwesii var. monostictus (Hiemalis Group)
G. elwesii var. monostictus
Syns. G. caucasicus, G. caucasicus var. hiemalis, G. caucasicus of gardens
Southern Turkey. Originally mistakenly named G. caucasicus in cultivation. Vigorous, free-flowering. Leaves broad, convolute, grey. Inner segments single apical mark. Common in cultivation, rare in wild. Early November–January. University of Cambridge Botanic Gardens, named by P.D. Sell, 1996. RHS AGM 1993. ↑15cm.

'Elworthy Bumble Bee'
Well rounded textured flowers. Outer segments rounded, bluntly pointed. Inner segments rounded, small green inverted 'U' at apex above sinus.

'Emerald Isle' (ikariae)
Attractive Irish snowdrop. Leaves supervolute, matt, mid-green. Outer segments long, bluntly pointed, pale-green lines above apex. Inner segments green mark

)almost covering segment, narrow white margin. Seed true. Ireland, naturalized in dry ditch.

'Enid Bromley' (*plicatus*)

Well shaped flowers. Leaves plicate, grey-green, paler median stripe. Outer segments rounded, bluntly pointed, goffered claw. Inner segments inverted 'V' at apex, bleeding on basal side, two paler, vertical ovals towards base. Very similar if not identical to *G.* 'Maidwell C'. ↑10cm.

'Envy'

Large flowers, slender pedicels, slender dark-green ovary. Outer segments boat-shaped, large, green mark above apex. Inner segments broad dark-green inverted 'V' to heart-shaped mark at apex, two paler green marks at base. ↑20cm.

'Epiphany'

Elegant flowers beneath long, slender, dark-green ovary. Leaves erect, pointed, dark-green. Outer segments slender, pointed, long, narrow claw. Inner segments dark-green small inverted 'V' at apex. January.

'Eric E'

Well shaped flowers, slight pink flush. Outer segments boat-shaped. Inner segments inverted 'V' with upturned arms at apex, diffusing almost to base.

'Eric Watson' (*plicatus*)

'Eric's Choice'

Very large, substantial, green-tipped flowers. Outer segments long, rounded, bluntly pointed, pale-green mark at apex. Inner segments broad inverted mid-green filled in 'U' at apex. Australian-raised selection.

'Ermine Ad Astra' (Hybrid semi-double)

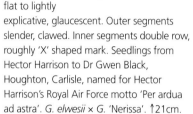

Open loose semi-double flowers with distinctive slender ovary. Leaves applanate-weakly supervolute, semi-erect, arching, flat to lightly explicative, glaucescent. Outer segments slender, clawed. Inner segments double row, roughly 'X' shaped mark. Seedlings from Hector Harrison to Dr Gwen Black, Houghton, Carlisle, named for Hector Harrison's Royal Air Force motto 'Per ardua ad astra'. *G. elwesii* × *G.* 'Nerissa'. ↑21cm.

'Ermine Farm' (Hybrid double)

Good regular double. Leaves applanate-supervolute, flat-explicative. Outer segments long, slender, pinched at apex. Inner segments neat regular ruff, good 'X' mark to base in small flowers, before base in larger flowers. Hector Harrison, Appleby, South Humberside. *G. elwesii* × *G.* 'Nerissa'. ↑16cm.

'Ermine House' (Hybrid double)

Good regular double. Leaves flat to explicative. Outer segments long. Inner segments broad inverted 'V' at apex, separate mark at base, occasionally joined. Hector Harrison, Appleby, South Humberside. ↑23cm.

'Ermine Joyce' (Hybrid double)

Double flowers. Leaves applanate-supervolute, semi-erect, flat-explicative, blue-green, glaucescent. Outer segments slender, pointed. Inner segments aberrant, irregular, inverted 'U' at apex, sometimes paler mark at base. Hector Harrison, Appleby, South Humberside, named after his wife. ↑27cm.

'Ermine Lace' (Hybrid double)

Beautiful, neat, regular double. Leaves applanate-supervolute, erect, variable margins, glaucous. Outer segments rounded,

clawed. Inner segment ruff, outermost whorl slightly misshapen, longitudinally incurved, narrow waisted 'X' mark, filled at base. Hector Harrison. Appleby, South Humberside. *G. elwesii* × *G.* 'Nerissa'. ↑17cm.

'Ermine Oddity' (*nivalis*)

Untidy spiky double. Small light-green marking. Similar to *G.* 'Boyd's Double'. Hector Harrison, Appleby, South Humberside, late 1980s.

'Ermine Ruby' (*nivalis*)

Slender ovary. Leaves applanate, erect, blue-green. Four neatly arranged outer and inner segments. January–February. Ruby Baker from Hector Harrison's garden, 1999. ↑15cm.

'Ermine Shuttlecock'

See 'Shuttlecock'.

'Ermine Spiky' (*nivalis*)

Thin, upward-facing spiky double. Almost tubular segments. Leaves applanate, erect, flat-subrevolute. Outer segments roughly three, tightly incurved, green. Inner segments variable, green, particularly towards apex. February–March. Hector Harrison, Appleby, South Humberside, early 1980s. ↑12cm.

'Ermine Street' (*nivalis*)

Tall, robust *G. nivalis*. Leaves applanate, erect, blue-green. Inner segments inverted green 'V' at apex. January–February. Hector Harrison, Appleby, South Humberside, 1970s. ↑18cm.

'Erway' (Hybrid cultivar)

Distinctive, very long, shiny olive-green ovary. Leaves semi-erect, glaucous. Outer segments short, rounded. Inner segments dark olive-green 'U' diffusing across segment towards base. Often second scape. February–March. Netta Statham's garden, Erway, Shropshire. Appears closely related to G. 'Ding Dong'. ↑16cm.

'Essie Huxley' (elwesii)
Large, single mark G. elwesii with well formed, textured flowers. Outer segments large, rounded, bluntly pointed. Inner segment deep filled-in inverted 'U' from apex to half of segment. Selected by Tasmanian grower and named after her by Marcus Harvey, Tasmania. ↑15cm.

'Esther Merton' (Hybrid double)
Excellent perfect double. Well rounded flowers. Outer segments large, broad, flaring, pointed. Inner segments neat ruff with inverted 'V' at apex.

'Ethiebeaton'
Leaves broad, grey-glaucous. Outer segments rounded, bluntly pointed. Inner segments upright rounded inverted 'V' at apex, two short narrow lines joining two small spots towards base. Ian Christie, Scotland.

'Eutopia' (plicatus)
Leaves plicate, broad, grey-green. Outer segments four, pointed at apex. Inner segments rounded, folded/split at sinus, small green mark.

'Eva Turner'
Name abandoned, same as G. 'Chadwick Cream'.

ex 'Blackthorn'
See 'Blackthorn'.

ex 'Cox' (Sandersii Group)
Yellow ovary and spathe. Leaves applanate, blue-green. Outer segments rounded, bluntly pointed. Inner segments narrow yellow inverted 'V' at apex. February. ↑14cm.

ex 'Robin Hall'
See 'Timpany Late'.

'Eye Candy' (Hybrid cultivar)
Elegant large flowers, erect scapes. Outer segments pointed at apex. Inner segments small inverted 'V' at apex, upturned ends.

'Fabian' (nivalis Poculiformis Group)
Slender poculiform, long slender ovary, inflated spathe. Outer segments slim, bluntly pointed, fractionally longer than inners, green mark at apex stretching towards base. Inner segment mark similar, smaller. Johan Mens, named after his son, c. 2007. ↑15cm.

'Fair Maid'
Leaves slender, arching, blue-green. Outer segments long, bluntly pointed. Inner segments rounded 'V' at apex, oval mark towards base. ↑14cm.

'Fairlight' (elwesii)
Smaller with funnel-shaped flowers. Leaves supervolute, erect, small, clasping. Outer segments clawed. Inner segments small dots either side of apex, shallow sinus, two paler dots towards base. March–April. Dorothy Underhill, garden at Colleton St Mary, Devon, 1970s, named after house. ↑10cm.

'Faith Stewart-Liberty' (plicatus hybrid)
Desirable. Large flowers. Outer segments large, boat-shaped, wide-spreading, strongly ribbed. Inner segments variable mid-green mark at apex, paler green margins. Mark Brown, Buckinghamshire garden, early 1980s, named after owner. ↑14cm.

'Falkland House' (Hybrid cultivar)
Shorter, similar but superior to G. 'Mighty Atom'. Leaves semi-erect, lightly explicative, glaucescent. Outer segments broad, rounded, bluntly pointed. Inner segments ridged at apex, broad dumpy inverted 'V'. Named after home of Mr and Mrs Ransom. ↑12–13cm.

Fanfare (nivalis)
Like G. 'Chatterbox', also named by North Green Snowdrops, has outward-facing flowers on erect stems. Named by John Morley, North Green Snowdrops.

'Fanny' (Hybrid cultivar)

Vigorous. Leaves semi-erect, broad, flat or explicative, glaucous. Outer segments long, slender, pointed, pale-green mark at apex. Inner segments large variable 'X' apex to base. Often three scapes on mature plants. Joy Bulford and Frank Rhodes, Ealing Wharf, Southampton, c. 1971, named after Joy Bulford's daughter. ↑21cm.

'Faringdon Double' (Hybrid double)

Vigorous, very early double. Flowers large, rounded, appear single until viewed closely. Leaves supervolute, semi-erect, grey-glaucous. Outer segments, smooth, pointed. Inner segments irregular, outer whorl often aberrant, strong heart to occasional 'X' shaped green mark diffusing towards base. December–January. David and Ruby Baker at Faringdon, Oxfordshire, 1988. ↑20cm.

'Farthingoe Beauty' (plicatus)
Possibly two snowdrops in circulation under this name. Originally named G. 'Ruth' by Richard Bashford and Valerie Bexley but when it was realised the name already applied they renamed it G. 'Farthingoe Beauty' as they had received it from Ruth Dashwood of Farthingoe.

'Fat Boy' (elwesii)
Inner segment uniform 'V' at apex, square ends. Originated with Elizabeth Parker-Jervis, distributed by Primrose Warburg. Earlier G. 'Fat Boy' described by E.A. Bowles as G. elwesii seedling from Myddelton House garden, Middlesex, 1914. Large rounded flowers, very short spathes, three or four or more flowers on ever lengthening spathes between same pair of leaves. Now appears lost.

'Fatty' (nivalis)
Smaller G. nivalis. Well rounded, balloon-like flowers. Leaves erect, slender,

blue-green. Outer segments broad, rounded, lightly ridged. Inner segments narrow Chinese-bridge mark at apex. January–February. ↑10cm.

'Fatty Arbuckle'
(*elwesii* var. *elwesii*)

Chunky, well rounded flowers, distinctive large ovary. Leaves supervolute, broad, erect, well developed at flowering, often three. Outer segments rounded, ridged. Inner segments unusual yellow-green variable 'X'. Seedling selected by C. Brickell from his garden, Pulborough, West Sussex, 1993. Named after the rotund actor Roscoe Conkling Arbuckle (1887–1933), whose stage name was 'Fatty Arbuckle'. ↑16cm.

'Fatty Puff'

Large, rounded, dimpled flowers. Outer segments broad, lightly ridged, dimpled. Inner segments green mark either side of sinus, larger mark towards base. Some consider this a snowdrop in its own right but John Grimshaw insists it is G. 'Diggory'.

'Federschwingen'
(*nivalis*)

Attractive, strong growing. Oblong ovary. Outer segments clawed lifting segment, pointed at apex, pale green lines from apex towards base. Inner segments broad inverted 'U' at apex, slightly fuzzy basal side. January–February. Germany. English translation: 'Spring Swing'. ↑23cm.

'Fee Clochette'
(*nivalis*)

Well rounded, balloon-like flowers. Leaves applanate, upright, blue-green. Outer segments longitudinally ridged, broadening towards apex, variable green marks at apex, one or two small dots or completely absent. Inner segments fractionally shorter than outer, large inverted 'V' at apex.

'Fenstead End'
(*elwesii* var. *elwesii*)

Beautiful large flowers, arching spathe. Leaves supervolute, long, upright. Inner segments incurved, slightly flared at apex, long broad dark green mark across segment, not to base, white margin. Early. Originated in Christopher Grey-Wilson's garden, Fenstead End, Suffolk. ↑23cm.

'Fieldgate A'
(Hybrid cultivar)

Leaves upright, slender, blue-green, paler median stripe. Outer segments rounded, broad claw and goffered at base. Inner segments inverted 'U' to 'V' at apex. February. Colin Mason, Kenilworth, Warwickshire.

'Fieldgate Allegro'
(Hybrid cultivar)

Fieldgate snowdrops' 'musical' introduction. Tall. Large, solid-looking flowers. Outer segments bluntly pointed. Inner segments broad 'U' at apex. February. Colin Mason, Kenilworth, Warwickshire.

'Fieldgate B'
See 'Fieldgate Superb'.

'Fieldgate Continuo'
(Hybrid cultivar)

Well shaped flowers, erect scapes. Outer segments pointed. Inner segments broad rounded inverted 'U' at apex. February. Colin Mason, Kenilworth, Warwickshire.

'Fieldgate E'
(Hybrid cultivar)

Elegant, stately, similar to G. 'Fieldgate Fugue'. Outer segments long, full, rounded, bluntly pointed. Inner

segments waisted green mark apex almost to base, slightly darker green upper side of marking. February. Colin Mason, Kenilworth, Warwickshire.

'Fieldgate Forte'
(Hybrid cultivar)

Leaves semi-erect, weakly supervolute, explicative, grey-glaucous. Outer segments pointed, longitudinally grooved, green marks apex and base. Inner segments green mark across segment diffusing slightly towards base. February. Colin Mason raised seedling from G. 'Modern Art', Kenilworth, Warwickshire, early 1990s. ↑26cm.

'Fieldgate Fugue'
(Hybrid cultivar)

Attractive rounded flowers, strong scapes. Leaves semi-erect, broad, glaucous. Outer segments textured, clawed. Inner segments roughly 'X' mark across segment, filled in base. Usually two scapes. February. Colin Mason, Fieldgate Lane, Kenilworth, Warwickshire. Origins mysterious as purported to have appeared in twin-scales of G. 'John Gray'. Similar to G. 'Fieldgate Superb'. ↑22cm

'Fieldgate L'
(Hybrid cultivar)

Elegantly shaped slender flower, slender pedicel, dark-green ovary. Outer segments recurved margins, pointed. Inner segments dark-green inverted 'V' at apex narrowly joining slender, dark-green oval towards base. Colin Mason, Kenilworth, Warwickshire.

'Fieldgate Prelude'
(*elwesii*)

Well shaped flowers, long dark-green ovary. Inner segment green 'V' at apex, upturned ends, joining

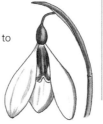

paler mark diffusing towards base. Vigorous, good. December. Colin Mason, Kenilworth, Warwickshire, from G. 'Mrs Macnamara' seedlings, 1990.

'Fieldgate Superb'
(Hybrid cultivar)
Syn. G. 'Fieldgate B' Bold, attractive. Large flowers. Leaves semi-erect, plicate, grey-green-glaucous. Outer segments long, slender, narrow claw. Inner segments roughly 'X' shaped green mark covering two-thirds, diffusing towards base. Often two scapes on established plants. March. Colin Mason, Kenilworth, Warwickshire, 1990. RHS PC 1998. G. plicatus. ↑23cm.

'Fieldgate Tiffany'
(elwesii)
Large snowdrop with substantial flowers. Leaves broad, grey-green. Outer segments broad, textured, pointed, short claw at base. Inner segments broad 'U' at apex. Colin Mason, Kenilworth, Warwickshire.

'Finale'
See 'Washfield Warham'.

'Finchale Abbey'
(nivalis)
Unusual almost tulip-shaped flowers. Leaves applanate, erect, thickly textured. Outer segments smooth, upturned, pointed at apex. Inner segments deeply ridged, small inverted 'U' or 'V' mark at apex. January–February. Barrie Carson Turner, near Finchale Abbey, Durham, 1982. ↑17cm.

'Fiona Mackenzie'
(nivalis)
Attractive green-tipped snowdrop. Olive-green ovary. Leaves erect, slender, blue-green.

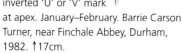

Outer segments lightly ridged, heavily marked green above apex to half of segment. Inner segments broad rounded 'U' at apex. January–February. Dr Ronald Mackenzie.

'Fiona's Gold'
(nivalis Sandersii Group)
Good yellow ovary and markings, upright green scape, spathe and leaves. Leaves applanate, green-yellow. Outer segments long, slender claw at base. Inner segments broad yellow inverted 'U' at apex. Primrose Warburg's garden. ↑11cm.

flavescens 'Flore Pleno'
(nivalis)
See 'Lady Elphinstone'.

'Flavescens'
(nivalis Sandersii Group)
Syn. G. nivalis Sandersii Group, also formerly G. nivalis 'Howick Yellow', G. nivalis 'Netherhall Yellow' Said to have better colouring than G. 'Sandersii'. Yellow ovary and yellow-green pedicel, spathe and scape. Outer segments pointed. Inner segments inverted yellow 'V' at apex. Yellow clones from Northumberland grouped under Sandersii Group. William Boyd, near Whittingham, Northumberland, 1889. See G. nivalis Sandersii Group.

'Flight of Fancy' (nivalis)
Attractive, unusual reflexed flowers. Leaves applanate, erect, slightly twisted. Outer segments recurving almost to base. Inner segment light-green Chinese-bridge to 'V' at apex. January–February. Alan Street at Shipton, Shropshire, 1997. Named by Ruby Baker. ↑15cm.

'Flocon de Neige' (nivalis)
Beautiful, double. Leaves erect to arching, slender, blue-green. Six delicate well

spaced outer segments surround symmetrically arranged inner segments marked small green inverted 'U'. February–March. Regular division. February. Mark Brown, 1980s. English translation: 'Snowflake'. ↑14cm.

'Flore Pleno' (elwesii × nivalis)
Well shaped, large, neat, double. Leaves supervolute, broad, glaucous. Very variable plants with double flowers but generally a better Flore Pleno than nivalis.

'Flore Pleno' (nivalis)
Syn. G. nivalis var. hortensis flore semipleno Common double nivalis. Robust, much loved, widespread. Variable flowers. Leaves applanate, narrow, grey-green, glaucous. Outer segments three to five. Inner segment tight irregular ruff, tipped green. Good. Sterile but produces pollen, increases quickly from offsets. February–March. Cultivated since early 1700s, widely naturalized. Most doubles have G. nivalis 'Flore Pleno' ancestry. RHS AGM 1993. ↑12–14cm.

'Florence Baker'
(plicatus)
Tall, handsome. Attractive, well shaped flowers. Leaves broad, arching, glaucescent, well developed at flowering. Inner segments roughly 'X' shaped two-tone green mark apex towards base. December–January. Ruth Stungo, in Michael and Caroline Baker's garden, Owletts, Kent. RHS PC 1999. ↑27cm.

'Fluff' (nivalis)
Small spiky flowers near ground before scape lengthens. Leaves erect, slender, blue-green. Outer segments three to five. Inner segments tight, uneven, heavily marked green. Late. Slow.

January–March. Alan Street at Collingbourne Kingston, Wiltshire, 1997. ↑12cm.

'Fly Away Peter'
Well shaped flowers on erect scapes. Outer segments long, bluntly pointed. Inner segments narrow inverted 'U' at apex.

'Fly Fishing'
Attractive G. 'Comet' seedling. Exceptionally long scape, upright spathe. Outer segments bluntly pointed. Inner segments green inverted 'V' at apex. Named for long pedicel suggesting fishing line.

'Fly Fly'
Slender flowers. Outer segments long, pointed, slender claw, reflexing. Inner segments narrow inverted pale-green 'V' at apex.

'Forge Double' (Hybrid double)
Tiny hybrid double, immature flowers dominate. Leaves erect, well developed at flowering. Outer segments slender, strongly incurved. Inner segments clasping, heart-shaped mark at apex, narrow line to base. February–March. Richard Britten, Chelsworth, Suffolk, 1988, named by Rod Leeds. ↑6cm.

fosteri (species)
Syn. *G. fosteri* var. *antepensis* Central and southern Turkey, Syria, Lebanon, Jordan. Leaves, supervolute, erect-recurving, hooded, broad, bright shiny-green, occasional longitudinal folds. Outer segments elongated. Inner segments green inverted 'U' or 'V' at apex or two small marks, large lighter

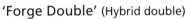

rectangular basal mark covering half of segment or with longitudinal divide. Uncommon. Dry, sandy soil, warm, better under glass. January–March. Named by John G. Baker, 1889, for Professor Sir Michael Foster (1836–1907). RHS PC 2009. ↑8–16cm.

fosteri var. *antepensis*
Very rare autumn-flowering *fosteri*. Inner segment clear Chinese-bridge at apex, separate basal mark. October. Best in pot.

'Fotini' (*reginae-olgae* subsp. *reginae-olgae*)
Unusual virescent G. *reginae-olgae*. Leaves applanate, narrow, green. Outer segments long, bluntly pointed, merging green lines well above apex to base. Inner segments green mark from apex diffusing towards base.

'Foundling'
Pale-green ovary. Outer segments broad, bluntly pointed. Inner segments scissor-shaped mark across segment filled in at base.

'Foursome'
A new four x four snowdrop with attractive, well-shaped flowers. Unusually having four outer segments and four inner.

'Fox Farm'
Attractive well shaped flowers, long ovary. Outer segments rounded, textured, bluntly pointed. Inner segments small green dot either side of sinus, narrowly joined, separate broad-green mark towards base.

'Foxgrove Magnet' (*nivalis*)
Long slender pedicel. Leaves applanate, semi-erect, flat, glaucous. Inner segments uniform inverted 'V' at apex. January–February. Like smaller G. 'Magnet'. Sold as

G. 'Magnet' by Foxgrove Plants, Berkshire, early 1990s, now renamed. ↑11cm.

'Foxton' (Hybrid cultivar)
Attractive, smaller snowdrop. Very erect scape. Leaves prostrate, glaucous, margins lightly explicative. Outer segments elongated. Inner segments inverted 'U' at apex, rounded ends, slightly fuzzy centre. Easy. Slow. Possibly from Sir Frederick Stern's garden, Highdown, Sussex, given to Don Sims, 1960s. Late. RHS PC 2000. ↑12cm.

'Framlingham Double' (Hybrid cultivar)
Rare, late, small double, similar to G. 'Forge', including dominant immature flower phase. Mature phase flowers undeveloped. Leaves erect. Outer segments slender, incurved. Inner segments longitudinally incurved, green heart-shaped mark at apex. February–March. Anglesey Abbey, Cambridgeshire.

'Francesca'
See 'Rosemary Burnham'.

'Francesca De Gramont' (*Poculiformis* Group)
Attractive poculiform with erect scapes and very uniform, slender white segments.

'Franz Josef'
Unusually shaped flowers, dark green ovary, inflated spathe. Outer segments broad across centre, narrowing towards pointed apex with mid-green mark above apex. Inner segments dark-green heart-shaped mark at apex, two paler 'eye' spots towards base. ↑12cm.

'Fred's Giant' (*elwesii* var. *elwesii*)
Large flowers, tall scapes. Leaves supervolute, broad, glaucous. Outer segments well shaped. Inner

segments broad vertical green 'V' at apex, two dots below base, sometimes joining but variable. January–February. Vigorous. Easy. Bulks up quickly. Fred Sutherland, then head gardener, Cruikshank Botanic Garden, Aberdeen, 1949. RHS PC 1992. RHS AM 1995. Numerous clones circulating under name, all originating from Cruikshank.↑35cm.

'Friedl' (*elwesii*)

Leaves supervolute, erect, broad, grey-green. Outer segments long, rounded, bluntly pointed. Inner segments solid green mark from apex to three-quarters of segment, notch at basal end. Australian-raised selection by Otto Fauser. ↑16cm.

'Funny Justine'

Quirky, unusual, upward-facing flowers heavily marked green on very short pedicel. Leaves broad, green-blue. Outer segments rounded, good olive-green mark above apex. Cathy Porter's alpine nursery, Belgium, named after youngest daughter. ↑10cm.

'Fuzz' (*nivalis*)

Very late, slender double *G. nivalis*. Long-lasting, sterile flowers. Elongated, thin dark-green ovary. Leaves applanate, erect, slender, blue-green. Outer segments variable, very slender pale green marks at apex and base. Inner segments shorter, broader, green mark at apex. March. Avon Bulbs. ↑15cm.

'G. Handel'
(*elwesii* var. *monostictus*)

Attractive, medium-sized flowers. Leaves supervolute, erect, dark-green, two or three. Outer segments lightly ridged. Inner segments blurred green inverted 'U' to half of segment. Early, from mid-November when established. Leo Schoorl's garden, Lisse, Netherlands, 1986, from Turkish stock. ↑10cm.

'G71' (Hybrid double)

Tall rounded Greatorex double. Leaves lax, spreading, arching, pointed, variable margins, glaucous. Outer segments rounded, bluntly pointed, clawed. Inner segments dark-green 'U' from apex to half of segment, slightly blurred centre on basal side. Sometimes single flowers. Occasionally two scapes. H.A. Greatorex, Brundall, Norfolk. ↑20cm.

'G75' (Hybrid cultivar)

Well rounded flowers without aberrant segments, unusually held at 45° angle on pedicel. Leaves semi-erect, revolute margins, glaucous, short at flowering. Inner segments uniform broad 'U' centre slightly fuzzy on basal side. H.A. Greatorex, Brundall, Norfolk. ↑15cm.

'G77' (Hybrid double)

Very irregular double, many aberrant segments. Leaves erect, variably narrowly explicative, glaucous, short at flowering. Inner segments often aberrant, green inverted 'U' above large sinus. H.A. Greatorex, Brundall, Norfolk. ↑19cm.

'Gabriel' (*elwesii* hybrid)

Flowers large, elegant. Outer segments strongly clawed, recurving in warmth. Inner segments green heart-shaped mark at apex. December. Occasional second scape. Alan Street, early 1980s, named as outer segments resemble angel's wings. ↑18cm.

'Galadriel'
(*elwesii* hybrid)

Large, well shaped flowers. Leaves broad, grey, pointed. Outer segments rounded. Inner segments, good crisp green 'Y' from apex across half of segment, shading yellow-green. Late. Often second scape. Possibly related to G. 'Cedric's Prolific'. Chance seedling found by David Ward, at Beth Chatto Garden, Colchester, mid-1990s. Named after Tolkien's Lady of the Woods. ↑25cm.

'Galatea'
(Hybrid cultivar)

Large shapely flowers from long slender kinked pedicel giving much movement. Leaves arching, grey-green, glaucescent, lightly explicative. Outer segments pear-shaped. Inner segments inverted green 'V' at apex. Often two scapes on established plants. Bulks up well. January. Similar to G. 'Magnet' but earlier. Original G. 'Galatea' one of the best from James Allen's garden, Shepton Mallet, pre-1890. However, probably different to modern stock from Ruth Birchall's Cotswold Farm garden, Gloucestershire, found again by Herbert Ransom, early 1970s. ↑25cm.

'Geerte Groote'

Tiny flowers around 1cm. Outer segments slender, bluntly pointed. Inner segments inverted 'V' at apex, pale-green mark towards base. Harry Pierick, near Windesheim, named after clergyman of 1387. ↑6cm.

'Geishaaugen'

Outer segments slender, pointed. Inner segments inverted 'U' or 'V' at apex, diffused pale green 'U' at base. Germany. ↑14cm.

'Geisterschwingen'

Leaves blue-green. Outer segments well shaped, long, textured, dimpled, broad, clawed. Inner segments pale-green 'X' to scissor-shaped mark across segment, stronger at apex. Germany. English translation: 'Ghost Swing'.

'Gelbe Marlu'
(Hybrid cultivar)

Pale-yellow ovary and pedicel. Outer segments pointed. Inner segments yellow inverted 'V' at apex merging into paler marks towards base. Günter Waldorf, Oirlicher Blumengarten, Germany.

'Gelber Clown'

Yellow-green spathe, pedicel and ovary. Outer segments slender. Inner segments pale yellow-green mark across segment.

Günter Waldorf, Oirlicher Blumengarten, Germany. English translation: 'Gold Clown'.

'Gemini' (*nivalis*)
Beautiful, elegant. Leaves applanate, erect, blue-green. Outer segments long, slender, pointed. Inner segments slender, tube-like, broad inverted 'V' at apex. Regularly two flowers to each scape from separate pedicels. January–February. ↑16cm.

'Genet's Giant' (*elwesii*)
A robust, vigorous, tall, Australian selection with large, well shaped flowers and good green marks.

'Genie'
Rounded, globular flowers. Outer segments rounded, bluntly pointed. Inner segments green mark from apex towards base.

'George Chiswell No 1' (Hybrid cultivar)
From George Chiswell, Porlock, Somerset.

'George Chiswell No 9' (Hybrid cultivar)
Small flowers, rounded ovary. Outer segments slender, incurved. Inner segments pale-green broad inverted 'U' at apex, paler lines towards base. From George Chiswell, Porlock, Somerset.

'George Elwes' (Hybrid cultivar)
Distinctive, tall, with large flowers beneath long hooded spathe arching above pedicel on erect scapes. Leaves, broad, sculptured, outer leaf flat, inner explicative. Outer segments slender. Inner segments tube-like, long waisted green mark, narrow white border, paler stripe lengthways from base. Vigorous. Regularly two scapes. January–February. *G. elwesii* × *G. plicatus* hybrid. Carolyn Elwes, Colesbourne, 1979, named after her late son. ↑16cm.

'Georgia' (*ikariae*)
Gerald Bauer Green-marked snowdrop.

'Gerard Parker' (*plicatus*)
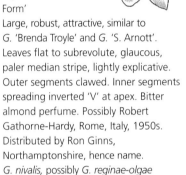
Syn. *G.* 'Warham' ex Lady Stern Good, strong, reliable *G. plicatus* cultivar. Very large, balloon-like flowers. Leaves broad, short, blue-green. Outer segments clawed, ridged, dimpled. Inner segments variable marks. Bulks up quickly. Lady Stern gave bulbs of *G.* 'Warham' to Primrose Warburg, who passed some to Ronald Mackenzie, who sold them under this name. Primrose Warburg also gave bulbs to John Morley as *G. plicatus* ex 'Gerard Parker', offered under this name, 1996. Despite slight variations in inner segment markings, Bishop, Davis and Grimshaw conclude the snowdrops are identical. Original name *G.* 'Gerard Parker' takes precedence. ↑16cm.

'Gerlinda'

Outer segments long, slender, rounded, slightly incurved. Inner segments pale-green mark across segment diffusing towards base.

'Ghost' (*nivalis*)
Alan Street snowdrop discovered in a cemetery, hence the name.

'Ghost Spirit' (*nivalis* Poculiformis Group)

Slender, elegant, attractive white poculiform flowers. Inner segments fractionally shorter than outer, all-white. Ehepaars Way, Hunton.

'Gill Gregory'
Elegant flowers. Outer segments well shaped, bluntly pointed. Inner segments green inverted 'V' at apex, two paler ovals shading towards base. ↑15cm.

'Gill's Special'

Well shaped flowers beneath pale-green ovary. Leaves slender, blue-green. Outer segments rounded, bluntly pointed.

Inner segments pale-green inverted 'V' at apex joining two pale-green marks extending towards base.

'Gilt Edge'
Good yellow. Inner segments marked yellow. Günter Waldorf, Germany.

'Ginn's Imperati' (*nivalis* hybrid)
Syn. *G. imperati* 'Ginns Form', *G.* 'Imperati Ginn's Form', *G. nivalis* subsp. *imperati* 'Ginn's Form'
Large, robust, attractive, similar to *G.* 'Brenda Troyle' and *G.* 'S. Arnott'. Leaves flat to subrevolute, glaucous, paler median stripe, lightly explicative. Outer segments clawed. Inner segments spreading inverted 'V' at apex. Bitter almond perfume. Possibly Robert Gathorne-Hardy, Rome, Italy, 1950s. Distributed by Ron Ginns, Northamptonshire, hence name. *G. nivalis*, possibly *G. reginae-olgae* associations. ↑18cm.

'Glacier' (*nivalis*)

Elongated white flower, oblong ovary, long slender pedicel, erect scape. Outer segments long, very slender. Inner segments wider, tiny green spot either side of sinus at apex, can be joined. January–February. ↑15cm.

'Gladysdale' (Hybrid cultivar)
Large attractively shaped flowers. Leaves erect, grey-green. Outer segments large, long, rounded at apex. Inner segments long, broad, inverted filled in 'U' from apex to half of segment. Australian-raised cultivar. ↑16cm.

'Glass Marble'
Attractive rounded flowers, rounded dark-green ovary, inflated spathe. Outer segments broad, bluntly pointed. Inner segments broad green inverted 'U' at apex diffusing into second paler mark at base.

'Glenchantress'
Rare large-flowered snowdrop. Outer segments green lines at apex. Inner segments deep-green. Wol and Sue Staines, Glen Chantry.

'Glooming'
Gert-Jan van der Kolk, 2001.

Gloria (*nivalis* Poculiformis Group)
Elegantly shaped poculiform. Leaves erect, blue-green. Outer segments slightly longer than inner, bluntly pointed. Inner segments sinus at apex. ↑18cm.

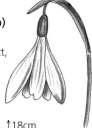

'Gloucester Old Spot' (*nivalis*)
Well shaped flowers. Leaves applanate, erect, slender, blue-green, glaucous. Outer segments bluntly pointed. Inner segments small rounded spot each side of large sinus. Bulks up well. Phil Cornish, 1990, at Hatherley Manor, Gloucestershire. Named after local Gloucester Old Spot pig. ↑13cm.

'Goblet' (*elwesii*)
Well shaped, rounded flowers. Outer segments longitudinally ridged, incurved margins, textured, bluntly pointed, clawed. Inner segments broad inverted 'U' at apex, paler green mark towards base, can be barely joined.

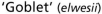

'Godfrey Owen' (*elwesii*)
Outstanding. Twelve segments forming symmetrical flower. Leaves supervolute, semi-erect, broad, two or three, well developed at flowering. Outer segments six, bluntly pointed. Inner segments six, occasionally more, two small marks at apex, can be joined, sometimes two paler

dots towards base. Bulks up well. December–early January. Margaret Owen, Acton Pigot, Shropshire, mid-1990s, named for her late husband. RHS AM 2009. RHS FCC 2011. ↑15cm.

'Gold Edge' (*plicatus*)
Good pear-shaped flowers. Leaves unusually variegated with yellow border. Outer segments clawed. Inner segments tube-like, straight-sided yellow-green mark from apex almost to base. Name derived from gold-edged leaves. ↑18cm.

'Goldcrest' (Hybrid cultivar)
Recently introduced, new yellow snowdrop with yellow marks on both inner and outer segments. Thetford, Norfolk.

'Golden Boy' (*nivalis* Sandersii Group)
Good yellow, slightly larger than some in group. Spathe yellow-green, ovary yellow. Leaves distinctive, applanate, erect, yellow-green. Outer segments longitudinally ridged. Inner segments lightly ridged, strong yellow inverted 'V' at apex, upturned ends. Grows well. Valentin Wijnen, Belgium, named for his son. ↑11cm.

'Golden Glow' (*nivalis*)
Named by John Morley, North Green Snowdrops.

'Golden Sunrise'
A Belgian introduction from Valentin Wijnen.

'Goldheart' (nivalis)
Named by John Morley, North Green Snowdrops.

'Goldmine'
Oblong ovary. Outer segments lightly ridged, bluntly pointed. Inner segments yellow-green inverted 'U' at apex, slightly staining on basal side. ↑14cm.

'Goliath' (*elwesii*)
Handsome flowers shown off to advantage by foliage. Large, rounded ovary. Leaves supervolute, broad, green-grey, pointed. Outer segments long claw. Inner segments inverted 'V' at apex narrowly joining long, broad oval towards base.

'Gone Fishing'
Well shaped flowers suspended from distinctive, exceptionally long arching pedicels. Leaves applanate, erect to arching, blue-green. Outer segments bluntly pointed. Inner segments inverted 'U' to 'V' at apex. ↑18cm.

'Grace' (*plicatus*)
Attractive flowers, small ovary. Leaves explicative, grey-green, paler median stripe. Outer segments good substance, pointed. Inner segments pale-green mark covering almost entire segment, narrow white margin. ↑23cm.

gracilis (species)
Syn. *G. graecus*
Greece, Bulgaria, Rumania, western Turkey, Ukraine. Flowers attractive, slender. Leaves applanate, narrow, twisted, blue-grey, glaucous, conspicuous median stripe. Inner segments slightly reflexed, 'U' or 'V' at apex or two small marks each side of sinus, occasionally 'X' shaped mark, also basal mark. Dry situation, full sun. Temperamental. February–March. ↑10–18cm.

gracilis Virescent Form
Handsome virescent snowdrop. Leaves upright-arching, blue-green. Outer segments merging green lines above apex towards base. Inner segments green mark apex to base, white margin. ↑12cm.

'Grakes Gold'
(*nivalis* Sandersii Group)

Strong yellow with yellow pedicel, spathe and ovary. Leaves initially yellow, greener in maturity. Inner segments strong yellow broad inverted 'V' at apex. Valentin Wijnen, Grakes Heredij, Belgium. Garden and series of snowdrops named after Valentin Wijnen's grandfather, Gerard Schoefs, nicknamed 'Grake'.

'Grakes Green Bells' (*nivalis*)

Well marked *G. nivalis*. Leaves applanate, erect, blue-green. Outer segments merging green lines on centre. Inner segments completely green, narrow white margin. Slow. Valentin Wijnen, old nursery, Belgium, 2005.

'Grakes Monster'

Very variable year to year. Inflated, curving spathe. Leaves applanate, erect, blue-green. Outer segments rounded. Inner segments inverted green 'V at apex. February. Valentin Wijnen, Grakes Garden, Belgium. ↑10cm.

'Grakes Yellow'
(*nivalis* Sandersii Group)

Yellow ovary and pedicel, yellow green spathe. Leaves applanate, blue-green. Outer segments long, bluntly pointed. Inner segments yellow inverted 'V' at apex. Good, grows well. Valentin Wijnen, Belgium. ↑9cm.

'Grandiflorus' (Hybrid cultivar)

See × *hybridus*.

× *grandiflorus*

See 'Grandiflorus'.

'Grandis'

See 'Straffan'.

'Gray's Child'
(Hybrid cultivar)

Beautiful, well shaped flowers. Leaves lax, two or three, flat to subrevolute, glaucous. Outer segments pear-shaped, clawed. Inner segments clasping, variably shaped and coloured roughly 'H' mark to half of segment. Usually two scapes. December–January. Graham Gough, 1996. ↑16cm.

'Grayling'

See 'Percy Picton'.

'Grayswood'
(*elwesii* var. *monostictus*)

Flowers medium. Leaves arching. Outer segments pointed, clawed. Inner segments inverted 'U' at apex, tiny sinus. Bulks up quickly. Geoffrey Pilkington's Grayswood garden, Haslemere, Surrey. Two clones, best of which and rightful bearer of name was given to Ray Cobb by Herbert Crook, Hertfordshire. ↑15cm.

'Green Arrow'

Elongated flowers. Leaves, long, erect, slender, blue-green. Outer segments large, long, bluntly pointed, mid-green mark at apex. Inner segments broad inverted 'V' at apex, rounded ends, diffusing towards base, narrow basal mark. ↑16cm.

'Green Brush' (*elwesii*)

Good green-marked *G. elwesii*. Striking, bold, broad waxy segments. Leaves broad, grey-green. Outer segments rounded, bluntly pointed, strong yellow-green mark at apex. Inner segments green mark covering most of segment. Well drained, sunny position. ↑18cm.

'Green Claw'

Double on erect scape. Leaves slender, erect to arching, blue-green. Outer segments large, long, pointed, strong green mark above apex. Inner segments neat whorl, inverted 'U' at apex. February–March. ↑15cm.

'Green Comet' (Hybrid cultivar)

Very large, attractive. Long pedicel. Flowers large, similar to *G.* 'Comet'. Leaves long, broad, grey-green. Outer segments bluntly pointed. Inner segments inverted 'U' at apex. John Morley, North Green Snowdrops, Suffolk. ↑18cm.

'Green Cross' (*elwesii*)

Variable snowdrop with well shaped flowers. Leaves broad, grey-green. Outer segments bluntly pointed. Inner segment green marks at apex and base joined with a green cross. December–January. 18cm.

'Green Diamond'
(*nivalis*)

Neat looking flowers, slender pedicel. Leaves applanate, erect, slender, blue-green. Outer segments bluntly pointed, merging green lines at apex. Inner segments broad green inverted 'V' at apex. February. Tom Koopman, W. Vieveen, Netherlands, 2010.

'Green Faun' (*nivalis*)

Attractive, heavily green-marked flowers, sturdy, erect scapes. Outer segments clawed and goffered at base, lightly longitudinally ridged, merging green lines running up lower half of segment. Inner segments solid green mark, narrow white margin. January–February.

'Green Fingers'
(Hybrid double)

Improved form of *G.* 'Blewbury Tart', lower growing, more floriferous. Leaves applanate, erect, grey-green. Outer segments three, tipped green at apex. Inner segments heavily

marked green on upper and lower sides of segment. February–March. ↑10cm.

'Green Flash'
Small with small flowers. Leaves supervolute, green-blue-glaucescent, well developed at flowering. Outer segments rounded, pointed, four merging green lines. Inner segments thin line joining small dot either side of sinus. Phil Cornish, Rodborough, Stroud, Gloucestershire, 1998. ↑10cm.

'Green Forest Fairy' (*nivalis*)
Slender virescent. Drooping flowers, erect scapes. Leaves applanate, slender, erect, blue-green. Outer segments long, incurved, pointed, pale-green lines following veins. Inner segments light-green mark across segment, narrow white margin.

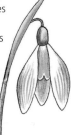

'Green Gauge'
Outer segments broad, rounded, broad goffered claw. Large bright-green mark above apex.

'Green Grey and White' (*elwesii*)
Often 'Siamese twin' flowers, or two flowers on separate pedicels. Leaves supervolute, broad, distinctively grey. Outer segments green mark at apex. Inner segments good, broad, green mark. January–March. ↑10cm.

'Green Hayes' (*plicatus*)
Beautiful, rare, with large flowers. Leaves shiny, grey-green. Outer segments pinched at apex, small pale-green shading at base. Inner segments green scissor-shaped mark diffusing, paling towards base. Primrose Warburg's garden, South Hayes.

'Green Horror'
See 'Boyd's Double'.

'Green Ibis' (*nivalis*)
Attractive, late. Leaves applanate, erect, arching, blue-green. Outer segments, long, rounded, bluntly pointed, around six

merging green lines on apical half. Inner segments squared inverted 'V' at apex slightly fuzzy basal side, two marginal lines towards base. March. ↑12cm.

'Green Ice'
Leaves applanate, erect, blue-green. Outer segments bluntly pointed. Inner segments broad pale-green mark across segment from apex towards base. February. ↑8cm.

'Green Lantern' (*plicatus*)
Beautiful Irish snowdrop with well shaped flowers. Leaves explicative, grey-green, paler median stripe. Outer segments large, thick, bluntly pointed. Inner segments small inverted green 'V' at apex pales oval towards base. Altamont Gardens, Eire.

'Green Leaf'
Delicate-looking snowdrop. As names suggests, leaves very green. Outer segments slender, clawed. Inner segments good inverted 'V' at apex.

'Green Light' (*nivalis*)
Well shaped *G. nivalis*. Leaves unusual, shiny, bright-green. Outer segments small merging green lines. Inner segments broad inverted 'U' at apex. January–February. 2004. ↑15cm.

'Green Man' (Hybrid cultivar)
Uncommon. Long ovary. Large well shaped flowers. Leaves semi-erect, flat to lightly explicative, glaucescent. Outer segments rounded, pointed, clawed. Inner segments strong green 'X' mark diffusing towards base. February–March. Probably *G. plicatus* × *G. nivalis*. ↑14cm.

'Green Mile' (Hybrid cultivar)
Very strongly green marked snowdrop. Outer segments spoon-shaped, heavily

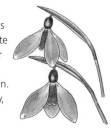

marked green across segment, small-white notch at apex. Inner segments green, narrow white margin. Green Miles Nursery, Belgium. ↑10cm.

'Green Necklace' (Hybrid cultivar)
Leaves applanate, flat to explicative, glaucescent. Outer segments light longitudinal ridging. Inner segments dark green inverted 'U' to 'V' shadowed above towards base. Easy. Bulks up well. Daphne Chappell in Ruth Birchall's garden, Cotswold Farm, 1970s, later at Hyde Lodge. ↑12cm.

'Green of Hearts' (Hybrid cultivar)
Outstanding, attractive, unusually shaped flowers. Leaves applanate, flat-explicative, glaucous. Outer segments incurved, light longitudinal ridging, dark-green heart-shaped mark at apex, lighter mark on underside stretching centrally to base. Inner segments clasping, only slightly shorter than outer, heart-shaped mark at apex. John Morley, North Green Snowdrops, Suffolk, 1997. *G. plicatus* 'Trym' parent. 'Trym' synonym 'Ace of Spades', suggested another card-based name. ↑13cm.

'Green Peace' (*plicatus*)
Well rounded flowers. Leaves explicative, green-glaucous. Outer segments rounded, textured, lightly ridged and dimpled, bluntly pointed. Inner segments broad green mark across segment towards base, narrow white margin. Often two scapes. Well perfumed. Derek Fox from Oliver Wyatt's former garden, Naughton, Suffolk. ↑18cm.

'Green Pips'

Elegant textured flowers, long, slender ovary. Outer segments thick, waxy, pointed. Inner segments broad green marking from apex towards base reminiscent of molar tooth, narrow white margin.

'Green Ribbon'
(*elwesii*)

Rounded, very white flowers, mid-green ovary. Leaves broad, grey-green. Outer segments long, large, bluntly pointed. Inner segments waisted green mark from apex towards base.

'Green Stripe' (*nivalis*)

Beautiful, well shaped flowers, erect, sturdy scapes. Leaves applanate, slender, erect, blue-green. Outer segments longitudinally ridged, green lines from apex towards base. Inner segments green mark across segment towards base. ↑18cm.

'Green Tear' (*nivalis*)

Good, stunning, sought-after virescent. Leaves applanate, semi-erect, blue-green. Outer segments broad green lines base towards apex. Inner segments strong green mark across segment. Possible *G. nivalis* × *G. plicatus*. January–February. Gert-Jan van der Kolk, Netherlands. Bulbs have sold for £320 on eBay. RHS PC 2009. ↑10cm.

'Green Teeth' (*plicatus*)

Delicate-looking flowers. Rounded, shiny bright-green ovary. Leaves explicative, green, paler median stripe. Outer segments long, boat-shaped. Inner segments flared, green inverted 'U'

at apex, smudged marks towards base. Sally Pasmore's garden, Limington, Somerset, c. 2000.

'Green Tip'
See 'Pusey Green Tip'.

'Green Tip Double'
See 'Pusey Green Tip'.

'Green Tipped'

Outer segments long, pointed, tapering towards apex, pale-green mark at apex. Inner segments dark-green mark, apex to three-quarters of segment. January–March. ↑20cm.

'Green Tips'
(*elwesii* var. *monostictus*)

Large, rounded, well shaped flowers. Leaves erect, arching, broad, grey. Outer segments rounded, bluntly pointed, tipped green at apex. Inner segments large waisted green mark across segment. Good. Free-flowering. January–March. Sometimes known as *G.* 'Michael Myer's Green Tipped'. ↑23cm.

'Green Tube'
(Hybrid cultivar)

Attractively shaped slender flowers. Outer segments pointed. Inner segments tube-like, broad green mark apex to three-quarters of segment, broken towards base.

'Green Wings'
(*elwesii* var. *elwesii*)

Attractive snowdrop with small, well rounded flowers. Leaves supervolute, erect. Outer segments rounded, green mark with nine merging lines covering half of segment from apex. Inner segments wide green mark squared before base. Slow. Seedling from 1970s *G. elwesii* planting, Katherine Boyd's garden, Cambridgeshire, 1990. ↑20cm.

'Green With Envy'
(*nivalis*)

Elongated, heavily green-marked flowers, large ovary. Leaves applanate, erect, slender, blue-green. Outer segments green mark across segment, narrow white margin. Inner segments green mark paling towards base, narrow white margin. January–February. Belgium.

'Green Woodpecker'
(*woronowii*)

Leaves broad, arching, green. Outer segments broad, pointed. Leaves supervolute, green, lightly pleated. Outer segments broad, rounded, bluntly pointed, green mark above apex. Inner segments small green inverted 'V' at apex or two small dots. Woodpeckers, Warwickshire. ↑10cm.

'Green X' (*elwesii*)

Leaves, broad, arching, grey-green. Outer segments bluntly pointed. Inner segments narrow inverted 'V' at apex joining into 'X' or scissor-shaped mark towards base. ↑18cm.

'Green Zebra' (*nivalis*)

Large flowers. Leaves applanate, erect to arching, slender, blue-green. Outer segments broad, longitudinally ridged, green lines following ridges. Inner segments green apex towards base, narrow white margin. M. Dreisvogt, found in Slovenia. ↑14cm.

'Greenfield'
See 'Greenfields'.

'Greenfields' (Hybrid cultivar)

Syn. *G.* 'Greenfield'
Attractive, smaller Irish snowdrop. Reflexed spathe, pale-green elongated ovary. Leaves semi-erect, silvery-glaucescent. Outer segments

smooth, spoon-shaped. Inner segments variable broad heart-shaped mark at apex. Regularly two scapes. Good, bulks up well. February. Liam Schofield, Ireland c. 1950s–60s in colonies of *G. nivalis* and *G. plicatus*. ↑14cm.

'Greenfinch'
(Hybrid cultivar)

Outstanding green-tipped flowers, strong scapes. Leaves applanate, erect-arching, silver-glaucescent. Outer segments spoon-shaped, bluntly pointed, merging green lines above apex. Inner segments spreading heart-shaped to inverted 'U' at apex. Often two scapes. Richard Hobbs in H.A. Greatorex's former garden, Brundall, Norfolk. Looks like strong *G. nivalis* but attractive, silvery-glaucous leaves show *G. plicatus* ancestry. PC 2008. ↑32cm.

'Greenish' (*nivalis*)

Attractive small virescent. Leaves applanate, prostrate, lightly explicative. Outer segments six to eight green lines on apical half. Inner segments inverted 'U' at apex shading to pale basal mark. Similar to *G. 'Virescens'* but earlier, lighter shading and easier to grow. Bulks up well. February–March. Fritz Kummert, Vienna, 1963. ↑13cm.

'Green-leaved hybrid ex R.D. Nutt' (Hybrid cultivar)

Leaves semi-erect, narrow, flat, applanate on small bulbs, mildly supervolute on larger. Outer segments clawed. Inner segments small inverted 'V' at apex, thinner in centre. Possible *G. woronowii* × *G. rizehensis*, though looking similar to *G. lagodechianus*. Richard Nutt from Hopa, Turkey, 1990s. ↑14cm.

'Greenshank' (Hybrid cultivar)

Elegant slender flowers. Leaves semi-erect, green. Outer segments slim, strongly clawed, faint green shadow at base. Inner segments strong inverted 'V' at apex with two arms extending, narrowing and diffusing towards base. John Grimshaw, Oxfordshire, 1996. ↑16cm.

'Greycott Greentip' (*nivalis*)

Spathe sometimes splits resembling *G. 'Scharlockii'*. Leaves applanate, semi-erect, lightly explicative margins. Outer segments solid mark at apex. Inner segments slightly fuzzy green inverted 'V' at apex. Matt Bishop, Surrey, 1987, named after parents' old home. ↑13cm.

'Gritt's Great'

Elongated flowers with slender segments.

'Grumpy'
(*elwesii* Edward Whittall Group)

Vigorous with well shaped flowers. Leaves supervolute, arching, grey-green. Outer segments clawed. Inner segments inverted 'V' at apex, two 'eye' dots towards base. January–February. Slow. Joe Sharman, in Sir Vivian Fuch's garden, Cambridge, 1990, named because marks resemble miserable face. ↑17cm.

'Grüne Ostern'

Large, strong, well shaped snowdrop. Outer segments large, rounded, bluntly pointed. Inner segments broad slightly waisted green mark covering almost entire segment apart from white triangle at base and narrow white border. Sometimes two scapes. Hagen Engelmann. Found just before Easter 2005. Probably *G. elwesii* × *G. nivalis*. English translation: 'Green Easter'.

'Grüne Ostern II'

Probably not a valid name as too close to *G. 'Grüne Ostern'*, but listed by some growers. Elegant flowers. Outer segments slightly narrower than *G. 'Grüne Ostern'*, small green mark above apex, sometimes absent. Inner segments slightly waisted broad green mark across segment. Hagen Engelmann, 2006.

'Grüne Pendelkugel'
(Hybrid cultivar)

Erect scapes and rounded flowers. Outer segments large, well rounded, green lines from apex diffusing towards base. Inner

segments broad, pale-green mark apex towards base, narrow white margin. Germany. English translation: 'Green Ball Pendulum'. ↑20cm.

'Grüne Perle'
(Hybrid cultivar)

Green-tipped snowdrop, slender pedicel, round, pale green ovary. Outer segments slender claw, pointed, pale green lines apex to half of segment. Inner segments green mark from apex paling towards base. Germany. English translation: 'Green Pearl'. ↑20–25cm.

'Grüne Schwerter'
(Hybrid cultivar)

Vigorous with beautifully shaped flowers, erect scapes, long slender ovary. Leaves erect to arching, grey-green. Inner segments pale-green scissor-shaped mark. Often two scapes. Possibly *G. elwesii* × *G. nivalis*. English translation: 'Green Sword'.

'Grüner Milan'
(Hybrid cultivar)

Long, slender pedicel. Leaves blue-green. Outer segments long, slender, pointed, brushed green. Inner segments green mark across segment almost to base, narrow white margin. Germany. English translation: 'Green Milan'. ↑25cm.

'Grüner Splitter' (*nivalis*)

Triangular flowers. Leaves applanate, erect-arching, green-blue. Outer segments large, white at apex diverging into merging pale-green lines running towards base. Inner segments solid green mark across segment, paling slightly at base, narrow white margin. Germany. English translation: 'Green Splitter'. ↑23cm.

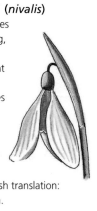

'Grünfrosch' (*nivalis*)

Well shaped flowers, long, slender ovary. Leaves applanate, erect, slender, blue-green. Outer segments slender, bluntly pointed, green stain above apex. Inner segments tube-like, large green mark, narrow white margin, central white mark. Germany. English translation: 'Green frog'.

'Günters Geist'
(*nivalis* Sandersii Group)

Yellow-green scape, pedicel, yellow ovary. Leaves applanate, variable yellow-green, some bordered yellow. Outer segments long, pointed, textured, longitudinally ridged. Inner segments smaller, ridged, puckered, no marking. Günter Waldorf. English translation: 'Gunter's Ghost'.

'Günter Waldorf'

Elegant flowers, erect scapes. Outer segments long, pointed at apex, slender claw at base. Inner segments dark-green filled 'V' at apex joining paler upright 'V' towards base. Joe Sharman, 2011, named for Günter Waldorf.

'H. Purcell'
(*elwesii* var. *monostictus*)

One of the 'Composer' snowdrops. Large flowers, arching pedicels. Leaves supervolute, short, arching, glaucous. Outer segments broad, rounded, bluntly pointed. Inner segments single roughly circular mark, small-white notch above sinus. January–March. Leo Schoorl's garden, Lisse, Netherlands, 1986, from Turkish stock. ↑14cm.

'Hacconby Green'

Large, long, rounded ovary. Outer segments slender claw. Inner segments good scissor-shaped mark.

'Haddon's Tiny'

Smaller, neat-looking snowdrop. Outer segments slender, incurved margins. Inner segments broad green inverted 'U' at apex. ↑8cm.

'Hainborn'
(Poculiformis Group)

Beautiful white poculiform with pointed segments. Leaves slender, erect to arching, green-blue. Inner segments slightly shorter than outer. Named after the town in Germany. ↑15cm.

'Half and Half'

Leaves erect, slender, blue-green. Outer segments long, slender, pointed. Inner segments inverted 'U' apex to half the segment. ↑16cm.

'Halfway'

Unusual in having four outer segments, bluntly pointed at apex. Inner segments variable inverted 'U' to 'V' at apex.

'Halo'

Leaves supervolute, upright, slender, glaucous. Outer segments ridged, pointed. Inner segments clasping, roughly 'X'-shaped mark with pronounced paler 'U' at base. Nicolas Top, Rhine Valley, Germany, c. 1992, in naturalized colony. ↑20cm.

'Hambutt's Brush'

Small irregular double. Outer segments pointed, variable pale-green marks at apex. Inner segments inverted 'V' at apex. Hambutt's Orchard, Gloucestershire. ↑15cm.

'Hambutt's Orchard'
(*nivalis*)

Strong double. Outer segment green marks at apex. Inner segments inverted 'V' at apex. Brig. Leonard Mathias at Hambutt's Orchard,

Stroud, Gloucestershire, named after garden, 1960s. Similar to G. 'Pusey Green Tip'. ↑15cm.

'Hanneke'
(Hybrid double)

Attractive regular neat double with flared segments. Outer segments narrow, reflex upwards. Inner segments neat, well formed ruff, broad inverted 'V' at apex. George Otter, 2009.

'Hanning's Horror' (*nivalis*)

Conspicuous with flowers well above leaves. Long straight pedicel above spathe. Leaves applanate, semi-erect, lightly explicative. Outer segments, three or four, incurved, pointed, thin green mark apex towards base. Inner segments lightly flared, rough inverted 'V' at apex, or mark to base. Martin Rickard, 1994, Kyre Park, Worcestershire. ↑16cm.

'Hans Guck In Die Luft'

Well shaped, attractive flowers. Leaves upright to arching, grey-green. Outer segments long, broad, rounded, bluntly pointed, longitudinally ridged and puckered. Inner segments triangular green mark either side of apex which can join, oval marks towards base. Johann Joschko. Name from German children's story book Struwwelpeter by Heinrich Hoffmann (1845).

'Hardwick' (*plicatus*)

Leaves explicative, grey-green, paler median stripe. Inner segment inverted 'V' at apex. Australian selection from Glad Patterson, Tasmania.

'Harewood Twin'

Attractive slender flowers. Leaves erect, broad, grey-green. Outer segments slender, incurved margins, opening wide. Inner segments mid-green inverted 'V' at apex thinly joining oval towards base. Regularly two flowers to each scape on separate pedicels. ↑18cm.

'Harlequin' (*nivalis*)

A *G. nivalis* which true to its name has unusually variegated foliage. Leaves applanate, narrow, variable with a strong yellow stripe. Phil Cornish.

'Harold Wheeler'
(*elwesii* Hiemalis Group)

See 'Howard Wheeler'.

'Hawkeye'

Elegantly shaped, good white flowers suspended from slender pedicel. Outer segments pointed. Inner segments green scissor-shaped mark.

'Hawkshead'

Standard-looking snowdrop. Leaves applanate, erect, blue-green. Outer segments bluntly pointed. Inner segments inverted 'V' at apex. ↑15cm.

'Haydn' (*elwesii* var. *monostictus*)

Good, small, neat. Flowers elongated, textured. Leaves short, wrapped around, finally separating part-way up scape, base wrapped around throughout season. Inner segments elongated, tube-like, inverted olive-green 'V' at apex diffusing towards base, tiny sinus. Late December–early January. Bulks up well. Best of Leo Schoorl's 'Composer' snowdrops, Lisse, Netherlands, 1986. ↑9cm.

'Hazeldene'
(*elwesii* var. *monostictus*)

Outer segments long. Inner segments yellowish-green mark. Australian selection.

'Headbourne' (Hybrid cultivar)

Beautifully shaped flowers, long pedicels. Leaves spreading, lightly explicative, glaucous. Outer segments longitudinally ridged,

bluntly pointed. Inner segments deeply ridged, spreading inverted 'V' at apex, narrow above sinus. Clumps up well. Michael Baron from garden of the Hon. Lewis Palmer, Headbourne, Winchester, Hampshire, 1987. ↑12cm.

'Hedgehog' (Hybrid double)

Shorter, quirky snowdrop with neat double, more upward-facing flowers. Leaves erect, slender, blue-green. Outer segments broad, pointed. Inner segments tight, neat ruff, green inverted 'V' at apex. Ian Christie, Scotland. ↑14cm.

'Heffalump' (Hybrid double)

Syn. *G.* 'Mrs Warburg's Double' Good, regular double. Leaves applanate or weakly supervolute, semi-erect, arching, flat-explicative, glaucescent. Outer segments narrow, splayed, strongly clawed. Inner segments clearly visible, inverted 'V' at apex narrowly joining filled-in 'U' towards base. Primrose Warburg, South Hayes, c. 1987, named for her late husband's nickname. ↑14cm.

'Helen Dillon's Whopper'

See 'Cicely Hall'.

'Helen Tomlinson' (*elwesii*)

Sturdy snowdrop with large, well shaped flowers. Leaves oblong-lanceolate, hooded. Outer segments boat-shaped, light longitudinal ridging. Inner segments light goffering at edges, broad inverted 'U' at apex. Good, reliable. Tight clumps. Named after John Tomlinson's wife. PC 2007. ↑14cm.

'Helios'

Snowdrop with strong yellow inner markings. Slow. Gert-Jan van der Kolks, Netherlands.

'Henham No 1' (*plicatus*)

Taller, later, larger flowers than *G.* 'Three Ships', though closely related and from same site. Narrow ovary. Leaves

semi-erect, wide, green. Outer segments rounded, pointed. Inner segments green 'Y' mark to base. Grows well. January. John Morley, under cork oak, Henham Park, Suffolk, 1984. ↑18cm.

'Henly Greenspot'
(*elwesii* var. *elwesii*)

Beautiful white flowers. Leaves supervolute, erect to arching, grey-green. Outer segments pointed, variable small green marks at apex. Inner segments clasping, no sinus, heart-shaped green mark at apex, separate smudges at base. Slow. Late, one of the last green-tips to flower. David and Ruby Baker in naturalized colony of *G. elwesii*, Surrey, 1992. ↑22cm.

'Henrietta'

Strong, vigorous, with erect scapes. Leaves erect-arching, blue-green. Inner segments green mark at apex. Clumps up well. Dick and Hillary Bird's garden, Rogers Rough, Kilndown, Kent, named after friend. ↑18cm.

'Henry's White Lady'
(*nivalis* Poculiformis Group)

Vigorous, slender-shaped poculiform. Leaves erect-arching, slender, green-blue. Outer segments bluntly pointed. Inner segments slightly shorter than outer, longitudinally ridged, usually white but occasionally small green spot either side of sinus. ↑15cm.

'Herbert Ransom'

See 'Ransom'.

'Hercule' (*elwesii*)

Leaves tall, erect, grey-green. Outer segments very long, rounded at apex. Inner segments broad inverted 'V' at apex. ↑18cm.

'Hiemalis'
(*elwesii* Hiemalis Group)

Syns. *G. caucasicus* Early form, *G. caucasicus* Hiemale, *G. caucasicus* var. *hiemalis*

Name covers numerous similar, smaller, early flowering clones with single inner segment mark. Leaves short at flowering. Outer segments long, slender. Inner segments variable small, narrow, green inverted 'V' at apex. Not the best, but useful for early flowering from November. Grows well. Sir Frederick Stern's garden, Highdown, Sussex, c. 1950s. RHS AM 1960. ↑25cm.

'Hiemalis ex Broadleigh Gardens'
Slender flowers. Outer segments slender, pointed. Inner segments tube-like, slightly flared at apex, narrow inverted 'V' at apex.

'Highdown' (*gracilis*)
Older snowdrop, smaller flowers. Pale olive-green-yellow ovary. Leaves distinctive, applanate, very narrow, grey-glaucous, twisted. Inner segment yellow-green 'X' or two separate marks at apex and base. Bulks up quickly, seeds well. Sir Frederick Stern, Highdown, Sussex. ↑10cm.

'Highdown 457 Dwarf' (*elwesii* Hiemalis Group)
Very short snowdrop with short stems. Early. Given to Michael Hoog by the late Sir Frederick Stern. ↑10cm.

'Hildegard Owen' (Hybrid cultivar)
Slender-looking flower and ovary. Outer segments tapering towards apex, bluntly pointed. Inner segments green mark apex towards base.

'Hill Poë' (Hybrid double)
Firm old favourite. Neat, fairly short double. Leaves spreading, flat-lightly explicative, glaucous. Outer segments regularly five. Inner segments uniform, tightly packed ruff, 'U' to 'V' mark. February–March. Sometimes two scapes. Grows well. James Hill Poe's garden, Riverston, Ireland, 1911. Known by E.A. Bowles, cultivated by D. Shackleton and the Giant Snowdrop Company. RHS PC 1974. RHS AM 1979. ↑14cm.

'Hippolyta' (Hybrid double)
Beautiful, shorter, distinctive, Greatorex double. Flowers neat, fully double, rounded, on short, erect scapes. Leaves broad, spreading, lightly explicative, grey-blue, glaucous, paler median stripe. Outer segments broad, rounded, showing inner ruff, sometimes tipped green at apex. Inner segments rounded, loose ruff, green heart-shaped mark at apex. Often second flower. February–March. Greatorex, Brundall, Norfolk. *G. nivalis* 'Flore Pleno' × *G. plicatus*, 1940s. RHS AM 1970. ↑15cm.

'Hobbgoblin'
Distinctive snowdrop with slender flowers. Outer segments slim, pointed, green marks above apex. Inner segments broad inverted 'V' with rounded ends. Richard Hobbs.

'Hobson's Choice' (*plicatus* × *nivalis*)
Strong, robust, prolific. Outer segments bluntly pointed. Inner segments longitudinally ridged, wide inverted 'U' at apex. Strong honey perfume. January–February. Richard Ayres, Anglesey Abbey, Cambridgeshire, c. 2000. Named after Thomas Hobson, a Cambridgeshire horse dealer, who supplied the horse regardless of your choice so it was 'Hobson's Choice' whether his horses were good or bad. Probably *G. plicatus* × *G. nivalis*. ↑30cm.

'Hoddles Creek' (*elwesii*)
Large, attractive, well shaped and textured flowers. Outer segments long. Clumps up well. Australian selection.

'Hollis' (*elwesii*)
Attractive flowers. Leaves broad, erect to arching, grey-green. Outer segments broad, pointed. Inner segments broad inverted 'U' at apex. ↑16cm.

'Hologram' (*nivalis* Poculiformis Group)
Stunning, beautiful, large poculiform with elegantly shaped segments and pure white flowers on slender pedicel. Leaves applanate, slender, upright to arching, blue-green. ↑14cm.

'Hololeucus' (*nivalis* Poculiformis Group)
See 'Danube Star'.

'Homersfield'
Attractive flowers, slender pedicel. Leaves erect, blue-green. Outer segments rounded, bluntly pointed, clawed. Inner segments small green Chinese-bridge mark at apex, two smudged marks towards base. February. ↑14cm.

'Honey Mouth'
Leaves upright, slender, blue-green. Outer segments well shaped, slender, pointed. Inner segments yellow-green inverted 'U' at apex. ↑15cm.

'Honeysuckle Cottage' (Hybrid cultivar)
Tall, vigorous, erect, showy. Outer segments bluntly pointed, clawed. Inner segments broad inverted 'V' at apex. Early. Sally Pasmore. *G. nivalis* × *G. plicatus*. ↑20cm.

'Hornet'
Very elongated, pointed, 'insect-like' flowers suspended from erect scapes. Outer segments very long, slender, longitudinally ridged, pointed.

Inner segments narrow inverted 'U' at apex, staining towards base, paler mark towards base. ↑16cm.

'Hörup'
Rounded balloon-like flowers. Outer segments broad, rounded, bluntly pointed. Inner segments dark-green rounded inverted 'V' at apex, rounded ends, two joined ovals towards base. Rita Thomsen, Hörup, Germany. ↑14cm.

'Horwick Yellow'
See G. 'Sandersii'.

'Hoverfly' (Hybrid cultivar)
Syn. 'William Ball No 1'
Neat rounded flowers suspended from slender pedicel. Leaves, erect, slim, flat-lightly explicative, glaucescent. Outer segments rounded, pointed, clawed. Inner segments small inverted 'V' merging into oval, not reaching base. Phil Cornish at Lapworth, Warwickshire, 1997. ↑28cm.

'Howard Wheeler' (elwesii Hiemalis Group)
Beautifully shaped flowers, dark green ovary. Leaves supervolute, glaucous. Outer segments slender, bluntly pointed. Inner segments dark-green inverted 'U' at apex. November–December. Phil Cornish, garden of late Howard Wheeler, Longlevens, Gloucestershire, 1998. ↑15cm.

'Howick'
See 'Sandersii'.

'Howick Starlight' (Hybrid cultivar)
Yellow-marked snowdrop.

'Howick Yellow'
See 'Sandersii'.

'Hugh Mackenzie' (nivalis)
Excellent snowdrop with large well shaped flowers. Leaves oblong-lanceolate, lightly hooded tip. Outer segments clawed, merging green lines from apex covering two-thirds of segment, fading towards base, narrow white margin. Inner segments dark-green Chinese-bridge mark at apex slightly spreading towards base. Late February. David Baker, named after Ronald Mackenzie's son, 2002.

'Hughes Emerald' (elwesii hybrid)
Large-flowered New Zealand hybrid. Leaves supervolute, broad, grey. Outer segments long, pointed, elegant claw, small merging green lines from apex. Inner segments broad inverted 'V' at apex, upturned ends, beneath two merging central ovals. Robust. Denis Hughes, Blue Mountain Nursery, New Zealand.

'Humberts Orchard'
See 'Hambutt's Orchard'.

'Hunton Early Bird' (nivalis)
Attractive, early snowdrop from David and Anke Way, Southover, Hunton.

'Hunton Giant' (elwesii)
Tall, sturdy, with well shaped, chunky flowers. Leaves unusually large, long, broad, blue-green, almost narcissus-like, long-lasting. Outer segments broad claw, bluntly pointed. Inner segments small dark green inverted 'V' at apex, dark-green band three-quarters way up segment. December. David and Anke Way, Southover, Hunton.

'Hunton Herald' (plicatus)
Outer segments rounded, lightly longitudinally ridged and dimpled, goffered claw. Inner segments mid-green 'X' filled at base. December. David and Anke Way, Southover, Hunton.

'Huttlestone' (elwesii var. elwesii)
Rounded ovary and flowers. Leaves supervolute, recurving, broad, arching, green, unusually puckered. Outer segments lightly ridged at base, goffered claw. Inner segments clasping, inverted heart-shaped mark at apex, small lines joining two merging ovals towards base. Joe Sharman at Anglesey Abbey, Cambridgeshire, 1992, named for first Lord Fairhaven. ↑16m.

× hybridus
Syns. G. × grandiflorus, G. × maximus
Probably G. elwesii × G. plicatus hybrid. Originally × grandiflorus, supposedly hybrid between G. nivalis and G. plicatus. Shows intermediate characteristics between G. elwesii and G. plicatus. Robust. Large attractively shaped flowers. Leaves explicative, erect, broad, glaucous. Inner segments generally large mark, can be almost entirely green. Cultivars include G. 'Merlin' and G. 'Robin Hood'.

'Hyde Lodge' (reginae-olgae subsp. reginae-olgae)
Tall, reliable, late autumn flowering. Flowers chubby, rounded. Leaves erect, short at flowering. Outer segments textured, lightly ridged. Inner segments green Chinese-bridge mark at apex. Almond perfume. Occasional second scape. Grown as G. corcyrensis by Herbert Ransom, who passed bulbs to the Giant Snowdrop Company, but bulbs probably originated from Gerald Rawinsky in the 1950s. ↑21cm.

'Icicle' (Hybrid cultivar)
Syn. G. 'Tony Colmer's Mighty Atom'
Shorter snowdrop with rounded flowers. Leaves erect, lightly explicative margins, glaucous. Outer segments strong, white, thick, rounded, clawed. Inner segments inverted olive-green 'U' to 'V' at apex, slimmer over sinus. Percy Picton's Old Court Nursery, Malvern,

Worcestershire, early 1970s, originally named G. 'Mighty Atom', renamed 'Icicle'. ↑12cm.

'Ida Maud'
Australian-raised selection.

'Igraine' (*elwesii*)
Well shaped flowers. Outer segments very rounded, pointed, slightly pinched at apex and small pale-green lines. Inner segments sharp waisted green mark apex almost to base, no sinus.

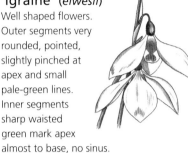

ikariae (species)
Syn. *G. ikariae* subsp. *snogerupii* Greece, Aegean islands. Well shaped flowers. Leaves supervolute, broad, recurving, dark, mat-green, rolled or occasional longitudinal folds. Outer segments occasional green mark at apex. Inner segments variable large broad-green mark covering roughly half segment. February–March. Collected on Ikaria, Greece, and sent to James Allen; passed to J.G. Baker, Royal Botanic Gardens, Kew, described as new species, 1893. ↑10cm.

ikariae 'Butts Form'
See 'Butts Form'.

ikariae subsp. *latifolius*
Syn. of *G. woronowii* and does not refer to *G. ikariae*.

'Ilse Bilse'
Leaves slender, spreading, blue-green. Outer segments rounded, bluntly pointed. Inner segments tube-like, thin yellow' V' at apex, yellow oval half to two-thirds towards base. ↑12cm.

'Imbolc'
(Hybrid cultivar)
G. 'Mighty Atom' group. Large, very white flowers, short scapes. Leaves applanate, semi-erect, variably explicative, glaucous.

Inner segments broad inverted 'U', 'V' to 'X' mark, usually two separate marks towards base. E.B. Anderson supplied *G.* 'Mighty Atom' to Primrose Warburg, this hybrid included, named by her after Celtic festival of spring. ↑12.5cm.

'Imitation'
Similar looking to *G.* 'Robin Hood' but wider outer segments. ↑23cm.

'Imperati' (*nivalis*)
Taller, older snowdrop with large flowers. Leaves long, erect, grey-green, lightly rolled edges but not explicative. Inner segment good green mark. Possible *G. nivalis* variant, central Italy, first offered 1875.

'Indiskretion' (*nivalis*)
Solid, weighty-looking flowers. Outer segments rounded, bluntly pointed. Inner segments narrow 'V' at apex, two pale eye spots at base. Germany. English translation: 'Indiscretion'. ↑23cm.

'Ingrid' (*nivalis* Poculiformis Group)
Erect stems, flattened spathe, pear-drop shaped flowers. Outer segments fractionally longer than inner, all with solid green mark above apex.

'Ingrid Bauer'
(Hybrid cultivar)
Attractive, vigorous. Leaves erect-arching, broad, grey-green. Outer segments slender, incurved margins. Inner segments green inverted 'U' at apex, paler second mark diffusing towards base. Rudi Bauer, 2007. Possibly *G. nivalis* × *G. elwesii*. ↑18cm.

'Ione Hecker'
Small plants with well shaped flowers from *G.* 'Mighty Atom' Group. Leaves erect, slender, blue-green. Outer segments bluntly pointed. Inner segments inverted 'V' at base. ↑12cm.

'Irish Green' (*nivalis*)
Rare, quirky, Irish spiky. Slender upright flowers. Leaves erect, flat. Outer segments three to five, variable green marks from palest to deepest green. Inner segments irregular ruff, curled, minus sinus, variable roughly heart to 'V' shaped green mark at apex, extending to base. Late. David and Ruby Baker at Ballintaggert, Co. Wicklow, Ireland, 1994. ↑10–12cm.

'Iseghem'
Well shaped flowers, long pedicel, split spathe. Outer segments incurved, large dark-green mark at apex, second paler mark towards base. Inner segments broad inverted 'V' at apex, paler shadow at base. Clumps up well. Ruben Billiet, Belgium.

'Ismail' (*rizehensis*)
Leaves mid-green, light shine, broad, semi-erect, short at flowering. Outer segments broad, bluntly pointed. Inner segments clasping, flared, large 'U' to 'V' at apex diffusing across segment towards base. Good perfume. December–January. Mark Berry selection named after Ismail Mentes, a friend. ↑11cm.

'Isobel Blakeway-Phillips'
(Hybrid cultivar)
Excellent, strong-growing snowdrop with attractive well shaped flowers. Leaves spreading, flat-lightly explicative, glaucescent. Outer segments clawed. Inner segments large inverted olive-green heart-shaped mark at apex, shadowed towards base. R.J. Blakeway-Phillips, Clun, Shropshire, 1997, named for granddaughter. ↑17cm.

'Ispahan' (*plicatus*)
Rounded flowers. Leaves lax, usually short at flowering. Outer segments clawed. Inner segments inverted

green 'V' extending towards base. Early. Rosie Steele, from colony of *G. plicatus*, Wells, Norfolk, 1995. Named after old rose variety, also has rare rose perfume. ↑12cm.

'Istrian Dwarf' (*nivalis*)

Tiny, delicate-looking dwarf snowdrop. Leaves applanate, prostrate, green-blue. Outer segments long slender claw. Inner segments small triangular mark either side of sinus. ↑6cm.

'Ivy Cottage Corporal'

Well shaped flowers. Outer segments bluntly pointed, clawed. Inner segments two strong inverted 'V' marks resembling army corporal's stripes. Michael Broadhurst, first of Ivy Cottage series.

'Ivy Cottage Green Tips' (*elwesii*)

Unusual *G. elwesii*. Leaves broad, grey-green. Outer segments light longitudinal ridging, variable green marks above apex. Inner segments bold green mark from apex to two-thirds of segment. Michael Broadhurst.

'Ivy Cottage No 6' (Hybrid cultivar)

Slender flowers on erect scapes. Outer segments long, slender, bluntly pointed. Inner segments lightly ridged, inverted green 'V' at apex, two merging ovals towards base. Possibly *G. plicatus* × *G. gracilis*.

'Jack Mead' (*elwesii*)

Attractive, rounded flowers. Leaves supervolute, broad, erect-arching, grey. Outer segments rounded, bluntly pointed. Inner segments broad inverted 'U' at apex, oval mark towards base. Early. Often three leaves. ↑15cm.

'Jack Percival' (*elwesii*)

Drooping, slender, pendant flowers, erect scapes. Leaves erect, broad, grey-green. Outer segments slim, pointed. Inner segments broad green mark covering two-thirds of segment from apex.

'Jade'

Sought-after virescent. Leaves erect, slender, blue-green. Outer segments green mark above apex, often line joining basal mark. Inner segments rounded inverted 'V' with upturned ends. Gloucestershire. ↑10cm.

'James Backhouse' (Hybrid cultivar)

Syn. *G.* 'Atkinsii of Backhouse' Curious, large, robust clone allied to *G.* 'Atkinsii'. Large, long, distinctively shaped conical flowers, often aberrant segments including from base of ovary. Leaves applanate, semi-erect-arching, pointed, glaucescent. Outer segments often aberrant. Inner segments uniform inverted green 'V' at apex. February. Prolific, bulks up well to good colonies. James Backhouse, York. ↑18cm.

'Jamie Broughton' (*elwesii* var. *elwesii*)

Beautiful flowers. Leaves supervolute, one broad, enclosing, second narrower. Outer segments broad, sharply pointed, lightly puckered. Inner segments longitudinally incurved, clasping, broad sharp inverted 'V' at apex, similar separate bluntly pointed mark at base. Anglesey Abbey, Cambridgeshire, named after Lord Fairhaven's eldest son. ↑17cm.

'Janet'

See 'Jenny Wren'.

'Janet Aspland' (*nivalis* Sandersii Group)

Good Sandersii Group yellow snowdrop with attractive flowers and good yellow marks.

'Janet's Gold' (Hybrid cultivar)

Yellow-marked snowdrop.

'Janis Ruksans'

See 'Oreana'.

'Janus'

Rounded ovary, slender pedicel. Outer segments incurved, lightly longitudinally ridged. Inner segments green inverted 'V' at apex, oval mark towards base.

'Jaquenetta' (Hybrid cultivar)

Syn. *G.* 'Jacquenetta' Robust, tall, distinctive, Greatorex double. Smaller, spreading, rounded flowers. Leaves semi-erect, explicative, narrow, grey-green. Outer segments rounded, variable green marks, often absent. Inner segment ruff broad, symmetrical, outer whorl often aberrant, dark-green 'U' from apex towards base. Vigorous, bulks up well. *G. nivalis* 'Flore Pleno' × *G. plicatus*. H.A. Greatorex, Brundall, Norfolk, 1940s. ↑18cm.

'Jean's Double' (Hybrid double)

Well rounded, neat, globular flowers. Outer segments broad, rounded, light longitudinal ridging. Inner segments broad mid-green mark apex to half of segment.

'Jedburgh'

Found by Joe Sharman, Kelso, Scotland, c. 2003.

'Jenny'

See 'Jenny Wren'.

'Jenny Owen' (*elwesii*)

Late. Hagen Engelmann, named after eldest daughter.

'Jenny Wren' (Hybrid cultivar)

Syn. *G.* 'Janet', G. 'Jenny' Attractive double, smaller flowers. Leaves flat, glaucous. Outer segments broad, rounded at apex, small green marks. Inner segments neat open ruff, either narrow 'V' or two small marks at apex. Fred Buglass, 1970s, from H.A. Greatorex garden, Brundall, Norfolk, but not the Greatorex hybrid, which appears no longer available.

'Jess Egerton'
Well shaped elongated, slender flower, long inflated spathe. Outer segments very long, slender, pointed, slender claw. Inner segments inverted rounded 'V' at apex, two small 'eye' dots towards base.

'Jesse Jane' (*elwesii*)
Rounded flowers. Leaves erect, broad, grey-green. Outer segments narrow, pointed, broadening towards base, narrow claw, pale-green lines above apex. Inner segments broad green mark across segment apex towards base.

'Jessica' (*elwesii* hybrid)
One of the best green-tipped *G. elwesii*. Leaves supervolute, broad, arching. Outer segments merging green lines at apex. Inner segments inverted heart-shaped mark at apex, strongly reversed and joined to second mark above, diffusing towards base. Slow. Phil Cornish, Wroxall, Warwickshire, 1997, named after his wife. ↑24cm.

'Jimmy Plat' (*elwesii* var. *monostictus*)
Convolute hybrid with attractive, well shaped, rounded flowers on very upright scapes. Leaves broad, grey-green. Outer segments broad, rounded. Inner segments inverted green 'U' at apex. March. Avon Bulbs. ↑30cm.

'Joan May'
Well rounded flowers, olive-green ovary. Outer segments broad, bluntly pointed, light longitudinal ridging. Inner segments broad mid-green inverted 'V' at apex.

'Joan Weighell' (Hybrid cultivar)
Leaves erect, slightly supervolute at base, glaucous. Outer segments flushed cream in bud caused by greenish-yellow shading on underside. Inner segments inverted 'V' at apex, yellow shadow towards base. Alan Street at South Hayes, Oxfordshire, 1997, named after Primrose Warburg's housekeeper. ↑19cm. Now thought probably extinct.

'Joe's Spotted'
Outer segments bluntly pointed, heavily marked green at apex. Inner segments pale-green mark at apex, two spots at base. February. ↑16cm.

'Joe's Yellow' (Sandersii Group)
Good yellow ovary and pedicel, yellow-green spathe. Outer segments bluntly pointed. Inner segments, narrow yellow, inverted, 'V' at apex. February. ↑15cm.

'John Gray' (Hybrid cultivar)
Excellent, handsome, robust, free-flowering. Flowers very large on short arching scapes, long slender pedicels. Leaves applanate, erect, long, narrow, grey-green-glaucous. Outer segments broad, spreading. Inner segments large green mark apex to base, diffusing towards base. Often two scapes. Can be difficult. January–March. E.B. Anderson from the late John Gray's garden, Benhall, Suffolk, named after him. RHS AM 1972. RHS FCC 1996. Appears closely related to *G.* 'Mighty Atom'. ↑18cm.

'John Long' (*plicatus*)
Very floriferous with beautiful, large white flowers. Outer segments thick, rounded, longitudinally ridged, clawed. Inner

segments olive-green inverted 'U' at apex with two paler curving lines towards base. Usually two scapes. Probably originally from the late John Long's garden, Morville, Shropshire, c. 1980s. He gave bulbs to Margaret Owen, who named it in his honour, 2000. ↑22cm.

'John Marr ' (*reginae-olgae* subsp. *vernalis*)
Elegant slender-looking flowers. Dark-green ovary. Outer segments long, slender, incurved margins. Inner segments long inverted 'V' at apex, narrowed ends. RHS PC 2009. ↑15cm.

'John Tomlinson' (*elwesii*)
Attractive, robust. Leaves supervolute, erect, pale-green, glaucous. Outer segments bluntly pointed, clawed, variable green lines at apex. Inner segments good olive-green heart-shaped mark covering around half segment. January–February. John Tomlinson, Weybridge, Surrey, named by C. Brickell, 1996. ↑18cm.

'Jonathan' (*elwesii* Edward Whittall Group)
Rounded flowers. Leaves supervolute, broad, grey-green. Outer segments broad, pointed, clawed, longitudinally ridged, textured. Inner segments inverted green 'U' to 'V' at apex, two paler 'eye' dots towards base. Michael Myers, North Yorkshire, 2000. ↑17cm.

'Joshua Jansen'
Well shaped flowers, erect scape, slender ovary. Outer segments broadening towards apex, small green mark. Inner segments rounded inverted 'V' at apex. Oirlicher Blumengarten, named after grandson.

'Josie' (*plicatus*)

Small rounded flowers, large, round, green ovary. Leaves explicative, grey-green-glaucous. Outer segments broad, rounded, longitudinal ridging, green mark above apex, lines extending short distance up veins, only slightly longer than inner segments. Inner segments green mark apex towards base. ↑16cm.

'Joy Cozens' (*elwesii* var. *elwesii*)

Unusual, distinctive pale orange colouring in bud, flowers fading to white when mature. Flowers well rounded. Leaves supervolute, broad, erect. Outer segments rounded bluntly pointed, flushed pale orange when first open. Inner segments clasping, uniform 'V' at apex, separate small rectangle at base. Mary Strood's Gloucestershire garden, 1997, named for friend.↑28cm.

'JRM 3139' (*nivalis*)

Small. Olive-green scape and ovary. Leaves applanate, spreading, glaucous, ridged, short at flowering. Outer segments narrow claw. Inner segments ridged, inverted 'V' at apex. February–March. ↑11cm.

'Jubilee Green' (*elwesii*)

Leaves bright green. Inner segments 'X'-shaped mark. From John Morley, North Green Snowdrops, Suffolk, named to commemorate their Silver Jubilee.

'Judith'

Outer segments rounded at apex. Inner segments dark-green inverted 'U' at apex.

'Jule Jansen' (*nivalis*)

Leaves applanate, spreading, blue-green. Outer segments rounded in centre, narrowing towards apex, longitudinally ridged, long goffered claw, broad green mark above apex. Inner segments, broad inverted 'U' at apex. Zlatko and Angelina Petrisevac, Croatia. ↑15cm.

'Julia' (Hybrid cultivar)

Exceptionally long, unusually horizontal pedicel. Leaves semi-erect to arching, explicative margins, glaucescent. Inner segments clasping, broad inverted 'V' above large, wide sinus. Late. Slow. Phil Cornish, Painswick, Gloucestershire, c. 1987, named for youngest daughter. ↑12cm.

'Julie' (*elwesii* var. *monostictus*)

Outer segments long. Inner segments small mark at apex. Australian-selected snowdrop.

'July' (*elwesii* var. *monostictus*)

Australian-selected snowdrop named after month of flowering in southern hemisphere.

'June' (*elwesii* var. *monostictus*)

Australian-selected snowdrop named after month of flowering in southern hemisphere.

'June Boardman' (*plicatus* hybrid)

Good yellow with yellow ovary, yellow-green pedicel and spathe. Outer segments long, elegant. Inner segments yellow-green mark at apex paling yellow towards base. Norwich. Named by Bill Boardman for his wife. ↑12cm.

'Kalum'

Strong, vigorous. Outer segments green mark at apex. Good grower. Mansfield Woodhouse, Nottingham. ↑15cm.

'Karla' (*nivalis* Sandersii Group)

Large rounded, yellow-marked creamy-white flowers, slender light-green ovary. Inner segments sharp yellow inverted 'V' at apex, slightly blurred on basal side.

'Karla Tausendschön' (*nivalis*)

Rounded creamy-white flowers. Ovary, spathe pale green. Outer segments bluntly pointed. Inner segments creamy-yellow with strong yellow 'V' at apex.

'Karneval' (Hybrid cultivar)

Well shaped flowers, long pedicel. Leaves supervolute, semi-erect to arching, glaucous, well developed at flowering. Outer segments smooth, thick. Inner segments variable green roughly 'X'-shaped mark across segment diffusing towards base. Nicolas Top, Rhine Valley, Germany, 1990. ↑16cm.

'Kastellorhizo' (*peshmenii*)

Attractive G. *peshmenii* from Greek island of Kastellorhizo. Leaves present at flowering. September–October. Good perfume. RHS AM 2007.

'Katarina' (*reginae-olgae* subsp. *reginae-olgae*)

Well shaped rounded flowers with erect scapes. Outer segments bluntly pointed. Inner segments narrow green 'U' at apex. Early.

'Kathleen Beddington' (Hybrid cultivar)

Outer segments broad, pointed, pale green mark above apex. Inner segments green mark from apex towards base, narrow white margin. Named for Galanthophile Kathleen Beddington.

'Kath Dryden' (Hybrid)

Attractive smaller snowdrop. Leaves erect blue-green. Outer segments well shaped, bluntly pointed. Inner segments inverted green 'V' at apex staining upwards on basal side. ↑12cm.

'Katie Campbell'

Similar but smaller to G. 'Magnet'. Well shaped flower suspended on long, slender pedicel. Outer segments long, rounded. Inner segments inverted green 'V' at apex. Australian-raised selection from Otto Fauser, pre-1984.

'Kedworth'

Vigorous. Large, slim, elegant flowers. Outer segments marked green to around half of segment. Inner segments heavy green mark at apex diffusing across segment. Often two scapes. David and Ruby Baker, Ireland, 1995.

kemulariae

See G. lagodechianus, of which this is now a synonym.

'Kencot Ivy' (*elwesii*)

Large shapely flowers. Leaves supervolute, broad, spreading, grey. Outer segments lightly ridged longitudinally, merging green lines above apex. Inner segments narrowing at apex, dark-green splayed 'V' at apex, two small, paler spots towards base. ↑16cm.

'Kencot Kali'

Good-looking snowdrop with well shaped flowers. Outer segments boat-shaped, pointed. Inner segments slightly waisted, broad green mark apex towards base. ↑15cm.

'Kencott Pip' (*elwesii*)

Substantial-looking, rounded flowers. Outer segments bluntly pointed, longitudinal ridging, merging green lines at apex, shadowed on underside. Inner segments green marks at apex and towards base. ↑18cm.

'Kennemerend'

Attractive, well shaped flowers. Leaves, erect, slender, green. Outer segments rounded, bluntly pointed. Inner segments light green pip either side of sinus, oval mark towards base. Wim Grannerman, 2011. ↑15cm.

'Kenneth Becket'

See 'Kenneth Beckett's AM Form'.

'Kenneth Beckett's AM Form' (*reginae-olgae* subsp. *vernalis*)

Strong scapes, elegant flowers. Leaves attractive, semi-erect to lax, short, silver-blue, paler median stripe, long lasting. Outer segments clawed. Inner segments, large dark-green broad 'U' at apex, slightly narrowed ends. December–January. Kenneth Becket, Montenegro, former Yugoslavia, *c.* 1970s. RHS AGM 2007. ↑15cm.

'Kenneth Hall'

Uninspiring Irish snowdrop, not well circulated as thought too poor. Named for snowdrop breeder Robin Hall's father.

'Kersen' (*nivalis*)

Leaves applanate, spreading, grey-green. Outer segments rounded, bluntly pointed. Inner segments narrow inverted 'V' at apex, rounded ends, resembling two cherries hanging from stalk. Nicolas Top, Cologne, Germany, 1996. Name is the Dutch word for cherries. ↑12cm.

'Ketton' (Hybrid cultivar)

Superb, strong, attractive with large flowers well above foliage. Leaves applanate, erect, very slender, variable explicative margins, grey-green, glaucescent. Inner segments triangular green marks at apex, one or two smaller smudges at base, sometimes joined. Popular, easy. February. E.A. Bowles introduction from Old Ketton, Leicestershire, 1948. RHS AM 1996. ↑16cm.

'Kew Green'

Attractive, well shaped flowers suspended from erect scapes. Outer segments bluntly pointed, light longitudinal ridging and dimpling. Inner segments slightly waisted broad-green mark from apex towards base. ↑15cm.

'Kildare' (Hybrid cultivar)

Good virescent Irish snowdrop, elegant, tall. Large well proportioned flowers. Leaves applanate, semi-erect-arching, glaucous. Outer segments long, slender, pale-green merging lines following veins at apex. Inner segments clasping, large dark-green mark at apex paling towards base. Vigorous, clumps up well. Often two scapes. David and Ruby Baker, Ireland, 1995. ↑24cm.

'Kingennie'

Discovered by inveterate snowdrop hunter Ian Christie on a country estate in Scotland.

'Kingston Double' (Hybrid double)

Beautiful, large, tall, brilliantly white double. Leaves supervolute, erect. Outer segments long, rounded . Inner segments untidy ruff, usually aberrant, olive-green inverted 'V' at apex, paler mark at base. Elizabeth Parker-Jervis, Kingston House, Kingston Bagpuize, Oxfordshire, early 1970s. ↑18cm.

'Kinn Macintosh' (*elwesii* Hiemalis Group)

Slender flowers. Leaves broad, erect, grey. Outer segments long, pointed. Inner segments small inverted green 'V' at apex. September–November. Kinn Mcintosh's garden, Kent, *c.* 1946. ↑20cm.

'Kinnaird' (*nivalis*)

G. nivalis × 'Kinnaird' has attractive flowers with distinctive green inner markings. Leaves applanate, erect, slender, blue-green. Outer segments bluntly pointed. Inner segments beautiful large green mark at apex, diffusing towards base. ↑25/30cm.

'Kirtling Tower' (*nivalis*)

Large, partly split inflated spathe, erect scapes. Outer segments bluntly pointed, lightly ridged, puckered, variable bright-green mark at apex. Inner segments, broad even inverted 'V' at apex. ↑14cm.

'Kite' (*elwesii* var. *elwesii*)

Syn. *G.* 'Maidwell A'
Unusual, rare. Noted for usually having two flowers to each scape on single pedicel, or two pedicels each bearing flower. Leaves supervolute, semi-erect, broad,

glaucescent. Outer segments medium/large. Inner segments broad inverted 'V' at apex joining two merging ovals towards base, creating almost 'X'-shaped mark. Oliver Wyatt selected seedling, Maidwell Hall, Northamptonshire, named by E.A. Bowles. ↑15cm.

koenenianus (species)
North-eastern Turkey. Leaves supervolute, erect, hooded, blue-grey, glaucous, conspicuous median stripe, under-surface ribbed. Inner segments green inverted 'U' at apex, occasional light yellow-green mark at base. Bitter almond scent. February–March. Uncommon. Can be difficult. Discovered 1988, named after Manfred Koenen, German botanist. ↑5–14cm.

'Krabat' (nivalis)
Distinctive large flowers. Leaves applanate, lax. Outer segments shaded green. Inner segments good mark extending and paling towards base. February–March. Selected by Jörg Lebsa, Germany, 1998, from Czech Republic. ↑14cm.

krasnovii (species)
North-eastern Turkey, western Georgia. Leaves supervolute, upper section broad, occasional light puckering and longitudinal folding, shiny-mat, mid-green. Outer segments clawed. Inner segments sinus absent or small, sharp green inverted 'U' at apex or two small marks, occasional lighter mark at base. Rare in the wild, rare and difficult in cultivation. Discovered north-eastern Turkey, 1908, named for Andrej Nikovaevich Krasnov (1862–1914), Russian scientist. ↑8–20cm.

'Kryptonite'
(elwesii var. monostictus)
Beautiful, well shaped flowers, heavily marked green. Outer segments rounded, pointed, long claw, large green mark above apex. Inner segments broad light-green mark apex almost to base, narrow white margin. Named after Superman comic book character whose strength came from green kryptonite. ↑16cm.

'Kubalach'
Large delicate flowers. Outer segments slender, bluntly pointed. Inner segments, broad mid-green mark across segment almost to base.

'Kullake' (nivalis)
Small yellow-marked nivalis from Estonia. Ovary yellow. Leaves applanate, upright, slender, blue-green. Outer segments slender, pointed. Inner segments yellow inverted 'V' at apex. ↑10cm.

'Kurt Kleisa'
Slender ovary. Leaves erect, blue-green. Outer segments rounded, bluntly pointed, strong merging green lines from apex to half segment. Inner segments green inverted 'V' at apex. ↑16cm.

'Kyre Park' (elwesii var. elwesii)
Rounded flowers. Leaves supervolute, broad, erect, grey. Inner segments green inverted 'V' at apex extending to oval below base, or 'X' mark filled in at base, shadowed underside of inner segments. Good perfume. December–January. Martin Rickard, Kyre Park, Worcestershire. ↑13cm.

'L.P. Long'
(Hybrid double)
Rarer Greatorex double. Leaves arching, flat to explicative. Outer segments variable merging green lines at apex. Inner segments flared, slightly diffused narrow inverted 'V'. H.A. Greatorex to Lewis Palmer, Headbourne Worthy, named by Richard Nutt, 1996. ↑30cm.

'L.P. Short' (Hybrid double)
Neat Greatorex double. Leaves arching, explicative margins. Outer segments long, flat, long goffered claw, green lines at apex. Inner segments neat rosette, mark from apex towards base, tiny sinus. One or two scapes. H.A. Greatorex to Lewis Palmer, Headbourne Worthy, named by Richard Nutt, 1996. ↑24cm.

'La Moriniere' (nivalis)
Vigorous, neat, double with slender flowers. Leaves erect, slender, blue-green.

Outer segments slender, pointed. Inner segments neat shapely, small green mark above apex. February. France. ↑15cm.

'Lac de Balcere' (nivalis)
Outer segments bluntly pointed, goffered claw, occasional small green mark at apex. Inner segments broad inverted 'U' at apex, rounded ends. January–February. Named after lake in French Pyrenees.

'Lacewing'
Attractive green-tipped snowdrop. Outer segments green mark above apex. Inner segments broad green inverted 'U' to 'V' at apex. Former H.A. Greatorex garden, Brundall, Norfolk.

'Lady Alice' (nivalis × plicatus)
Very attractive, pristine, well rounded flowers. Leaves distinctive, strong blue colour. Outer segments rounded, bluntly pointed. Inner segments slightly waisted green mark across segment apex towards base. Ian Christie, Brechin Castle, Angus, Scotland. ↑15cm.

'Lady Bacon's Spiky Single'

'Lady Beatrix Stanley' (Hybrid double)
Syns. G. caucasicus 'Flore Pleno', G. caucasicus double Superb, strong, well proportioned. Leaves supervolute, long, semi-erect, recurving, grey-green, glaucous. Outer segments narrow, small compared to inner. Inner segments tightly packed ruff, often aberrant, green marks at apex. Mid-January. Easy, reliable, bulks up well. Originally considered G. caucasicus, now thought hybrid. Possibly Lady Beatrix Stanley's garden, Sibbertoft, via her daughter, Barbara Buchanan, renamed by Richard Nutt in 1981. RHS AM 1982. ↑15cm.

'Lady Dalhousie' (plicatus × nivalis)
Beautifully shaped flowers, erect scapes. Leaves plicate. Outer segments long, boat-shaped. Inner segments bold inverted 'U' above

rounded apical notch. January–February. Ian Christie, Brechin Castle, Angus, Scotland, named for Lady Dalhousie. *G. plicatus* × *G. nivalis*. PC 2008. ↑20cm.

'Lady Elphinstone' (*nivalis*)
Syn. *G. nivalis* flavescens flore pleno, *G. nivalis* 'Flavescens flore pleno' Good, distinctive *G. nivalis* 'Flore Pleno'. Ovary olive-green-yellow. Leaves applanate, semi-erect, grey-green. Inner segments flushed apricot, stronger when established, narrow inverted apricot-coloured 'V' at apex, can revert to green, especially after transplanting, eventually settles again. Sometimes aberrant segments. Slow. January–February. Sir Graeme Elphinstone, Heawood Hall, Cheshire, c. 1890, passed to Samuel Arnott, who named it *G. nivalis* 'Flavescens', later *G.* 'Lady Elphinstone'. ↑15cm.

'Lady Fairhaven' (*elwesii*)
Attractive regular, neat double. Leaves supervolute, erect, blue-grey. Outer segments broad, rounded. Inner segments neat ruff, broad, inverted green 'V' at apex, separate rounded mark towards base. Anglesey Abbey, 1998. RHS PC 2009. ↑10cm.

'Lady Lorna'
Large, balloon-like, well textured flowers. Outer segments broad, rounded, heavily longitudinally ridged, textured, rounded at apex. Inner segments broad 'H' mark from apex towards base. January–February. Ian Christie, Brechin Castle, Angus, Scotland. ↑12cm.

'Lady Mary Grey' (*nivalis*)
Mid-way between poculiform and standard. Leaves, semi-erect. Outer segments pointed. Inner segments furrowed, generally white, shorter than outer, rounded at apex, occasional small green dot either side of sinus. January–February. David and Ruby Baker, Northumberland, 1998, named after Lady Mary Grey, Howick. ↑9cm.

'Lady Moore' (*plicatus*)
Irish snowdrop with large, triangular flowers on erect scapes. Leaves plicate, upright-arching, broad, grey-green. Outer segments clawed, bluntly pointed. Inner segments roughly 'X' shaped mark across segment with solid base. Named after wife of Sir Frederick Moore, former director of Glasnevin Botanic Gardens, Dublin. Passed to Mrs Rutherford, 1940s, grown by her daughter, Miss Rita Rutherford. ↑18cm.

'Lady Scharlock'
Slender, delicate albino with pure-white segments. Long split spathe. Outer segments slender, incurved. Inner segments sender, rounded, all-white. February. Harry Pierik, Hidden City Garden, Netherlands. ↑8cm.

'Lady X' (Hybrid cultivar)
Well shaped flowers, erect scapes. Outer segments pointed. Inner segments broad inverted 'V' at apex joining larger mark towards base. January–February.

'Ladybird' (*elwesii*)
Outer segments spreading, slightly nipped at apex, pointed, tipped green. Inner segments broad inverted 'U' at apex. Phil Cornish.

lagodechianus (species)
Syns. *G. artjuschenkoae*, *G. cabardensis*, *G. kemulariae*, *G. ketzkhovelii* Caucasus. Well shaped small flowers. Leaves applanate, narrow, shiny, mid-green. Recurving or lax at maturity. Inner segments small green inverted 'U' or 'V' at apex. Research on-going into Caucasian snowdrops. This remains distinct species. Hardy, flowers well. February–March. Described by L.M. Kemularia-Nathadze, Georgian botanist, 1947. ↑4–20cm.

'Lake Garda' (*nivalis*)
Well rounded flowers. Outer segments broad, longitudinal ridging. Inner segments mid-green, inverted 'V' at apex, upturned ends. January–February. Lake Garda, Italy.

'Lambrook Green'
Leaves slender, upright to arching, green. Outer segments broad, rounded with green lines above apex. Inner segments broad dark-green, inverted 'U' at apex covering half segment. January–February. East Lambrook Manor, Somerset. ↑12cm.

'Lambrook Greensleeves' (*plicatus*)
Vigorous, shorter, *G. plicatus* hybrid. Leaves distinctive and different, bright shiny green. Inner segments mid-green inverted 'U' at apex, small sinus. East Lambrook Manor, Somerset, c. 1960s, not named until 2000. ↑10cm.

'Lammermuir Snow White' (*nivalis*)
See 'Snow White'.

'Lanarth' (*elwesii* var. *elwesii*)
Excellent with attractive large flowers. Leaves supervolute, semi-erect, arching. Outer segments clawed. Inner segments green inverted 'V' at apex, separate second 'V' above, occasionally joined. January. ↑15cm.

'Langenweddinger Knuddel'
Elegantly shaped snowdrop on slender pedicel. Outer segments bluntly pointed. Inner segments broad with

rounded green 'U' at apex. Germany. English translation: 'Long Wedding Hug'.

'Lapwing' (Hybrid cultivar)

Syn. *G.* 'William Ball No 2' Outstanding, distinctive snowdrop. Medium-sized triangular-shaped flower suspended from long pedicel. Leaves blue-grey, glaucous. Outer segments rounded. Inner segments broad, distinctive 'X' to scissor-shaped mark diffusing towards base. Early, reliable, increases well. Phil Cornish, Lapworth, Warwickshire, 1997. ↑15cm.

'Largest of All'
See 'Naughton'.

'Latest of All'
(*elwesii* var. *monostictus*)
Rare, very late flowering snowdrop. Outer segments long. Inner segments inverted 'V' at apex. March–April. Oliver Wyatt.

latifolius
See woronowii.

'Laubfrosch'
Recent introduction from Jörg Lebsa.

'Lavinia'
(Hybrid double)
Taller Greatorex double. Leaves erect, lightly explicative. Outer segments rounded, incurved, occasional mark at apex. Inner segments regular, can be aberrant, incurved, variable green 'U' at apex. Mid-January. Shy. H.A. Greatorex, Brundall, Norfolk, 1940s. Similar to *G.* 'Cordelia' but usually fewer, more incurved, inner segments. ↑28cm.

'Leckford form'
(*elwesii*)
Name in circulation but not valid. Leaves erect, broad, grey-green. Outer segments long, slender, pointed. Inner segments broad green mark from apex across three-quarters of segment towards base. ↑20cm.

'Lefki'
(*reginae-olgae* subsp. *vernalis*)
Strong, vigorous, tall with well shaped flowers. Leaves absent at flowering. Inner segment green rounded inverted 'U' at apex. December–January. ↑30cm.

'Lemon' (*elwesii*)
Olive-green ovary, upright scapes. Outer segments bluntly pointed. Inner segments olive-green mark at apex. January.

'Lenin' (*woronowii*)

'Lerinda'
(Hybrid cultivar)
Large, well shaped flowers. Leaves green, short at flowering. Outer segments well rounded. Inner segments inverted 'V' at apex, rounded ends. January–February. Bulks up well. Ken Aslet, former rock garden superintendant at Kew, 1970. ↑12cm.

'Lichtgeel'
Newer yellow snowdrop with good yellow marks.

'Light Bulb' (Hybrid cultivar)
Distinctive rounded shape. Leaves erect, explicative margins, glaucous. Outer segments rounded, ridged, clawed. Inner segments tube-like, flared at apex, heart-shaped mark diffusing across segment to horizontal patch at base. February–March. Mark Brown, South Hayes, Oxfordshire. *G. gracilis* in parentage. ↑17cm.

'Limetree'
(Hybrid cultivar)
Syn. *G.* 'Limetrees' Similar to 'Atkinsii' but slimmer, earlier flowering. Slender pear-shaped flowers. Leaves upright, narrow, grey-green. Outer segments slender. Inner segments green mark above apex. Numerous similar variants. Oliver Wyatt, under lime tree, Maidwell Hall, Northamptonshire, although original hybrid probably lost. ↑18cm.

'Limetrees'
See 'Limetree'.

'Limey' (*plicatus*)
Large flowers with distinctive pale yellow-green ovary. Leaves upright, glaucescent. Outer segments thickly textured. Inner segments flared, dark-green inverted 'V' at apex, two small triangular marks towards base. Phil Cornish from E.B. Anderson's former garden, Lower Slaughter, Gloucestershire, early 1990s. ↑17cm.

'Linnett Green Tips' (*elwesii* var. *elwesii*)
Shorter snowdrop with attractive, substantial flowers. Leaves supervolute, erect, small at flowering. Outer segments pointed, green lines above apex. Inner segments heart-shaped mark at apex, two small joined marks at base. Difficult. Basil Smith from imported *G. elwesii*, Linnett Farm, Hertfordshire, 1989. ↑14cm.

'Little Ben'
(Hybrid cultivar)
Syn. *G.* 'Mighty Atom' One of the best *G.* 'Mighty Atom' group. Large flowers, long arching pedicels. Leaves applanate, erect, explicative, grey-green-glaucous. Inner segments broad 'V' at apex bleeding slightly upwards. Possibly South Hayes but origins confusing as originally incorrectly named *G.* 'Mighty Atom'. Ray Cobb renamed it *G.* 'Little Ben'. RHS PC 1996. ↑12cm.

'Little Bitton'
Delicate-looking flowers. Outer segments slim, clawed. Inner segments broad inverted 'V' to heart-shape at apex. January–February.

'Little Dancer' (*nivalis*)

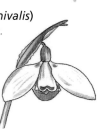

Curious small *G. nivalis*. Flowers tend to face outwards from slender pedicel. Scape and pedicel vary from normal to non-existent, leaving flower among leaves. Leaves slender, upright to arching, green. Outer segments bluntly pointed. Inner segments narrow inverted 'V' at apex. January–February. Phil Cornish, Yanworth, Gloucestershire, 1995. ↑8cm.

'Little Dorrit' (Hybrid cultivar)

Short snowdrop with well shaped rounded flowers. Leaves semi-erect, glaucescent. Outer segments well rounded, clawed. Inner segments strongly ridged, inverted 'U' at apex diffusing into scissor-shaped mark towards base. John Morley, North Green, Suffolk, early 1990s. *G. plicatus* in parentage. ↑10cm.

'Little Drip' (Hybrid cultivar)

Small, floriferous plants with well shaped flowers. Leaves erect. Inner segments inverted 'V' at apex, lighter in centre. Usually two scapes, occasionally third on mature plants. Late. Michael and Carol Baron in Sotheby's garden, Summers Place, Sussex, 1993, named for flower shape. ↑14cm.

'Little Emma'
(*nivalis* × *plicatus*)

Broad balloon-shaped flowers. Outer segments well rounded, textured. Inner segments scissor-shaped mark filled in towards base. January–February. Ian Christie, Brechin Castle, Angus, Scotland, named for his granddaughter. ↑10cm.

'Little Joan' (*nivalis*)

Tiny snowdrop with unusually rounded flowers for nivalis. Leaves applanate, glaucous. Outer segments, broad, well rounded. Inner segments narrow inverted 'U' or 'V' at apex. January–February. Cliff and Joan Curtis, The Cottage, Ketton, Rutland, 1995. ↑9cm.

'Little John'
(Hybrid cultivar)

Syn. *G.* 'Maid Marian'
Tall with large, substantial, smooth flowers. Leaves semi-erect, mainly explicative, distinctively pale, glaucous. Outer segments slender claw. Inner segments solid slender 'X' apex towards base. Vigorous. February. Phil Cornish in E.B. Anderson's former garden, Lower Slaughter, Gloucestershire, 1992. ↑20cm.

'Little Late Comer'

Outer segments well shaped, rounded at apex, goffered at base. Inner segments small green spot either side of sinus. February–March.

'Little Magnet'
(Hybrid cultivar)

Generally larger than *G.* 'Magnet'. Well shaped rounded flower, long thick pedicel. Leaves spreading, revolute to explicative, glaucescent. Inner segments heavy texture, uniform, deep-green 'V' at apex. January–February. Alan Street, Blewbury, Oxfordshire, 1980s. ↑20cm.

'Livia' (*nivalis*)

Dainty flowers, oblong green ovary. Leaves applanate, erect, slender, blue-green. Outer segments long, slender, bluntly pointed, merging green lines above apex. Inner segments broad even inverted 'V' at apex. January–February.

'Llo 'n' Green' (*nivalis*)

Well formed, rounded flowers. Leaves mid-bright green, paler median stripe. Outer segments variable green lines at apex. Inner segment heart-shaped green mark at apex. December–January. Joe Sharman and Dr Alan Leslie, Gorge de Llo, Mount Louis, French Pyrenees.

Originally thought to be *G. reginae-olgae* subsp. *vernalis* as leaves have pale median stripe. PC 2008. ↑11cm.

'Lodestar'
(*elwesii* var. *elwesii*)

Upright, tall, robust. Well proportioned flowers, slender pedicels. Leaves supervolute, arching, grey-green, hooded, lax at maturity. Outer segments brilliant white, boat-shaped, strongly clawed. Inner segments inverted rounded 'U', minute sinus. Clumps up well. Richard Ayres, Anglesey Abbey, Cambridgeshire, early 1980s. ↑24cm.

'Lohengrin'

Round green ovary, erect scape. Outer segments broad, rounded. Inner segments broad 'X'-shaped mark. January–February.

'Long Drop' (*elwesii*)

Handsome, long flowering snowdrop with large flowers, long thin ovary. Leaves supervolute, arching, narrow, pointed, well developed at flowering. Outer segments slender, variable green lines at apex. Inner segments broad 'U' to 'V' at apex. Possibly Primrose Warburg's garden, South Hayes, early 1990s. ↑21cm.

'Long Guy'

Long slender ovary. Outer segments long, slender. Inner segments green inverted 'U' or 'V' at apex.

'Long John'
(Hybrid cultivar)

Particularly fine. Leaves slender, erect to arching, green. Outer segments boat-shaped, bluntly pointed. Inner segments slightly waisted green mark across segment, deep white 'V' from base. Good, prolific. ↑23cm.

'Long Leys'

Large flowers, erect scapes. Leaves supervolute, erect to arching, broad, grey-green. Outer segments bluntly pointed. Inner segments rounded inverted 'V' at apex, oval mark towards base. January–February. ↑18cm.

long pedicelled ex 'Herbert Ransom'
See ex Herbert Ransom.

'Long Tall Sally' (*plicatus* cultivar)
Distinctive, tall, attractive, with small rounded flowers. Inner segments strong green heart-shaped mark at apex, thin lines towards base. Two scapes held well above foliage. Christopher Brickell selection. ↑30cm.

'Long Wasp' (Hybrid cultivar)
Elongated flowers similar to *G.* 'Wasp'. Long pedicel. Outer segments elongated, narrow, insect-like. Inner segments tube-like, green mark at apex, green mark at base which can joined. John Morley, North Green Snowdrops, Suffolk. ↑25cm.

'Longfellow' (*plicatus*)
Attractive, sturdy, bold. Large flowers. Leaves arched, revolute from base towards middle. Outer segments bluntly pointed. Inner segments small green inverted 'U' at apex, short arms. Phil Cornish in E.B. Anderson's old garden, Lower Slaughter, Gloucestershire, 1992. First mistakenly distributed as *G.* 'Gerard Parker'. ↑17cm.

'Longnor Hall'
Well shaped, broadly triangular flowers. Outer segments long, bluntly pointed. Inner segments inverted 'V' at apex. January–February. Longnor Hall, Shropshire.

'Longstowe'
Free-flowering, prolific. Leaves narrow, erect, grey-green. Outer segments well shaped, rounded at apex. Inner segments dark-green inverted 'V' at apex to half of segment. February–March. Possible *G. plicatus* × *G. nivalis*. ↑14cm.

'Longworth Double' (Hybrid double)
Good regular double. Leaves supervolute, erect, incurved margins. Outer segments occasional green lines at apex. Inner

segments neat ruff, outer whorl usually aberrant, inverted 'V' at apex, paler mark at base, sometimes absent. Elizabeth Parker-Jervis and Primrose Warburg at old Longworth Hospital, Kingston Bagpuize, Oxfordshire. Similar to *G.* 'Kingston Double'. ↑19cm.

'Look Up Twin' (*elwesii*)
Large, unusually angled flowers looking outwards and upwards at 45° from pedicel. Outer segments broad, rounded, bluntly pointed. Inner segments inverted green 'V' at apex, paler green mark at base. November–January. ↑15cm.

'Looking Around' (*nivalis*)
Outward-facing double flowers held horizontally on pedicel. Small, narrow ovary. Outer segments long, pointed. Inner segments well rounded, neat ruff, narrowly joined inverted 'V' with green line towards separate basal mark. January–February. Named as flowers project out from pedicel. Valentin Wijnen.

'Loose Spirit' (*nivalis*)
Attractive, slim, delicate-looking flowers on short scapes tending towards poculiform. Leaves applanate, erect, slender, shiny, green. Outer segments slender. Inner segments shorter than outer, tiny green spot either side of sinus. January–February. ↑10cm.

'Lord Kitchener' (Hybrid cultivar)
Large, vigorous snowdrop with well shaped flowers. Inner segments good mark. Highly perfumed. ↑18cm.

'Lord Lieutenant' (Hybrid cultivar)
Distinctive, attractive snowdrop with upright scapes and more outward-facing flowers. Leaves semi-erect, explicative at base. Outer segments ridged, clawed. Inner segments

large part-filled roughly 'X'-shaped mark across segment, not to base. Carolyn Elwes, Colesbourne, Gloucestershire, 1994, named in honour of Henry Elwes's post as Lord Lieutenant of Gloucestershire. ↑23cm.

'Lord Monostictus' (*elwesii* var. *monostictus*)
Although this name is in circulation with some suppliers, it is not valid. Beautiful snowdrop. Large bulbs, well shaped flowers. Leaves bold, broad, convolute, blue-green. Outer segments well shaped, rounded. Inner segments inverted 'U' at apex. Originally sold as *G. caucasicus*.

'Louise Ann Bromley' (*elwesii*)
Strong with attractive flowers. Leaves, broad, erect-arching, grey-green. Outer segments long, broad, bluntly pointed. Inner segments slightly waisted dark-green mark apex almost to base. David Bromley, Wellington, Shropshire, named for his late sister. ↑20cm.

'Lowick' (*nivalis* Sandersii Group)
Good, strong yellow ovary, pedicel, yellow-green spathe and scape. Outer segments rounded, bluntly pointed. Inner segments strong yellow inverted 'V' at apex, yellow lines following veins, paler mark at base. January–February (formerly Cambo Estate form). ↑10cm.

'Lucifer'
Large slender ovary. Outer segments well shaped, small green marks above apex. Inner segments green mark covering almost entire segment.

'Luke'
Upright, slender spiky snowdrop with narrow segments heavily marked green. ↑12cm.

'Lulu'

Long, slender, curving pedicel. Outer segments rounded, bluntly pointed, light longitudinal ridging. Inner segments lightly ridged, small inverted 'V' at apex. Michael Baron, Brandy Mount.

'Lutea' (*nivalis*)

Yellow-marked *G. nivalis*.

'Lutescens' (*nivalis*)

See *G. nivalis* Sandersii Group. 'Lutescens' originally applied by James Allen to yellow snowdrops sent by Mr Sanders. Name reverted to correct *G*. 'Sandersii', 1993. ↑12cm.

'Lutescens Flore Pleno'

See 'Lady Elphinstone'.

'Lutz Bauer'
(*nivalis* Poculiformis Group)

Slender rounded poculiform flowers with long pedicel and split spathe. All segments equally sized with large green mark above apex. February. Rudi Bauer, 2006. ↑12cm.

'Lydiard Diana'
(*nivalis* Poculiformis Group)

Beautiful slender poculiform with bluntly pointed, all-white segments. Inner segments slightly shorter than outer. January–February.

'Lyn' (Hybrid cultivar)

Vigorous *G*. 'Atkinsii' clone with very large flowers. Outer segments long, slender claw. Inner segments heart-shaped mark at apex. Bulks up well, quickly. December–January. Lyn Sales, Perrot's Brook, Cirencester, Gloucestershire, 1981. ↑20cm.

'Lyzzick'
(Hybrid cultivar)

Clean-looking with dark-green ovary. Well shaped flowers. Outer segments long. Inner segments crisp, dark-green, broad

rounded 'U' at apex diffusing slightly towards base. January–February. Melvyn Jope, Cumbria. *G. nivalis* × *G. plicatus*.

'M. Myer's Green Tipped '

See 'Green Tip'.

'M5287'
(*reginae-olgae* subsp. *vernalis*)

Dainty, neat. Bulbs small. Leaves lax. Inner segments low green inverted 'U' at apex. Early. Brian Mathew, Montenegro, 1969. ↑12cm.

'Madeleine'
(*plicatus*)

Good vigorous yellow. Ovary greenish-yellow. Leaves bright-green, plicate edges. Inner segments yellow mark at apex diffusing towards base. Colour varies depending on site. January–February. Joe Sharman, 2002, named for his niece.

'Mafangza' (*nivalis*)

Erroneously named. Bulbs and seeds distributed with this name but appears to be standard *G. nivalis*.

'Magnet' (Hybrid cultivar)

Good, vigorous, one of the oldest and best. Large flowers on tall scapes. Exceptionally long arching pedicel creates distinctive movement. Leaves erect, narrow, flat-lightly explicative, grey-green-glaucescent. Outer segments long. Inner segments inverted 'V' at apex. Strong honey perfume. Easy, bulks up well, sterile. January–February. Originally '*G. elwesii* with long pedicel'. Raised from seed of *G*. 'Melvillei' by James Allen, pre-1894. RHS AM 1967. ↑20cm.

'Magnus' (*elwesii* var. *elwesii*)

Standard-looking *G. elwesii* snowdrop. Leaves supervolute, semi-erect. Outer segments, long, rounded, pointed. Inner

segments distinctive elongated heart to 'Y' mark not reaching base. First listed Long Acre Plants, 1997, but origins obscure prior to this. ↑17cm.

'Maid Marian' (*elwesii*)

See 'Little John'.

'Maidwell'
(*elwesii* var. *elwesii*)

Popular, tall, strong growing. Short scape, large elongated flower, broad segments. Leaves attractive, broad, blue-grey. Inner segment well shaped dark, strong 'X' mark. Oliver Wyatt, from Maidwell Hall, Northamptonshire. ↑25cm.

'Maidwell 1'

See 'Maidwell C'.

'Maidwell A'

See 'Kite'.

'Maidwell C' (plicatus hybrid)

Syn. *G*. 'Maidwell 1'
Distinctive rounded ovary, slender arching pedicel, rounded flowers. Leaves arching, explicative, glaucescent. Outer segments clawed. Inner segments pale inverted 'U' or 'V' at apex, or variable 'X' extending towards base. Usually two scapes. Oliver Wyatt, Maidwell Hall, Northamptonshire, c. 1940s. ↑17cm.

'Maidwell L' (*elwesii* var. *elwesii*)

Syns. *G*. 'Oliver Wyatt', *G. caucasicus* 'Maidwell L'
Popular, tall, attractive, vigorous snowdrop. Flowers large, long, very white. Leaves supervolute, broad, erect to arching, glaucous. Outer segments slender, clawed. Inner segments solid green 'X' across segment. Slow, good when established. December–January. Oliver Wyatt, Maidwell Hall, Northamptonshire. ↑24cm.

'Major Pam' (*nivalis*)

Syns. *G*. 'Pamski's Double', *G*. 'Major Pam's Double'
Neat, regular double similar to 'Flore Pleno' but flowers unique. Leaves applanate, erect, blue-green. Outer

segments rounded. Inner segments lightly flared ruff, generally aberrant, outer whorl variable 'U'-shaped mark, inner whorls wide 'V' at apex. Major Albert Pam, Broxbourne, Hertfordshire. ↑14cm.

'Major Pam's Double'
See 'Major Pam'.

'Mandarin'
(*elwesii* Edward Whittall Group)
Syns. G. 'Coolie', G. 'Mandarin's Hat' Vigorous, eye-catching with extremely white flowers, bright olive-green ovary. Leaves supervolute, erect, broad. Outer segments long claw, opening wide in warmth. Inner segments variable inverted 'V', shallow sinus, occasional lighter marks toward base which can join. Phil Cornish in garden, Longlevens, Gloucestershire, 1993, old colony of imported wild *G. elwesii*. ↑18cm.

'March Sunshine' (*nivalis*)

'Margaret Biddulph' (*elwesii*)
Beautiful snowdrop with elegant flowers, rounded green ovary. Leaves broad, erect, grey-green. Outer segments pointed, light-green merging lines apex towards base. Inner segments solid mid-green mark apex to base, narrow white margin. Named by Simon Biddulph, Rodmarton Manor, Gloucestershire, for his grandmother. ↑14cm.

'Margaret Ford'
Elongated flowers. Outer segments long, boat-shaped, pointed. Inner segments broad mid-green mark from apex to two-thirds of segment.

'Margaret Owen'
(Hybrid cultivar)
Beautiful snowdrop with elegantly shaped flowers. Outer segments long, large, rounded, bluntly pointed. Inner

segments dark-green mark from apex spreading on basal side. January–February. Named for Galanthophile Margaret Owen, Acton Pigot, Shropshire. ↑28cm.

'Margery Fish' (*nivalis*)
Unusual, easily recognized, very distinctive spathe curving backwards, sometime split. Long, straight pedicel. Leaves applanate, semi-erect, lightly explicative. Outer segments long, slender, green marks towards apex. Inner segments slightly flared, green mark apex to base, edged white. January–February. Margery Fish's East Lambrook Manor Garden, Somerset, 1987, named after her. ↑16cm.

'Maria' (*reginae-olgae* subsp. *reginae-olgae*)
Elegant, beautiful, with distinctively shaped flowers, long pedical. Leaves short or absent at flowering. Outer segments long, slender, textured, clawed. Inner segments spreading, narrowing at apex, large sinus, inverted 'U' at apex. Early. ↑16cm.

'Marielle' (*elwesii*)
Dark-green mark and ovary enhances very white flowers. Leaves broad, grey-green. Outer segments longitudinally ridged. Inner segments green mark across segment from apex towards base. From Bernard Tickner, Coddenham, Suffolk.

'Marijke'
Outer segments broad, pointed, recurved margins, pale-green lines above apex, shadowed on underside. Inner segments broad heart-shaped mark at apex. Easy, good. January–February. Wim Snoeijer, Gouda, Netherlands, 2005, named for Marijke van Dijk, 2009. ↑18cm.

'Marjorie Brown'
(*elwesii* var. *monostictus*)
Vigorous, good. Leaves supervolute, arching, blue-grey, glaucous. Outer

segments clawed. Inner segment inverted olive-green 'V' at apex. February–March. In bulbs purchased by John Parry, Marjorie Brown's nephew, from bulb merchant Van Tubergen, 1958. Named after his aunt. ↑17cm.

'Mark Solomon'
(*nivalis* Poculiformis Group)
Beautiful white poculiform with well balanced flowers. Leaves applanate, slender, erect, blue-green. Segments slender, all-white, bluntly pointed. January–February. ↑14cm.

'Mark's Tall'
(*nivalis* × *plicatus*)
Attractive Irish snowdrop. Outer segments bluntly pointed, clawed, lightly longitudinally ridged. Inner segments mid-green heart-shaped mark at apex. Prolific. Bulks up well. ↑35cm.

'Marlene Uhlhaas'
(*elwesii* var. *monostictus*)
Beautifully rounded flowers on long scapes. Leaves upright, slender, blue-green. Outer segments well rounded, large, bright-green heart-shaped mark above apex. Inner segments bright-green, rounded heart-shaped mark at apex. Rudi Bauer, 2007. ↑20cm.

'Marlie Raphael'
(*elwesii* var. *elwesii*)

Eye-catching with large, elegant flowers. Leaves supervolute, semi-erect-arching, broad, green. Outer segments strongly clawed, greenish yellow lines at apex. Inner segments pale yellow-green part-filled ''X', occasionally separate apical and basal marks. Francis and Virginia Grant, Kingston Bagpuize House, Oxfordshire, 2003, named after previous owner. ↑15cm.

'Martha Maclaren'
(Hybrid cultivar)
Strong, robust snowdrop with rounded flowers. Leaves erect, broad, slightly supervolute, flat margins, glaucous. Outer segments good goffered claw. Inner segments clasping, inverted 'V' at apex merging with oval, indented white mark at base. South Hayes, Oxfordshire, named for John Grimshaw's niece. ↑24cm.

'Martyn Rix' (peshmenii)
Leaves large, broad, grey. November–December. Dry situation. G. 'Kastellorhizo' clone.

'Mary Ann Gibbs'
(elwesii var. elwesii)
Attractive, dazzling white flowers. Leaves supervolute, erect, pointed, hooded. Outer segments large, rounded, overlapped until spreading, clawed. Inner segments tube-like, small green spot either side of sinus, separate oblong at base. Slow. Mrs Gibbs, Hampshire, c. 1960s. ↑23cm.

'Mary Biddulph'
(elwesii var. elwesii)
Large flower, unusually crooked spathe. Inner segments good inverted 'V' at apex, two small ovals towards base which can merge. Early. Oliver Wyatt, named for him by the Hon. Mary Biddulph, name previously applied so renamed G. 'Mary Biddulph'.

'Mary Hely-Hutchinson'
(plicatus)
Very early, small, elegant, beautiful, Irish G. plicatus. Leaves lax. Outer segments hooded, slender, rounded. Inner segments well shaped large broad-green mark across segment from inverted 'V' at apex. Probably earliest G. plicatus, flowering October–December. Can be difficult. Robin Hall's garden, Primrose Hill, Co. Dublin from Lady Mary Hely-Hutchinson. ↑8–9cm.

'Mary O'Brien'
(elwesii)
Leaves broad, erect, grey. Outer segments pointed. Inner segments 'V'-shaped mark joining oval towards base. Robin Hall, Co. Dublin.

'Maskenball'
Well shaped flower. Outer segments broad, rounded, bluntly pointed. Inner segments scissor-shaped green mark from apex towards base. Germany. English translation: 'Masked Ball'.

'Matt-adors'
(Hybrid cultivar)
Unusual, upward-facing flowers. Leaves applanate, semi-erect, glaucescent. Outer segments slender, pointed, green mark at apex, also on underside. Inner segments goffered margins, inverted 'U' at apex with small legs. Richard Hobbs in former H.A. Greatorex's garden, Brundall, Norfolk, 1999, named for Matt Bishop as he 'adored' it. ↑17cm.

'Maximus' (nivalis)
Supposed to be extinct, and the plant being sold as G. 'Maximus' is almost certainly not the original cultivar. However, it is still listed by some growers and therefore included here. A substantial G. nivalis generally taller and later than the norm. Outer segments rounded. Inner segments small inverted 'U' at apex. The name is now classed as a syn. of G. 'Yvonne Hay', although the markings are different. Tom Koopman, Netherlands.

'MBAC 93' (nivalis)

'Megan'
Well shaped G. 'Trym' seedling. Outer segments paddle-shaped, broad at apex, green mark above apex. Inner segments green heart-shaped mark at apex. January–February.

'Melanie Broughton'
(Hybrid cultivar)
Tall with beautifully shaped rounded flowers. Leaves erect, broad, flat-explicative, blue-grey. Outer segments rounded, strong claw. Inner segments green mark from apex towards base. Often two scapes. February–March. Anglesey Abbey, Cambridgeshire, 1998, named for Lord Fairhaven's youngest daughter. ↑29cm.

'Melanie S' (Hybrid double)
Well shaped regular double. Outer segments rounded, lightly longitudinally ridged, clawed. Inner segments neat ruff, flared at apex, dark-green inverted 'V' mark. Valentin Wijnen, Belgium, named after his wife.

'Melbourne'
(elwesii var monostictus)
Australian-raised selection named after city.

'Melnik'
Slender light-green ovary, inflated spathe. Outer segments long, bluntly pointed, pale-green-yellow lines above apex. Inner segments pale-green-yellow inverted 'V' at apex, upturned ends.

'Melot'
Shapely flowers. Leaves grey-green. Outer segments long, pointed, green mark at apex. Inner segments small inverted 'V' at apex.

'Melvillei' (nivalis hybrid)
Syns. G. 'Dunrobin Seedling', G. 'Melvillei Major', G. nivalis var. melvillei Flowers large, rounded, gleaming white. Leaves applanate, broad, glaucescent. Inner segment green inverted 'V' at apex. Although there are descriptions for G. 'Melvillei' similar to G. 'Atkinsii', name is probably misapplied and G. 'Melvillei' now appears extinct. Dunrobin Castle, Sutherland 1879, named G. 'Dunrobin seedling', later renamed for head gardener, David Melville. RHS FCC 1879. ↑25cm.

'Melvillei Major'
See 'Melvillei'.

'Merlin' (Hybrid cultivar)
Beautiful old snowdrop with large, long, well marked flowers. Leaves semi-erect, broad, ridged, variable explicative margins, grey-green, glaucous. Outer segments large, substantial, short claw. Inner segments slightly waisted dark-green mark across segment, narrow white margin. Strong, bulks up well. Mid-January–February. James Allen, 1891. *G. elwesii* × *G. plicatus*. RHS AM 1971. ↑23cm.

'Mette'
(***reginae-olgae* subsp. *reginae-olgae*)
Elegant, with large, well shaped flowers and long pedicel giving good movement. Leaves absent or short at flowering, subrevolute margins. Outer segments thick, ridged, clawed. Inner segments spreading, incurved margins, Chinese-bridge mark at apex, large sinus. Early. ↑15cm.

'Michael Holecroft' (*elwesii*)
Elegant snowdrop. Elongated flowers, slender ovary, arching spathe. Leaves supervolute, broad, grey, channelled. Outer segments long, slender, pointed, dimpled. Inner segments good, crisp 'U' to 'V' at apex. ↑20cm.

'Michael Myer's Green Tipped'
See 'Green Tips'.

'Midge' (*plicatus*)
Well shaped flowers, erect scapes, inflated spathe. Leaves erect to arching, blue-green. Outer segments slender, bluntly pointed. Inner segments broad inverted 'V' at apex, rounded ends, narrowly connected to larger mark diffusing to base. February. ↑12cm.

'Mighty Atom' (Hybrid cultivar)

Outstanding, strong growing, later snowdrop in 'Mighty Atom' group. Very large, white, rounded flowers. Leaves broad, erect, grey. Outer segments clawed. Inner segments incurved, ridged, dark-green inverted 'V' at apex, often with one or two white veins. February–March. John Gray raised seedling, named by E.B. Anderson. Numerous similar clones under this name create difficulties establishing definitive type, but above now accepted. ↑14cm.

'Milkwood'
See 'Mrs Macnamara'.

'Mill House'
See 'Viridapice'.

'Mill View'
(*elwesii* var. *monostictus*)
Short, sturdy snowdrop with rounded flowers, one of the last *G. elwesii* in bloom. Leaves supervolute, erect, well developed at flowering. Inner segments narrow inverted 'U' at apex. March–April. Bob Taylor, garden at Mill View, Shepshed, Leicestershire, 1994. ↑11cm.

'Miller's Late'
(*elwesii* var. *monostictus*)
Elongated flowers, arching spathe. Leaves supervolute, arching. Outer segments long, lightly ridged and textured. Inner segments broad green inverted 'U' at apex. Slow. Very late, one of last to flower. March–April. Primrose Warburg's garden, but possibly from Giant Snowdrop Company, *c.* 1967. ↑15cm.

'Min'
Delicate flowers, long arching spathe. Outer segments concave. Inner segments broad dark-green inverted 'V' at apex, paler mark towards base. January–February.

'Mini Me' (*nivalis*)
Variable and, as its name implies, miniature snowdrop from Ireland. Outer segments pointed. Inner segments small inverted green 'V' at apex. Slow. January–February. ↑6cm.

'Miss Adventure'
(*reginae-olgae* subsp. *vernalis*)
Distinctive white petaloid spathe. Leaves erect. Outer segments broad, unmarked, clawed. Inner segments green inverted 'U' or 'V' at apex, occasional green stain at base. Early. Anglesey Abbey, Cambridgeshire, early 1990s. ↑10cm.

'Miss Behaving'
(*reginae-olgae* subsp. *vernalis*)
Unusual as flowers held upright and open. White petaloid spathe. Leaves semi-erect. Outer segments green mark at apex. Inner segments incurved margins, shallow sinus, green 'V' slightly upturned at apex. December–January. Joe Sharman selection, 1995. ↑10cm.

'Miss Willmott'
An attractive, robust and early snowdrop found by Ailsa Wildig in an old abandoned garden in Essex, 2003. ↑18cm.

'Missenden Slender' (*nivalis*)
Slender-flowered *G. nivalis*. Outer segments long, slender. Inner segments inverted green 'V' at apex. January–February. Mark Brown, Missenden Abbey, Buckinghamshire, mid-1980s. ↑12cm.

'Mmm' (*elwesii*)
Creamy-coloured flowers, yellow-green ovary. Leaves supervolute, broad, grey. December–January. ↑12cm.

'Mocca's'
See 'Moccas'.

'Moccas' (Hybrid cultivar)
Syns. *G.* 'Atkinsii Moccas Form', *G.* 'Atkinsii Moccas Strain', *G.* 'Mocca's'

Similar to G. 'Atkinsii'. Outer segments long claw. Inner segments large broad inverted 'U' at apex. Rarely aberrant segments, flowers earlier than G. 'Atkinsii'. Moccas Court, Herefordshire. ↑18cm.

'Modern Art'
(Hybrid cultivar)
Very distinctive large, upright, leafy spathe, split at apex. Leaves applanate, erect, long, explicative, glaucous. Outer segments long, narrow, incurved, clawed, green mark apex and base. Inner segments tube-like, variable yellow-green inverted 'U' diffusing slightly towards base, two vertical bands paling towards base. E.B. Anderson selected seedling, 1950s. Similar to 'G. Viridapice' and G. 'Warei', slight variations. ↑19cm.

'Molly Watts'
(elwesii var. elwesii)
Leaves supervolute, erect. Outer segments distinctive with joined green lines at apex forming roughly circular mark. Inner segments heart to 'V' at apex, two small joined ovals towards base. Ruby Baker in David and Molly Watt's garden, Goring, Oxfordshire, early 1990s.

'Mona' (nivalis × plicatus)
Beautiful very delicate-looking flowers, pale-green ovary. Outer segments large, bluntly pointed. Inner segments, almost completely white with a hint of pale-green marking at apex. January–February. Ian Christie, Brechin Castle, Angus, Scotland, named after friend's daughter. ↑10cm.

'Monica' (nivalis)
Attractive flowers, erect scapes. Leaves applanate, erect, slender, blue-green. Outer segments bluntly pointed, merging green lines. Inner segments, broad squared inverted 'U' at apex. January–February. ↑15cm.

'Monk'
Elegant, slender flowers. Outer segments long, incurved, longitudinally ridged. Inner segments small narrow inverted green 'V' at apex, paler mark towards base.

'Moonlight'
Erect scapes, pale yellow-green ovary. Inner segments, broad pale-green mark, central white notch at apex and base.

'Moortown'
(Hybrid cultivar)
Syn. G. 'Mighty Atom'
Large, well shaped flowers, strong scapes. G. 'Mighty Atom' group. Leaves semi-erect, glaucescent. Outer segments clawed. Inner segments dark-green inverted 'V' at apex blurring slightly on basal side. Given to David Bromley as G. 'Mighty Atom' by E.B. Anderson, 1968, renamed after David Bromley's garden, Moortown, Wellington, Shropshire. ↑18cm.

'Morag' (plicatus)
Vigorous snowdrop with large flowers and good single inner segment mark.

'Mordred'
(Hybrid double)
Neat, solid-looking double. Leaves applanate, slender, erect, blue-green. Outer segments brushed green at apex, shadowed on underside. Inner segments good neat ruff, green mark above apex. ↑15cm.

'Moreton Mill'
(Poculiformis Group)
Beautiful, elegant, albino poculiform with equal-sized segments. Leaves erect to arching, blue-green. January–February. ↑12cm.

'Moses Basket' (elwesii)
Quirky flowers, slender ovary, long spathe and scape which can be weak. Outer segments with short claw that raises segment then sharply incurves at apex, like parrot's beak,

forming a lantern or basket shape. Inner segments small yellow-green mark. Found by David Jordan, assistant head gardener at Anglesey Abbey, Cambridgeshire, 2004, growing at the edge of G. elwesii. Named by Richard Todd and David Jordan for the late grandson of a visitor to Anglesey Abbey. ↑30cm.

'Mosquito' (nivalis)
Small double G. nivalis. Leaves applanate, slender, erect, blue-green. Outer segments slender. Inner segments small green inverted 'V' at apex. January–February. ↑10cm.

'Mothering Sunday' (plicatus)
Large, balloon-like, rounded flowers. Leaves explicative, green. Outer segments broad, bluntly pointed. Inner segments very narrow inverted green 'V' at apex, spreading at ends. Very late flowering, March–April. Avon Bulbs, 2007, named by Hagen Engelmann. ↑20cm.

'Mountain Sunrise' (elwesii)
Well shaped with segments flushed light orange. Belgium.

'Moya's Green' (elwesii)
Slim flowers. Outer segments slender, light-green mark above apex to half of segment. Inner segments slightly waisted dark-green mark across segment almost to base. February. ↑18cm.

'Mr Beaney' (elwesii)
Large flowers. Leaves erect, broad, grey-green. Outer segments pointed, green marks above apex, shadowed on underside. Inner segment green 'U' mark at apex diffusing towards base. Similar to G. 'Big Boy' with smaller mark. ↑18cm.

'Mr Blobby' (elwesii)
Flowers rounded, variable aberrant segments. Leaves supervolute, arching, grey-green. Outer segments clawed. Lightly ridged, textured. Inner segments rounded

heart-shaped mark at apex. Joe Sharman, the late Sir Vivian Fuchs' garden, Cambridge, 1990. ↑14cm.

'Mr Courages Early'

'Mr Fraylings Double' (*nivalis*)
Double *G. nivalis*. Outer segments spreading. Inner segments ruff marked green. January–February. ↑15cm.

'Mr Spoons'
(Hybrid cultivar)
Attractive rounded flowers. Outer segments strongly tipped green. Inner segments large strong inverted 'V' to 'U' at apex. Simon Savage, in H.A. Greatorex's former garden, Brundall, Norfolk, 1997.

'Mr Thompson'
Strong, vigorous and attractive snowdrop. Inner segments have a single 'U' to 'V' shaped mark at apex. Easy. January–February.

'Mr. Winkler'
(*nivalis* Scharlockii)
Snowdrop with quirky extra segment. Outer segments four, very long, slender, green marks apex towards base. Inner segments broader heart-shapedgreen mark at apex. January–February. Rudi Bauer, 2007.

'Mrs Backhouse'
See 'Mrs Backhouse No 12'.

'Mrs Backhouse No 12'
(Hybrid cultivar)
Syns. *G.* 'Mrs Backhouse', *G.* 'Backhouse No 12'
Large, well shaped flowers. Leaves blue-grey, glaucescent, flat or lightly explicative. Outer segments ridged. Inner segments inverted olive-green 'V' at apex. *G.* 'Atkinsii' type, similar to *G.* 'Backhouse Spectacles'. Probably Mr and Mrs Backhouse, Sutton Court, Herefordshire. Possible *G. nivalis* × *G. plicatus*. Past

misidentification and confusion means present type may not be original cultivar. ↑21cm.

'Mrs Backhouse's Spectacles'
See 'Backhouse Spectacles'.

'Mrs McNamara' (*elwesii*)
Syn. *G.* 'Milkwood'
Tall, elegant, robust. Well shaped flowers. Leaves supervolute, blue-green, glaucous. Outer segments long, slender, textured. Inner segments narrow 'V' at apex. December–January. Named for Mrs McNamara, Dylan Thomas's mother-in-law. Two snowdrops circulated as *G.* 'Mrs McNamara', one from C. Brickell, and *G.* 'Dylan Thomas's mother's snowdrop', later named *G.* 'Milkwood', from Richard Nutt. When discrepancy discovered, *G.* 'Mrs McNamara' applied as more fitting. ↑20cm.

'Mrs Thompson'
(Hybrid cultivar)
Syn. *G.* 'Yorkshire Cottage'
Rare, striking, curious and erratic, varying each year. Often two scapes, first having two pedicels each with flower, second usually only one flower. Flowers fuse and vary in segment number. There can be five equal outer segments and four inner segments, although can revert to three outer and three inner. Leaves semi-erect, glaucescent. Outer segments often misshapen. Inner segments, light-green, inverted 'V' at apex. January–February. Mrs N.G. Thompson, Escrick, York, *c.* 1940–1950. ↑18cm.

'Mrs Tiggywinkle' (*nivalis*)
Dark green double spiky. Ovary wrinkled, spathe split. Leaves applanate, erect, pointed. Outer segments three or four, slender, incurved, merging green lines from apex. Inner segment ruff, outermost whorl usually aberrant, roughly

shaped 'V' at apex. January–February. Joe Sharman, from Frank Condon, Orchard Nurseries, Cambridgeshire, 1997, named for Beatrix Potter's hedgehog character. ↑10cm.

'Mrs W.M. George'
Attractive, well shaped flowers. Leaves erect, slender, blue-green. Outer segments long rounded. Inner segments inverted 'V' at apex. ↑16cm.

'Mrs Warburg's Double'
See 'Heffalump'.

'Mrs Wrightson's Double'
(Hybrid double)
Sought-after, vigorous, full double. Leaves supervolute, two or three, grey. Outer segments cup-shaped. Inner segments longitudinally incurved, inverted 'V' at apex, small mark towards base, undersides striped green. Mrs David Wrightson, Ward's Moat, Kent, 1975. ↑16cm.

'Mrs. Wrightson's No 2'
(Hybrid cultivar)

'MT4027'
(*reginae-olgae* subsp. *vernalis*)
Syn. MT5297
Leaves semi-erect, subrevolute margins. Outer segments slender. Inner segments small inverted 'U' at apex, small sinus. Early. Brian Mathew and John Tomlinson, Montenegro, 1965. ↑8cm.

'Munchkin' (*nivalis*)
Small snowdrop on erect scape. Leaves applanate, upright, slender, blue-green. Outer segments pointed. Inner segments inverted heart-shaped green mark at apex. Small in stature but clumps up well. ↑8cm.

'Mustang Sally'
(Hybrid cultivar)
Tall, beautiful snowdrop with long elegant flowers. Leaves, long, green-glaucous. Outer segments slender, elongated, textured. Inner segments rounded

inverted 'U' at apex, two small joined ovals towards base. Early. Somerset. Probably *G. nivalis* × *G. plicatus*. ↑18cm.

'Mystra' (*reginae-olgae* subsp. *reginae-olgae*)
Outer segments long, pointed. Inner segments large green inverted 'V' apex almost to base. David and Ruby Baker, Mystra, Peloponnese, Greece, c. 1997. ↑10cm.

'Nancy Lindsay'
See 'Sutton Courtenay'.

'Napoleon' (*nivalis*)
Slender flower, long pedicel, strong, upright scape. Leaves applanate, erect slender, blue-green. Outer segments long, slender. Inner segments inverted 'U' at apex, rounded ends. January–February. ↑14cm.

'Narrengesicht' (*nivalis*)
Well shaped flowers with small, rounded ovary. Leaves applanate, erect, blue-green. Outer segments pointed. Inner segments mid-green inverted 'V' at apex joining two paler marginal lines towards base. January–February. Germany. English translation: 'Fool's Face' (said to resemble carnival mask). ↑20cm.

'Narwhal'
Another *G.* 'Walrus'-type snowdrop with outward-facing flowers. Outer segments very long, thin, incurved with green marks at apex, paler at base. Inner segments small ruff, marked green. Late flowering, well into April. ↑14cm.

'Natalie Garton' (*elwesii*)
Attractive, vigorous, rounded semi-double. Leaves broad grey-green. Outer segments globular, well rounded. Inner segments broad, inverted 'U' at apex. Named after Natalie Garton, Ramsden, Oxfordshire, pre-1996. ↑16cm.

'Naughton' (*elwesii* var. *elwesii*)
Syns. *G.* 'Largest of All', *G.* 'Oliver Wyatt's Giant' Excellent, large, eye-catching snowdrop. Beautifully shaped flowers, arching spathe. Leaves supervolute, arching. Outer segments rounded, ridged, textured, delicate claw. Inner segments inverted 'V' at apex, paler 'U' at base. Slow, replant regularly. Rod Leeds in Oliver Wyatt's garden, Naughton, Suffolk, early 1970s, named by Rod Leeds. ↑19cm.

'Neill Fraser' (Hybrid cultivar)
Slender flowers. Leaves erect, narrow, linear, flat-lightly explicative, glaucous. Outer segments rounded, clawed. Inner segments rounded inverted 'U' at apex. February. Similar to *G.* 'Straffan' but smaller, more rounded flowers. Selected by P.N. Fraser, Murrayfield, Edinburgh, c. 1905, named by E.A. Bowles, who grew it in his Myddelton House garden. ↑22cm.

'Nellie Brinsley' (*nivalis*)
Very similar to *G.* 'Pusey Green Tips'. Well proportioned double. Outer segments pointed, green mark at apex. Inner segments green marks at apex. January–February. ↑15cm.

'Nerissa' (Hybrid double)
Shorter Greatorex double. Leaves semi-erect, lightly explicative. Outer segments clawed. Inner segments broad ruff, outer whorl often aberrant, variable marks from apex to half of segment, fuzzy on basal side. H.A. Greatorex, Brundall, Norwich. Similar to *G.* 'Cordelia' but smaller marks. ↑14cm.

'Netherhall Yellow' (*nivalis* Sandersii Group)
Good old yellow. Selected by Timothy Clark, 1960s, at Netherhall Manor, Cambridgeshire. Although named separately, John Grimshaw considers this to be *G.* 'Lady Elphinstone' as similar in all respects. See also *G.* 'Ceri Roberts'.

'Never Before'
Leaves broad, grey-green. Outer segments paddle-shaped, two small marks or broad inverted 'V' at apex. Inner segments green inverted 'V' at apex.

'Newby' (*nivalis* Poculiformis Group)
Unusual poculiform. Large, leaf-like spathe, long pedicel. Outer segments teardrop-shaped mark from apex, slender line towards base. Inner segments slightly shorter than outer, heart-shaped mark at apex. January–February. Rudi Bauer, 2006. ↑12cm.

'Nigel Chadwick'

Erect scapes, chunky, rounded flowers. Outer segments spoon-shaped, variable merging green lines at apex. Inner segments broad green inverted 'U' to 'V' at apex. Honey perfume. ↑18cm.

'Nightowl'

Rounded ovary, long curving spathe. Outer segments long, rounded, bluntly pointed. Inner segments, small, narrow inverted 'V' at apex, second mark halfway up segment. ↑15cm.

nivalis (species)
The common snowdrop. Covering widest natural area of genus, predominantly growing in deciduous woodland. Widely cultivated and naturalized into vast colonies. Leaves applanate, blue-green-glaucescent. Outer segments three. Inner segments smaller, green inverted 'U' or 'V' at apex. December–March. Many divisions and subdivisions, including numerous clones, hybrids, etc. RHS AGM 1993. ↑15–20cm.

'Nobody's Perfect'
Beautiful green-marked flowers. Outer segments paddle-shaped, broad inverted 'V' at apex. Inner segments broad inverted 'V' at apex.

'Norfolk Blonde' (*nivalis* Sandersii Group)
Slender yellow-green ovary. Leaves silver, applanate, erect, short at flowering. Outer

segments slender. Inner segment yellow-green mark. Can be difficult but increases when established. January–February. Rosie Steele's garden, Norfolk, in *nivalis* colony. ↑10cm.

'Norfolk Small' (*nivalis*)
Smaller *G. nivalis* clone from Norfolk, possibly now extinct.

'Norm's Late'
Australian-selected snowdrop.

'Norris' (*nivalis*)
Syn. *G.* 'Lady Norris'
Short, arching pedicel. Leaves applanate, glaucous, spreading, subrevolute margins. Inner segments green inverted 'U' at apex. January–February. First listed by John Morley, North Green Snowdrops, 1991. ↑15cm.

'Northgrange' (*nivalis*)
Well shaped flowers suspended beneath inflated spathe. Outer segments bluntly pointed. Inner segments green inverted 'U' at apex, upturned ends.

'Nothing Special'
Similar to *G.* 'S. Arnott' but shorter and flowers larger and slimmer. Leaves erect, blue-green. Outer segments rounded, bluntly pointed. Inner segments narrow inverted 'U' at apex, rounded ends. Free-flowering. February. ↑15cm.

'November Merlin'
See 'Remember Remember'.

'November Snow' (*transcaucasicus*)
Attractive, modest, autumn-flowering transcaucasicus from northern Iran. Leaves supervolute, green. Inner segments inverted 'V' at apex. November–December. ↑8cm.

'Nutt's Double'
Quirky little double flowers, thin ovary. Outer segments bluntly pointed.

Inner segment ruff outer whorl slightly reflexed, green inverted 'V' at apex.

'Nutts Early' (*elwesii* Hiemalis Group)
Excellent early flowering snowdrop usually out before Christmas. Outer segments bluntly pointed. Inner segments inverted 'V' at apex. Clumps up well. Originally given to friends by the late Richard Nutt. ↑18cm.

'O Mahoney'
Irish snowdrop, similar to and possibly same as *G.* 'Straffan'.

'Octopussy' (*nivalis*)
Long, often divided spathe. Large double flowers. Leaves applanate. Outer segments four, slender, tipped green at apex. Inner segments sometimes aberrant, inverted 'V' at apex. February. Phil Cornish, Gloucestershire, 1997. ↑16cm.

'Oirlicher Elfe' (Hybrid cultivar)
Elegant, gleaming white flowers, dark-green ovary, curving spathe. Outer segments rounded, bluntly pointed at apex. Inner segments tube-like, flared at apex, small green spot either side of sinus. Oirlicher Blumengarten, Germany.

'Old Court' (*elwesii*)
Well shaped flowers. Leaves broad, grey-green. David Bromley, Moortown, Shropshire.

'Old January' (*plicatus*)
Named by John Morley, North Green Snowdrops, with reference to Chaucer's Canterbury Tales.

'Oliver Wyatt'
See 'Maidwell L'.

'Oliver Wyatt's Giant'
See 'Naughton'.

'Oliver Wyatt's Green' (*plicatus*)
Later, well rounded flowers. Leaves erect, explicative at base. Outer segments

rounded at apex. Inner segments large mark across segment, finishing before base. Given by Oliver Wyatt to Leo Baxendale at The Old Manor, Naughton, Suffolk, 1972, named for Oliver Wyatt.

'Oliver Wyatt's Green Tip'
Slightly inflated spathe. Outer segments rounded, green lines at apex. Inner segments broad 'U' mark at apex.

'One Drop or Two' (Hybrid cultivar)
Unusual snowdrop with additional segments and two pedicels and flowers to each scape. Outer segments six. Inner segments dark-green rounded inverted 'V' at apex, smaller mark immediately above.

'Oosterhouw' (*nivalis*)
Dutch snowdrop named after the garden. Green-tipped, petaloid segments from ovary. Can be difficult. January–February.

'Ophelia' (Hybrid double)
Vigorous, large, Greatorex double. Neat, rounded flowers, tall scapes. Leaves semi-erect, narrow, grey-green, glaucous, lighter median stripe. Outer segments large. Inner segments tight ruff, outer whorl often aberrant, inner usually perfect, large, variable 'U' mark. Often two scapes. One of earliest Greatorex doubles to bloom, January–early February. Easy. Bulks up well. H.A. Greatorex, Brundall, Norfolk, 1940s. *G. nivalis* × *G. plicatus*. ↑23cm.

'Orange'
Distinct orange blush to well shaped flowers.

'Oreanda' (*plicatus*)
Syn. *G.* 'Janis Ruksans'
Inflated spathe. Outer segments rounded. Inner segments green broad inverted 'U' or

'V' at apex. Collected near the village of Oreanda, Crimean Peninsula.

'Orion'
(elwesii var. monostictus)
Elegant, tapering crisp white flowers set off by dark-green ovary. Outer segments long, slender, bluntly pointed. Inner segments green inverted 'U' at apex. ↑16cm.

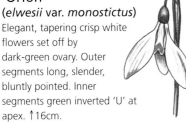

'Orleton'
Clean-looking white flowers against green foliage. Inner segments green heart-shaped mark at apex. Vigorous. Clumps up well. Shropshire.

'Orwell Greentip' (nivalis)
Rare clone, difficult to obtain. Outer segment green mark at apex. Inner segments inverted green 'V' at apex. January–February. Revd R.J. Blakeway-Phillips' garden, Orwell Rectory, Cambridgeshire, 1970s.

'Otto Fauser' (Hybrid cultivar)
Large, rounded flowers. Outer segments spoon-shaped, bluntly pointed, long claw. Inner segments broad inverted 'V', upturned ends. Australian-raised snowdrop named for Galanthophile Otto Fauser. ↑18cm.

'Paddy's Ketton' (Hybrid cultivar)
Substantial and good with large flowers. Outer segments long, well shaped. Inner segments good mark. Vigorous. February. ↑18cm.

'Pagoda' (nivalis)
Slightly larger than G. 'Flight of Fancy'. Leaves applanate, semi-erect, faintly explicative, short at flowering. Outer segments' delicate upward curve said to resemble pagoda. Inner segments broad inverted 'U' at apex. Simon Savage, in Old Vicarage garden, Wrockwardine, Shropshire, 1994. RHS PC 1994. ↑23cm.

'Palava' (nivalis)
Well shaped flowers with yellow-green ovary, pedicel and spathe. Leaves erect, blue-green. Outer segments long, rounded, bluntly pointed, reflex in sunlight. Inner segments yellow 'V' at apex. February. ↑10cm.

'Pale Cross' (Hybrid cultivar)
Attractive yellow-marked snowdrop. Inner segments soft yellow marks above apex.

'Pale Face' (Hybrid cultivar)
Newer yellow-marked snowdrop. Inner segments pale yellow marks above apex.

'Pamski's Double'
See 'Major Pam'.

'Pan'
Beautiful upright pure-white flowers, small green ovary. Leaves slender, erect to arching, green-blue. Inner segments slightly shorter than outer. ↑12cm.

panjutinii (species)
Western Transcaucasus. Leaves supervolute, narrow, conspicuous median rib, two to four longitudinal folds, bright mid-green, oily sheen. Outer segments clawed. Inner segments rounded at apex, variable marks from inverted 'U', two small marks, or no mark, small or absent sinus. Occasional paler mark at base. March–June. Named 2012 by A.P. Davis and D. Zubov in honour of Platon Sergeyevich Panjutin, chemist and botanist. Similar to G. krasnovii and G. platyphyllus and closely related to G. platyphyllus. ↑18–25cm.

'Paradise Giant'
(elwesii var. elwesii)
Undistinguished G. elwesii. Leaves supervolute, broad, pale-green, sometimes three. Outer segments long, slender, pointed. Inner segments pale-green elongated 'U' or roughly 'H'-shaped mark covering three-quarters of segment. Bulks up well. January–February. c. 1993. Similar to G. 'Sickle'. ↑20cm.

'Pastures Green' (nivalis)
Similar to G. 'Anglesey Abbey' without variable or poculiform flowers. Leaves erect,

bright-green. Outer segments bluntly pointed. Inner segment green mark at apex. January–February. Richard Hobbs, Bourton, Shropshire, 1996. ↑13cm.

'Pat Mackenzie'
(elwesii var. elwesii hybrid)
Outstanding snowdrop with well rounded flowers. Leaves supervolute, semi-erect. Outer segments smooth, thick texture, bluntly pointed, narrow green lines above apex. Inner segments green 'X'-shaped mark, filled base on mature plants, immature flowers heart-shaped mark merging into basal oblong. Ruby and David Baker in G. elwesii colony, Surrey, 1991. ↑25cm.

'Pat Mason' (elwesii var. elwesii)
Good green-tipped snowdrop with large attractive flowers and erect spathe. Leaves broad, erect, incurved margins, grey-green. Outer segments broad, rounded, bluntly pointed, small green mark at apex. Inner segments broad green 'X' from apex to three-quarters of segment. ↑16cm.

'Patricia Ann'
(plicatus subsp. byzantinus)
Large, elegant flowers. Leaves erect, slender, blue-green. Outer segments spoon-shaped, large, long, broad, bluntly pointed, light longitudinal ridging. Inner segments flared with small 'V' at apex, two merging ovals towards base. Carolyne Elwes gave this to Ronald Mackenzie, named after his wife. ↑20cm.

'Peardrop' (Hybrid cultivar)
Strong growing snowdrop with very beautiful peardrop-shaped flowers. Leaves erect to arching, grey-green. Outer segments rounded, pointed. Inner

segments flared at apex, dark green inverted 'V' diffusing towards base. Vigorous. Clumps up well. Highly perfumed. March. Found and named by Cliff Curtis at Ketton. ↑18cm.

'Pearl Drops'
As the name implies, elegant pearl drop-shaped flowers. Outer segments rounded. Inner segments pale-green inverted 'U' at apex diffusing across segment.

'Peg Sharples'
(Hybrid cultivar)
Excellent, rare, with well shaped flowers. Leaves applanate, slender, grey-glaucous, well developed at flowering. Outer segments long, rounded, clawed. Inner segments pale green 'X' diffusing towards base. March. Peg Sharples, Grange-over-Sands, Cumbria, seed from E.B. Anderson, 1960s. Probably *G. elwesii* × *G. nivalis*. ↑19cm.

'Pelican' (*elwesii* var. elwesii)
Standard-looking elwesii var. elwesii. Leaves supervolute. Large, rounded. Inner segments clasping, tube-like, green marks apex and base. Origins obscure, possibly South Hayes, named as buds resemble pelican's bill. ↑16cm.

'Penelope Ann' (*elwesii*)
Strong, striking, very rare, with large flowers and delicately arching pedicel. Leaves erect, broad, grey-green. Outer segments very long, bluntly pointed. Inner segment broad mid-green mark at apex to three-quarters of segment above large sinus. ↑20cm.

'Percy Picton' (*plicatus*)
Syns. *G.* 'Grayling', *G. plicatus* ex Percy Picton.
Excellent, with large attractive flowers. Tall arching scape, long slender pedicel. Leaves broad, arching, channelled. Inner segments

bright-green 'V' at apex, shadowed above by similar 'V' outlined in green. Usually two scapes flowering together. Bulks up well. Percy Picton, Malvern, Worcestershire, c. 1970s, named in his memory by son Paul Picton. ↑23cm.

'Perrott's Brook'
Outer segments rounded, pointed at apex, goffered claw. Inner segments pale-green mark across segment fading at base. Perrot's Brook, Cirencester, Gloucestershire. ↑18cm.

peshmenii (species)
Kastellorhizo, Greece, southern Turkey. Autumn-flowering. Leaves applanate, narrow, glaucescent to glaucous, grey median band, absent or short at flowering, lax at maturity. Inner segments variable 'U', 'V' or heart-shape at apex, occasionally small spot either side of sinus. October–November. Well drained, sheltered position. First collected c. 1973, named for Hasan Pesmen, Turkish botanist, described by Aaron Davis and Christopher Brickell, 1994. ↑12cm.

'Peter Gatehouse'
(*elwesii* var. elwesii)
Short, upright snowdrop. Symmetrical, triangular flowers, short pedicel. Leaves supervolute, erect, grey-green, mainly after flowering. Outer segments textured, clawed. Inner segments heavy olive-green mark from apex, paling towards base. One of the earliest *G. elwesii* clones to flower, mid-November. Given by the late Peter Gatehouse to Elizabeth Strangman, Washfield Nursery, Hawkhurst, c. 1994. ↑10cm.

'Peter Pan' (*plicatus* hybrid)
Small, dainty. Slender flowers. Leaves spreading. Outer segments clawed. Inner segments 'Y'-shaped green mark. Phil Cornish in E.B. Anderson's former garden, Lower Slaughter, Gloucestershire, 1994. ↑14cm.

'Pewsey Green'
See 'Pewsey Green Tips'.

'Pewsey Green Tips' (*nivalis*)
Syn. *G.* 'Pewsey Green'
G. nivalis 'Flore Pleno' variant. Outer segments marked green at apex. Inner segments large, rounded at apex, large sinus, small, squared inverted 'V' at apex. Netheravon valley, Wiltshire. ↑15cm.

'Pewsey Vale'
(*nivalis*)
Attractive miniature *G. nivalis*. Small bulbs. Leaves applanate, narrow, grass-like, glaucous. Inner segment inverted 'U' at apex. January–February. Hilda Davenport Jones, Washfield Nurseries, from Pewsey Vale, Wiltshire. ↑7cm.

'Phantomas' (*nivalis*)
Leaves applanate, erect, flat or slightly explicative, blue-green. Outer segments concave. Inner segment inverted 'V' at apex, paler indistinct oval above. February. Mark Brown at Gustingthorpe Hall, Suffolk, 1980s. ↑15cm.

'PHD 33643' (*plicatus*)
Beautifully proportioned snowdrop. Outer segments brilliant white, rounded. Inner segments clear, dark-green heart-shaped mark at apex. Beautiful fragrance. Dr Peter Davis, Georgia, 1970s.

'Phil Bryn'
(*elwesii* Edward Whittall Group)
Large, late flowering. Leaves supervolute, arching, two or three, pale blue-green. Outer segments broad, strongly clawed. Inner segments heart-shaped mark at apex, usually two pale marginal marks at base which can be absent. One of the latest *G. elwesii*, March–April. Matt Bishop in collection of Dutch *G. nivalis* bulbs, 1990, named for father of old friend. ↑21cm.

'Phil Cornish'
(Hybrid cultivar)
Beautifully shaped flowers. Outer segments paddle-shaped, rounded at apex, clawed, large green mark

above apex, paler mark at base. Inner segment green mark apex to base, paler basal indentation. Named for Galanthophile Phil Cornish.

'Phil's Fancy' (Hybrid cultivar)
Well shaped, 'Trym'-type. Recurved flowers. Outer segments broadening towards apex, flared, green merging lines above apex, paler smudge towards base. Inner segments broad green mark across segment apex almost to base, narrow white margin.

'Phuk'
See *G.* 'Gunter Waldorf'
Although this name is in circulation, it is invalid and started with a misnomer when Joe Sharman was asked what a new snowdrop should be called and he answered '****', not realizing he had been taken seriously!

'Picton's Mighty Atom'
See 'Bill Bishop'.

'Pink Panther' (*reginae-olgae*)
Rare, decidedly pink-flushed flowers. One of a number of seedlings found by Joe Sharman in the Taygetos Mountains.

'Pixie'
Small flowers with curving spathes. Outer segments very slender, pointed, goffered claw, green mark above apex. Inner segments slender, tube-like, green heart-shaped mark at apex. ↑10cm.

platyphyllus (species)
Syns. *G. ikariae* subsp. *latifolius, G. latifolius*
Southern Russia, Georgia. Leaves supervolute, broad, noticeably narrowed at base, erect to semi-erect or recurving, occasional longitudinal pleating, light-mid green, prominent central rib. Inner segment sinus absent or very small, inverted 'U' or two small marks at apex, often small light-green basal mark. March–April. Slow. Named by H.P. Traub and H.N. Moldenke, 1948. ↑10–20cm.

'Plemy Green' (*elwesii*)
Attractive flowers. Leaves broad, erect, grey-green. Outer segments long, pointed. Inner segments large 'X' mark across segment. February–March. Originally from the late Sir Frederick Stern, Highdown, Sussex, given to Michael Hoog. Re-released 2009. ↑18cm.

plicatus (species)
Northern Turkey, southern Russia, Romania. Described on Crimean Peninsula, 1808. Very variable species with large bulbs. Flowers large. Leaves, plicate, dark green, sometimes silver median stripe. Inner segment mark variable, inverted 'U' or 'V', sometimes large basal mark, or mark covering most of segment. December–March. Seeds well. Named by F.A. Marschall von Bieberstein, German botanist. RHS AGM 1993. ↑10–20cm.

plicatus subsp. byzantinus (subspecies)
Syns. *G. byzantinus, G. plicatus* var. *byzantinus*
North-western Turkey. Differs from *G. plicatus* subsp. *plicatus* in having two green marks. Not so widely cultivated. Inner segments inverted 'U' or 'V' at apex, larger basal mark spreading across segment. December–March. Named by botanist J.G. Baker, 1893. RHS AGM 1993. ↑10–20cm.

plicatus subsp. *plicatus* (subspecies)
Northern Turkey, Romania, southern Russia. Inner segment always single variable green 'U', 'V' or 'X' mark which can spread towards base. December–March. RHS AGM 1993. ↑10–20cm.

'Pocahontas'
White flowers, tending to poculiform, on erect scapes. Outer segments, long, rounded, pointed. Inner segments slightly shorter, variable, green marking on underside of segment.

'Poculiformis' (*nivalis*)
Discovered by David Melville at Dunrobin Castle, Scotland. See *G. nivalis* Poculiformis Group.

'Poculiformis Group' (*nivalis*)
Syn. *G.* 'Poculiform'
Mutation in which segments are all roughly equal, although variations in length and marking. Occurs in wild populations as well as cultivated. First poculiform noted by head gardener David Melville, Dunrobin Castle, Scotland, named by Revd H. Harpur-Crew, 1880. Poculiform = 'little cup', as flowers cup-shaped.

'Polar Breeze'
Long, slender pear-shaped flowers. Leaves upright to arching, grey-green. Outer segments long, slender, rounded, bluntly pointed. Inner segments narrow pale-green 'V' at apex. ↑14cm.

'Pom Pom' (Hybrid double)
Attractive, neat double. Outer segments three, white. Inner segments neat ruff, inverted 'V' at apex, spreading arms, some aberrant segments.

'Porlock No 2'
Well shaped pendant flowers. Leaves semi-erect, blue-green, glaucous. Outer segments stiff, long claw. Inner segments inverted 'U' at apex diffusing towards base. George Chiswell, West Porlock, Somerset. Variation of *G.* 'White Wings'. ↑18cm.

'Poseidon' (Hybrid double)
Regular Greatorex double with rounded flowers. Leaves erect, mainly explicative, glaucous. Outer segments rounded. Narrow inverted 'U' at apex diffusing towards base. Distinctive green ring on outer and inner segments beneath minute ovary. Originally from Frank Whaley to the late Molly Grothaus, Oregon, USA. His bulb died. *G.* 'Poseidon' reintroduced into UK late 1990s. ↑14cm.

'Potter's Prelude' (*elwesii* var. *monostictus*)
From USA. Excellent, vigorous, large, well

shaped flowers. Leaves supervolute, broad, recurved, spreading, grey-green. Outer segments long, bluntly pointed. Inner segments large mid-green inverted 'U' at apex. November–January. Jack Potter, 1960s. ↑25cm.

'Powelltown' (Hybrid cultivar)
Shapely Australian snowdrop. Elongated flowers. Outer segments long, slender, pointed. Inner segments broad green mark across segment.

'Prague Spring' (nivalis)
Beautiful virescent snowdrop. Leaves applanate, blue-green. Outer segments long, broad green lines from apex to half of segment. Inner segments deep inverted 'U' at apex, paler mark towards base. February. John Morley from seed collected from woods in Prague, selected and named by John Morley, North Green Snowdrops. ↑16cm.

'Prestwood White' (nivalis)
Leaves applanate, slender, blue-green. Pure white, unmarked outer and inner segments. ↑14cm.

'Pretty Close'
Small, slender, very green snowdrop. Outer and inner segments all green, including undersides, except for narrow white margin. ↑10cm.

'Pride o' the Mill' (Hybrid cultivar)
Smaller, well proportioned, rounded flowers, yellow-green ovary. Leaves variable revolute margins, blue-grey, glaucous, reclining in maturity. Outer segments slender, bluntly pointed. Inner segments tube-like, green inverted 'U' or 'X' across segment, paler centre. Early. Can be easy or difficult. Daphne Chappell's former garden, Mill House, Gloucestershire, 1987. *G. gracilis* (possibly × *G. plicatus*) hybrid. ↑10cm.

'Primrose Hill' (plicatus hybrid)
Outer segments boat-shaped, well textured, bluntly pointed. Inner segments broad mid-green inverted 'U' at apex, two marginal lines extending towards base.

'Primrose Hill Special'
See 'Cicely Hall'.

'Primrose Warburg' (Hybrid cultivar)
Coveted yellow *G. plicatus* with yellow ovary. Leaves applanate, semi-erect, variable flat-explicative, pale yellow-glaucescent. Outer segments rounded at apex. Inner segments yellow 'U' at apex. Not vigorous. Origins uncertain, but grown in the late Primrose Warburg's garden, South Hayes, c. 1990s. Possibly *G. plicatus* × *G. nivalis* 'Sandersii'. Similar to but slightly smaller than *G.* 'Spindlestone Surprise'. ↑9cm.

'Princeps'
Elegant, long, slender-looking 'hovering' flowers. Outer segments long, very slender, pointed, slender claw. Inner segments inverted mid-green 'U' to 'V' at apex.

'Pringle' (elwesii)
Attractive *G. elwesii*. Strong erect scapes. Leaves supervolute, broad, grey-green. Outer segments rounded, pointed. Inner segments inverted green 'V' at apex, two small marks towards base. ↑18cm.

'Priscilla Bacon' (plicatus)
Outstanding. Attractive, well textured, balloon-like flowers. Leaves supervolute, broad, arching, grey-green. Outer segments full, long, rounded, longitudinally ridged, dimpled. Inner segments ridged, mid-green 'V' at apex diffusing towards base, two smaller ovals at base. ↑14cm.

'Proliferation' (Hybrid cultivar)
Extremely thick scapes making flowers appear small. Leaves arching, glaucescent. Outer segments bluntly pointed. Inner segments inverted 'U' at apex diffusing palely towards base. Westbury on Trym, Bristol, named because eight scapes appeared on one bulb. ↑22cm.

'Propellerköfchen'
Leaves applanate, erect, slender blue-green. Outer segments clawed, broad. Inner segments green inverted 'U' or 'V' at apex, can divide into two spots, second mark towards base. English translation: 'Propeller Head'. ↑14cm.

'Puck' (nivalis)
Quirky, small, irregular semi-double. Leaves applanate, erect, slender, blue-green. Outer segments variable, marked green, also segments from top of ovary. Inner segments well marked green at apex. January–February. ↑10cm.

'Pummelchen' (Hybrid cultivar)
Beautifully shaped flowers. Leaves slender, erect, blue-green. Outer segments spoon-shaped, bluntly pointed, lightly longitudinally ridged. Inner segments lightly ridged, inverted 'V' at apex upturned and rounded ends above large sinus. Germany. English translation: 'Podge'. ↑14cm.

'Pumpot'
Recent introduction from Jörg Lebsa.

'Purcell'
See 'H. Purcell'.

'Pusey Green Tip' (nivalis)
Syn. *G. nivalis* Flore Pleno 'Green Tip' Attractive, irregular double. Well proportioned flowers. Leaves applanate, grey-green, semi-erect, lightly explicative. Outer segments often aberrant, merging

green lines at apex. Inner segments neatly clustered ruff in mature flowers, narrow green inverted 'V' at apex. Easy. Bulks up well. February–March. By River Thames, Faringdon, Oxfordshire, 1938. ↑14cm.

'Pyramid' (*elwesii*)

Elongated triangular flowers. Leaves erect to arching, grey-green. Outer segments long, slender, pointed, clawed at base. Inner segments tube-like, broad mid-green inverted 'U' at apex.

'Quad' (*nivalis*)

Distinctive double with extra segment. Leaves applanate, erect, clender, blue-green. Outer segments four. Inner segments and then full central ruff of smaller segments.

'Quadriga'

Rounded flower on slender pedicel. Four segments. Leaves slender, erect to arching, blue-green. Outer segments clawed, rounded, bowl-shaped. Inner segments small green dot either side of large sinus.

'Quatrefoil' (*elwesii*)

Beautiful snowdrop with attractive, weighty-looking flowers and extra segments. Leaves erect, grey-green. Outer segments four, long, broad, bluntly pointed. Inner segments broad, wide inverted 'U' at apex. Margaret Owen, Acton Pigot, Shropshire. ↑28cm.

'Quintet' (*nivalis*)

Leaves applanate, short, erect. Outer and inner segments, five, occasionally four, nicely spaced forming a 'skirt', held well above leaves. January–February. Richard Hobbs, 1998, in H.A. Greatorex's former garden, Brundall, Norfolk. ↑11cm.

'Rabbits Ears' (*elwesii*)

Strange, distinctive-looking snowdrop with only two outer segments, hence name. Australian selection by Mitchell Carle, 2000.

'Ragamuffin' (*nivalis*)

Small, variable, untidy, spiky double. Loose segments, variable marks. Leaves applanate, erect, flat. Outer segments three, narrow, pointed, variable green mark apex to base. Inner segments thin, small sinus, variable green mark at apex, usually one or two spots, may diffuse towards base. Central segments white. Barrie Carson Turner, Norfolk–Suffolk border, 1992. ↑8cm.

'Ragini'

Handsome snowdrop. Good, regular-shaped flowers beneath slender ovary. Outer segments bell-shaped, hazy green mark. Inner segments inverted 'V' at apex. Harry Pierick, Netherlands. ↑20cm.

'Rainbow Farm Early' (*elwesii* Hiemalis Group)

Attractive flowers, slender green ovary. Outer segments lightly ridged, bluntly pointed. Inner segments broad inverted 'U' at apex. October.

'Ransom' (Hybrid cultivar)

Leaves erect, glaucescent. Outer segments rounded at apex, clawed. Inner segments narrow inverted 'V' at apex, rounded ends. Herbert Ransom and E.B. Anderson in Hyde Lodge garden, Gloucestershire, late 1950s. ↑14cm.

'Ransom's Dwarf' (*elwesii* var. *elwesii*)

Small, sturdy, with large, well formed flowers. Leaves supervolute, erect, incurved. Outer segments slender, pointed. Inner segments clasping, inverted 'U' to 'V' at apex, separate smudge at base. Late. Bulks up well. Dr Ronald Mackenzie obtained bulbs from Herbert Ransom, 1990s, origins obscure prior to that. ↑8cm.

'Ransom's Late' (*plicatus*)

Less attractive flowers. Leaves broad, large. Inner segments olive-green 'U' or 'V' at apex. Mid-late March–April. Herbert Ransom.

'Raveningham' (Hybrid cultivar)

Quality, rounded flowers usually all-white apart from tiny spot, sometimes joined, either side of sinus on inner segments. Late. Supplied to Priscilla (Lady) Bacon by Philip Ballard, as G. 'Mighty Atom', later named after her garden, Raveningham, Norfolk. ↑14cm.

'Ray Cobb' (*nivalis* Sandersii Group)

Small, elegant, superior Sandersii with yellow ovary. Scape and spathe yellow-green. Leaves subrevolute, semi-erect, green. Outer segments rounded, bluntly pointed. Inner segments yellow inverted 'V' at apex. February. Origins uncertain, named for Galanthophile Ray Cobb. ↑12cm.

reginae-olgae (species)

Syn. G. *nivalis* subsp. *reginae-olgae*
Autumn species, similar to and related to G. *nivalis*. Leaves applanate, narrow, green, conspicuous, glaucous median stripe, absent or short at flowering. Inner segments green inverted 'U' or 'V' at apex. Very early, mid-September–November. Strong perfume. Well drained, sunny situation. ↑10cm.

reginae-olgae subsp. *reginae-olgae* (subspecies)

Syns. G. *corcyrensis*;
G. *reginae-olgae* subsp. *corcyrensis*
Greece, Sicily, Corfu. Leaves small or absent at flowering, lengthening at maturity. Autumn-flowering, September–December. RHS AGM 2002. ↑10cm

reginae-olgae subsp. *vernalis* (subspecies)

Former Yugoslavia, Greece, Sicily. Occasional white petaloid top to spathe. Flowers large. Leaves green, usually present at flowering.

December–March. Seeds freely. Numerous clones. Named by Georgia Kamari, Greek botanist, 1982. ↑10–13cm.

'Remember Remember' (elwesii)
Syn. G. 'November Merlin' Substantial flowers weigh down scapes. Leaves supervolute, erect, small at flowering. Outer segments pointed, light longitudinal ridging, dimpled, edged cream in bud. Inner segments longitudinally incurved, deep-green mark to almost half segment, blurring towards base. Early November. Better with protection. John Morley, North Green Snowdrops, 1992, named for flowering around 5 November. Probably Hiemalis Group, but distinct differences, also possible G. reginae-olgae parentage. ↑20cm.

'Reverend Hailstone' (elwesii hybrid)
Large, strong, robust. Flowers exceptionally long. Outer segments double length of inners. Inner segments pale-green inverted 'V'. Early. Anglesey Abbey, Cambridgeshire, named after former rector of local church. ↑30cm.

'Rheingold'
Ovary yellow, scape yellow-green, crooked spathe. Leaves applanate, erect, blue-green. Outer segments pointed. Inner segments yellow inverted 'V' at apex. March. Nicolas Top, Cologne, Germany, 1996. ↑12cm.

'Rib in White' (nivalis)
Large albino snowdrop. Leaves erect, grey-green. Outer segments long, rounded, longitudinally ridged. Inner segments longitudinally ridged, large sinus.

'Richard Ayres' (Hybrid double)
Good, vigorous, tall, double G. elwesii. Leaves supervolute, semi-erect, arching, slender, glaucous, well developed at flowering. Outer segments variable, three to six. Inner segment ruff variable 'X' mark or smaller mark at apex and base. Early.

Easy. Bulks up well. Richard Nutt in Anglesey Abbey garden, 1987, named by National Trust after head gardener. Probably G. nivalis 'Flore Pleno' × G. elwesii. ↑30cm.

'Richard Blakeway-Phillips' (plicatus subsp. byzantinus)
Beautiful, large flowers. Outer segments rounded, pointed, clawed. Inner segments thin green inverted 'V' at apex narrowly joining roughly circular mark towards base. Often two scapes. October. Named for Revd Richard Blakeway-Phillips, Clun, Shropshire.

'Richard Nutt'
Slender ovary. Outer segments bluntly pointed. Inner segments broad green 'V' at apex to half of segment, staining slightly on basal side.

'Rings Rum' (nivalis)
Outer segments long, well textured, pointed. Inner segments strangely twisted, split at apex making thin mark appear circular. January–February.

'Rita Rutherford' (plicatus)
Rounded mid-green ovary. Outer segments broadening towards apex, bluntly pointed. Inner segments slightly waisted light-green mark apex almost to base.

rizehensis (species)
Black Sea area, western Georgia, north-east Turkey. Leaves applanate, green, erect or recurving, lax at maturity, shiny-matt, mid-green, lighter underside. Inner segments inverted 'U'

or 'V' at apex. January–February. Named by Sir Frederick Stern after Black Sea town Rize, Turkey, 1956. ↑8–12cm.

'Robert Berkeley'
See 'Berkeley'.

'Robert Wijnen' (nivalis Sandersii Group)
Good yellow snowdrop with slender yellow to olive-green ovary. Outer segments rounded, bluntly pointed. Inner segments strong yellow inverted 'V' at apex, rounded ends, lines following veins to base. Valentin Wijnen, Belgium, 2006, named for his father who encouraged his love of gardening. ↑12cm

'Robin Hall' (elwesii var. monostictus)
Attractive Irish snowdrop. Leaves supervolute, broad, arching blue-grey. Inner segments large, well rounded, inverted 'U' to 'V' at apex. Very floriferous, bulks up well. Seedling from Robin Hall's garden, Primrose Hill, Lucan, Ireland, late 1970s, named for him. ↑18cm.

'Robin Hood' (Hybrid cultivar)
Tall, erect, strong. Leaves applanate-supervolute, glaucous, two or three. Outer segments long, shallow, long claw. Inner segment waisted roughly 'X'-shaped mark (also likened to spanner or crossed swords). January–February. Origins obscure, name applied to slightly different clones in the past. First mentioned by James Allen, 1891. Modern stock from E.A. Bowles to R.D. Trotter, father of Elizabeth Parker-Jervis. G. plicatus × G. elwesii. ↑23cm.

'Robyn Janey' (Hybrid cultivar)
Distinctive-looking with elegant flowers suspended from long slender pedicel. Leaves

erect to arching, blue-green. Outer segments rounded, bluntly pointed, clawed. Inner segments narrow 'V' or spot either side of sinus which can be joined, two elongated eyespots towards base. Often two scapes. ↑18cm.

'Rodmarton' (Hybrid double)
Sturdy, tall, large double. Distinctive inflated spathe. Leaves semi-erect, explicative, two or three. Outer segments variable, broad, longitudinally ridged, clawed, green mark at apex. Inner segment ruff, outer whorl larger, often one aberrant segment, broad 'U' at apex, diffusing towards base. One of the earliest flowering double hybrids. Bulks up well. Mary Biddulph, Rodmarton Manor, Gloucestershire, mid-1970s. *G. plicatus* × *G. nivalis* 'Flore Pleno'. ↑26cm.

'Rodmarton Arcturus' (Hybrid cultivar)
Elegant, rounded flowers. Leaves slender, erect, blue-green. Outer segments spoon-shaped, bluntly pointed. Inner segments broad green mark across segment from apex, paling at base. Simon Biddulph, Rodmarton Manor, Gloucestershire. RHS Preliminary Commendation 2011. ↑10cm.

'Rodmarton Capella' (*woronowii*)
Attractive, very tall snowdrop with bright green leaves, well shaped flowers and good mark. Simon Biddulph, Rodmarton Manor, Gloucestershire. ↑30cm.

'Roger's Rough' (*elwesii* var. *monostictus*)
Large, well shaped flowers. Leaves supervolute, erect, broad, grey. Outer segments long, rounded, pointed. Inner segments broad mid-green 'U' to 'V' at apex. February. ↑15cm.

'Romeo' (Hybrid cultivar)
Original *G. plicatus* 'Romeo' raised by James Allen, with very broad glaucous, plicate leaves, large spreading outer segments and tube-like inner segments with bold green mark, but this may now be extinct. There is possibly another snowdrop circulating under this name.

However, first name must take precedence.

'Ron Ginns' (*plicatus*)
Thin, olive-green ovary. Leaves semi-erect, channelled. Outer segments pointed, lightly puckered. Inner segments tube-like, green inverted 'U' at apex extending towards base. Ron Ginns, from Turkish-raised stock. Many snowdrops sold with this name have single inner segment mark and are simply *G. nivalis*. ↑15cm.

'Ronald Mackenzie' (*nivalis*)
Good, slender, yellow ovary and pedicel. Spathe, scape, leaves yellow-grey-green. Outer segments rounded, pointed. Inner segments flared at apex, two narrowly joined yellow spots either side of sinus, broad yellow mark top half of segment towards base. Vigorous yellow. RHS PC 2009. ↑14cm.

'Rose Baron'
Rounded green ovary. Outer segments spoon-shaped. Inner segments narrow inverted 'V' at apex, two smaller joining ovals towards base. ↑15cm.

'Rose Lloyd' (*elwesii*)
Well shaped flowers on erect scapes. Leaves supervolute, erect, broad, grey-green. Outer segments broad, rounded, longitudinally ridged, textured, pointed, slender claw, small green mark above apex. Inner segments roughly 'X'-shaped green mark apex towards base. Michael Baron, Brandymount. ↑16cm.

'Rosemary Burnham' (*elwesii* var. *elwesii*)
Syn. *G.* 'Francesca' Good virescent. Leaves supervolute, erect. Outer segments incurved margins, green lines apex to base. Inner segments green mark from apex paling towards base, narrow white margin. Rosemary Burnham in old garden, Burneby, British Columbia, 1960s. RHS PC

2006. Bulbs did not survive in UK, neither did similar snowdrop found in Robert Marshall's garden, Norwich, 1994, named *G.* 'Marshalls Green'. In 1998 the Canadian snowdrop reappeared at RHS show. ↑13cm.

'Rosie' (Hybrid double)
Classic double. Outer segments lightly recurved margins, bluntly pointed and small pale-green mark at apex. Inner segment ruff neat, broad, inverted 'U' mark at apex, paler mark towards base. Hugh and Hilary Purkess's garden, Welshway, Cirencester, Gloucestershire, 1995, named after granddaughter.

'Roudnice'
Attractive flowers, large, yellow-green ovary. Outer segments long, bluntly pointed, broad yellow-green mark. Inner segments inverted yellow-green 'V' at apex, spreading at ends. Named after town on banks of River Elbe in Czechoslovakia.

'Roulade'
Elongated, slender flowers. Leaves erect, slender, blue-green. Outer segments long, slender, bluntly pointed. Inner segments slightly waisted green mark from apex almost to base. ↑16cm.

'Roundhead' (Hybrid cultivar)
Outer segments rounded, longitudinal ridging, bluntly pointed, variable small green mark. Inner segments, spreading inverted 'U' at apex, rounded ends.

'Rowallane' (*elwesii* var. *elwesii*)
Rounded flowers. Leaves supervolute, spreading, broad, distinctive grey. Outer segments rounded, textured. Inner segments slightly flared at apex, large roughly 'X'-shaped to oval mark apex to base. Co. Down, Ireland, in bulbs purchased from Dutch grower Van Tubergen by Mike Snowden, head gardener of Rowallane, early 1990s. John Sales of National Trust singled snowdrop out. ↑18cm.

'Rowan Russell' (*elwesii*)
Slender flowers. Leaves supervolute, broad, grey-green. Outer segments slender claw. Inner segments broad green mark across segment.

'Ruby Baker'
(Hybrid cultivar)
Excellent Irish snowdrop. Pale yellow-green ovary and attractive, well shaped flowers. Leaves supervolute, erect, broad, glaucous. Outer segments broad. Inner segments single spot either side of apex, two merging ovals at base. David and Ruby Baker, in Robin and Cicely Hall's garden, Primrose Hill, Lucan, 1994, named by Robin Hall for Ruby Baker. ↑17cm.

'Ruby's Geburtstagsblumen'
(*peshmenii* hybrid)
Rounded, globular flowers. Outer segments broad, rounded, tipped green. September–October. Hagen Engelmann, Germany, named in honour of Ruby Baker. English translation: 'Ruby's Birthday Flowers'.

'Ruby's Gold'
(*nivalis* Sandersii Group)
Green foliage creates a good contrast to the yellow-marked white flowers. Yellow ovary and pedicel, yellow-green spathe. Leaves applanate, erect, green-blue. Outer segments well shaped, bluntly pointed. Inner segments yellow inverted 'V' at apex. ↑14cm.

'Ruby's Surprise'
Shapely flowers, erect scapes, light-green ovary. Outer segments bluntly pointed, light longitudinal ridging. Inner segments mid-green inverted 'V' at apex, two small merging ovals towards base. ↑12cm.

'Ruksans'
See 'Christmas Wish'.

'Rumenoglavi'
(*nivalis* Sandersii Group)
Striking snowdrop with yellow scape, spathe, ovary and pedicel. Leaves upright, slender, yellow. Outer segments pointed. Inner segments broad yellow 'V' at apex. January–February. University BG Ljubljana, Slovenia.

'Rumpelstiltskin'
(*nivalis*)
Shorter-growing snowdrop. Leaves blue-green. Outer segments long, slender, elegant. Inner segments large green mark apex almost to base. January–February. ↑23cm.

'Rupert Golby' (*plicatus*)
Conspicuous olive-green ovary. Leaves semi-erect, explicative margins. Outer segments clawed. Inner segments inverted olive-green 'V at apex. Late. Rupert Golby at Sorbrook Manor, Oxfordshire, c. 1990, in large mixed snowdrop colony. Named by Ronald Mackenzie. ↑19cm.

'Rushmere Green'
(Hybrid cultivar)
Well shaped flower, upright pedicel, erect scape. Leaves applanate, spreading, flat-explicative, glaucous. Outer segments bluntly pointed, green lines at apex. Inner segments green apex towards base, narrow white margin. March–April. Mark Brown at Rushmere, Buckinghamshire, 1990s. ↑16cm.

'Ruth' (*nivalis*)
Similar to *G.* 'Greenish', but taller. Leaves erect, flat-subrevolute. Outer segments green smudge at apex with stronger green lines. Inner segments broad heart-shaped mark. Matt Bishop, Brixton, Devon, named after Ruth James. There may be two snowdrops circulating under this name. One was renamed *G.* 'Farthingoe Beauty' when realized *G.* 'Ruth' already applied, and some Galanthophiles refer to a *G. plicatus* 'Ruth'. ↑20cm.

'Ruth Birchall' (*elwesii*)
Elegant flowers. Leaves erect, broad, grey-green. Outer segments, broad, incurved margins, pointed. Inner segments clasping, tube-like, wide dark green filled in 'U' at apex to half of segment. ↑16cm.

'Ruth Dashwood' (*plicatus*)
Attractive flowers. Outer segments longitudinally ridged, dimpled, bluntly pointed. Inner segments waisted green mark apex towards base.

'Ruth MacLaren' (*plicatus*)
Elegant snowdrop. Leaves narrow, erect. Outer segments shallowly rounded, flaring in sunshine. Inner segments narrow inverted 'V' at apex, two lines running towards base. Often two scapes. Bulks up well. John Grimshaw from the late Primrose Warburg's garden, South Hayes, Oxford, named for his niece. Originally *G.* 'Warburg No 3'. ↑12cm.

'Ryszards Grün' (Hybrid cultivar)
Elongated flowers, slender ovary. Outer segments bluntly pointed, pale green lines apex towards base. Inner segments solid green mark apex towards base, narrow white margin. Germany. English translation: 'Ryszards Green'. ↑20cm.

'Ryton Ruth' (Hybrid double)
Shorter semi-double. Leaves supervolute, incurved margins, short at flowering. Outer segments clawed. Inner segments variable, regular or irregular ruff, small inverted 'V' at apex faintly joining two pale marks towards base. Daphne Chappell, Ryton, 1995, named after village and lady in whose garden it was found. ↑11cm

'S. Arnott'
Syns. *G.* 'Arnott's Seedling', *G.* 'Sam Arnott', *G.* 'Samuel Arnott'
One of the best and oldest. Classic

all-rounder. Tall, vigorous, free-flowering. Flowers large, graceful, bell-shaped. Leaves erect, long, grey-green, glaucescent. Outer segments pure white, rounded. Inner segments dark-green heart-shaped mark at apex. Bulks up well. Strong honey perfume. February. Originally G. 'Arnott's Seedling' which should take precedence, but because later name so long standing and widely accepted it creates exception. Probably Samuel Arnott sent bulbs to Henry J. Elwes, Colesbourne, Gloucestershire. RHS AM 1951. FCC 1991. ↑20cm.

'St Annes'
(Hybrid cultivar)
Delicate-looking, slender flowers. Unusually in sheath rising above ground before leaves break. Leaves lax, spreading, lightly explicative, blue-glaucescent. Outer segments long, slender, tapering, delicate claw. Inner segments tube-like, Chinese-bridge mark, separate mark at base. February–March. Norfolk, named after St Anne's Church, Sutton Bonington, Nottinghamshire. ↑16cm.

'St Boniface'
Distinctive rounded flowers with four outer segments. Inner segments dark-green inverted 'V' at apex.

'St Pancras'
(Hybrid double)
Good, tall, robust. Well rounded, weighty-looking flowers. Leaves supervolute, erect, grey. Outer segments rounded, pointed, goffered claw. Inner segments variable 'V' at apex, roughly 'U'-shaped mark towards base, often three white segments from centre. Alan Street at West Bagborough, Somerset, 1994, named after local church. In colony of G. elwesii and G. nivalis 'Flore Pleno'. ↑22cm.

'Sally Ann' (Hybrid cultivar)
Well proportioned, rounded flowers, long pedicels. Leaves semi-erect to arching, explicative, glaucous. Outer segments thick, rounded at apex, clawed. Inner segments dark 'X' mark part filled at base. (Variable markings can cause confusion.) February. E.B. Anderson and Herbert Ransom, Hyde Lodge, Gloucestershire, named after one of Ransom's daughters. G. plicatus parentage. ↑17cm.

'Sally Pasmore' (plicatus)
Slender, elegant, long-lasting flowers. Leaves plicate, glaucous. Outer segments clawed. Inner segments tube-like, solid green mark from apex diffusing to base, white margin. Late. Sally Pasmore's Somerset garden, named after her, 1999. ↑22cm.

'Sally Wickenden'
(Hybrid cultivar)
Syn. G. 'Bellacorolla' Chunky flowers. Leaves semi-erect, subrevolute-explicative margins. Outer segments thick, waxy, rounded, clawed. Inner segments tube-like, small dot either side of large sinus at apex can be joined by narrow band. Margaret Owen in daughter's garden, Kent. ↑20cm.

'Sam Arnott'
See 'S. Arnott'.

'Samuel Arnott'
See 'S. Arnott'.

'Sandersii' (nivalis)
Syns. G. nivalis 'Howick Yellow', G. nivalis 'Horwick Yellow', G. nivalis 'Lutescens', G. nivalis var. lutescens Small to medium snowdrop, yellow ovary. Inner segment markings yellow. Beautiful but can be difficult. G. 'Sandersii' originally named G. nivalis var. Sandersii by Harpur-Crew for Mr Sanders who discovered first yellow, Northumberland, 1877. ↑12cm.

'Sandersii Cambo Estate Form' (nivalis)
See 'Lowick'.

'Sandersii Group' (nivalis)
Syns. G. 'Sandersii', G. 'Lutescens', G. 'Flavescens' Heavily veined flowers, yellow ovaries, green-yellow scapes. Coloration varies from pale yellow-green to apricot. Leaves pale yellow-green, semi-erect. Inner segment yellow inverted 'U' or 'V' at apex. Slow, better on acidic soils. Yellow snowdrops first found in naturalized colonies of G. nivalis, Belford, Northumberland, 1877, by Mr Sanders. All yellow clones of G. nivalis are in Sandersii Group, though certain distinct clones retain original names.

'Sandhill Gate'
(nivalis Poculiformis)
Excellent poculiform with ovary tapering towards pedicel. Large, perfect, pearl drop flowers, reminiscent of G. 'Atkinsii'. Leaves semi-erect, lightly explicative. Segments slender, usually equal. Distinctive pink flush from anthers in sunlight. Revd R.J. Blakeway-Phillips, Sandhill Gate Garden, Sussex, 1960s. ↑14cm.

'Santa Claus' (Hybrid cultivar)
Similar to single-marked G. elwesii. Leaves semi-erect, two or three, glaucous. Outer segments rounded, pointed. Inner segments flared, heart-shaped mark at apex. Usually two scapes on mature bulbs. December. Timothy Clarke, Netherhall Manor, Cambridgeshire, c. 1980, named 1998 as usually flowers for Christmas. ↑14cm.

'Sarah Dumont'
(plicatus)
Yellow ovary, pedicel. Leaves plicate, grey-green. Outer segments long, pointed. Inner segments broad inverted yellow 'U' to 'V' at apex.

'Savill Gold'
(nivalis Sandersii Group)
Syn. G. Saville Yellow, 'Windsor Form'. An older snowdrop, now becoming rare.

Pale yellow ovary, yellow-green pedicel and spathe. Leaves splayed, slightly twisted, possibly *G. gracilis* genes. Inner segment broad inverted 'U' at apex. Sir Frederick Stern's garden, Highdown, Sussex. Later distributed by Savill Garden, Windsor. ↑11cm.

'Savill Yellow'
(*nivalis* Sandersii Group)
Similar to *G. nivalis* 'Sandersii'.

'Scharlockii' (*nivalis*)
Syns. *G. nivalis* 'Scharlokii', *G. nivalis* forma *scharlockii*, *G. nivalis* var. *scharlokii*, *G. nivalis* var. *shaylockii* Small, 'donkey-eared' snowdrop. Very distinctive, long split spathe forming two 'ears' above slender flowers. Very variable. Leaves erect, lightly explicative, blue-green. Outer segments merging green lines towards apex. Inner segments inverted 'V' at apex. February–March. Easy. Bulks up well. Named by Professor Caspary, 1868, after Herr Julius Scharlock, who discovered snowdrop in 1818. Seedlings raised by James Allen, named *G.* 'Elise Scharlock' and *G.* 'Jason Scharlock'. ↑14cm.

'Scharlockii Flore Pleno'
(*nivalis*)
See 'Doncaster's Double Scharlock'.

'Scharlockii Group' (*nivalis*)
The 'donkey-eared' snowdrop with very conspicuous split spathe forming two long 'ears' above slender flowers.

'Schattenwinkel'
(Hybrid cultivar)
Outer segments lightly ridged, bluntly pointed. Inner segments dark-green inverted 'V' at apex joining paler 'V' shadowed above. Germany. English translation: 'Shadow Angle'. ↑20–25cm.

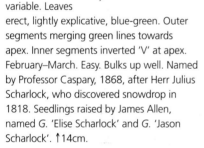

'Schneeweisschen'
(Hybrid cultivar)
Very elegant and beautiful albino with all-white segments. Outer segments slender, pointed. Inner segments pure white, lightly ridged, large sinus, no mark. Germany. English translation: 'Little White Snow'.

'Schorbuser Blut' (*nivalis*)
Large flowered virescent. Outer segments large, broad, large green mark from apex to half of segment, shadowed on underside. Inner segments green mark across segment, narrow white margin. Bulks up well, quickly. January–February. Hagen Engelman, Germany. English translation: 'Dragon's Blood'.

'Schorbuser Irrlicht'
(*plicatus* subsp. *byzantinus*)
Well shaped, rounded flowers. Yellow pea-like ovary. Leaves plicate. Outer segments lightly ridged, bluntly pointed. Inner segments narrow egg-yolk yellow 'V' at apex beneath yellow oval paling towards base. English translation: 'Dragons Wisp'. ↑12cm.

'Scissors' (*plicatus*)
Elegant, well shaped flowers. Outer segments hooded at apex, long claw. Inner segments bright green variable scissor-shaped mark across segment. Revd R.J. Blakeway-Phillips, Clun, Shropshire, *c.* 1980s. ↑15–16cm.

'Seagull' (Hybrid cultivar)
Similar to *G.* 'Mighty Atom', possibly better. Flowers chunky, textured. Leaves striking, semi-erect, broad, explicative margins, glaucous. Outer segments long, clawed. Inner segments clasping, large dark-green inverted 'V' at apex stretching towards base. Strong honey perfume. Easy. Usually two scapes. George Chiswell, West Porlock, Somerset, late 1980s. ↑23cm.

'Seersucker'
(*ikariae*)
Dark-green ovary enhances very white flowers. Leaves broad, short, green, puckered. Outer segments slender claw, pointed, longitudinally ridged, puckered. Inner segments inverted dark-green 'U' from apex to halfway up segment. January–March. ↑12cm.

'Selborne Green Tips'
(*elwesii* var. *elwesii*)
Leaves supervolute, erect, three. Outer segments merging green lines towards apex. Inner segments rounded inverted 'V' at apex, square smudge towards base. Often second perfect flower, separate pedicel, same scape. December–January. Regular division maintains twin flowers. David and Ruby Baker, Selborne, Hampshire, 1982. ↑20cm.

'Selina Cords' (Scharlockii)
Small slender flowers, long pedicel, split spathe. Outer segments elongated, narrow, incurved, large green mark apex almost to base, shadowed through to underside. Inner segments broad heart-shaped mark at apex. Rudi Bauer, 2006, named for his granddaughter.

'Senne's Sunrise' (*nivalis*)
Excellent 'orange' snowdrop. Flowers lightly flushed orange, especially in bud. Leaves applanate, slender, erect, blue-green. Outer segments broad, slender claw. Inner segments small inverted 'U' at apex, two oval basal marks which can merge. Slow. February–March. Valentin Wijnen, Grakes Heredij, Belgium, named after his son, Senne. ↑14cm.

'Sentinel' (Hybrid cultivar)
Excellent, strong and vigorous. Large flowers, enlarged spathe. Leaves applanate, arching, variable flat-explicative,

glaucous. Outer segments longitudinally ridged, clawed. Inner segments clasping, flared at apex, dark green 'U' to heart-shaped mark at apex, two small ovals at base. Often two scapes. Daphne Chappell at Sutton Court, Herefordshire, 1994. ↑24cm.

'Seraph'
(*plicatus* Poculiform)
Elegant, attractive, rare, *G. plicatus* poculiform. At one time *G.* 'Seraph' was thought to be extinct. Leaves plicate, blue-green. Well shaped outer and inner segments of equal length, white.

'Shackleton'
See 'David Shackleton'.

'Shades of Green'
Leaves erect, slender, green. Outer segments long, clawed. Inner segments mid-green broad inverted 'V' at apex, paler oval towards base.

'Shadow' (*elwesii* var. *elwesii*)
Excellent virescent. Large, well shaped flowers. Leaves attractive, supervolute, erect, spreading at apex. Outer segments pale green lines, less on underside. Inner segments tube-like, slightly waisted broad green mark apex almost to base, darker at apex, narrow white margin. Ruby and David Baker in colony of *G. elwesii*, Surrey, 1998. ↑20cm.

'Shaggy' (*nivalis*)

'Sharman's Late' (Hybrid cultivar)
Yellow ovary, yellow green spathe and pedicel. Outer segments well shaped, pointed. Inner segments yellow mark either side of large sinus. February–March. Joe Sharman, Cambridge.

'Sheila McQueen'
Well rounded flower beneath slightly inflated spathe. Outer segments light longitudinal ridging, bluntly pointed, broad claw. Inner segments very broad

dark-green inverted 'U' at apex, diffusing towards base. February.

'Shellbrook Giant'
(*elwesii*)
Large snowdrop with rather ragged-looking flowers. Outer segments spoon-shaped, rounded at apex, uneven margins. Inner segments mid-green mark from apex almost to base, narrow white margin. ↑22cm.

'Shepton Merlin'
Well shaped flower, rounded ovary, inflated spathe. Outer segments longitudinal ridging. Inner segments broad green mark across segment to base, narrow white margin.

'Shrek'
Elongated, semi-poculiform with green-marked flowers. Leaves upright, slender, blue-green. Outer segments long, slim, large, pale-green mark above apex, shadowed on underside. Inner segments pale-green merging lines forming roughly inverted 'U' at apex. Green colouring strengthens as plant matures. Named after green giant in a children's film. ↑12cm.

'Shropshire Queen'
(Hybrid cultivar)
Outstanding, beautiful and one of the best recent introductions with very attractive, well shaped flowers. Leaves erect to spreading, slender, blue-green, lighter median stripe. Outer segments elegantly spoon-shaped, bluntly pointed. Inner segments flared at apex, dark-green, rounded, inverted 'V' at apex. ↑20cm.

'Shrubbery Special'
(Hybrid cultivar)
Rare, vigorous, single hybrid with rounded flowers. Inner segments four marks, two at apex, two at base. Probably *G. gracilis* and *G. elwesii* genes. Seedling, Rod and Jane Leeds garden.

'Shuttlecock' (*nivalis*)
Syn. *G.* 'Ermine Shuttlecock'
Spiky intermediate double. Upward-facing flowers. Leaves semi-erect, margins flat or slightly explicative. Outer segments six, slender, light longitudinally incurved, variable marking across segment, darker at apex and base. Inner segments variable, untidy, often reflexed, variable inverted 'V' diffusing towards base, undersides all green, narrow white margin. Hector Harrison in woodland, Appleby, South Humberside, 1980s. ↑10cm.

'Sibbertoft'
See 'Sibbertoft Manor'.

'Sibbertoft Magnet'
(*elwesii* var. *elwesii*)
Distinctive, long, arching pedicel, long spathe, slender ovary. Leaves supervolute, semi-erect, grey-green. Outer segments clawed. Inner segments variable heart-shaped mark at apex, paler reversed shadow above, can join. 'Sibbertoft Bank' in Primrose Warburg's garden, South Hayes, Oxfordshire. ↑23cm.

'Sibbertoft Manor'
(*plicatus* hybrid)
Syn. *G.* 'Sibbertoft'
Excellent snowdrop with strong scapes and large weighty flowers. Leaves broad, glaucous, explicative margins. Outer segments long, large, well rounded, bluntly pointed. Inner segments mid-green waisted mark from apex paling towards base. Primrose Warburg, South Hayes, Oxford.

'Sibbertoft No 2' (Hybrid cultivar)
G. 'Atkinsii' clone but perfect flowers with no aberrant segments. Leaves erect, slender, green-blue. Outer segments long, slender, bluntly pointed. Inner segments broad filled-in 'V' at apex. Lady Beatrix Stanley's former garden, mid-1980s.

'Sibbertoft White' (*nivalis*)
Elegant albino following standard *G. nivalis* form. Delicate, slender flowers.

Leaves applanate, erect, slender, blue-green. Outer segments slender, pointed. Inner segments often completely white or very small green spot either side of sinus. February. Richard Nutt in Lady Beatrix Stanley's garden, Sibbertoft Manor, Northamptonshire. ↑12cm.

'Sickle' (*elwesii* var. *elwesii*)

Rare, tall cultivar. Arching spathe. Leaves attractive, prominent, broad, arching, grey-green, often three. Outer segments elongated, strongly clawed, reflexing in sun. Inner segments large dark-green mark resembling two inverted skittles from apex towards base. Slow. Possibly from the late Phil Ballard's nursery, Malvern, Worcestershire, named as spathe resembles sickle. ↑18cm.

'Silverwells' (Hybrid cultivar)

Similar to *G.* 'Atkinsii', less triangular, no aberrant segments. Leaves applanate, slender, erect to arching, blue-green. Outer segments long, slender, bluntly pointed, long slender claw. Inner segments broad 'U' to 'V' at apex. March. Probably Edrom Nursery, Berwickshire, *c.* 1980s. ↑15cm.

'Silvia'

A snowdrop from Germany, *c.* 2000, with yellow-green colouring.

'Simon Lockyer' (*elwesii*)

Long, rounded flowers on upright scapes. Leaves erect, broad, grey-green. Outer segments long, rounded, tapering to point and green marks at apex. Inner segments inverted green 'V' at apex, second mark towards base. ↑16cm.

'Simplex' (*nivalis*)

Leaves applanate, erect, slender, blue-green. Inner segments inverted green 'V' at apex. January–February. ↑14cm.

'Simply Glowing'

Beautiful, striking, virescent snowdrop. Outer segments broad, pointed, large vivid green mark across segment above apex to base, literally glows. Inner segments broad green mark apex to base, paling at base, narrow white margin. February. Alan Street, Avon bulbs. ↑20cm.

'Sir Edward Elgar' (*elwesii*)

Leaves supervolute, erect to arching, grey-green. Outer segments long, bluntly pointed, light longitudinal ridging. Inner segments flared at apex, inverted 'U' to 'V' at apex above tiny sinus. ↑16cm.

'Sir Henry BC'

Attractive green-tipped snowdrop. Outer segments bluntly pointed, merging green lines above apex. Inner segments inverted filled in 'U' from apex to half of segment. Matt Bishop at East Lambrook Manor, Somerset, 2006, named after the late Margery Fish's nephew, Sir Henry Boyd-Carpenter. ↑15cm.

'Sir Herbert Maxwell' (Hybrid cultivar)

Attractive, large flowers, long green ovary. Leaves applanate, erect, lightly explicative, glaucous. Outer segments long, rounded, bluntly pointed, broad claw. Inner segments ridged, spreading inverted 'V' at apex, rounded arms. Often two scapes. January–February. Sir Herbert Maxwell, Montreith, Galloway, Scotland, named by E.A. Bowles. Probably *G. nivalis* × *G. plicatus*. ↑17cm.

'Sky Rocket'

Tall. Well shaped flowers, erect scapes. Leaves erect to arching, blue-green. Outer segments long, bluntly pointed, light green mark. Inner segments broad green mark from apex to two-thirds of segment. ↑23cm.

'Skyward' (*elwesii*)

Tall. Erect scapes. Flowers well above foliage. Altamont Gardens, Ireland, named by Paul Cutler, head gardener. ↑30cm.

'Slim Jim' (*plicatus*)

Elegant, slender flowers. Leaves semi-erect, narrow. Inner segment unusual double lines extending from heart-shaped apical mark up centre. Phil Cornish, from E.B. Anderson's former garden, Lower Slaughter, Gloucestershire, 1992. ↑22cm.

'Smagg' (Hybrid double)

Good, rounded double. Leaves erect, blue-green. Outer segments broad, flaring. Inner segments outer whorl aberrant, inners small greenish-yellow inverted 'V' at apex.

'Smelthouses' (Hybrid cultivar)

'Smurf'

Smaller snowdrop. Well shaped flowers. Outer segments green mark above apex. Inner segments broad inverted 'V' at apex, two smaller dots at base. Johan Mens. Belgium. ↑10cm.

'Snocus' (*elwesii* Poculiform)

Unusual, sturdy *elwesii* poculiform on erect scape. Leaves supervolute, semi-erect, pointed. Outer segments pointed, clawed. Inner segments similar in shape and size to outer. Al and Shirley Smith, Victoria, British Columbia.

'Snogerupii'

See *G. ikariae* subsp. *snogerupii*.

'Snoopy'

Attractive, well rounded flowers. Outer segments, broad, rounded, bluntly pointed. Inner segments inverted 'V' at apex, paler narrow mark towards base. Named by Ian Christie, Scotland.

'Snow Queen'

Good, neat regular double. Leaves applanate, erect, slender, blue-green. Outer segments long, bluntly pointed, strongly incurved. Inner segments tightly packed neat ruff, narrow green 'V' at apex. March. ↑14cm.

'Snow White' (*elwesii*)

Syn. *G.* 'Lammermuir Snow White'
Similar to *G.* 'Sandhill Gate', ovary more

rounded. Leaves arching, semi-erect. Inner segments slightly shorter than outer. Late. Lyn Bezzant, Berwickshire, 1992. (See also 'Bohemia White'.) ↑12cm.

'Snow White's Gnome' (*nivalis*)

True miniature albino but unusual in still retaining green lines on underside of inner segments. Flowers held high above low leaves. Inner segments occasional tiny green dot each side of sinus. January–February. Wolfgang Kletzing, Czechoslovakia, 1990. ↑5cm.

'Snowball' (*nivalis*)

Rare albino with rounded ovary and large, slender, elegant flowers. Leaves semi-erect. Outer segments long, slender. Inner segment mark completely absent, or two tiny green marks, one each side of sinus. Difficult. Phillip Ballard, origins obscure. ↑16cm.

'Sofia' (*reginae-olgae* subsp. *reginae-olgae*)

Outstanding. Tall upright scape, attractive textured flowers. Leaves absent at flowering. Outer segments rounded, textured, opening wide. Inner segments tube-like, goffered towards apex, broad inverted 'V' at apex. Often two scapes. ↑20cm.

'Sophie North' (*plicatus*)

Neat, sturdy with large bulbs and well textured, rounded flowers. Leaves very broad, blue-green, glaucous, margins rolled inward, often three. Outer segments boat-shaped. Inner segments green inverted 'V' merging into oval towards base. Bulks up well. Often

two scapes. Dr Evelyn Steven's garden, Dunblane, 1970s. Originally *G. plicatus* subsp. *byzantinus*, renamed *G.* 'Sophie North', 1997, in memory of one of the children killed in Dunblane Primary School tragedy. Bulbs sold and proceeds donated to 'Snowdrop Fund' for the victims and local community. RHS PC 1997. ↑13cm.

'South Hayes' (Hybrid cultivar)

Distinctive, unusually shaped flowers. Leaves applanate, semi-erect, variable margins, glaucous. Outer segments flattish, light longitudinal ridging, broadening towards apex, flared, variable narrow green mark apex towards base. Inner segments large green mark across segment, narrow white border. Primrose Warburg, South Hayes, 1990s, named after garden. RHS PC 2000. Probably *G.* 'Trym' seedling. ↑13cm.

'Spanish Swan' (*nivalis*)

Attractive long, rounded flowers. Small ovary. Leaves, long, slender, erect-arching, matt green-blue. Elegant slender white segments. March. ↑14cm.

'Sparkler'

Well shaped flowers beneath curving spathe. Outer segments bluntly pointed, pale green mark. Inner segments inverted 'V' at apex barely joining oval towards base.

'Spetchley'

Slender flowers, inflated spathes. Outer segments slim, pointed. Inner segments small inverted 'V' at apex. Spetchley Park, Worcestershire.

'Spetchley Cassaba'

Attractive flowers, rounded ovary. Outer segments pointed, clawed at base. Inner segments

narrow inverted green 'V' at apex, rounded ends, broad mark top half of segment to base. Spetchley Park, Worcestershire.

'Spetchley Yellow' (*nivalis* Sandersii Group)

Well shaped dainty flowers with greenish-yellow ovary. Outer segments bluntly pointed. Inner segment yellow inverted 'U' at apex. Spetchley Park, Worcestershire.

'Spindlestone Surprise' (*plicatus*)

Vigorous, reliable, with yellow-green marks, maturing yellow. Large flowers, yellow ovary. Leaves applanate, erect, lightly explicative. Outer segments rounded at apex, clawed. Inner segments yellow-green variable 'U' at apex. Bulks up well, damper, shadier conditions. Ron McBeath and Jim Jermyn in Diana Aitchison's garden, Spindlestone, Northumberland, c. 1990s. Probably *G. plicatus* × *G. nivalis* 'Sandersii'. RHS AM 1998. ↑20cm.

'Spindlestone Yellow'

See 'Spindlestone Surprise'.

'Splendid Cornelia' (*nivalis*)

A Dutch introduction from Tom Koopman and W. Vieveen, 2010. ↑12cm.

'Spot' (*nivalis*)

See 'Gloucester Old Spot'.

'Spring Coat'

Outer segments long, slender, pale-green above apex towards centre. Inner segments pale-green inverted 'U' at apex.

'Spring Greens' (*elwesii* var. *elwesii*)

Leaves supervolute, large, long, broad, arching, well developed at flowering. Outer segments clawed. Inner segments large green, 'H' to 'X' mark across three-quarters of segment, sometimes two marks with 'V' at apex, two paler spots at base. January. Primrose Warburg, c. 1995. ↑23cm.

'Spring Pearl'
(*elwesii* var. *elwesii*)
Leaves supervolute, erect, broad, grey-green. Outer segments rounded, pointed. Inner segment green mark at apex, separate mark at base which can join. Peter Nijssen, Heemsteede, Netherlands, late 1990s.

'Springvale' (Hybrid cultivar)
Elegant, long pedicel suspending flower at good angle. Leaves applanate, semi-erect, two or three, third leaf lightly explicative. Outer segments smooth, bluntly pointed. Inner segments clasping, narrowly joined green dot either side of sinus towards solid mark towards base. Sometimes two scapes. Michael Baron in Lewis Palmer's garden Headbourne, Winchester, Hampshire, 1987, named for nearby hamlet. ↑16cm.

'Springwood Park'
(*nivalis* Poculiformis Group)
Good, large, well shaped, neat poculiform. Very large flowers suspended beneath slightly split spathe. All segments of equal length and usually white but occasional small green mark at apex. Joe Sharman, Spring Park, Kelso, Scotland. ↑14cm.

'Sprite'
Attractive, recently introduced, green-tipped snowdrop. Leaves erect, slender, blue-green. Outer segments broad, rounded, bluntly pointed, green lines above apex, slight shading between. Inner segments broad green band from apex to two-thirds of segment. Avon Bulbs.

'Squib' (*nivalis*)
Interesting, variegated foliage *G. nivalis*. Leaves applanate, erect, slender, prominent cream stripes. Inner segments inverted green 'V' at apex. Weak, slow to increase, but interesting for variegated foliage. Joe Sharman, 2000.

'Squire Burroughs'
(Hybrid cultivar)
Syn. *G.* 'Aldgate 16'
Tall, with large rounded flowers. Leaves applanate, erect, broad, flat margins apart from lightly folded third leaf. Outer segments light longitudinal ridging, textured. Inner segments tube-like, flared at apex, two narrowly joined marks at apex, solid mark towards base. Regularly two scapes. Cliff and Joan Curtis, from The Cottage, Rutland, where *G.* 'Ketton' originally found, named after owner of cottage at that time. Probable *G. plicatus* hybrid. ↑18cm.

'Stargazer' (*nivalis*)
See 'Elfin'.

'Stavroula' (*reginae-olgae* subsp. *reginae-olgae*)
Elegant, smaller cultivar. Slender flowers, erect scapes. Leaves absent at flowering. Outer segments lightly concave. Inner segments uniform green inverted 'U' at apex. ↑10cm.

'Stefan' (*reginae-olgae* subsp. *reginae-olgae*)
Leaves applanate, erect, slender, blue-green, paler undersides, small at flowering. Inner segments broad, infilled 'U at apex. October–November. ↑10cm.

'Steve's Yellow' (*nivalis*)
Light yellow-green ovary and pedicel. Leaves applanate, erect, green-yellow. Outer segments long, slender, pointed, incurved margins. Inner segments pale yellow inverted 'V' at apex. January–March. ↑12cm.

'Stork' (*nivalis*)
As the name implies, a rather lanky snowdrop with slender scapes and flowers. John Morley, North Green Snowdrops.

'Straffan' (Hybrid cultivar)
Syn *G.* 'Cool Ballintaggart',
G. 'The O'Mahoney',
G. nivalis grandis
Beautiful, vigorous Irish snowdrop. Large flowers, short scapes. Leaves semi-erect, flat to explicative, glaucous. Outer segments large, long. Inner segments rounded 'U' at apex. Often second, shorter, smaller-flowered scape as first fades. Easy. Bulks up well. February–March. Third oldest cultivar still grown. Possibly *G. nivalis* × *G. plicatus* from colonies originating in Crimea. Lord Clarina's garden, Straffan House, Kildare, Ireland, found by head gardener George Bedford, 1858. E.A. Bowles called it 'the most beautiful of all forms'. RHS AM 1968. ↑15cm.

'Sulphur Ramblings'
(Hybrid cultivar)
Large, stately flower. Outer segments broad, clawed, narrowing to point at apex. Inner segments strong green inverted 'V' at apex, raised ends, shadowed towards base.

'Sutton Court'
(Hybrid cultivar)
Syn. *G.* 'Sutton Supreme'
Outstanding, similar to *G.* 'S. Arnott' but better. Leaves erect, strong, glaucous. Outer segments bluntly pointed. Inner segments deep-green inverted 'V' at apex. Veronica Cross at James and Alison's Page's garden, Sutton Court, Herefordshire, 1995, former home to R.O. Backhouse. ↑30cm.

'Sutton Courtenay'
(*gracilis* Hybrid)
Syn. *G.* 'Nancy Lindsay'
Good, robust. Olive-green to yellow ovary and large, rounded flowers. Leaves applanate, erect, glaucous, explicative, short at flowering. Outer segments broad. Inner segments slightly flared at apex, narrow green 'V', separate broad paler mark at base. Very early. Nancy Lindsay's garden, Sutton Courtenay, Oxfordshire. Probably *G. gracilis* × *G. plicatus*. ↑15cm.

'Sutton Supreme'
See 'Sutton Court'.

'Swanton' (Hybrid cultivar)
Well rounded, weighty flowers, upright scapes. Leaves erect to arching, slender,

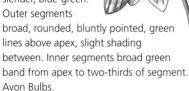

twisted, grey-green. Outer segments boat-shaped, dimpled, pointed, slender claw. Inner segments narrow green mark at apex, broad green mark across top half of segment to base. Named after village of Swanton. *G.* 'Diggory' × *G. plicatus*. ↑14cm.

'Sweet Alice'
(*elwesii*)

Beautiful large, rounded, green-tipped flowers. Leaves broad, grey-green. Outer segments broad, round, recurved margins, pale-green mark above apex. Inner segments broad 'V' at apex joining horizontal band towards base. Valentin Wijnen, private garden, Belgium, 2009, named after his mother.

'Sybil Roberta'
See 'Dionysus'.

'Sybil Stern'
(*elwesii*)
Syn. *G.* 'Lady Stern's False Hiemalis' Heavy, substantial-looking flowers. Leaves supervolute, broad, arching, grey-green. Outer segments broad, clawed, extending as flower matures. Inner segments spreading 'V' at apex. Origins obscure, possibly Sir Frederick Stern, Highdown, Sussex, named for his wife. ↑15cm.

'Sylvie' (*reginae-olgae* subsp. *reginae-olgae*)

'Tall Prague Spring' (*nivalis*)
A larger version of *G.* 'Prague Spring'. Named by John Morley, North Green Snowdrops. ↑20cm.

'Tante Käthe'
(*nivalis* Scharlockii)
Elegant, slender flowers. Spathe split. Outer segments slender, bluntly pointed. Inner segments small green mark either side of sinus. Rudi Bauer, Germany. English translation: 'Aunt Kath'.

'Tatiana' (*nivalis*)
Rounded flower suspended from erect scape. Leaves erect-arching, blue-green,

subrevolute. Outer segments concave, lifted at base. Inner segments furrowed, narrow inverted 'V' at apex. Immature plants have one dot each side of sinus. February–March. Slow. Czechoslovakia, 1990, named for Wolfgang Kletzing's wife. ↑16cm.

'Taubenei'
Reminiscent of a pigeon's egg with its rounded whiteness. Outer segments long, bluntly pointed, pure white. Inner segments narrow green 'V' at apex. Germany. English translation: 'Pigeon'.

'Taynton Squash'
(*elwesii*)
Outer segments, slender, rounded, short claw. Inner segments broad-green inverted 'V' at apex joining heart-shaped mark towards base. Slow to increase.

'Teresa'
(*elwesii* var. *elwesii*)
Excellent snowdrop with attractive flowers. Leaves supervolute, erect-arching, two or three, well developed at flowering. Outer segments broad, veined green towards apex. Inner segments green mark from apex paling towards base. Phil Cornish in garden at Longlevens, Oxfordshire, named after his daughter. ↑21cm.

'Teresa Stone'
(*elwesii* var. *elwesii*)
Tall, robust, attractive. Sometimes extra perfect inner and outer segment on large bulbs, one extra segment on smaller bulbs. Leaves supervolute, erect, clasping, three. Inner segments tube-like, wide-spreading inverted 'V' at apex, horizontal blotch towards base. Louise Parsons, Corvallis, Oregon, 1975, named for previous owner of garden. ↑27cm.

'Terry Jones'
Slender flowers, erect scapes. Outer segments long, slender. Inner

segments, broad green mark from apex, paling and feathering towards base.

'Tessera'
(*reginae-olgae* subsp. *reginae-olgae*)
Beautiful flowers with four well shaped inner and outer segments. Leaves short or absent at flowering. Outer segments tapering towards apex. Inner segments inverted green 'V' at apex. October–November. ↑10cm.

'The Apothecary'
(Hybrid cultivar)
Outer segments bluntly pointed, slender claw. Inner segments neat inverted 'V' at apex. December. *G. nivalis* × *G. plicatus*.

'The Bride'
(*elwesii* Poculiform)
Beautiful, all-white poculiform. Rounded flowers weighed down by weak scapes. Leaves supervolute, erect, incurved margins. Inner segments slightly shorter than outer. Difficult. Phil Cornish at Foxcote Farm, Cheltenham, Gloucestershire, 1975. ↑15cm.

'The Charmer' (*nivalis*)
Well shaped, green-tipped flowers. Leaves applanate, erect, slender. Outer segments slender, bluntly pointed, good mid-green mark with merging lines above. Inner segments broad ruff, deep inverted 'V' at apex. February–March. ↑12cm.

'The Groom'
(*elwesii* Inverse Poculiform)
Unusual inverse poculiform. Small flowers beneath large green ovary on erect scapes. Leaves erect, broad, grey-green. Six identical segments all with inner segment markings, inverted 'V' at apex above sinus and oval towards base. Completely opposite to poculiform, now called inverse poculiform. ↑18cm.

'The Linns'
(Hybrid cultivar)

Attractive rounded flowers. Very floriferous. Outer segments rounded, bluntly pointed. Inner segments spreading inverted 'V' at apex. Clumps up well. Dr Evelyn Stevens' garden, near Dunblane, Perthshire, Scotland, mid-1980s.

'The O Mahoney'

See 'Coolballintaggart'.

'The O'Mahony'

See 'Coolballintaggart'.

'The Pearl' (*plicatus*)

Elegant pearl drop flowers on slender pedicel move well in breeze. Leaves broad, erect to semi-erect, dark-green. Outer segments long, slender, clawed. Inner segments mid-green mark across segment almost to base, visible when flower closed. Slow. Sir Frederick Stern's garden, Highdown, Sussex, c. 1960s. At least two other snowdrops in circulation with this name, with minor differences in shape of inner segment marking.

'The Stalker'

See 'Cicely Hall'.

'The Turban'

Outer segments broad, rounded, pale green lines at apex. Inner segments large green mark above sinus extending across segment to base

'The Whin's Yellow'
(Hybrid cultivar)

Yellow-marked snowdrop.

'The Whopper'

See 'Cicely Hall'.

'Three Leaves'
(*elwesii* var. *monostictus*)

Large, attractive, unusually shaped flowers. Leaves supervolute, erect, regularly three, grey-green, glaucous. Outer segments long, rounded, tapering to point at apex. Inner segments green inverted 'V' at apex joining oval basal mark. ↑20cm.

'Three Musketeers' (Scharlockii)

Interesting snowdrop with split spathe. Outer segments long, spiky, curling, heavily marked green. Gert-Jan van der Kolk.

'Three Ships'
(*plicatus* subsp. *plicatus*)

Usually Christmas flowering. Leaves broad, folded margins, deep green, glaucescent median stripe. Outer segments textured. Inner segments flared, inverted 'V' at apex joining oval fading towards base. Open situation. December. John Morley, under cork oak, Henham Hall, Suffolk, 1984. RHS AM 2008. ↑12cm.

'Three Spur'

Slender ovary. Outer segments slender, pointed.

'Tilebarn Jamie'
(*reginae-olgae* subsp. *reginae-olgae*)

Vigorous, floriferous, autumn snowdrop. Flowers large, weighty, rounded. Leaves narrow, short or absent at flowering. Outer segments thick, rounded, prominently clawed. Inner segments variable broad, spreading inverted 'V' at apex. Usually shorter second scape. October–November. Named by Peter Moore for his father in the 1980s. ↑13cm.

'Till E' (Hybrid cultivar)

Long slender ovary. Outer segments bluntly pointed. Inner segment mark similar to crossed swords reminiscent of Meissen porcelain mark, darker green above sinus. Two scapes on mature bulbs. Germany. ↑24cm.

'Till Sonnenschein'
(*nivalis*)

Attractive flowers, erect scapes, inflated spathes. Leaves blue-green, hooded. Unusual pale yellow-green colouring.

Outer segments merging yellow-green lines apex to half of segment. Inner segments yellow-green inverted 'V' at apex, rounded ends, staining towards base, two pale spots towards base. Late. Vigorous. Germany. English translation: 'Sunshine Till'. ↑10cm.

'Timpany Late'

Syn. *G.* ex Robin Hall
Late flowering Irish snowdrop. Inner segments large green 'X' mark. Robin Hall, named after Susan Tindall's Nursery, Ireland. ↑25cm.

'Tiny' (*nivalis*)

Slightly smaller *G. nivalis* but standard-looking flowers. Leaves applanate, erect, narrow, blue-green. Outer segments bluntly pointed. Inner segment Chinese-bridge mark at apex. February–March. *See also G.* 'Tiny Tim', which appears identical. ↑10cm.

'Tiny Tim' (*nivalis*)

Smaller, late flowering *G. nivalis*. Leaves applanate, narrow, erect. Outer segments bluntly pointed. Inner segments Chinese-bridge mark above apex. February–March. This is probably *G.* 'Tiny', but some Galanthophiles maintain they are different and often grow both. ↑10cm.

'Tippy Green' (*nivalis*)

Strong growing *G. nivalis* with upward-facing flowers. Leaves applanate, erect, blue-green. Outer segments long, bluntly pointed, small green mark at apex. Inner segments inverted green 'V' at apex. Vigorous. February. Gerard Oud, 2007. ↑15cm.

'Titania'
(Hybrid double)

Good, regular, Greatorex double. One of the best. Full, neat, rounded flowers, rarely aberrant segments. Leaves semi-erect, spreading, narrow, lightly explicative, glaucescent, short at flowering. Outer segments clawed.

Inner segments neat ruff, green inverted 'U' at apex. Grows well. February. H.A. Greatorex, Brundall, Norfolk, c. 1940s. Probably *G. plicatus* × *G. nivalis*. ↑22cm.

'Todered'
(Poculiform)

Elegant, rounded poculiform with well shaped, all-white, equally sized segments. February. ↑14cm.

'Tom Watkins'
(Hybrid cultivar)

Leaves applanate, spreading, glaucescent. Outer segments clawed, merging green lines above apex. Inner segments broad dark-green heart-shape or inverted 'V'. Often two scapes. Joe Sharman in R.O. Backhouse's former garden, Sutton Court, Herefordshire, 1996, named by owner for head gardener. Similar to *G.* 'Viridapice'. Possibly *G. nivalis* and *G. plicatus* ancestry. ↑23cm.

'Tommy'

Leaves applanate, erect-arching, blue-green. Outer segments broad, rounded. Inner segments dark-green inverted 'V' at apex. February. Tom Koopman, W. Vieveen, 2009. ↑15cm.

'Topaz'
(*reginae-olgae* subsp. *vernalis*)

Long slender ovary. Leaves erect, dark-green, central median stripe. Inner segments broad 'Y' mark at apex. Mid-February. Janet Lecore, Judy's Snowdrops, named for her Labrador dog.

transcaucasicus (species)

Syn. *G. caspius*
Armenia, Azerbaijan, northern Iran. Leaves supervolute, broad, occasional longitudinal folds, shiny to mat dark-green upper surface, pale green underside. Inner segments inverted green 'U' or 'V' at apex. January–March. Rarely cultivated so little known, probably hardy. Named by A.V. Fomin, Russian botanist. ↑4–12cm.

'Treasure Island'

Recently introduced yellow-marked *G.* 'Mighty Atom' type snowdrop with very large, rounded flowers. Rounded yellow ovary. Outer segments long, bluntly pointed, clawed at base. Inner segments clear strong yellow mark at apex. Grows well.

'Tricorn' (*elwesii*)

Outer segments tipped green, flicked back resembling tricorn hat. Matt Bishop, seedling from The Garden House, Devon.

'Trimmer' (*plicatus*)

Beautiful, vigorous *G.* 'Trym' seedling, similarly shaped flowers. Outer segments flared, broadening towards apex with broad green mark above apex, separate oval towards base. Inner segments broad green mark from apex almost to base, white 'V' notch at base. ↑18cm.

'Trojan' (Hybrid cultivar)

Rounded flowers beneath slender ovary. Outer segments broad, rounded at apex, goffered claw at base. Inner segments broad green inverted 'U' at apex, rounded ends.

trojanus (species)

North-western Turkey. Leaves applanate, broad, mat, mid-dark green, glaucous upper surface, shiny lighter green lower surface. Inner segments green Chinese-bridge to 'V' shape at apex or small mark either side of sinus, occasionally two small marks at base. January–February. Seed collected by Royal Botanic Garden, Kew, and University of Istanbul botanists, 1994. ↑15–22cm.

'Trotter's Giant Plicate'

Leaves plicate, green. Outer segments long, shapely, pointed. Inner segments broad mid-green inverted 'U' mark at apex. ↑20cm.

'Trotters Merlin'
(Hybrid cultivar)

Handsome, vigorous. Beautiful flowers, similar to *G.* 'Merlin'. Leaves erect, linear, glaucous. Outer segments elongated, clawed. Inner segments tube-like, flared at apex, waisted green mark across segment. February–March. Originally from Richard Trotter as *G.* 'Merlin', renamed by John Morley, 1990. ↑17cm.

'Trumpolute'
(Hybrid cultivar)

Rare. Leaves convolute. Outer segments flat, 'V'-shaped mark at apex, paler oval at base, variable until plants establish. Inner segments large green mark. First good *G. plicatus* 'Trym' × *G. elwesii*. North Green Snowdrops, Suffolk, 2001.

'Trumps' (Hybrid cultivar)

Leaves applanate, semi-erect, variable margins, glaucescent. Outer segments broad, spreading at apex, green heart-shaped mark, shadowed on underside, small sinus. Inner segments green heart-shaped mark at apex. Early. Related to *G.* 'Green of Hearts' but earlier. Matt Bishop in North Green Snowdrops garden, Suffolk, late 1999. RHS AGM 2011. ↑17cm.

'Trym' (*plicatus*)

Distinctive, unusually shaped flowers. Leaves semi-erect, plicate, mat-green, glaucescent median stripe. Outer segments broad, reflexed, particularly in maturity, resemble enlarged inner segments, large variable heart-shaped green mark. Inner segments flared, ridged, green mark above sinus. Vigorous, bulks up well and sets seed. Jane Gibb's garden, Westbury on Trym, Bristol, c. 1987, named by C. Brickell. ↑22cm.

'Trym Baby'
(Hybrid cultivar)

One of an increasing number of *G.* 'Trym' seedlings. Outer segments broad, boat-shaped, broad claw, small merging green lines at apex. Inner segments broad 'U' to 'V' at apex. ↑16cm.

'Trymest' (Hybrid cultivar)

G. 'Trym' seedling with paddle-shaped segments and good green marks at apex. ↑18cm.

'Trymlet' (*plicatus*)

G. 'Trym' seedling with pagoda-shaped flower, not as flared as 'Trym'. Outer segments flat, clawed, pale-green 'U' above apex. Inner segments pale-green 'U' to 'V' above apex. G. 'Sally Ann' pollen-bearing parent, seedling selected by Kathleen Beddington, Rippingale, Lincolnshire, 1995, named by Wol and Sue Staines. ↑13cm.

'Trymming' (*plicatus*)

Leaves erect, blue-green. Outer segments large, broadening towards apex, dark-green mark above sinus. Inner segments large, dark-green inverted 'U' at apex diffusing towards base. Avon Bulbs. ↑18cm.

'Trymposter' (*plicatus*)

Vigorous, shorter G. 'Trym' seedling. Beautifully shaped flower, erect scape. Leaves erect, broad, grey-blue. Outer segments wide, paddle-shaped, splayed, inverted green 'V' at apex. Inner segments shorter, upright inverted green 'V' at apex. RHS Preliminary Commendation 2011. ↑16cm.

'Tubby Merlin' (Hybrid cultivar)

Neat, rounded flowers, olive-green ovary. Leaves lax, spreading, flat-lightly explicative, grey-glaucous. Outer segments rounded. Inner segments waisted olive-green mark across segment, white margin. Usually two scapes. Honey perfume. February–March. Clumps up well. Related to G. 'Merlin',

shorter. E.B. Anderson, Lower Slaughter, Gloucestershire, 1960s. Probably G. *gracilis* parentage. ↑11cm.

'Tuesday's Child' (*elwesii*)

Tall. Slender flowers and ovary. Leaves narrow, well developed at flowering. Inner segments variable inverted 'V' at apex, upturned pointed ends, paler mark above. Distinctive primrose perfume. Daphne Chappell from Helen Milford's former garden, Chedworth, Gloucestershire, 1995. ↑21cm.

'Tuff'

Unusual light brown-green ovary and mark. Leaves slender, splayed, green.

'Turncoat' (Hybrid cultivar)

Elegant flowers, erect scapes, slender rounded ovary. Outer segments broadening towards apex, bluntly pointed, broad green mark. Inner segments broad inverted 'U' to 'V'-shaped mark at apex. Good, vigorous. ↑18cm.

'Tutu' (*nivalis*)

Attractive, smaller, tightly packed double resembling ballet dancer's tutu. Flowers held at right angles from the scape. Leaves applanate, erect, slender, blue-green. Outer segments four or five. Inner segments tight neat ruff tipped green at apex. January–February. ↑12cm.

'Twins' (*elwesii*)

Large flowers on erect scapes. Regularly two good, well shaped flowers to each scape. Often two scapes. Leaves supervolute, broad, erect to arching, grey. Outer segments rounded, bluntly pointed. Inner segments broad dark-green mark apex towards base, white margin. January–March. ↑18cm.

'Two Eyes' (*elwesii* Edward Whittle Group)

Large flowers, distinctive with variable green mark at apex of outer segments.

Leaves supervolute, arching. Outer segments bluntly pointed, variable green lines at apex. Inner segments heart-shaped mark at apex, two small 'eye' dots towards base. Good, vigorous. February–March. Christopher Brickell's former private garden, Woodside, RHS Wisley, Surrey. ↑23cm.

'Uncle Dick' (Hybrid cultivar)

Leaves upright, slender, blue-green. Outer segments long, ridged, boat-shaped. Inner segments solid green 'X', filled in base. February–March. Named for nurseryman Richard Trotter, Brin, Inverness-shire. ↑16cm.

'Upcher' (*plicatus*)

Attractive small-flowered plicatus. Leaves green, slightly explicative. Outer segments strongly clawed. Inner segments tube-like, dark-green inverted 'V' at apex. Late Tom Upcher's garden, Sheringham Hall, Norfolk, c. 1950s. ↑18cm.

'Utrecht Gold' (*nivalis*)

Good yellow. Erect yellow-green scape, spathe, yellow ovary. Leaves applanate, erect, yellow-green. Outer segments strongly incurved at margins, pointed. Inner segments yellow inverted 'V' at apex. January–February. Jörg Lebsa, 2002, named after town of Utrecht, Netherlands. ↑12cm.

'Utrecht Lime' (*nivalis*)

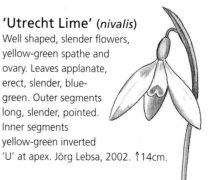

Well shaped, slender flowers, yellow-green spathe and ovary. Leaves applanate, erect, slender, blue-green. Outer segments long, slender, pointed. Inner segments yellow-green inverted 'U' at apex. Jörg Lebsa, 2002. ↑14cm.

'Valentine's Day'
(*nivalis* Poculiformis Group)
Elegant full poculiform with unusually shaped, equal-sized segments. Outer segments clawed at base, rounded, broadening towards apex, inverted green 'U' at apex. Inner segments broad, inverted 'U' at apex. February. Valentin Wijnen, Belgium, 2006. ↑12cm.

'Valerie Finnis'
(*elwesii* var. *elwesii*)
Tall, sturdy. Large flowers. Leaves supervolute, erect, very broad, three or four, grey-green. Inner segments 'X' mark, rounded ends, in-filled base. Sometimes two scapes. Slow. Valerie Finnis's garden, The Dower House, Boughton House, Kettering, Northamptonshire, possibly originating in the Warburgs' garden, South Hayes, Oxfordshire. ↑19cm.

'Vasiliki'
(*reginae-olgae* subsp. *reginae-olgae*)
Short ovary and pedical. Outer segments spoon-shaped, rounded at apex. Inner segments mid-green inverted 'V' at apex, rounded ends. September–October. Bulks up well. Frequent division. ↑12cm.

'Vera Trum'
(*plicatus*)
Attractive, large, puckered flowers, upright scapes. Leaves wide, minus plicate folding. Outer segments rounded, bluntly pointed. Inner segments flared, narrow green 'V' at apex. John Morley, under cork oak, Henham Hall, Suffolk. ↑13cm.

'Vertigo' (*nivalis*)
Similar to G. 'Viridapice' but flowers upright in spathe before becoming pendant, hence name. Leaves erect, lightly explicative. Outer segments slender, green mark above apex, lighter basal mark. Inner segments inverted 'V' to 'W' mark. January–February. Barrie Carson Turner, Polstead, Suffolk, 1996. ↑12cm.

'Vic Horton' (*gracilis*)
Small, neat, pear-shaped flowers. Leaves applanate, slender. Outer segments rounded. Inner segments small triangle each side of sinus, larger basal mark. Vic Horton passed bulbs to Thuja Alpine Nursery, Gloucestershire, 1960s, named for him. ↑10cm.

'Victor'
Attractive, well shaped flowers. Outer segments rounded, bluntly pointed at apex. Inner segments have a broad 'U' or heart-shaped mark at the apex, bleeding slightly on the basal side.

'Virescens' (*nivalis*)
Syns. G. *caucasicus* var. *virescens*, G. *caucasicus virescens*
Good, slender, virescent cultivar. Outer segments narrow, pointed, green shading apex towards base. Inner segments dark-green mark apex to base, narrow white margin. March–April. Difficult, slow. Professor Eduard Fenzl, Vienna Botanical Garden, 1870s, passed via Max Leichtlin to James Allen and Revd H. Harpur-Crew. ↑9cm.

'Viridapice'
(*nivalis*)
Syns. G. *nivalis* var. *viridapicis*, G. *nivalis* 'Viridi-apice', G. *nivalis* 'Viridiapicis', G. 'Mill House'
Tall snowdrop with dainty flowers beneath hooded spathe which sometimes splits. Leaves erect to arching, glaucescent. Outer segments large, long, pale-green mark at apex shadowed on underside. Inner segment green inverted 'V' at apex. Vigorous, reliable, bulks up well. February. Probably J.C. Hoog, Netherlands, exhibited 1922. Numerous green-tipped clones. ↑18cm.

'Viridapicis'
See 'Viridapice'.

'G. Viridi-apice'
See 'Viridapice'.

'W.O. Backhouse' (*nivalis*)
Enlarged spathe forms grey hood above pendant flowers. Similar in shape to 'Modern Art'. Outer segments slender. Joe Sharman, former Backhouse garden, Sutton Court, Herefordshire, 1997. ↑13cm.

'W. Thomson'
See 'William Thomson'.

'Wake-up-Call'
(Hybrid cultivar)
Attractive flowers, long green ovary, slender pedicel. Outer segments rounded, bluntly pointed, lightly ridged. Inner segments flared, broad inverted 'V' at apex, two small ovals towards base. ↑16cm.

'Walker Canada'
(*plicatus*)
Elegant flowers with slender green ovary. Leaves arching, grey-green, paler median stripe. Outer segments long, lightly ridged, pointed at apex. Inner segments 'X' mark to three-quarters of segment, base filled in. Origins obscure but grown by Richard Nutt. ↑15cm.

'Walloping Whopper'
Syn. 'Cronkhill Selection'
Large rounded, very white flowers enhanced by mid-green ovary. Leaves long, broad, erect, grey-green. Outer segments large, rounded, spoon-shaped, with long goffered claw. Inner segments narrow inverted 'V' at apex with two paler green marks above which can merge, diffusing towards base. ↑20cm.

'Walrus' (*nivalis*)

Unusual pendant double. Spathe sometimes split, flattened. Leaves semi-erect. Outer segments brushed green, long, thin, tubular, resembling walrus's 'tusks', occasionally broader but generally revert to type. Inner segments long, slender, tightly clustered ruff, heart-shaped mark at apex. Can be slow. Seedling selected by Oliver Wyatt at Maidwell Hall, Northamptonshire, 1960s. ↑10cm.

'Walter Fish' (*plicatus*)

Straight pedicel. Leaves semi-erect. Outer segments long, slender, flat, spoon-shaped, clawed, green mark at apex. Inner segment mark covering roughly half, paling towards base, white margin. Andrew Norton, former owner, East Lambrook Manor, Somerset, 1988, near group of G. 'Margery Fish', named for Margery Fish's husband. ↑20cm.

'Waltham Place 2'

Long green ovary, slender flowers. Leaves slender, erect, blue-grey. Outer segments bluntly pointed. Inner segments broad green 'V' at base joining oval towards base. February. ↑12cm.

'Waltham Place 3'

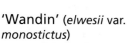

Leaves erect, broad, blue-grey. Outer segments long, slender, bluntly pointed. Inner segments broad green 'V' at apex joining oval towards base. February. ↑12cm.

'Wandin' (*elwesii* var. *monostictus*)

Large, well shaped flowers. Leaves erect, broad, grey-green. Outer segments well rounded, bluntly pointed. Inner segments large inverted 'U' at apex up to three-quarters of segment. Bulks up well, quickly. Australian-raised selection. ↑18cm.

'Wandlebury Ring' (*plicatus*)

Good yellow with slender flowers and yellow ovary and pedicel. Leaves arched,

semi-erect. Outer segments incurved. Inner segments broad yellow inverted 'U' to 'V' at apex. Seedling cross by Bill Clark, 1991, with G. 'Wendy's Gold' as seed parent. Varies from G. 'Wendy's Gold' in size and shape of ovary and segment marking. ↑28cm.

'Warande's Groenpunt' (*elwesii* cultivar)

Leaves erect, broad, grey. Outer segments broad, pointed, clawed, green mark above apex. Inner segments solid inverted 'V' at apex, separate or narrowly joining broad mark towards base. From De Warande garden, Netherlands. English translation: 'Warande's Green Point'.

'Warande's Grootste' (*elwesii* cultivar)

Heavy-looking balloon-like flowers, curved spathe. Outer segments large, broad, bluntly pointed, small pale-green lines at apex. Inner segments 'X' mark across segment, in-filled base. From De Warande garden, Netherlands. English translation: 'Warande's Largest'.

'Warande's Sieraad' (*elwesii* cultivar)

Leaves erect to arching, broad, light-green. Outer segments long, slender, incurved margins, clawed at base. Inner segments scissor-shaped mark across segment towards base, in-filled at base. From De Warande garden, Netherlands. English translation: 'Warande's Jewel'. ↑16cm.

'Warburg No 1' (Hybrid cultivar)

Elegant flowers, erect scapes. Leaves broad, erect to arching, blue-grey. Outer segments spoon-shaped, bluntly pointed, small green mark above apex. Inner segments green mark apex towards base, narrow white margin. February. ↑14cm.

'Warburg No 2' (Hybrid cultivar)

Yellow ovary, pedicel, yellow-green spathe. Outer segments bluntly pointed. Inner segments broad inverted yellow 'U' at apex. February. ↑14cm.

'Warburton'

Australian-raised snowdrop with well shaped flowers. Clumps up well and seeds freely.

'Warei' (*nivalis*)

Similar to larger G. 'Viridapice' but exceptionally long, well developed spathe. Leaves semi-erect, lightly explicative. Outer segment green mark toward apex. Inner segments green inverted 'V' at apex. February. Mr Ware to W. Boyd, to James Allen. Originally thought to be G. 'Scharlockii' because of large spathe. ↑25cm.

'Warham' (*plicatus*)

Syn. G. 'Warham Variety' Older cultivar. Leaves large, semi-erect, bright-green, glaucous, paler median stripe. Outer segments thick. Inner segments broad inverted 'U' or 'V' at apex. February. Various stories regarding origins. Revd Charles Digby, Norfolk, obtained bulbs brought back after Crimean War, 1855, sent some to E.A. Bowles in 1916; alternatively seedlings from Northgate Hall, Norfolk. Various bulbs sold under this name, but only G. 'Ceres Esplan' resembles Bowles's original illustration. RHS AM 1928. FCC 1937. ↑20cm.

'Warham Rectory' (*plicatus*)

Good, vigorous, easy. Flowers large, well shaped. Leaves erect to arching, broad, glaucous. Outer segments well shaped, rounded, bluntly pointed. Inner segments good green mark. Bulks up well. February. Origins obscure. ↑18cm.

'Warham Variety'

See 'Warham'.

'Warley Belles' (*plicatus*)

Bell-shaped flowers. Outer segments clawed, variable green mark at apex. Inner segments broad inverted 'U' at apex. After her death, house and garden of Ellen Wilmott (1858–1934), Warley Place, Chelmsford, Essex, became derelict. Bulbs survived and naturalized. Now Essex Wildlife Trust nature reserve. Derek Fox selected and named this G. *plicatus* seedling. ↑15cm.

'Warley Duo'
(Hybrid cultivar)
Nicely rounded, well shaped flowers. Outer segments long, well shaped, bluntly pointed. Inner segment green inverted 'V' at apex bleeding on basal side. Ellen Wilmott's garden, Warley Place, Essex. ↑18cm.

'Warley Longbow'
(Hybrid cultivar)
Attractive snowdrop with upright scape and spathe, slender green ovary. Leaves applanate, slender, grey. Outer segments long, slender, clawed. Inner segments inverted olive-green 'V' at apex, paler marginal stains towards base. Derek Fox, from Ellen Wilmott's garden, Warley Place, Essex, 1980s, named 1996. ↑22cm.

'Warwickshire Gemini'
(elwesii var. monostictus)
Robust, attractive with large elegant flowers. Often two scapes when established or two flowers to a single scape on separate pedicels. Leaves erect, broad, grey-green. Outer segments pointed. Inner segments heart-shaped mark at apex.

'Warwickshire Gremlin' (elwesii)
Good, vigorous and often two flowers to a scape when established. Leaves broad, grey-green. Outer segments long, spoon-shaped, bluntly pointed. Inner segments inverted 'U' at apex. ↑18cm.

'Washfield Colesbourne'
(Hybrid cultivar)
Beautiful flowers on strong scapes. Leaves supervolute, erect to spreading, broad, flat to explicative, grey-glaucous. Outer segments bluntly pointed, clawed. Inner segment tube-like, green mark across segment almost to base. Seedling from Elizabeth Strangman's

Washfield Nursery, Hawkhurst, Kent, c. 1981, sold as G. 'Colesborne', renamed when discrepancy discovered. ↑24cm.

'Washfield Titania'
(Hybrid double)
Showy, neat double. Leaves erect to arching, blue-green, silver median stripe. Outer segments rounded, bluntly pointed. Inner segments neat ruff, inverted green 'U' at apex, large sinus. February. Washfield Nursery, Kent. ↑18cm.

'Washfield Warham'
(plicatus)
Syn. G. 'Finale'
Large, well shaped flowers. Leaves spreading, broad, glaucous, partly plicate. Outer segments bluntly pointed. Inner segments narrow inverted 'V' at apex. Often two scapes. Late. Confusion with G. 'Warham' snowdrops but G. 'Washfield Warham' first recorded by Monksilver Nursery, Cambridge, 1996 and takes precedence. Originated with Ray Cobb from bulbs received as G. 'Warham' from E.A. Bowles, 1954. ↑18cm.

'Wasp'
(Hybrid cultivar)
Vigorous, with slender, elongated flowers suspended from long pedicel. Leaves applanate, erect, flat to explicative, glaucescent. Outer segments long, narrow, incurved, clawed, resembling insect wings. Inner segments variable inverted olive-green 'U' at apex, roughly 'H'-shaped mark below base, sometimes lightly joined. Grows well. February. Veronica Cross, Sutton Court, Herefordshire, 1995. ↑27cm.

'Waverly Aristocrat'
(Hybrid cultivar)
Attractive Irish snowdrop. Outer segments long, slender, bluntly pointed. Inner segments broad green mark across segment towards base,

white margin. Often two scapes. Bulks up well. February–March. Harold McBride, Ireland. ↑16cm.

'Waves' (nivalis)
Standard G. nivalis, green-tipped but different shape. Leaves applanate, erect, slender, blue-green. Outer segments slender, sharply pinched above apex giving very unusual shape, merging green lines at apex. Inner segments inverted 'U' at apex. January–February. ↑15cm.

'Wayside'
Small flowers, thick scapes and spathes. Outer segments long, slender, incurved, bluntly pointed, green lines apex towards base, shadowed on underside. Inner segments tight ruff heavily marked green. February. ↑16cm.

'Weather Hill'
Well rounded, balloon-like flowers. Outer segments broad, rounded, textured, bluntly pointed. Inner segments inverted 'U' at apex.

'Webb's Gold' (Hybrid cultivar)
Yellow-marked snowdrop.

'Wedding Dress'
(nivalis Poculiformis Group)
Elegant poculiform with well shaped, all-white segments. Leaves applanate, erect, slender, blue-green. Outer segments slightly longer than inner. ↑12cm.

'Wee Betty'
(nivalis × plicatus)
Attractive, robust. Leaves shiny green. Outer segments rounded, longitudinally ridged. Inner segments scissor-shaped mark, base filled in. January–February. Ian Christie, Brechin Castle, Angus, Scotland, named for the SRGC Honorary President. ↑15cm.

'Wee Grumpy'
Outer segments narrow, reflexed well above horizontal. Inner segments tube-like, two narrowly joined eyespots at apex, two small ovals towards base. ↑10cm.

'Weisse Pendelkugel'
(Hybrid cultivar)
Well shaped, rounded flowers on slender pedicel. Outer segments rounded, pointed, lightly ridged. Inner segments small pale-green spot either side of large sinus. English translation: 'White Ball Pendulum'. ↑14cm.

'Weisses Läuten' (Hybrid cultivar)
Very attractive, rounded flower. Outer segments well shaped, rounded, bluntly pointed. Inner segments small pale-green dot either side of sinus. English translation: 'White Ring'. ↑15cm.

'Welshway'
(Hybrid double)
Good, neat, regular double. Small rounded flowers, tall upright scapes. Leaves supervolute, erect. Outer segments long, narrow. Inner segment ruff outermost whorl ruffled, inverted 'V' at apex, small paler mark at base. Hugh and Hilary Purkess's garden, Welshway, Cirencester, Gloucestershire, 1995. *G. elwesii* × *G. nivalis* 'Flore Pleno'. Similar to taller *G.* 'Heffalump'. ↑12cm.

'Wendover Green Tip'
(*nivalis*)
Said to be slightly later than *G.* 'Pusey Green Tips' but in all other respects similar. Irregular double. Leaves applanate, grey-green, semi-erect, lightly explicative. Outer segments often aberrant, green lines at apex. Inner segment ruff green 'V' at apex. February–March. Mark Brown, Wendover, Buckinghamshire, 1980s. ↑15cm.

'Wendy's Gold'
(*plicatus* subsp. *plicatus*)
Yellow ovary and pedicel. Leaves broad, plicate. Outer segments short, rounded. Inner segments, large long yellow mark fading towards base, white margin. Colour stronger in good light. Bulks up well. Sometimes two scapes. Grows well. February. Mrs Sharman and Bill Clarke from Wandlebury Ring, Cambridgeshire, 1985, named after his wife. Joe Sharman of Monksilver Nursery propagated bulbs, exhibited at RHS Spring Show, 1987. University of Cambridge Botanic Garden also successful with propagation. RHS PC 1992. RHS AM 1996. NB. E.A. Bowles noted he acquired a yellow *G. plicatus* from Cambridge Botanic Garden in 1917. ↑15cm.

'West Porlock No 7/8/9'
See 'White Wings'.

'Westburn'
(*elwesii* var. *monostictus*)
Leaves erect, broad, grey-green. Inner segment large mark across most of segment. Australian-selected snowdrop. ↑16cm.

'Whirlygig'
Outer segments slender, bluntly pointed. Inner segments broad, rounded, inverted 'U', narrow ends at apex, variable lines, staining towards base.

'White Admiral'
(Hybrid cultivar)
Tall, attractive snowdrop with strong scapes, between two and four spathe valves, and additional segments. Leaves erect, flat margins, glaucous. Outer segments three to six, rounded, clawed. Inner segments three to five, inverted 'V' at apex. John Grimshaw in Sir George and Lady Meyrick's garden, Hinton Admiral, Hampshire. ↑28cm.

'White Cloud' (*nivalis*)
Leaves applanate, erect, slender, blue-green. Outer segments broad, rounded, bluntly pointed. Inner segments small inverted 'V' at apex. Two scapes. Bulks up well into good clumps. February–March. Jan Van de Sijpe in parents' garden, Belgium. ↑14cm.

'White Dream' (*nivalis*)
Similar to normal *G. nivalis* but more rounded, strikingly white flowers. Leaves unusual, erect, slender, prominent pale median stripe. Outer segments rounded, incurved, pointed. Inner segments green inverted 'U' at apex. Grows well, bulks up quickly. March. T. Koopman, Netherlands, 2003. ↑15cm.

'White Gem'
Beautiful albino enhanced by mid-green ovary and green-blue leaves. Outer segments slender, rounded, bluntly pointed. Inner segments pure white, lightly ridged. Jörg Lebsa. ↑15cm.

'White Kay' (*nivalis*)
Attractive, neat semi-double with rounded flowers. Leaves applanate, slender, erect to arching, blue-green. Outer segments four or five large, well rounded, bluntly pointed. Inner segments neat ruff, inverted 'V' at apex. February. Gerard Oud, 2004. ↑12cm.

'White Lady'
See 'Henry's White Lady'.

'White Perfection' (*elwesii* Poculiformis Group)
Attractive and rare. Upright, albino poculiform snowdrop with rounded flowers and all white segments. Increases slowly over time. Named by Rod Leeds, Suffolk. 15cm. .

'White Stag' (*nivalis*)
A *G. nivalis* which never shows its flowers as they stay trapped inside an embracing spathe. Named by John Morley, North Green Snowdrops.

'White Swan'
(Hybrid double)
Elegant Greatorex double. Large triangular flowers, tall scapes. Leaves arching, lax, flat to explicative. Outer segments sometimes green lines at apex. Inner segment ruff, outer whorl often aberrant,

semi-circular to heart-shaped mark. Originally H.A. Greatorex, Brundall, Norfolk, modern stock via Philip Ballard may not be same. *G. nivalis* 'Flore Pleno' × *G. plicatus*. ↑25cm.

'White Wings'
(Hybrid cultivar)
Syn. *G.* 'West Porlock No 7/8/9'
Elegant, slender flowers. Leaves semi-erect, flat to explicative, glaucous. Outer segments hint pale-green at base. Inner segments pronounced inverted 'U' from apex, across segment, diffusing towards base. Often second scape. George Chiswell, West Porlock, Somerset, late 1980s. ↑19cm.

'Whittallii'
See Edward Whittall Group.

'Whittington'
Leaves applanate, erect, slender, blue-green. Outer segments bluntly pointed. Inner segments narrow green inverted 'V', rounded ends, at apex. ↑12cm.

'Wilhelm Bauer'
(*nivalis*)
Sharlockii-type spathe. Outer segments long, slender, incurved, broad green mark above apex. Inner segments rounded, large heart-shaped mark at apex. Found by Rudi Bauer, at the Eifel, Germany, named after his father. ↑16cm.

'William Ball No 1'
See 'Hoverfly'.

'William Louis'
Elegant flowers, long pedicels. Outer segments well shaped, bluntly pointed. Inner segments inverted mid-green 'V' at apex, separate paler mark towards base.

'William Thomson'
(Hybrid cultivar)
Syn. *G.* 'W. Thomson'
Later flowering *G. nivalis* clone. Leaves broad, flat-explicative, glaucous. Outer segments rounded, bluntly pointed. Inner segments dark-green 'V' or two small dots

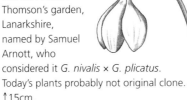

at apex. February–March. William Thomson's garden, Lanarkshire, named by Samuel Arnott, who considered it *G. nivalis* × *G. plicatus*. Today's plants probably not original clone. ↑15cm.

'Wim' (*elwesii*)
Good, large triangular flowers. Leaves semi-erect. Inner segments wide olive-green 'U' covering around half of segment. December–January. Michael Baron, Wim Lemmers from Leo Schoorl's garden, 1995, in imported wild Turkish bulbs. ↑15cm.

'Wind Turbine'
Outer segments well splayed, small notch at apex, small green mark. Inner segments narrow green inverted 'V' at apex, spreading ends, broad oval towards base. Named as reflexed flowers resemble shape of wind turbine.

'Windesheim'
(*nivalis* Sandersii Group)
Small snowdrop. Yellow-green spathe, yellow ovary. Leaves applanate, erect, blue-green. Outer segments rounded, bluntly pointed. Inner segments strong yellow mark at apex. February. ↑8cm.

'Windmill' (*nivalis*)
Irregular, semi-erect, spiky double. Numerous roughly tiered segments, small, pale-green mark at apex. Leaves applanate, semi-erect. Outer segments three to five, lightly concave, pear-shaped, three pale-green lines. Inner segments around thirty, reducing in size to centre, 'V'-shaped green mark at apex. January–February. Hector Harrison, Appleby, North Humberside, late 1970s. ↑24cm.

'Windsor Yellow'
(Sandersii)
Well shaped, pearl drop-shaped flowers. Yellow ovary, yellow-green spathe. Outer segments rounded, bluntly pointed. Inner segments yellow mark at apex. ↑10cm.

'Winifrede Mathias'
(Hybrid cultivar)
Similar but inferior to *G.* 'S. Arnott'. Thin olive-green ovary, slender arching pedicel, small flowers. Leaves semi-erect, slender, glaucescent. Outer segments bluntly pointed. Inner segments inverted 'V' to heart-shaped mark. Good. February–March. Seedling beneath *G.* 'S. Arnott'. E.B. Anderson and Herbert Ransom in garden of Hyde Lodge, Stroud, Gloucestershire, named after Mrs Mathias, proprietor of the Giant Snowdrop Company. ↑18cm.

'Wishbone' (*elwesii*)
Good-looking *G. elwesii*. Leaves erect, broad, grey-green. Outer segments bluntly pointed. Inner segments inverted 'V' at apex, topped by small oval on basal side resembling a wishbone. ↑16cm.

'Wisley Magnet'
(Hybrid cultivar)
Long pedicel as in *G.* 'Magnet' but *G.* 'Wisley Magnet' projects 45° before bending. Leaves glaucescent, lightly explicative. Inner segments inverted 'V' at apex. Christopher Brickell at RHS Wisley, Surrey, early 1960s. *G.* 'Wisley Magnet' and *G.* 'Galatea' confused, making true *G.* 'Wisley Magnet' identity unclear. ↑16cm.

'Wisp' (Hybrid cultivar)
Long, very slender flowers, erect scapes, pale yellow-green ovary. Outer segments long, slender, pointed. Inner segments small pale yellow-green mark at apex. ↑15cm.

'Wispy' (*elwesii*)
Elegant, long, pointed flowers, upright scapes. Leaves broad, grey-green. Outer segments long, slender, pointed. Inner segments small inverted 'V' or single dot either side of sinus.

'Witchwood' (*nivalis*)
Delicate-looking flowers, erect scapes. Leaves applanate, erect to arching, slender, blue-green. Outer segments bluntly

pointed, large pale-green mark. Inner segments inverted dark-green 'U' at apex, diffusing towards base. January–February. ↑12cm.

'Wodny Muž' (nivalis)
Distinctive, smaller flowers. Leaves supervolute, developed at flowering. Outer segments seven dark-green lines. Inner segments large green mark extending and paling towards base. ↑12cm.

'Wolfgang' (nivalis)
Very rare, desirable, green-tipped nivalis. Triangular-shaped flowers. Leaves long, lax, glaucous. Outer segments green lines at apex. Inner segments deep furrowing. Very late flowering. Wolfgang Kletzing, Czechoslovakia, 1990. ↑17cm.

'Wolfgang's Gold' (elwesii)
Unusual yellow G. elwesii. Slender yellow ovary, yellow pedicel, yellow-green spathe. Leaves supervolute, grey-green. Inner segments yellow marks at apex merging into basal mark. Wolfgang Kletzing, from imported wild Turkish stock, c. 2000. ↑12cm.

'Wonston Double' (nivalis)
Good, neat, full double G. nivalis. Leaves applanate, erect, slender, blue-green. Outer segments rounded, bluntly pointed. Inner segments neat, tightly packed ruff, green inverted 'U' at apex, paler oval towards base. February. Lewis Palmer's garden, Winchester. ↑15cm.

'Woodpeckers' (nivalis Sandersii Group)
Well shaped flowers. Yellow ovary, yellow-green spathe. Leaves upright, slender. Inner segments yellow 'V' at apex.

'Woodtown'
Large, rounded pear-shaped flowers. Leaves erect to arching, blue-green. Outer segments broad, rounded, bluntly pointed. Inner segments

mid-green inverted 'V' at apex, two paler spots towards base which can join. Vigorous. ↑16cm.

'Woozle' (nivalis)
Quirky, green-tipped double spiky with dense, rounded, outward-facing flowers. Frequent additional segments and often growing from ovary. January–February. ↑14cm.

woronowii (species)
Syns. G. ikariae subsp. latifolius, G. latifolius Southern Russia, Georgia, north-eastern Turkey. Smaller species snowdrop. Gently curved spathe and pedicel. Leaves supervolute, broad, semi-erect, shiny, bright-green. Outer segments tapered. Inner segments square horseshoe-shaped mark at apex. January–March. Damper soil. Seeds, bulks up well when established. Named by A.S. Losina-Losinskaya, Russian botanist, 1935. RHS AGM 2002. ↑12cm.

× allenii (Hybrid cultivar)
G. × allenii Large, rounded, very white flowers. Leaves supervolute, broad, green-glaucescent, short at flowering. Outer segments rounded, bluntly pointed. Inner segments inverted green 'V' at apex. Almond perfume. Slow. Can be difficult. February–March. G. alpinus × G. woronowii. Named by J.G. Baker, 1891, for James Allen. ↑12cm.

'X Files' (elwesii)
Syn. G. 'Early Bird' Large flowers. Leaves supervolute, erect, well developed at flowering. Outer segments bluntly pointed. Inner segments green 'X'-shaped mark apex towards base. January. Phil Cornish. ↑15cm.

× valentinei
Syn. G. nivalis 'Valentine' Hybrids between nivalis and plicatus. × valentinei nothosubsp. subplicatus Wild hybrid between G. nivalis and G. plicatus subsp. byzantinus. Leaves applanate to explicative, grey-green, glaucescent, grey median stripe. Inner segments inverted 'V' at apex, one or two marks at base which can be absent, occasionally mark across segment. January–March. ↑7cm.

× valentinei nothosubsp. valentinei
Cultivated hybrid between G. nivalis and G. plicatus subsp. plicatus, giving rise to numerous named cultivars. Leaves grey-green. Inner segments generally single mark at apex, occasional small basal mark or mark across segment diffusing towards base.

Yaffle (plicatus)
Attractive, vigorous, creamy flowers enhanced by lime-green ovary. Leaves arching, erect. Outer segments long, slender, light longitudinal ridging, textured. Inner segments variable green mark apex towards base, white margin. Often second scape. Clumps up well. January. Richard Hobbs, Wells, Norfolk, 1992.

'Yamanlar' (gracilis)
(incorrect syn. G. 'Cassaba') Attractive, large, long flowers. Leaves applanate, broad, semi-erect, twisted. Inner segments small green dot either side of sinus, larger mark extending towards base. Sometime two scapes. Colin Mason, near Izmir, Turkey, 1972, incorrectly named G. elwesii 'Cassaba'. Seedlings sold under this name until renamed by Colin Mason. ↑15cm.

'Yarnton'
Attractive smaller flowers on tall erect scapes. Leaves erect, slender, blue-green. Outer segments bluntly pointed, green mark at apex. Inner segments inverted 'U' at apex. ↑20cm.

'Yashmak' (*elwesii*)

Large, attractive flowers with yellow-green ovary. Leaves supervolute, semi-erect to arching. Outer segments long, clawed. Inner segments no mark at apex, two very pale yellow-green 'eye' dots towards base, sometimes joined. David and Ruby Baker, Surrey in naturalized *G. elwesii* colony, 1998, named as 'eye' dots appear to be behind veil. ↑18cm.

'Yellow Angel'

Not validly published name so far. Flowers hint of creamy-yellow, pale yellow-green ovary. Outer segments long, rounded at apex. Inner segments all-white, no mark. ↑14cm.

'Yellow Trym'
(Hybrid cultivar)

Recently introduced yellow form of *G*. 'Trym', not yet officially named or validly published, but included here as mentioned by some growers. Yellow-green ovary. Outer segments broad, longitudinally ridged, broad and flared at apex, broad yellow-green mark. Inner segments broad yellow-green 'U' at apex. ↑18cm.

'Yeti'

Rounded flowers. Leaves erect, slender, blue-green. Outer segments long claw then well rounded, bluntly pointed, longitudinally ridged, seersucker texture. Inner segments spreading green 'V' at apex, slightly upturned ends. February. ↑12cm.

'York Minster'

Recent introduction from Jörg Lebsa.

'Yorkshire Cottage'

See 'Mrs Thompson'.

'Yuletide' (*elwesii*)

Well shaped flowers. Leaves broad, arching, well developed at flowering. Inner segments beautiful heart-shaped marking to around half of segment. December. Phil Cornish from E.B. Anderson's former garden, Lower Slaughter, Gloucestershire, 1985. ↑17cm.

'Yvonne'
(*nivalis* × *plicatus*)

Leaves erect, blue-green. Outer segments long, pear-shaped, longitudinally ridged, dimpled, bluntly pointed. Inner segments scissor-shaped mark filled in at base. January–February. Ian Christie, Brechin Castle, Angus, Scotland. RHS PC 2009. ↑12cm.

'Yvonne Hay'
(*elwesii*)

Syn. *G*. 'Maximus' Very large snowdrop, large bulbs, large, well shaped flowers. Leaves very broad, three or four. Outer segments occasional green mark at apex. Inner segments strong heart-shaped mark from apex shading towards base. January. Harry Hay, Surrey. Originally *G*. 'Maximus' but name already applied, renamed 'Yvonne Hay' for his wife. ↑37cm.

'Zarnikova' (*nivalis*)

Light-green scape, spathe. Yellow-green ovary. Outer segments yellow-green lines above apex. Inner segments yellow-green inverted 'U' to 'V' at apex, two smaller, paler ovals towards base. February. University BG Ljubljana, Slovenia.

'Zlatko' (*nivalis*)

Good, robust *G. nivalis*. Outer segments bluntly pointed. Inner segments broad mark across segment diffusing to base. Zlatko and Angelina Petrisevac, named for him. ↑16cm.

'Zwanenburg' (*elwesii*)

Light green spathe and ovary. Leaves supervolute, erect. Inner segments light-green mark at apex and base which can join into roughly scissor-shape. Second scape from mature bulbs. Possibly named after Zwanenburg Nursery, Holland. Possible *G. elwesii* × *G. gracilis*. ↑14cm.

EXTINCT GALANTHUS

There are many reasons why snowdrops disappear from commercial use. They may simply die out and become extinct, inferior forms may not be worth cultivating further, or names are misspelt, duplicating another known snowdrop still in cultivation. Occasionally an 'extinct' snowdrop has been growing quietly in its own corner until someone notices it and it reappears.

A.P. Davis, *The Genus Galanthus* (1999), and Bishop, Davis and Grimshaw, *Snowdrops – A Monograph of Cultivated Galanthus* (2001) aided the compilation of this list.

Acme
Aestivalis
Afterglow
Aiden
Albus
Allen's Perfection
Allen's Seedling
Anacreon
Anamus
Angustifolius
Aurora
Balloon
Beauty
Belated
Biflorus
Biscapus
Boydii
Breviflos
Candidus
Cassaba Boydii
Cathcarti
Cathcartiae
Chapeli
Charmer
Charmer Flore Pleno
Claudia
Cloven
Coquette
Creole
Cupid
Curio
Delight
Demo
Distinction
Dora Parker
Dragoon
Early Bird

Elegenas
Elise Scharlock
Elsae
Emerald
Empress
Ermine Green
Erythrae
Esmerelda
Excelsior
Faldonside
Fascination
Fenella
Flavus
Fortuna
Frazeri
Gem
Gimli
Globosus
Gottwaldi
Grandiflorus
Grandior
Grenadier
Gusmusi
Hololeucus
Hortensis
Hybridus
Jason Scharlock
Kew
Kilkenny Giant
King
Ladham's Variety
Lanarth
Lazybones
Leopard
Loiterer
Longiflorus
Lop Ears

Lyminghame
Macedonicus
Maculatus
Majestic
Major
Majus
Marshall's Green
Marvel
Maximus
Minnie Warren
Minnierren
Miriam Ledger
Miss Hassell's
Mystra
Newry Giant
Nicana
Novelty
November
Ochrospeilus
Octobrensis
Olivia
Omega
Pallidus
Paris
Pat Schofield
Pearl
Pendulus
Perfection
Phaenika Samos
Pictus
Platytepalus
Plenissimus
Plover
Poculiformis
Praecox
Pumilis
Punctatus

Quadripetala
Rachelae
Raphael
Rebecca
Redoutei
Reflexus
Robin
Robustus
Romeo
Saundersi
Serotinus
Silvia
Spot
Stenopetalus
Steveni
Talisman
Tauricus
Taurus
Titania (*single*)
Tomtit
Trifolius
Umbrensis
Umbricus
Unguiculatus
Valentinae
Valentine
Valentinei
Van Houttei
Victor
Victoria Gibbs
Virgin
Viridans
Whittallii
Winner
Wraysbury

GLOSSARY OF TERMS

Aberrant Malformed.
Acuminate Tapering to a point.
Acute Terminating in a sharp point.
AGM Royal Horticultural Society Award of Garden Merit, awarded to plants with outstanding qualities in the garden.
Albino All-white, with rounded flower shape.
Alpine Plant native to the Alpine zone, suitable for growing in rock garden conditions.
AM Royal Horticultural Society Award of Merit for worthy plants exhibited at shows.
Anthers Part of stamen containing pollen.
Apex Tip of a plant formation, as in leaf, root or perianth segment.
Applanate Vernation of leaf where two leaves are held flat against each other.
Base The lowest point of a structure, according to its place of insertion.
Basal plate Base of bulb from which roots grow.
Binomial Two-part naming system employed in Linnaean plant classification, first part denoting genus, second part denoting species.
Bulb Underground storage organ composed of fleshy leaf bases enclosing the growing point.
Bulbil Immature bulb formed at base of parent bulb.
Bulblet Small bulb or 'offset' growing from parent bulb.
Capsule Dry or semi-fleshy fruit containing seeds.
Classification Arrangement of plants and other organisms into groups,. ie. species grouped into genera, then families, etc.
Clone Identical plants obtained from a single parent by vegetative propagation.
Corm Thickened stem base forming plant storage organ.
Cross Hybridization of plant by

transferring pollen from anthers of one plant to stigma of another.
Cucullate Hooded, as in leaf or spathe.
Cultivar Variant of a plant selected for its merits in cultivation. Cultivars can also be selected directly from wild populations.
Cuneate Triangular or wedge-shaped.
Deciduous Usually referring to trees, shrubs and bulbous plants which lose their leaves at the end of each season.
Distribution Geographical areas in which wild plants grow.
Dormant Applied to a resting plant, usually when it makes little or no growth.
Double flowered Flowers with additional segments.
Elaiosome Small appendage on seed with substances attractive to insects aiding distribution.
Escape Plant escaped from cultivation, now growing in the wild.
Evergreen Applied to plants which retain foliage throughout the year.
Explicative Vernation of leaf showing margins sharply rolled under.
f. Abbreviation of forma.
FCC Royal Horticultural Society First Class Certificate, awarded at shows.
Filament Stalk of stamen which carries the anthers.
Forma Botanical term for a minor variation from the norm that is rather rare and does not usually reproduce as a population, eg double flowers.
Galanthophile A person with a passion for snowdrops.
Genus Botanical classification category containing allied species. May also be subdivided into further sections within the genera.
Geophyte A plant that spends much of its lifecycle underground.
Germination The emergence of a shoot and roots from a seed.

Glaucescent Leaves and stems with green-grey colouring and light waxy bloom.
Glaucous –Leaves and stems with silvery-grey-blue colouring and light waxy bloom.
Globular Rounded, spherical, ball-like.
Goffering Refers to the light crimping on edges at base of segments.
Green-tipped Snowdrop flowers having green marks on the outer segments, usually towards the apex.
Habitat A plant's natural environment.
Herbaceous Plants which die down in autumn and reappear in spring.
Humus Friable, dark-brown substance resulting from decayed vegetable matter.
Hybrid New plant produced by crossing two distinct species or subspecies.
ICBN International Code of Botanical Nomenclature, covering plant-naming procedures.
ICNCP International Code of Nomenclature for Cultivated Plants, covering naming of cultivated plants.
Inflorescence Flowering parts of plant.
Insecticide Liquid or powder substances for killing injurious insects.
Introduction A plant occurring in the wild through human intervention but also used in a horticultural sense to mean brought into cultivation.
Leaf mould Peat-like matter formed from decayed leaves.
Loam Combination of sand, clay, silt, humus and minerals to create a friable, fertile soil.
Longitudinal Running lengthways.
Matt Dull, not shiny.
Microclimate Area with a climate differing from the normal prevailing conditions.
Midrib Centre vein of leaf.
Morphology Appertaining to physical characteristics of plant or organism.
Mulch Decayed organic or other matter

applied to ground to conserve moisture, add nutrients and suppress weeds.

Native Plant or organism that occurs specifically in a particular region or country.

Naturalized Introduced species which has successfully adapted and reproduces in its new situation.

Naturalizing Bulbs and other plants grown in conditions simulating their natural habitats.

Nectar Sweet substance usually found in flowers which attracts insects to aid pollination.

Nectary Gland secreting nectar.

Notch Small indentation at apex of segment, also referred to as a sinus.

Obtuse Blunt or rounded (applied to apex).

Offset Naturally occurring new plant easily separated from parent plant, as in numerous bulbs.

Ovary Female part of flower which produces seeds after fertilization.

Ovules Contained in the ovary.

PC Royal Horticultural Society Certificate of Preliminary Commendation, for plants exhibited in shows.

Pedicel Stalk of individual flower.

Perennial Plants that live for a number of years.

Perianth Term covering sepals and petals when they are indistinguishable from each other.

Perianth segment Individual section of perianth.

Perlite Lightweight, granular form of volcanic rock used in potting or lightening soil.

Petal Modified leaf form, often coloured, surrounding and protecting stamens and attracting insects for pollination.

Petaloid Usually of stamens or sepals, taking on the appearance of petals.

Pistil Entire female organs of flower.

Plunge Setting pots to the rim in soil, sand or peat.

Poculiform Cup-shaped flower formed when segments are all of equal length.

Pollen Male plant cells contained in anthers or pollen sacs.

Pollination Transfer of pollen grains onto female stigma, either naturally by wind or insects, or artificially by hand.

Propagation Method of increasing plants, either by seed or vegetative processes.

Prostrate Lying flat to the ground.

Reflexed Usually referring to leaves or petals, sharply bent back on themselves.

Rhizome Storage organ composed of horizontal creeping underground stem.

Scape Single leafless flower stem, particularly in bulbs.

Scree Coarse gravel, chippings or other loose rocky detritus mixed with soil or peat to form specific growing conditions for certain plants.

Seedling Plants raised from seed, or a young single unbranched stemmed plant after germination.

Segment Term used when petal and sepal cannot be distinguished from one another (e.g. perianth segment).

Sinus Small notch at apex of segment.

Spathe Structure composed of modified leaf or leaves enclosing bud or flower.

Species Classification term applied to a single plant or a group of closely related plants in a genus which breed true to type from seed.

Spiky With reference to a snowdrop flower, having narrow segments that point upwards or nearly so, rather than being pendant.

Spp Species.

Stamen Complete male reproductive unit of flower containing filament and two anther lobes with pollen grains.

Sterile Plants which do not (or rarely) set seed. Many double flowers are sterile as reproductive organs have become petals.

Stigma Tip of female reproductive organ which secretes a sticky solution prior to pollination.

Style Stalk linking the ovary and stigma in female flower.

Sub-alpine Mountainous plant whose native habitat is just below the alpine zone.

Supervolute Vernation with one leaf fully or partially wrapped around the other.

Subsp. Subspecies.

Subspecies Nomenclature group immediately below species, used for a population of wild plants differing in some definable way from the norm.

Synonym Alternative plant name where plant has been renamed or reclassified. Oldest name always takes priority if validly published.

Taxonomy Study of plant classification.

Tepal Individual perianth segment that cannot be differentiated into petal or sepal.

Transplanting Moving plants from one area to another.

Tunic Papery outer layer of compressed leaf scales surrounding bulb. New scales are continually formed inside bulb, pushing older scales gradually outwards.

Unguiculate Narrowed at base into claw shape.

Var. Variety.

Variety Next rank below subspecies in plant classification for plants showing minor but consistent variations from the norm.

Vegetative Propagation of plants by cuttings, division, layering or grafting, rather than seed.

Vernation Arrangement of leaves in bud.

Virescent Green-stained segments.

BIBLIOGRAPHY AND FURTHER INFORMATION

Bishop, M., Davis, A.P. and John Grimshaw, *Snowdrops: A Monograph of Cultivated Galanthus* (Griffin Press, 2006)

Brickell, Christopher, *Royal Horticultural Society Encyclopaedia of Garden Plants* (Dorling Kindersley, 2003)

Brickell, Christopher, *Royal Horticultural Society Encyclopaedia of Plants and Flowers* (Dorling Kindersley, 2006)

Davis, A.P., *The Genus Galanthus* (Royal Botanic Gardens, Kew, in association with Timber Press, Oregon, 1999)

Diduch, J.P., *Red Book of Ukraine: Plant Kingdom* (Globalkonsalting, Kyiv, 2009)

Griffiths, Mark, *The New RHS Dictionary Index of Garden Plants* (Macmillan, 1997)

IUCN *Red List of Threatened Species* (2011)

Larsen, M.M., Adsersen, A., Davis, A.P., Lledo, M.D., Jager, A.K. and Ronsted, N., 'Using a phylogenetic approach to selection of target plants in drug discovery of acetylcholinesterase inhibiting alkaloids in Amaryllidaceae tribe Galantheae', *Biochemical Systematics and Ecology* (2010).

Lord, Tony, Flora, *The Gardener's Bible* (Cassell, 2003)

Phillips, Roger, and Rix, Martin, *Bulbs* (Pan Books, 1989)

Sharman, Joe, *Galanthus Gala Transcripts* (1997–2011)

Sterndale-Bennet, Jane, *The Winter Garden* (David & Charles, 2006)

Van Dijk, Hanneke, *Galanthomania* (Terra, 2011)

Waldorf, Günter, *Schneeglökchen* ('Snowdrops – White Magic') (August 2011).

Zobov, Dimitriy A. and Davis, Aaron, *Galanthus panjutinii* (Magnolia Press, 2012)

Daffodil, Snowdrop and Tulip Year book available from the RHS.

RHS Horticultural Database www.rhs.org.uk

Societies

UK

Alpine Garden Society
AGS Centre, Avon Bank, Pershore, Worcestershire, WR10 3JP
www.alpinegardensociety.net
Promoting interest in alpines and small hardy plants and bulbs. Quarterly journal *The Alpine Gardener*, online discussion, seed exchange.

Cottage Garden Society
The Cottage Garden Society, 'Brandon', Ravenshall, Betley, Cheshire, CW3 9BH, UK
www.thecottagegardensociety.org.uk

Cottage Garden Society Snowdrop Group
Founded 1994, organizes visits to private snowdrop gardens, lectures, plant sales and twice yearly newsletter. Members must belong to CGS before eligible to join snowdrop group. Contact Toby Jarvis: tjmail99-cgs@yahoo.co.uk

E.A. Bowles of Myddelton House Society
www.eabowlessociety.org.uk
Registered charity (No. 1020908), 1992, promoting interest and awareness of E.A. Bowles and Myddelton House Garden. Works with gardeners and volunteers to restore and maintain the gardens. Contact: Mr A. Pettitt, 2(A) Plough Hill, Cuffley, Potters Bar, Herts, EN6 4DR.

Friends of Bank Hall and Bank Hall Action Group
Bank Hall, Liverpool Road, Bretherton, Chorley, PR26 9AT.
www.bankhouseonline.2ye.com
Helping to save Bank Hall and its surrounding pleasure grounds. Contact: Mrs Janet Edwards, Hall Green Farm, Hall Carr Lane, Longton, Nr Preston, Lancashire, PR4 5JN

Friends of Kings Arms Garden
Kings Arms Garden, Ampthill, Bedfordshire, MK45 2PP. Helping manage the garden on behalf of Ampthill Town Council. Contact: Ampthill Town Council.

Hardy Plant Society
www.hardy-plant.org.uk
Contact: Pam Adams, The Hardy Plant Society, Little Orchard, Great Comberton, Pershore, Worcestershire, WR10 3DP.

Hardy Plant Society Galanthus Group
www.hardy-plant.org.uk
Founded 2012. Newsletter, garden visits, lectures and snowdrop sales. Members must belong to the HPS before eligible to join Galanthus Group. Contact: Rob Cole, Secretary, Meadow Farm, 33 Droitwich Road, Feckenham, Worcestershire, B96 6RU. Tel. 01527 821156.

Lingen Davies Cancer Relief Fund
The Appeals Office, Hamar Centre, Royal Shrewsbury Hospital, Mytton Oak Road, Shrewsbury, Shropshire, SY3 8XQ. A registered charity helping improve services for cancer sufferers in Shropshire and mid-Wales.

Multiple Sclerosis Trust
Spirella Building, Bridge Road, Letchworth Garden City, Hertfordshire, SG6 4ET. Tel: 01462 476700. Free Phone Information Service: 0800 032 3839. Charitable trust helping people and families affected by MS.

National Gardens Scheme
Hatchlands Park, East Clandon, Guildford, Surrey, GU4 7RT. Promoting gardens opening for charity across the UK since 1927. Special snowdrop gardens. Yellow Book lists gardens with information. www.ngs.org.uk

Royal Horticultural Society
80 Vincent Square, London, SW1P 2PE. The

UK's leading horticultural society devoted to advancing horticulture and good gardening. Monthly journal *The Garden*. RHS gardens: Harlow Carr, Yorkshire; Hyde Hall, Essex; Rosemoor, Devon; and Wisley, Surrey; free to members.
www.rhs.org.uk

Scottish Rock Garden Club
PO Box 14063, Edinburgh, EH10 4YE. Founded 1993 for those interested in alpines and rock garden plants. Twice yearly journal *The Rock Garden*, online forum, seed exchange.
www.srgc.org.uk

Greece
Mediterranean Garden Society
Sparoza, PO Box 14. GR–190 02 Peania, Greece. International society, founded 1994, based in Greece, for all those interested in Mediterranean plants and gardens. Highly acclaimed quarterly journal, garden visits, seed exchange, scientific committee, and headquarters garden near Athens.
www.themediterraneangardensociety.org

Czech Republic
Rock Garden Club of Prague
Klub Skalnickaru Praha, Marikova 5, 162 00 Praha 2, Czech Republic.

USA
American Horticultural Society
7931 East Boulevard Drive, Alexandria VA 22308.
www.ahs.org
The AHS is one of the oldest societies in the country.

Great Lakes Bulb Society
www.shieldsgarden.com

International Bulb Society
Dept W, PO Box 92136, Pasadena, CA 91109-2136, USA.
www.bulbsociety.org

North American Rock Garden Society
NARGS, PO Box 67, Millwood, NY 10546. USA.
www.nargs.org

Pacific Bulb Society
www.pacificbulbsociety.org
Inaugurated 2002 for all those interested in bulbs. Newsletter The Bulb Garden.

Canada
Alpine Garden Club of British Columbia
38 Bowen Island, B.C. V0N 1G0. Canada.

New Zealand
New Zealand Alpine Garden Society
NZAGS, PO Box 2984, Christchurch, New Zealand.

Otago Alpine Garden Group
PO Box 1538, Dunedin, New Zealand.

Shows for Snowdrops
Royal Horticultural Society Shows RHS Horticultural Halls, Greycoat Street and Vincent Square, London, SW1P 2PE.

Alpine Garden Society
AGS Centre, Avon Bank, Pershore, Worcestershire, WR10 3JP.
www.alpinegardensociety.net

The Scottish Rock Garden Club
PO Box 14063, Edinburgh, EH10 4YE.
www.srgc.org.uk

Useful Names and Addresses

Addresses for the Statutory Agencies Responsible for Plant Conservation
Joint Nature Conservation Committee, Monkstone House, City Road, Peterborough, PE1 1JY

England: English Nature, North Minster House, Peterborough, PE1 1UA

Wales: Countryside Council for Wales, Plas Penrhos, Fford Penrhos, Bangor, Gwynedd, LL57 2LQ

Scotland: Scottish Natural Heritage, 2-5 Anderson Place, Edinburgh, EH6 5NP

Northern Ireland: Environment and Heritage Service, Commonwealth House, 35 Castle Street, Belfast, BT1 1G0

Republic of Ireland: Department of the Environment, Heritage and Local Government, 7 Ely Place, Dublin 2, Eire

International Union for the Protection of New Varieties of Plants
www.upov.int

UK: DeFRA, Plant Variety Rights Office and Seed Division, White House Lane, Huntingdon Road, Cambridge, CB3 0LF. Tel. 01223 342381.
www.defra.gov.uk/plants/pvs

USA: The Commissioner, Plant Variety Protection Office, Agricultural Marketing Service, Department of Agriculture, Beltsville, Maryland 20705-2351. Tel. (1-301) 5045518.
www.ams.usda.gov./science/pvpo/pvpindex

Germany: Bundessortenamt, Postfach 61 04 40, D-30604, Hannover, Germany. Tel. (49-511)9566-5.
www.bundessortenamt.de

Australia: The Registrar, Plant Breeders Rights, IP Australia, PO Box 200, Woden A.C.T. 2602. Tel. (61-2) 6283 2999.
www.ipaustralia.gov.au/pbr/index

International Code of Nomenclature for Cultivated Plants (ICNCP)
ISHS Secretariat, PO Box 500, 3001 Leuven 1, Belgium. Tel. +32 16229427.
www.ishs.org

International Cultivar Register Authority
ISHS Secretariat, PO Box 500, 3001 Leuven 1, Belgium. Tel. +32 16229427.
www.ishs.org
Koninklijke Algemeene Vereeniging voor Bloembollencultuur (KAVB)
www.kavb.nl

Twin-Scaling Services
For further information please contact Colin Mason, Fieldgate Twinscaling, email: cmason@twinscaling.com

INDEX

General Index

SNOWDROP INDEX